DINOSAURS

THE TEXTBOOK

SECOND EDITION

DINOSAURS
THE TEXTBOOK

—🐾🐾🐾—

Spencer G. Lucas

NEW MEXICO MUSEUM OF NATURAL HISTORY
UNIVERSITY OF NEW MEXICO

Wm. C. Brown Publishers

Dubuque, IA Bogota Boston Buenos Aires Caracas Chicago Guilford, CT
London Madrid Mexico City Seoul Singapore Sydney Taipei Tokyo Toronto

Project Team

Editor *Lynne M. Meyers*
Developmental Editor *Daryl Bruflodt*
Production Editor *Karen Baumann Nickolas*
Designer *Barb Hodgson*
Art Editor *Renee Grevas*
Photo Editor *Nicole Widmyer*
Permissions Coordinator *Patricia Barth*

WCB **Wm. C. Brown Publishers**

President and Chief Executive Officer *Beverly Kolz*
Vice President, Director of Editorial *Kevin Kane*
Vice President, Sales and Market Expansion *Virginia S. Moffat*
Vice President, Director of Production *Colleen A. Yonda*
Director of Marketing *Craig S. Marty*
National Sales Manager *Douglas J. DiNardo*
Marketing Manager *Keri L. Witman*
Advertising Manager *Janelle Keeffer*
Production Editorial Manager *Renée Menne*
Publishing Services Manager *Karen J. Slaght*
Royalty/Permissions Manager *Connie Allendorf*

A Times Mirror Company

Copyedited by Jeff Putnam

Cover illustration © Doug Henderson

Library of Congress Catalog Card Number: 96–84634

ISBN 0–697–27995–2

Printed in the United States of America by Times Mirror Higher Education Group, Inc.,
2460 Kerper Boulevard, Dubuque, IA 52001

10 9 8 7 6 5 4 3 2 1

FOR

Toons, Henry,

Dickens, and the City

Kitty (r. i. p.), keen students of

the descendants of

dinosaurs...

CONTENTS

CHAPTER 4

A PRIMER OF DINOSAUR ANATOMY 33

CHAPTER 5

THE ORIGIN OF DINOSAURS 43

CHAPTER 6

PREDATORY DINOSAURS 59

Chapter 7

Chapter 8

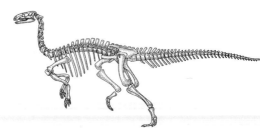

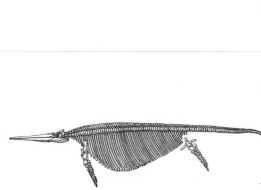

LIST OF BOXED READINGS

FOREWORD

D inosaurs have been a source of fascination for students of all ages since their discovery over 150 years ago. For a hundred years dinosaurs epitomized failure. But as we now know, it was simply a failure of science to recognize the group's successes. In the early years of discovery, interpretation of dinosaurs as animals was based on preconceived notions concerning reptiles. Reptiles were generally thought of as stupid, sluggish animals that had survived almost accidently. Dinosaurs, thought of at the time as "good reptiles," were burdened with the same misconceived notions of science as were other reptiles. Reptiles drag their tails when they walk, so dinosaurs must also have dragged their tails. Reptiles are cold-blooded and sluggish in cool weather, so dinosaurs must also have been cold-blooded and sluggish. But, reptiles survived and the dinosaurs did not, so in the minds of many, dinosaurs were thought of as unfit animals that were simply waiting for a place in time to go extinct.

Fortunately, over the years many more dinosaur specimens were found, and together with some very careful studies of their morphology, phylogeny, and ecology, it has been determined that dinosaurs were a highly specialized group of animals related not only to other reptiles, but also to birds. And although the dinosaurs are extinct, we now know that they represented one of the greatest evolutionary success stories of all time. *Dinosaurs: The Textbook* is a monument to our present understanding of these wonderful creatures. It is a book that will take the student on a journey through nearly every aspect of dinosaur biology, geology, and the history of their discovery. It is a text that presents facts together with current ideas, notions, and controversies. Dr. Lucas presents dinosaurs as successful, living creatures that were merely different in appearance from animals living today.

Dr. Lucas has written a comprehensive book that is easily read and understood by students with little scientific background—a book that teaches students not only how to use scientific methods, but how to synthesize data to create their own ideas. In contrast with many dinosaur books from the past, Dr. Lucas, although indicating his own views, allows students the opportunity to think for themselves.

This is an incredible achievement for future learning about past mysteries.

John R. Horner
Curator of Paleontology
Museum of the Rockies
Montana State University
Bozeman, Montana

Spencer Lucas received his Bachelor of Arts degree in Anthropology from the University of New Mexico in 1976 and his Ph.D. in Geology from Yale University in 1984. Since 1988 he has served as Curator of Paleontology and Geology at the New Mexico Museum of Natural History and as Adjunct Associate Professor of Geology at the University of New Mexico. Spencer is also an active member of several professional organizations. He has served as Vice President (1990) of the Albuquerque Geological Society, President (1991) of the New Mexico Academy of Science, President (1991) of the Rocky Mountain section of the Paleontological Society, and has been a voting member of the International Union of Geological Sciences' Subcommission on Triassic Stratigraphy since 1990. The recipient of several research grants and awards, Spencer remains a very active participant in this ever-changing field of study.

PREFACE

Seven years ago the geology faculty at the University of New Mexico, at my suggestion, initiated an introductory level course on dinosaurs. As the lone vertebrate paleontologist on campus, I, of course, was to teach this course. I had several years of teaching introductory geology—both physical and historical geology—under my belt. But now a problem faced me: no textbook existed for a dinosaur course. Furthermore, in a decade-long stint as a university student—from freshman to doctorate—I never took a course on dinosaurs. Few colleagues were teaching dinosaur courses at that time, and all they could offer was a syllabus with a suggested list of readings. Not fully satisfied with their offerings, I set out to design a course and provide reading material from available sources to suit my own prejudices about how to teach college freshmen and sophomores about dinosaurs.

Although the students were enthusiastic the first time I taught the course, I was not satisfied. I had tried to teach about dinosaurs within the broader context of vertebrate evolution and used Edwin Colbert's excellent survey book, *EVOLUTION OF THE VERTEBRATES*, as the text. But it seemed to me the course was too diffuse—not enough of a focus on dinosaurs—and the book lacked needed depth on the drawing card of the course, the dinosaurs themselves. So, I shifted gears and subsequently taught a course more focused on dinosaurs, using Alan Charig's stimulating book, *A NEW LOOK AT THE DINOSAURS*. This worked better, but after a couple of years, I realized that Charig's book was neither broad enough nor sufficiently detailed to suit the course. Fortunately, David Norman's outstanding *THE ILLUSTRATED ENCYCLOPEDIA OF THE DINOSAURS* appeared. It is the one dinosaur book I hope to have if ever marooned on a desert island. Norman's book provided excellent coverage of dinosaur details and lore for the students. But it did not meet head on the most interesting topics—dinosaur extinction, hot-blooded dinosaurs, and so forth—that had become the causes celebres of my course.

The book I have written is the semester-long course I teach as it has been honed by years of experimentation and student feedback to a lean but comprehensive introduction to the dinosaurs. This book thus fulfills my selfish need for a textbook. But I also believe that it will meet the needs of the growing number of paleontologists teaching introductory-level dinosaur courses across the United States. My reviewers share this belief, and I hope we are right.

There is, however, a second reason why I wrote this book. It represents my attempt to slog through the available morass of information and ideas about dinosaurs, some controversial, others ridiculous, to stand on the firm ground of established facts and reasonable inference. Much of what Americans think they know about dinosaurs is wrong, and some of what they are being told today, in some popular books by "experts," is baloney. This book tries to right the wrongs and slices up the baloney by going out of its way to not promote unreasonable speculation about dinosaurs. Not everything in it is above debate, but nothing here is science fiction. As such, I want this book to teach many people about dinosaurs and the science of studying dinosaurs as few other books do.

These are heady times for dinosaur science. Almost daily, new discoveries, novel methods, and innovative ideas are pushing forward the frontiers of our knowledge of dinosaurs. Americans seem to have an insatiable appetite for information on dinosaurs. This book provides a "first course," and I hope it fosters an accurate understanding of the dinosaurs and a deep appreciation of dinosaur science in all who read it.

ORGANIZATION

The table of contents essentially divides the book into three parts. The first part, Chapters 1–5, is designed to provide the beginning student with the minimum background in geological, biological, and anatomical concepts necessary to understand the remainder of the text. In the second part, Chapters 6–10, I have you "meet the dinosaurs." These chapters review each group of dinosaurs. Each chapter focuses on two or three well-known taxa that are exemplary of the group. The remaining discussion covers aspects of phylogeny, diversity, distribution, and functional morphology. The third part, Chapters 11–18, covers a variety of thought-provoking "topics." These chapters discuss everything from the history of the great dinosaur hunters to the extinction of the dinosaurs. The emphasis in many of the chapters will be on concepts of broad applicability, in other words, concepts also relevant to subjects other than dinosaurs. Thus, for example, I believe that the history of dinosaur collecting and study can be used to tell the student much about how scientific perceptions change through time. Finally, I have included a dinosaur dictionary and a glossary for ease in locating definitions and identifying information.

I have strived to present a balanced review of competing ideas in controversial areas. For example, I believe the weight of evidence suggests that some dinosaurs had a higher metabolic rate than that of living ectotherms, whereas there is no evidence of such a heightened metabolic rate in other dinosaur groups. I intend to present the range of evidence on this subject, not push a particular point of view not justified by the evidence.

ACKNOWLEDGMENTS

I wish to extend my thanks and appreciation to the reviewers whose thoughtful comments, criticisms, and encouragement have helped tremendously in revising and improving the final draft. Reviewers of the first edition were Bonnie Blackwell, Purdue University; Matthew J. James, Department of Geology, Sonoma State University; Norman R. King, University of Southern Indiana; John H. Ostrom, Yale University; John M. Renserger, Department of Geological Sciences and Burke Museum, University of Washington; J. Keith Rigby, Jr., University of Notre Dame; André Wyss, Department of Geological Sciences, University of California–Santa Barbara; William J. Zinsmeister, Department of Earth & Atmospheric Sciences, Purdue University. Reviewers for this edition include: Robert Cox, University of Michigan–Ann Arbor; Norman R. King, University of Southern Indiana; George (Rip) Rapp, Jr., University of Minnesota–Duluth; Robert Thorson, University of Connecticut; Craig B. Wood, Ph.D., Providence College.

Several colleagues, museums, and other institutions provided photographs that add to the quality of instruction in this textbook. Their contributions are acknowledged, where appropriate, throughout the text.

Many people at Times Mirror Higher Education helped make this book possible. Karen Nickolas, of course, is without an equal in my estimation. I owe a special thanks to Bob Fenchel for his wise and patient counsel and friendship. His thoughtful suggestions and writing schedule made it possible for my wife, Mimi, to set deadlines for my writing and hold me to them. She also listened patiently to my chatter and provided much needed emotional support. Four house cats taught me the fascination of birds and also "were there" when I needed them. Extra catnip is on order.

Over the years, I learned much about dinosaurs from my colleagues and students. Heavy hitters on my scorecard in this regard are John Ostrom, who long ago tried to convince me, without success, that dinosaurs are more interesting than mammals; Adrian Hunt, with whom I have dug and studied many dinosaurs; Barry Kues and Jeff Froehich, who first taught me vertebrate paleontology and still put up with me; Niall Mateer, who has kept me in touch with the Cretaceous; Bob Sullivan, who forced me to think hard about dinosaur extinction after I had ceased to care; Jack McIntosh, who taught me everything I know about sauropods; J. Keith Rigby, Jr., and Bob Sloan, who believe in Paleocene dinosaurs and know that I don't; Martin Lockley, who convinced me that dinosaur footprints really are important; and Zhen Shuonan, who opened up the world of Chinese dinosaurs to me. Each of the aforementioned have made invaluable comments and suggestions throughout the development of this project. To the rest of you who collect dinosaurs, do the research, give the talks, and write the papers, thanks for teaching me so much. Finally, I thank the hundreds of undergraduate students at the University of New Mexico who have sat through my dinosaur course. You were the guinea pigs upon which I experimented. This is the book you asked for.

Three years ago, in the preface to the first edition of this textbook, I spoke of the rapid pace of new dinosaur discoveries and the American public's insatiable appetite for information on dinosaurs. Since I wrote those words, the pace has picked up, and that appetite appears at best to have only been whetted.

The second edition of this textbook thus updates many areas, large and small, to keep current in one of the most rapidly moving fields of scientific discovery and research that I know of. This new edition also corrects as many sins of commission and omission as I could beat out of the first edition; there were a few! Several new illustrations and full color also set this edition off from the first.

Many of the improvements in this edition are due to the thoughtful and constructive reviews I received from Robert S. Cox, Norman R. King, George Rapp, Jr., and Craig B. Wood. Although I did not heed all their advice, much of it did move ink. Ben Creisler, Andy Farke, Gerry Forney, George Olshevsky, John Ruben, and Chris Whittle also offered substantive input towards revision. I thank them and many other colleagues who took the time to talk to me about the book and offer suggestions for its improvement. Blame me for any remaining mistakes!

Spencer G. Lucas

INSTRUCTOR'S MANUAL

Many who teach dinosaur courses are not vertebrate paleontologists, and few if any of the instructors ever had the opportunity to enroll in a dinosaur course during their college-student careers. The first edition of this book was the first textbook written specifically for a dinosaur course. For these and other reasons, I have written an Instructor's Manual to accompany the text.

The Instructor's Manual includes a suggested syllabus along with a description of the text's organization and chapter interdependence to assist the instructor in planning how best to use the text to meet the needs of their course. The manual provides a description of the material covered in each chapter as well as suggestions for presenting the material. The suggestions discuss what material should be emphasized and methods for overcoming potential difficulties. Answers to all of the review questions are also provided for each chapter.

A list of books which the instructor may find helpful in gathering additional information for teaching the course is provided along with a list of suggested videos that may be used to supplement the text.

A selected bibliography of technical articles beyond those listed under "Further Reading" in the text is provided for those teachers or students who wish to explore topics more deeply.

Finally, the Instructor's Manual includes a test item file with 25 to 30 multiple choice and true-false questions for each chapter.

INTRODUCTION

In 1842, British comparative anatomist **Richard Owen** (1804–1892) coined the word **dinosaur,** from the Greek words *deinos,* meaning "terrible" (Owen actually read it to mean "fearfully great"), and *sauros,* meaning "lizard" or "reptile." To Owen, the "terrible lizards" were large, extinct reptiles known from only a handful of fossils discovered in western Europe since the 1820s. Today, dinosaur fossils are known from all the continents and represent hundreds of distinct types of dinosaurs.

This chapter briefly answers some very basic questions about dinosaurs and introduces some topics discussed at greater length later in this book.

WHAT ARE DINOSAURS?

Many people apply the term dinosaur to any large, extinct animal. To most people, any large extinct reptile qualifies as a dinosaur. Many people even identify large, extinct mammals, such as woolly mammoths, as dinosaurs (figure 1.1). Some authors and toy manufacturers perpetuate inaccurate ideas about what is a dinosaur by presenting to the public a variety of non-dinosaurs as dinosaurs. The mammal-like reptile (pelycosaur) *Dimetrodon* and the flying reptile *Pteranodon* are examples.

Dinosaurs are most easily thought of as a group of extinct reptiles having an **upright posture.** They first appeared about 225 million years ago and became extinct 65 million years ago. Birds, the descendants of dinosaurs, are still with us. Dinosaurs can be identified as reptiles because of their reptilian skeletal features and because dinosaurs, like many other reptiles, reproduced by laying hard-shelled eggs. Dinosaurs' upright posture, in which the legs extend directly underneath the body, distinguishes them from reptiles that hold their limbs out to their sides in a **sprawling posture** (figure 1.2). Largeness is not a prerequisite for being a dinosaur; some dinosaurs were no larger than a chicken. In fact, skeletal features of one group of dinosaurs are remarkably like those of modern birds, which indicates that dinosaurs were the ancestors of birds. Specific skeletal features unique to dinosaurs will be discussed in Chapter 5. But for now, we can define dinosaurs as reptiles having an upright posture, and thereby identify them as a group with an evolutionary history distinct from that of other reptiles.

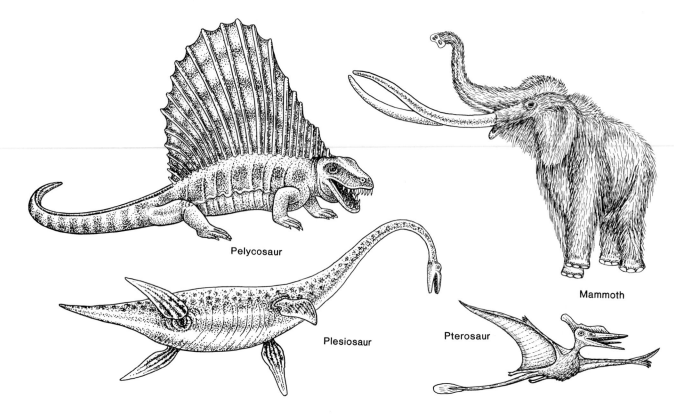

FIGURE 1.1

Although these kinds of animals are thought by many people to be dinosaurs, they are not. The pelycosaur is more closely related to mammals than to dinosaurs. The mammoth is a mammal. The plesiosaur is a kind of reptile very different from dinosaurs. The pterosaur is a close relative of dinosaurs.

Pelycosaur

Mammoth

Plesiosaur

Pterosaur

WHEN AND WHERE DID DINOSAURS LIVE?

We have already noted that dinosaurs first appeared about 225 million years ago and became extinct 65 million years ago, which means that dinosaurs lived on earth for about 160 million years (figure 1.3). Most paleontologists date the origin of humans at 2 or 3 million years before the present. This means that dinosaurs persisted 50 to 80 times as long as we have been on earth. Movies and cartoons that portray humans and dinosaurs living side by side are, therefore, inaccurate.

The first discovery of dinosaur remains in Antarctica was in 1989, so that we now have dinosaur fossils from all the continents (figure 1.4). The broad geographic distribution, survival for about 160 million years, variety in shapes and sizes, and, in many instances, extremely large size identify dinosaurs as one of the most successful groups of land animals in the history of life.

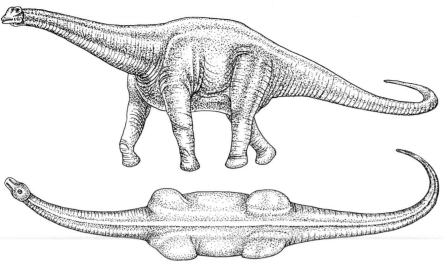

FIGURE 1.2

Dinosaurs are a group of extinct reptiles having an upright limb posture. In contrast, other reptiles such as lizards hold their limbs out from the sides of their bodies in a sprawling posture.

Dinosaur (upright posture)

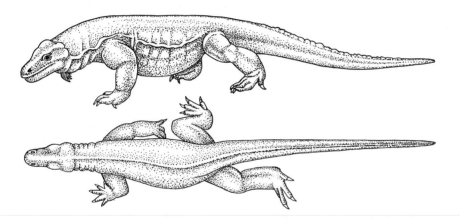

Lizard (sprawling posture)

WHY STUDY DINOSAURS?

Dinosaurs fascinate most people, including young children. This fascination stems from the large size, strange shapes, and long-past extinction of dinosaurs. Some dinosaurs, such as *Tyrannosaurus rex*, the largest meat-eating land animal to have walked the earth, terrify us. Other dinosaurs, such as *Stegosaurus*, puzzle us with their unusual body shapes and "armor." Clearly one reason to study dinosaurs is because they are interesting.

FIGURE 1.3

Dinosaurs became extinct 65 million years ago, more than 60 million years before humans appeared on Earth.

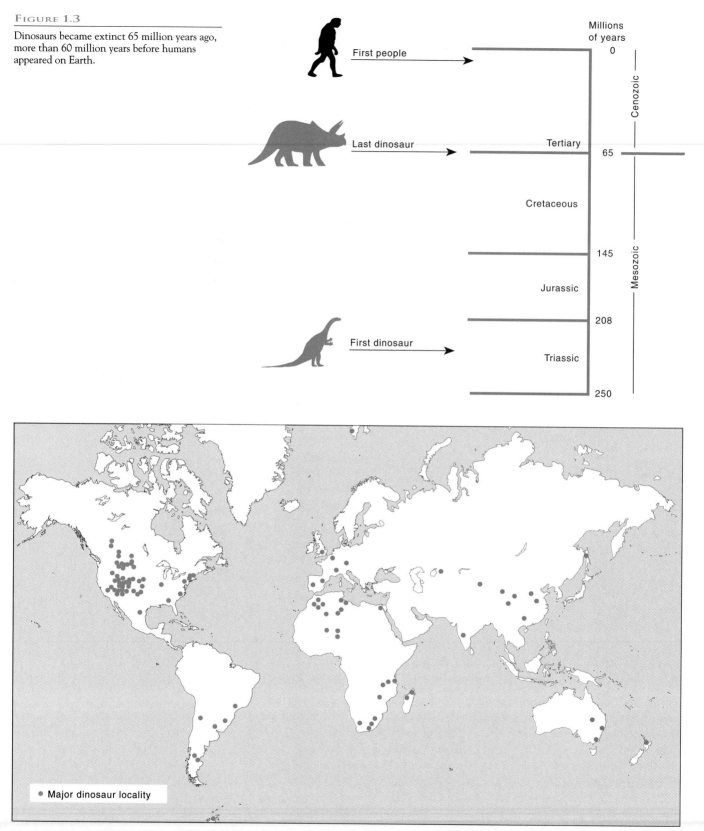

FIGURE 1.4

Dinosaur fossils have been collected on all the continents.

Dinosaurs also are worth studying because they represent a unique episode in the history of life on this planet. They appeared some 225 million years ago, evolved into some of the largest and the most successful land animals of all time, and then disappeared 65 million years ago. Dinosaurs have much to teach us about evolution and extinction, especially of large animals. Dinosaurs remind us of our own vulnerability to extinction, and understanding the extinction of dinosaurs may help us to understand ongoing extinctions and avoid our own extinction.

We study dinosaurs for two reasons: first because they interest us, and second because they were an important part of the evolutionary history of life.

KEY TERMS

dinosaur
Richard Owen

sprawling posture
upright posture

REVIEW QUESTIONS

1. Identify two characteristics that preclude the pelycosaur and the mammoth from being dinosaurs.

2. When and where did dinosaurs live?

3. What can the study of dinosaurs teach us?

EVOLUTION, PHYLOGENY, AND CLASSIFICATION

Paleontologists, scientists who study fossils, base their understanding of the history of life on the **fossil record,** which comprises all the fossils discovered as well as those awaiting discovery. The fossil record of dinosaurs indicates that they existed for about 160 million years. During that time, many types of dinosaurs evolved. Key to understanding this **evolution** is to determine the family tree, or genealogy, of dinosaurs. Which dinosaurs were closely related to each other and which were only distant relatives? Answering these questions requires some understanding of the principles of evolution and of phylogeny. Knowing how scientific names are given to dinosaurs or to groups of dinosaurs requires an understanding of the basic ideas and methods of biological classification.

EVOLUTION

Evolution, simply defined, is the origin and change of groups of organisms over time. Today, biologists and paleontologists believe that evolution occurs in the specific way formulated by **Charles Darwin.**

In his 1859 book, *On the Origin of Species by Means of Natural Selection,* Darwin argued that organisms adapt to the environments in which they live. In other words, each organism has a specific way of living and interacting with its environment. When the environment changes, those organisms that are better able to cope with the changed environment are more successful—which, in Darwinian terms, means they reproduce more than those organisms less able to cope with the change. The most successful organisms are thus "selected for" and those least successful are "selected against" in the jargon of what is called **natural selection.** Another phrase that has been used to describe this is "survival of the fittest," where "fittest" refers to the most successful organisms, or those having more offspring than the least successful.

In Darwin's view, certain organisms are more successful than others when faced with environmental change because of the variation that occurs in any population of organisms. We see this variation most easily by recognizing that no two people are alike, and the same is true of any population of animals or plants. So, when the environment changes, some individuals in a population are able to better cope with the change than others. Which organisms are better or less able to cope, however, is not something that the organisms themselves control, because they cannot anticipate what type of environmental change might occur.

For example, in a population of dinosaurs, we would expect to find a range of body sizes (figure 2.1). If climate were to change to favor larger dinosaurs in the population, the larger variants would be selected for. Because they would reproduce more successfully than the smaller dinosaurs, we would expect dinosaurs to become

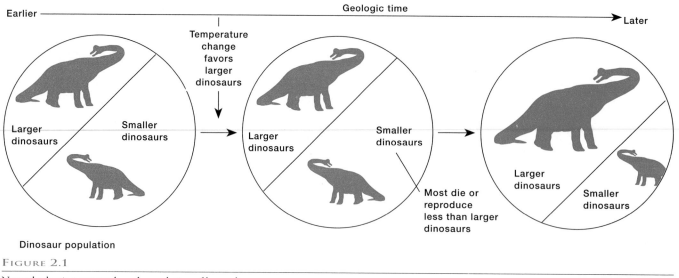

Temperature
change
favors
larger
dinosaurs

Larger
dinosaurs

Smaller
dinosaurs

Larger
dinosaurs

Smaller
dinosaurs

Most die or
reproduce
less than larger
dinosaurs

Larger
dinosaurs

Smaller
dinosaurs

Dinosaur population

FIGURE 2.1

Natural selection can produce the evolution of larger dinosaurs.

larger in the next generation, provided that the trait of larger size could be passed on from one generation of dinosaurs to the next. In this way, larger dinosaurs might evolve by the process of natural selection.

Evolution by natural selection is also called "Darwinian" evolution. In Darwinian evolution, the evolutionary history of a group of organisms is diagrammed by a family tree (or genealogy) of populations undergoing natural selection. The family tree emphasizes the fact that there are ancestors, descendants, and other relationships among organisms. Because organisms change as a result of natural selection, Darwinian evolution can also be described in Darwin's own phrase as "descent with modification."

The family tree of a group of evolving organisms is also termed its **phylogeny,** from the Greek words for "tribe" (*phylum*) and "birth" (*genos*). On a phylogeny, each branch, or each bundle of branches with a common stem, is called a **clade** (*clados* is Greek for "branch"), whereas a horizontal slice through a phylogeny is called a **grade** (figure 2.2). When a new type of organism appears, we speak of **origination,** and a new clade or segment of a clade is drawn on a phylogeny. When a type of organism disappears, we speak of **extinction.** When one clade splits into two we speak of **divergence,** and the evolution of similar features in two unrelated clades is **convergence.** The populations of organisms shown on a phylogeny are usually assigned to groups called **taxa** (singular, *taxon*). For example, each different type of dinosaur in the phylogeny of dinosaurs is a dinosaur taxon, and these taxa can be grouped into larger dinosaur taxa based on their relationships to each other. When we speak of how taxa are related to each other, we are referring to their **phylogenetic relationships.**

PHYLOGENY

A phylogeny, as stated previously, is a family tree or genealogy of taxa. How do paleontologists construct a phylogeny of a group of extinct taxa like dinosaurs?

Until recently, the most common method was to examine the timespan and overall similarity of the fossils of taxa as keys to their phylogenetic relationships. This method, called stratophenetic, from the words for "layer" (of rock) and "population" (of organisms), identifies ancestral taxa as those older than descendant taxa resembling their ancestors closely in one or more features (figure 2.3). Critical to a **stratophenetic phylogeny** is the notion that the changes that took place between the ancestor and its descendant are not so great as to seem implausible during the time interval between ancestor and descendant.

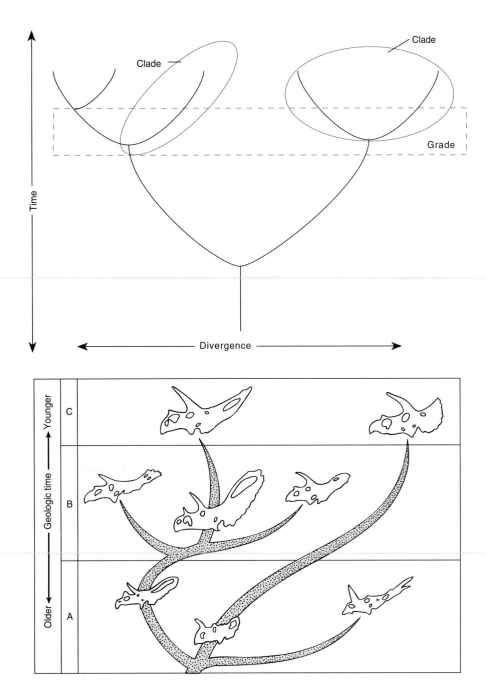

FIGURE 2.2

A phylogeny is an evolutionary family tree consisting of distinct clades. A horizontal slice through a phylogeny is called a grade.

FIGURE 2.3

A stratophenetic approach to phylogeny identifies ancestors and descendants as time-successive, similar taxa. This diagram of skulls of horned dinosaurs is a stratophenetic phylogeny.

From E. H. Colbert, *The Age of Reptiles.* Copyright © 1966 W. W. Norton & Company, Inc., New York, NY; and Weidenfeld and Nicolson, London, England. Reprinted by permission.

The problem many paleontologists, especially those who study dinosaurs, have with stratophenetic phylogeny is that it makes a great assumption about the completeness of the fossil record, namely that the ancestor will be represented by fossils older than the fossils of the descendant. In theory this would be the case, but in practice the known fossil record of many taxa, especially dinosaurs, is very incomplete. Because of this, we can almost never be certain when older fossils represent the ancestors of younger fossils, and we cannot assume that we have discovered all the ancestors and descendants in a phylogeny.

Because the known fossil record of dinosaurs lacks many ancestors and descendants, most paleontologists who study dinosaurs no longer use the stratophenetic method to construct phylogenies. Instead, they use a different method that makes fewer assumptions about the completeness of the fossil record. This method is called cladistics, and the resultant **cladistic phylogeny** is called a **cladogram** (figure 2.4). The phylogenies of dinosaurs presented in this book are cladograms.

FIGURE 2.4

A cladistic phylogeny is a cladogram. A monophyletic group is all the branches that share a common stem. A polyphyletic group is formed by uniting branches with different stems.

Monophyletic group

Polyphyletic group

FIGURE 2.5

This cladogram indicates that a horse and a whale are more closely related to each other than either is to a trout.

A cladogram does not incorporate information about the time ranges of taxa. Instead, it is based only on the similarities of taxa. But neither overall similarity nor just any similarities are used to construct a cladogram. The similarities of value to cladistics are those features that are **evolutionary novelties.** An evolutionary novelty is an inherited *change* from a previously existing structure. Cladistics argues that two taxa are closely related when they share evolutionary novelties. Taxa sharing the most such novelties are most closely related and are shown on the cladogram as diverging from a common ancestor (figure 2.4). In cladistic terms, these taxa form a **monophyletic group** and share two or more clades with a single ancestor. In contrast, groups lacking a common ancestor on a cladogram are termed **polyphyletic** (figure 2.4).

A good example of a cladistic phylogeny (see box 2.1) is provided by trying to construct a cladogram of the three taxa trout, horse, and whale (figure 2.5). Based on many similarities, we might conclude that a trout and a whale are more closely related to each other than either is to a horse. But, if we focus on evolutionary novelties that distinguish mammals, such as the horse and whale, from bony fishes, such as the trout, then the cladogram that identifies the horse and whale as members of a monophyletic group is well-founded. These evolutionary novelties include warm-bloodedness, hair, and giving live birth, which are features shared by horses and whales but not by trout.

Thus, evolutionary novelties allow us to distinguish a monophyletic group on the cladogram for whales and horses distinct from the clade for trout. But how do we identify evolutionary novelties to be used in constructing cladograms? In other words, what features shared by two taxa are evolutionary novelties and what features are not? No simple answers to these questions exist, but we can get a feel for how evolutionary novelties are identified by examining the theoretical basis for their identification.

BOX 2.1

A CLADOGRAM OF DINOSAURS AND BIRDS

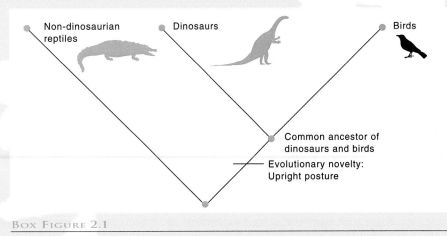

BOX FIGURE 2.1

This cladogram indicates birds and dinosaurs are more closely related to each other than either is to non-dinosaurian reptiles.

Once we understand the principles and methods behind cladistics, we should be able to construct a cladogram for any taxa, including the dinosaurs. Here, we will construct a basic cladogram of dinosaurs, birds, and non-dinosaurian "reptiles." To do so, we ask the question, which of these taxa are most closely related to each other?

Because we have to start somewhere, let's begin with some longstanding ideas, treating them as reasonable assumptions within which to direct our cladistic efforts. These are that reptiles are descended from amphibians and that dinosaurs are descended from some other group of reptiles. This allows us to identify the sprawling posture of most reptiles, in which their limbs are held out from the sides of the body, as a primitive feature of reptiles inherited from their ancestors, the amphibians. The upright posture of dinosaurs, in which their limbs are held under the body, thus must be an evolutionary novelty of dinosaurs with respect to their reptilian ancestors. Birds share the upright posture with dinosaurs, so this shared evolutionary novelty (if it did not evolve convergently) suggests that birds and dinosaurs are more closely related to each other than either is to non-dinosaurian reptiles. We thus can construct a cladogram in which non- dinosaurian reptiles form one clade and birds plus dinosaurs the other. For the sake of convenience, we can indicate the evolutionary novelty shared by birds and dinosaurs (upright posture) on the cladogram (box figure 2.1).

When we view the origination and evolution of a taxon, we can see that it must inherit some features from its ancestor. The inherited features can be identified as primitive. But the features that arise for the first time in a new taxon—its evolutionary novelties—are thought of as derived. These derived features, not the primitive features, unite the organisms into a group of closely related organisms, but only if the evolutionary novelties in question arose only once. Evolutionary convergence is when they arose more than once in separate taxa not descended from a single close ancestor. For example, the wings of bats and of birds, though they are similar evolutionary novelties, arose in two taxa with very different ancestors, and thus are convergent. Convergence presents the greatest threat to arriving at the correct cladistic phylogeny of a group of taxa.

Once we have constructed a cladogram, we can add information to this phylogeny to turn it into a **phylogenetic tree.** The information we add usually is intended to turn the vertical axis of the cladogram into a geological time scale and to indicate which taxa may have been ancestors and which may have been descendants (figure 2.6).

Cladistics makes no assumptions about the completeness of the fossil record; it simply tries to identify closely related taxa by their shared evolutionary novelties. However, cladistics does not lack problems. Some of those problems arise from convergence, when a shared evolutionary novelty thought to unite two taxa

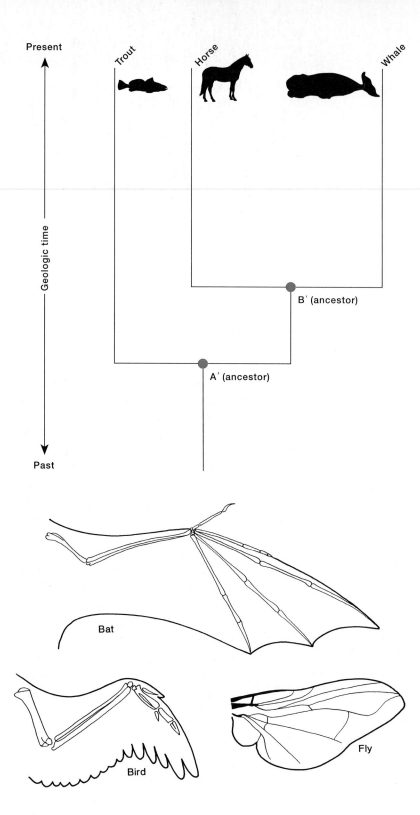

FIGURE 2.6

A cladogram can be turned into a phylogenetic tree by changing its vertical axis into a geologic time scale and indicating possible ancestors and descendants.

FIGURE 2.7

Convergence can produce evolutionary novelties in distinct clades that do not indicate close relationship. The wings of birds, bats, and flies are superficially similar, but evolved in distinct clades. They are a classic example of evolutionary convergence.

turns out not to be that at all (figure 2.7). Also, not all paleontologists may agree that a particular feature is an evolutionary novelty rather than a primitive feature inherited from an ancestor. This leads to debate and disagreement among paleontologists attempting to construct cladistic phylogenies of extinct organisms. As we shall see in this book, such debates and disagreements currently are taking place over certain aspects of dinosaur phylogeny.

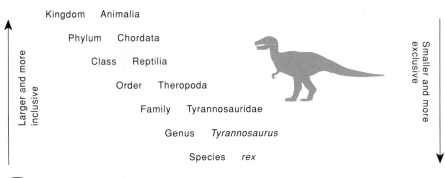

Kingdom   Animalia

Phylum   Chordata

Class   Reptilia

Order   Theropoda

Family   Tyrannosauridae

Genus   *Tyrannosaurus*

Species   *rex*

Larger and more inclusive →

Smaller and more exclusive →

FIGURE 2.8

The Linnaean hierarchy groups organisms into progressively more inclusive groups. The major categories in the hierarchy—Kingdom, Phylum, Class, Order, Family, Genus, Species—can be easily memorized with this mnemonic: "King Phillip Can Order Fresh Green Salad."

CLASSIFICATION

Constructing a phylogeny based on shared evolutionary novelties is the fundamental basis for classifying taxa. This is because the biological classification of organisms is the grouping of them into taxa that share a common ancestry. In other words, closely related taxa are placed in the same group so that the classification reflects their phylogenetic relationships.

Thus, the principal information paleontologists use to classify extinct organisms is their phylogeny. Based on their phylogeny, organisms are grouped into categories called taxa, and those taxa are named. For the **classification** of animals, living and extinct, the categorical system used is a hierarchy first formulated in the eighteenth century by **Carolus Linnaeus,** a Swedish naturalist. A set of international rules governs the method of naming the categories (taxa) (see box 2.2).

The **Linnaean hierarchy** (figure 2.8) is a system of classification in which smaller (lower) taxa are nested into larger (higher) taxa. The categories of this classification extend from large and very inclusive to small and very exclusive. Each of these categories has a category name. Thus, a phylum is a very large category in the Linnaean hierarchy. It contains one or more classes, and each class contains one or more orders and so on.

The name assigned to a taxon follows the international rules that mandate endings and forms of Latinization of most names. For example, the rules specify that family names must end with the suffix "-idae." So, the name of the **family** containing *Tyrannosaurus* and closely related dinosaurs is Tyrannosauridae.

The name of a species of organisms, the lowest rank in the Linnaean hierarchy, always has two parts and is called a **binomen.** These are the **genus** (plural, *genera*) name followed by the specific (or **species**) name. Thus, the name of the species to which all readers of this book belong is *Homo* (the generic name) *sapiens* (the species name), a Latin name that literally means "man the wise." Another way to explain this is to say living humans belong to the genus *Homo* and to the species (plural, *species*) *Homo sapiens*. The specific name *sapiens* cannot stand alone as the name of a species, which must be a binomen—therefore *Homo sapiens*.

The international rules of zoological nomenclature set standards for naming taxa that allow scientists worldwide to name taxa in a consistent way to facilitate communication. But, because different ideas exist about the phylogenetic relationships of many organisms, the process of constructing classifications from phylogenies is full of disagreements that are useful in an active science. Once it comes time to name taxa, however, the rules that govern their naming ensure uniformity in the construction of the names and their endings. Nevertheless, the naming of taxa is a creative enterprise in which biologists and paleontologists are free to base the name on some attribute of the organism or organisms to be named, or on anything else.

As an example, place yourself in the shoes of paleontologist Henry Fairfield Osborn in 1905, presented with the huge skeleton of a meat-eating dinosaur found in Montana. In the Linnaean hierarchy, dinosaurs belong to the phylum Chordata,

BOX 2.2

THE INTERNATIONAL RULES: PRIORITY AND SYNONYMS

The *International Code of Zoological Nomenclature* dictates the rules by which the scientific names of animals are constructed. A central rule is the "principle of priority." This rule mandates that the oldest correctly proposed scientific name for an animal has priority over later names proposed for that animal. In other words, if an animal received a proper scientific name in, say, 1900, and a second name was properly proposed for the same animal in 1980 (mistakes like this do occur!), the 1900 name should be used because it has priority. The 1980 name is identified as a "synonym" of the 1900 name and should not be used.

The dinosaur generic names *Apatosaurus* and *Brontosaurus* provide a good example of the **principle of priority.** Paleontologist O. C. Marsh coined the name *Apatosaurus,* "deceptive lizard," in 1877, for gigantic dinosaur hip and back bones from Colorado. In 1879, Marsh named an almost complete gigantic dinosaur skeleton from Wyoming *Brontosaurus,* "thunder lizard." Marsh believed *Apatosaurus* and *Brontosaurus* were different types of dinosaurs, so his proposal of two different names made sense. But comparisons made many years later revealed that the bones from Colorado and the skeleton from Wyoming belonged to the same type of dinosaur. So *Brontosaurus* is really a **synonym** of *Apatosaurus,* and the latter is the correct scientific name for this type of dinosaur. Despite this, *Brontosaurus,* which is a much more colorful name for this gargantuan dinosaur than *Apatosaurus,* gained wide use, especially in popular books. Indeed, many people continue to use the name *Brontosaurus*—it even appeared on a stamp issued by the U.S. Postal Service in the 1980s—even though the name is technically incorrect.

重庆龙属（新属） *Chungkingosaurus gen. nov.*

（图版 40—43）

属的特征 中小个体的剑龙。头骨较高，下颌骨厚实。牙齿细小，排列密集，互不重叠。齿冠不对称。背椎和尾椎为双平型的椎体。荐椎4—5个完全愈合，附有一加强椎体，荐部背面封闭不全。骨板呈棘板状，大而厚实。股骨骨干圆直，第四转节不明显，股骨与胫骨之比：1.61—1.68。

该属目前包括一个种，两个未定种：

1. 江北重庆龙（新属新种） *Chungkingosaurus jiangbeiensis gen. et sp. nov.*
2. 峨岭的重庆龙（未定种一） *Chungkingosaurus sp. 1*
3. 重庆的重庆龙（未定种二） *Chungkingosaurus sp. 2*

江北重庆龙（新属新种） *Chungkingosaurus jiangbeiensis gen. et sp. nov.*

（图版 40—42）

种属名称解释 化石因发现于重庆市江北区而命名：江北重庆龙（新属新种）（*Chungkingosaurus jiangbeiensis gen. et sp. nov.*）。

特征 小个体的剑龙。头骨吻端较高，下颌骨厚实，牙齿细小，排列紧密，齿冠不对称，齿环不发育。背椎和尾椎均为双平型的椎体，荐椎4个和一个加强腰椎完全愈合一起，荐部背面封闭不全。骨板棘板状，大而厚实。肱骨有不明显的骨干。肠骨髋臼窝浅平，股骨圆直，无第四转节。胫骨近端显著扩粗，关节面圆形，胫、腓骨远端同距骨和跟骨完全愈合。

标本 一不完整的骨架，计有：头骨吻端，10个背椎，较完整的腰带和荐椎，23个相连续的尾椎，一对完整的股骨和一胫骨，一肱骨远端，5个骨板，3个掌骨。（标本登记号：CV00206）。

BOX FIGURE 2.2

This portion of an article describing a new dinosaur from China follows the *International Code of Zoological Nomenclature* by naming the new genus and species in Latinized words.

Source: Dong Zhiming, et al., *The Dinosaurian Remains from Sichuan Basin, China.* Science Press, New York, Ltd.

The rules in the *International Code of Zoological Nomenclature* cover even the details of how to spell the scientific names of animals. These names must take Latin endings, and many of them have Greek or Latin roots. The genus and species names are always italicized. Such rules may seem a bit arbitrary, but they ensure uniformity in the scientific names of dinosaurs and other animals. This uniformity facilitates communication among scientists worldwide. So even though a dinosaur may be discovered in China and described by a Chinese paleontologist in an article written in Chinese, the dinosaur's scientific name is two Latinized words (box figure 2.2). This makes it possible for those paleontologists who do not read or write Chinese to understand and use the dinosaur's name.

animals with a flexible cord or rod running down the middle of their backs. Within Chordata, dinosaurs belong to the subphylum Vertebrata, in which the rod is segmented into vertebrae. The class Reptilia, vertebrates that lay hard-shelled eggs, have scaly skin and limb structures for fully terrestrial locomotion, includes the dinosaurs. Reptilia is one of several classes in the subphylum Vertebrata. Dinosaurs can be more precisely classified within Reptilia as members of an infraclass Archosauria (the "ruling reptiles," discussed in Chapter 5). Most meat-eating dinosaurs belong to an order called Theropoda (see Chapter 6).

But Osborn's new meat-eating dinosaur differed from all other known theropods, so he had to name a new genus and species for this huge predator. The name he coined, *Tyrannosaurus rex*, was constructed in accordance with the rules of zoological nomenclature. It is Latin for "king" (*rex*) of the "tyrant lizards" (*Tyrannosaurus*), an appropriate and colorful name for the largest land-living predator of all time. The next year, 1906, Osborn created the family Tyrannosauridae for this dinosaur, because he realized it was quite different from most of the other dinosaurs in the order Theropoda.

DINOSAURS AND EVOLUTION

Paleontologists view evolution as taking place at two levels. Evolution at the species level, or **microevolution**, is the evolution of populations of organisms that results in the origination of new species and takes at least thousands or ten-thousands of years. Evolution above the species level, or **macroevolution**, is the origination and evolution of taxa larger than species, including genera, families, and orders and usually takes millions of years.

To decipher microevolution from fossils requires a large number of fossils that are dated close to each other in geologic time. Only with such a dense fossil record can paleontologists document the variation and small changes of extinct organisms during relatively short intervals of geologic time (100,000 years or less), the types of changes that lead to the origination of new species.

In contrast, to study macroevolution does not require such an extensive fossil record. A good example of a macroevolutionary problem relevant to dinosaurs is the origin of birds. Fossils of dinosaurs and those of the earliest birds provide extensive insight into the origin of a higher taxon, the birds (Class Aves), from the dinosaurs, as will be discussed in Chapter 16. This is the case even though a dense fossil record of the evolutionary changes from a species of dinosaur to the first bird species is far from being documented.

The fossil record of many shelled invertebrates (animals without backbones, such as clams) and of some mammals is extensive enough to allow paleontologists to study microevolution. But the fossil record of most dinosaurs is not. Dinosaur fossils are rarely abundant enough or close enough to each other in time to allow paleontologists to study the microevolution of dinosaurs. Instead, dinosaur fossils do document the macroevolution of some of earth history's largest and most bizarre animals.

SUMMARY

1. Evolution is the origin and change of groups of organisms over time. It can also be described by Darwin's phrase "descent with modification."

2. Darwinian evolution occurs by natural selection. This means that variants in a population of organisms better adapted to their environment will reproduce more successfully than less adapted variants.

3. The stratophenetic method of phylogeny reconstruction requires a much more complete fossil record than exists for dinosaurs. Therefore, most paleontologists who study dinosaurs do not use this method.

4. The cladistic method of phylogeny, which constructs cladograms, is favored instead. Cladistics identifies closely related taxa as those that share evolutionary novelties.

5. Problems with using the cladistic method arise from evolutionary convergence and difficulties in identifying features as evolutionary novelties.

6. Biological classification groups organisms into taxa according to their phylogenetic relationships.

7. The names of taxa are constructed according to international rules.

8. The fossil record of dinosaurs is best applied to problems of macroevolution.

KEY TERMS

binomen
clade
cladistic phylogeny
cladogram
classification
convergence
Charles Darwin
divergence
evolution
evolutionary novelty
extinction

family
fossil record
genus
grade
Linnaean hierarchy
Carolus Linnaeus
macroevolution
microevolution
monophyletic group
natural selection

origination
paleontologist
phylogenetic relationships
phylogenetic tree
phylogeny
polyphyletic group
principle of priority
species
stratophenetic phylogeny
synonym
taxa (taxon)

REVIEW QUESTIONS

1. Explain the central ideas behind Darwinian evolution.

2. Why do paleontologists who study dinosaurs favor cladistics instead of the stratophenetic method of phylogeny reconstruction?

3. Why does convergence pose a problem to cladists?

4. Construct a cladogram for the three taxa frog, dog, and cat. What shared evolutionary novelties led you to construct the cladogram?

5. What is the basis of biological classification?

6. What is the principle of priority and how is it applied to the scientific names of dinosaurs? What problems are alleviated by applying this principle?

7. What are the strengths and weaknesses of the dinosaur fossil record for studying evolution?

FURTHER READING

Eldredge, N. and Cracraft, J. 1980. *Phylogenetic Patterns and the Evolutionary Process.* New York: Columbia University Press. 349 pp. (An excellent introduction to the principles and methods of cladistics.)

Futuyma, D. J. 1986. *Evolutionary Biology* (second edition). Sunderland, Massachusetts: Sinauer Associates, Inc. 600 pp. (An intermediate-level college textbook on evolution.)

International Commission on Zoological Nomenclature. 1985. *International Code of Zoological Nomenclature* (third edition). London, International Trust for Zoological Nomenclature. 338 pp. (The international rule book for the construction of the scientific names of animals.)

Stanley, S. M. 1979. *Macroevolution.* San Francisco: W. H. Freeman and Company. 332 pp. (An advanced college text on evolution that heavily emphasizes the fossil record.)

Wiley, E. O., Siegel-Causey, D., Brooks, D. R., and Funk, V. A. 1991. *The Compleat Cladist: A Primer of Phylogenetic Procedures.* Lawrence, Kansas: The University of Kansas Museum of Natural History Special Publication 19, 158 pp. (A comprehensive how-to manual of cladistics.)

FOSSILS, SEDIMENTARY ENVIRONMENTS, AND GEOLOGIC TIME

Dinosaurs have been extinct for 65 million years, so we must study the fossils of dinosaurs to understand the history of this fascinating group of animals. Dinosaur fossils were formed in the environments in which the dinosaurs lived and died. The rocks that contain dinosaur fossils provide clues to the climate and habitats in which they lived. The reign of the dinosaurs began 225 million years ago. In this chapter, we examine the nature of dinosaur fossils, the relationship between rocks and ancient environments, and the geologic time scale for dinosaur evolution.

FOSSILS

The word **fossil** literally means "something dug up." Now the word generally refers to any physical trace of past life. Most dinosaur fossils are mineralized bones. But dinosaur fossils also include tracks, eggs, skin impressions, stomach stones (**gastroliths**) and fossilized feces (**coprolites**) (figure 3.1). These fossils are called **trace fossils** (or ichnofossils, from the Greek word *ichnos*, which means "trace") in contrast to mineralized dinosaur bones, which are termed "body fossils." Chapter 13 of this book discusses dinosaur trace fossils.

How are fossils formed? How long does it take for a bone to become a fossil? These are common questions asked of paleontologists, the scientists who study fossils. Key to the process of fossilization (figure 3.2) is burial in sediment (rock particles) of the dinosaur bone (or footprint, egg, etc.). When a dinosaur died, either it was buried immediately in sediment, or its remains, perhaps after scavenging, weathering, or transport by running water, were buried somewhat later (box 3.1). The soft tissues of the dinosaur—skin, muscles, internal organs—rotted away quickly whether or not it was buried immediately or long after death. Only rarely are soft tissues preserved, as in the case of a mummified duckbill dinosaur found in Alberta, Canada (figure 3.3).

FIGURE 3.1

Dinosaur fossils comprise bones and skeletons, footprints, eggs, skin impressions, gastroliths, and coprolites.

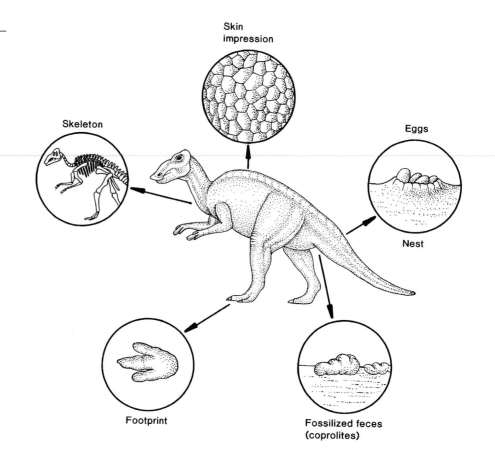

After burial, the remaining bones and teeth must usually undergo some form of **mineralization** to become fossils. Bones and teeth are not just inorganic minerals, but contain a significant amount of organic matter. This matter either decays and is replaced by minerals such as silica, calcite, or iron, or forms complex compounds by combining with these minerals. The replacement or combining takes place on a microscopic scale, so that tiny spaces around the inorganic matrix of the bone are filled with the new minerals. The resulting mineralized bone is thus a combination of the original inorganic bone matrix (a mineral called **calcium phosphate**) and the new minerals. However, in some cases the original inorganic bone matrix is also partly or completely replaced by the new minerals. In most mineralized bones the quality of microscopic structures is very high, so they can be studied under the microscope (figure 3.4).

Death

Decay

Burial

Mineralization

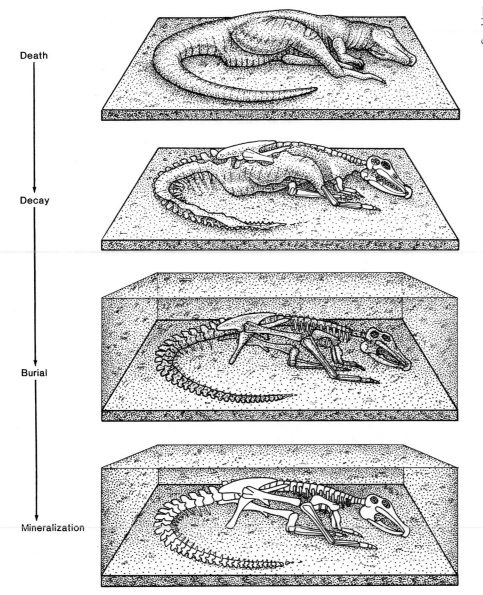

FIGURE 3.2

The process of fossilization involves death, decay, burial, and mineralization.

Fossils, Sedimentary Environments, and Geologic Time

BOX 3.1

TAPHONOMY

In 1943, Soviet paleontologist Ivan Efremov combined the Greek words *taphos*, meaning "burial" and *nomos*, meaning "laws," to describe a branch of paleontology he called **taphonomy**. Taphonomy is the study of how fossils are formed and what biases are inherent in the fossil record. By undertaking taphonomic studies, paleontologists gain insight into the behavior and ecology of extinct organisms. They also come to grips with the kinds of information contained in a collection of fossils. They do these things by trying to understand the processes that have taken place between the time an organism, or group of organisms, was alive and the present, when we collect fossils of those organisms.

If we imagine a population of dinosaurs alive, say, 100 million years ago, the first step toward fossilization of these animals is, of course, their death (box figure 3.1). If they die in an accident and their bodies are buried rapidly, such as in a flash flood, the dinosaurs immediately become a "burial assemblage." Most dinosaurs, however, probably died in other ways that did not cause immediate burial of their bodies. They may have been preyed upon by other dinosaurs or died from disease or old age,

or in other accidents. Also, many dinosaur carcasses must have been scavenged by other animals long before burial. Because most forms of death for dinosaurs did not include burial, taphonomists speak of a "death assemblage" made up of all the dead dinosaurs—whether they were whole carcasses or partial, preyed upon and/or scavenged carcasses—that were not buried at the time of death. Only later, usually through geologic processes such as the accumulation of river sediments around and over bones, did burial occur. The death assemblage eventually is converted to a burial assemblage.

This is an important distinction. We would expect the fossils of dinosaurs that enter the burial assemblage immediately upon death to be complete or virtually complete skeletons. But, by contrast, we would expect the fossils of dinosaurs that did not immediately enter the burial assemblage to be much less complete skeletons. Indeed, the fossils of such dinosaurs would be mainly parts of skeletons, isolated bones, and bone fragments. This is because any number of taphonomic processes, including surface weathering of bone, destruction of bone by

predators and scavengers, and damage to bone by running water and moving sediment, would have reduced the integrity of a dinosaur skeleton prior to burial. These simple observations show that complete dinosaur skeletons are mostly those of animals buried immediately upon death or very soon after. Many dinosaurs are represented by less complete specimens, whereas the overwhelming majority of dinosaurs left no fossils at all, simply because their skeletons were totally destroyed before they were buried.

Just because a dinosaur skeleton or bone was buried does not mean it became a fossil. Other taphonomic processes may intervene between the burial assemblage and the fossil assemblage (see box figure 3.1). For example, buried dinosaur bones could be exhumed by erosion and weather away before being fossilized. Or, even though buried, a skeleton might not become a fossil because the chemistry of the soil and groundwater was of the wrong type to lead to fossilization.

We can see that many factors may prevent a dinosaur from becoming a fossil that we can collect and study. Taphonomists stress this aspect of the fossil

FIGURE 3.3

This mummy of a duckbill dinosaur found in Alberta, Canada is a rare case of the fossilization of dinosaur soft tissues.

Courtesy Department of Library Services, American Museum of Natural History (Neg. #330491).

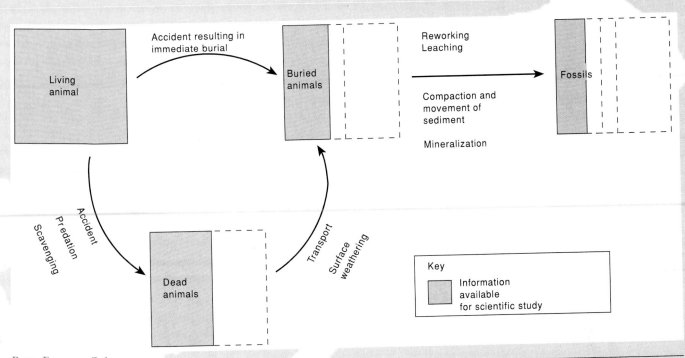

Living animal → Accident resulting in immediate burial → Buried animals

Living animal → Accident / Predation / Scavenging → Dead animals

Dead animals → Transport / Surface weathering → Buried animals

Buried animals → Reworking / Leaching / Compaction and movement of sediment / Mineralization → Fossils

Key

Information available for scientific study

BOX FIGURE 3.1

Taphonomic processes destroy information between the life of a dinosaur and the dinosaur fossils we collect and study.

record by pointing out how much information taphonomic processes have destroyed between the living dinosaur and its fossil in a museum. When the dinosaur was alive—a flesh-and-blood, moving animal—it was in a state of 100 percent information. But, as death, burial, and fossilization take place much information is lost, leaving us with only a small percentage of the original information available from the living dinosaur. Taphonomy helps paleontologists to understand how much information has been lost between the life of a dinosaur and the dinosaur fossils we collect and study.

FIGURE 3.4

This cross section of a fossilized dinosaur bone seen under high magnification shows the microscopic detail preserved. Here you can see small passages that were filled with blood and soft tissue.

The length of time it takes to fossilize bone is not well established. Most paleontologists believe it takes 10,000 years or more to fossilize a bone. This is because most bones that are 10,000 years old or younger—mainly those excavated at archaeological sites—show little or no mineralization. However, some bones much older than 10,000 years are little mineralized as well. Clearly, the rate at which a bone is mineralized depends on the type and chemistry of the sediment, the amount of water in the sediment, and other aspects of the sedimentary environment in which the bone is buried. This makes it difficult to generalize about the rate at which fossilization takes place. But, 10,000 years still remains a good minimum estimate of the time it takes most bones to fossilize.

The preservation of delicate organic structures, such as dinosaur skin or eggs, requires a special type of sedimentary environment where these structures are not damaged or destroyed. Dinosaurs must have made literally trillions of footprints during the 160 or so million years of their existence. But, with few exceptions, only those footprints made in moist sediment and buried quickly, before they could erode away, were preserved as fossil footprints.

Dinosaur fossils of all types are discovered and collected by fossil hunters worldwide. People who collect and study fossils professionally are called *paleontologists*, from the Greek words for "ancient-life studies." Dinosaur fossils collected by paleontologists are cleaned and studied in laboratories in museums and universities.

SEDIMENTARY ENVIRONMENTS

Geologists recognize three types of rock on the surface of the earth. **Igneous rocks** are those that cool from a molten state. They include all volcanic rocks. **Metamorphic rocks** are those that have been altered (metamorphosed) by temperature and/or pressure. Common metamorphic rocks are marble, which is limestone before metamorphism, and quartzite, which is sandstone before metamorphism. **Sedimentary rocks** are those formed by the accumulation and cementation of mineral grains or by chemical (including organic) precipitation. Sandstone, limestone, shale, and siltstone are common sedimentary rocks. Fossils are very rarely found in igneous or metamorphic rocks. Almost all fossils, and those of dinosaurs are no exception, are found in sedimentary rocks.

The type of sedimentary rock a dinosaur fossil is found in contains much information about the environment in which the dinosaur lived and died. This is because different types of sedimentary rocks are characteristic of the distinct **sedimentary (depositional) environments** in which the rocks formed. The process of rock formation encompasses the deposition of sediment (sedimentation) and its subsequent compaction and cementation.

The study of sedimentary rocks and their formation is called sedimentology. Sedimentologists make a broad distinction between marine (in the sea) and nonmarine (on the land) sedimentary environments (figure 3.5). Dinosaurs did not live in the sea, so their fossils are seldom found in marine sedimentary rocks. Therefore, we need not concern ourselves very much with marine sedimentary environments. Instead, we can focus mainly on the nonmarine (also called terrestrial) sedimentary environments—fluvial, lacustrine, eolian and deltaic—where almost all dinosaurs were fossilized.

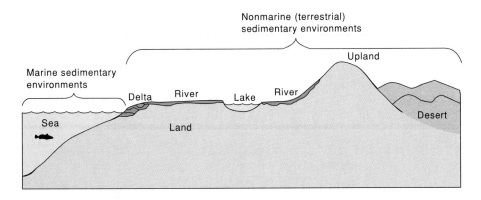

Nonmarine (terrestrial)
sedimentary environments

Marine sedimentary
environments

Upland

Delta   River   Lake   River

Sea   Desert

Land

FIGURE 3.5

Sedimentologists distinguish marine (in the sea)
from nonmarine or terrestrial (on the land
surface) sedimentary environments.

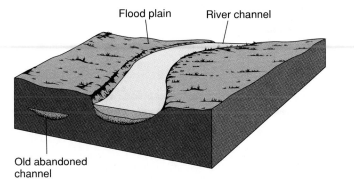

Flood plain   River channel

Old abandoned
channel

FLUVIAL ENVIRONMENTS

Fluvial environments (figure 3.6) are those where rivers and streams are the dominant agents of sedimentation (deposition). Because the water is moving in one direction, often quite rapidly, sediments deposited in fluvial environments are typically made up of relatively large particles of sand and gravel. These particles, when cemented, become sandstone and conglomerate. Fluvial sandstones and conglomerates often display structures characteristic of running water, such as ripple marks formed by currents or crossbeds formed on underwater dunes (figure 3.7). Coarse particle size and these sedimentary structures are the primary features by which geologists identify fluvial sedimentary rocks.

Most dinosaur fossils are found in fluvial sedimentary rocks (figure 3.8). This is because rapid deposition of sediments is typical of fluvial sedimentary environments. These environments bury the large bones of dinosaurs most rapidly, which would be most conducive to their fossilization.

LACUSTRINE ENVIRONMENTS

Lacustrine sedimentary environments are those where deposition takes place in or on the margins of lakes (figure 3.9). There the action of water is much gentler than in rivers, so lacustrine sedimentary rocks have much smaller particle sizes (clay and silt) than fluvial sedimentary rocks. Lacustrine rocks also have different sedimentary structures than fluvial rocks. Typically, they are laminated in thin layers whose

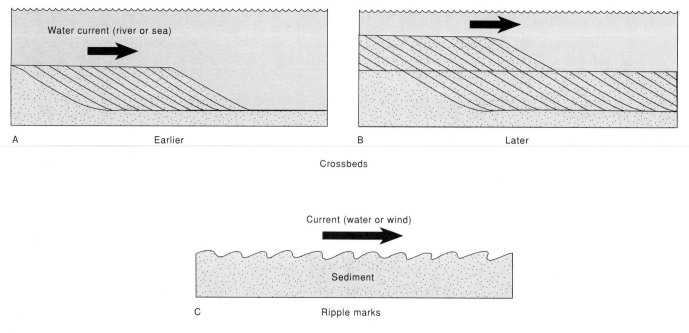

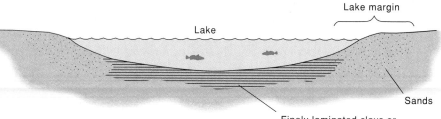

FIGURE 3.7

Running water produces ripple marks and crossbeds. (A.) Earlier; (B.) Later; (C.) Ripple marks.

From Charles C. Plummer and David McGeary, *Physical Geology*, 5th ed. Copyright © 1991 Times Mirror Higher Education Group, Inc., Dubuque, Iowa. All Rights Reserved. Reprinted by permission.

FIGURE 3.8

This dinosaur bone in a crossbedded sandstone in New Mexico is from a fluvial sedimentary environment.

FIGURE 3.9

Lacustrine environments are those in which sedimentation takes place in a lake.

FIGURE 3.10

This 150-million-year-old crossbedded sandstone in western Oklahoma was deposited in an eolian environment.

FIGURE 3.11

These dinosaur tracks near Moab, Utah were preserved in a desert.

Photo by Martin Lockley.

varying thicknesses reflect periodic (sometimes seasonal) fluctuations in deposition. And in lakes where not much mud or silt is involved in deposition, chemical precipitation of calcium carbonate, silica, or gypsum can become the dominant mode of deposition.

A fair number of dinosaur fossils have been found in lacustrine sedimentary rocks. Most of these dinosaur fossils, however, were found in the rocks that represent shoreline or river-delta deposits on the lake margins. This suggests that few, if any, dinosaurs were actually aquatic and lived in lakes.

EOLIAN ENVIRONMENTS

Eolian environments are those where the wind is the major agent of deposition. Wind-blown sediments typically display the same types of sedimentary structures— ripple marks and crossbeds—as fluvial sediments. But the wind generally cannot move larger particles as does running water, so eolian sedimentary rocks are fine-grained sandstones and siltstones. Also, the wind tends to sort and abrade the particles it moves, giving them a more even size distribution and a rounder shape than particles moved by water. Crossbedded and ripple-marked, well-sorted, rounded, fine-grained sandstones are typical rocks formed in ancient deserts (figure 3.10).

Few body fossils of dinosaurs were formed in eolian sediments because very little water was available for mineralization, but fossil footprints of dinosaurs abound in some eolian sedimentary rocks (figure 3.11).

DELTAIC ENVIRONMENTS

A delta is a triangular body of sediment formed where a river enters a large, quiet body of water, either a sea or a lake. So, **deltaic** sediments and fluvial sediments share many features. But the overall shape (geometry) of deltaic sediments and their proximity to lacustrine or **marine** sediments reveals their place of origin. Because deltas are often places where deposition is rapid, many dinosaur fossils, especially those of dinosaurs that lived near or along seashores, are preserved in deltaic deposits (figure 3.12).

FIGURE 3.12

These rocks in New Mexico, formed by river deltas about 70 million years ago, are loaded with dinosaur fossils.

Era	Period	Epoch	
Cenozoic	Quaternary	Holocene	
			0.01
		Pleistocene	
			1.6
	Tertiary	Pliocene	
			5
		Miocene	
			25
		Oligocene	
			34
		Eocene	
			54
		Paleocene	
			65
Mesozoic	Cretaceous		
			145
	Jurassic		
			208
	Triassic		
			250
Paleozoic	Permian		
			290
	Pennsylvanian		
			323
	Mississippian		
			362
	Devonian		
			408
	Silurian		
			439
	Ordovician		
			510
	Cambrian		
			570
Precambrian			

FIGURE 3.13

This geologic time scale shows both the major divisions of relative geologic time and the approximate numerical ages in millions of years of the division boundaries.

GEOLOGIC TIME

When we talk about the when and how fast (or slow) in dinosaur evolution, we must think in terms of geologic time—millions of years. Paleontologists and geologists, however, don't think about geologic time just in terms of numbers, but also in terms of a **relative time scale.** In a relative time scale, the goal is simply to determine whether one event is older or younger than another. The statement of the age of an event is thus an age relative to the age of another event. For example, *Stegosaurus* lived before, or is geologically older than, *Tyrannosaurus*. This is a statement of the relative geologic age of the two dinosaurs.

This contrasts with a **numerical time scale** in which the goal is to assign a numerical age, usually expressed in millions of years, to an event. In a numerical time scale we say *Stegosaurus* lived 150 million years ago, whereas *Tyrannosaurus* lived 67 million years ago. It might seem simplest and most precise to assign numerical ages to all the events in the age of dinosaurs. But the fact is that this is not possible, although most events in dinosaur evolution can be dated to within about 5 million years. Because of this general inability to assign more precise numerical ages, paleontologists use a relative geologic time scale to discuss the age of a dinosaur or an event involving dinosaurs.

The relative geologic time scale is a hierarchy of names applied to intervals of geologic time (figure 3.13). These names resemble the names of the months of the year or the names of the days of the week. In a given week, we know Thursday is after Tuesday, and, in a given year, we know March follows February. The names and their succession on the relative geologic time scale similarly allow paleontologists to be certain that the Cretaceous followed the Jurassic and that the Triassic was before the Cenozoic.

BOX 3.2

A DINOSAUR-BASED STRATIGRAPHIC CORRELATION

Today, Tanzania, in eastern Africa is tens of thousands of kilometers from the western United States. But during the Late Jurassic, when dinosaurs lived in these two areas, the locations were somewhat closer together because of continental drift, though still thousands of kilometers apart. In the western United States, especially Wyoming, Colorado, Utah, and Oklahoma, Late Jurassic dinosaurs are now found in a sequence of rocks called the Morrison Formation. In Tanzania, similar dinosaurs have been collected from a different sequence of rocks geologists call the Tendaguru Series. It is mostly because of the similarity of the dinosaur fossils from the Morrison Formation and the Tendaguru Series that paleontologists believe both rock sequences are of approximately the same age. The dinosaur fossils provide an important correlation of two rock sequences widely separated geographically, then and now.

Dinosaurs from the Morrison Formation are among the most familiar to the American public: Brontosaurus (properly called Apatosaurus), Diplodocus, Brachiosaurus, Allosaurus, and Stegosaurus. These and other Morrison Formation dinosaurs were first collected by American paleontologists during the late 1800s. Imagine the surprise of many paleontologists when several of the same types of dinosaurs, such as Brachiosaurus and Allosaurus, were discovered in the Tendaguru Series of East Africa by German paleontological expeditions just before the First World War. According to the principle of biostratigraphic

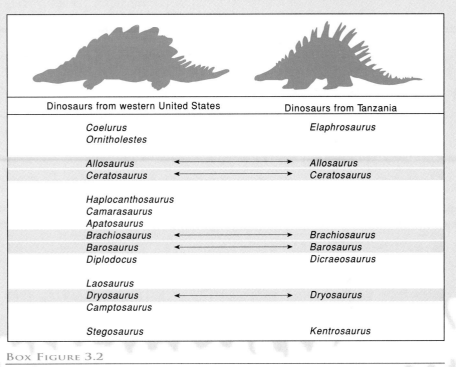

Dinosaurs from western United States		Dinosaurs from Tanzania
Coelurus Ornitholestes		Elaphrosaurus
Allosaurus	←———→	Allosaurus
Ceratosaurus	←———→	Ceratosaurus
Haplocanthosaurus Camarasaurus Apatosaurus		
Brachiosaurus	←———→	Brachiosaurus
Barosaurus	←———→	Barosaurus
Diplodocus		Dicraeosaurus
Laosaurus		
Dryosaurus	←———→	Dryosaurus
Camptosaurus		
Stegosaurus		Kentrosaurus

BOX FIGURE 3.2

Dinosaurs from rocks as far apart as the western United States and Tanzania are similar and support the correlation of these rocks.

correlation, this means that the Morrison Formation and the Tendaguru Series are of the same relative age.

The Tendaguru Series, however, has additional importance to the correlation of these dinosaur faunas. This is because the dinosaur-bearing rocks in Tanzania were deposited along the shore of a Late Jurassic sea, and some of the dinosaur bones from the Tendaguru Series have the fossils of marine clams attached to them. Apparently, the clams grew on these bones in the shoreline lagoons and estuar-

ies after the dinosaurs died. These clams are Late Jurassic in age because they are the same types as clams found in other marine rocks of well-accepted Late Jurassic age. So we can now say that the same types of dinosaurs lived in the western United States and eastern Africa during the Late Jurassic when certain types of clams lived in the sea. This gives paleontologists a more complete picture of the Late Jurassic world, on the land and in the sea.

The construction of a relative geologic time scale by geologists and paleontologists was heavily rooted in two principles. The first, the **principle of superposition,** states that in layered rocks (strata) the oldest rocks are at the bottom and younger layers are on top. The second, the **principle of biostratigraphic correlation,** states that rocks containing the same types of fossils are of the same age. This principle is one of the basic ideas of **biostratigraphy,** which is the identification and organization of strata based on their fossil content and the use of fossils in stratigraphic correlation. Stratigraphic correlation is the process of determining the equivalence of age or position of strata in different areas (box 3.2). It is one of the fundamental goals of stratigraphy, the study of layered rocks.

Geologists and paleontologists long ago realized that much of the vast thickness of **strata** exposed on the earth's surface is full of fossils, many of which only occur in specific layers and are thus considered to represent organisms distinctive of a particular interval of geologic time. The study of strata and fossils began in western Europe during the late 1700s, so many of the names used in the relative geologic time scale (see figure 3.13) were coined by European geologists and based on European rocks and fossils.

One useful aspect of the time scale is that it is a hierarchy of time intervals from long to short. For the purposes of this book, the longest intervals used are the eras. During the past 570 million years, there have been three eras: the **Paleozoic,** "ancient life," **Mesozoic,** "intermediate life," and **Cenozoic,** "recent life." The boundaries of these eras coincide with major extinctions, such as the Permo-Triassic extinction, which eliminated many characteristic Paleozoic organisms, and the terminal Cretaceous, or Cretaceous-Tertiary, which eliminated the dinosaurs and other characteristic Mesozoic organisms. Because dinosaurs lived only during the Mesozoic, we need only concern ourselves with the three geologic periods of the Mesozoic: the **Triassic, Jurassic,** and **Cretaceous.**

THE TRIASSIC PERIOD

German geologist Friedrich August von Alberti coined the term *Triassic* in 1834. In studying the salt deposits of Germany, Alberti found three different rock sequences, an older one dominated by sandstone, an intermediate one mostly of limestone, and a younger one mostly of shale. All three sequences were younger than rocks identified as Permian but older than Jurassic rocks. Thus, Alberti established a distinct time interval between the Permian and Jurassic, naming it Triassic (*triad* is Latin for "three") for the three rock sequences in Germany. The Triassic, of course, is subdivided into three time intervals, the Early, Middle, and Late Triassic. Geologists, however, refer to Triassic rocks, not time intervals, as Lower, Middle, and Upper Triassic rocks. This convention, using Lower and Upper for rocks, but Early and Late for time, and Middle for both, is applied to all portions of the rock record and geologic time.

Today, rocks of Triassic age are recognized worldwide. The Triassic Period lasted more than 40 million years, from about 250 to 208 million years ago (see figure 3.13). Dinosaurs did not appear until the Late Triassic, about 225 million years ago. They appeared at almost exactly the same time as the first turtles, crocodiles, pterosaurs (flying reptiles), plesiosaurs (long-necked marine reptiles), and mammals.

THE JURASSIC PERIOD

Many of us know Alexander von Humboldt as a famous explorer and geographer of the late eighteenth century. But von Humboldt was also a trained geologist who, in 1799, first used the name Jura for a distinctive limestone in the Jura Mountains of Switzerland. This became the basis for the word *Jurassic*, used by geologists to refer to the time period between the Triassic and the Cretaceous, 208 to 145 million years ago (see figure 3.13).

Like the Triassic, the Jurassic is divided into Early, Middle, and Late intervals of time and Lower, Middle, and Upper rock intervals. Dinosaurs flourished everywhere on Earth during the Jurassic and were very abundant and diverse.

THE CRETACEOUS PERIOD

In parts of western Europe, especially in Great Britain, France, and Belgium, rocks that are younger than Jurassic and older than Tertiary are mostly chalk. For this reason, the Belgian geologist J. J. D'Omalius d'Halloy used the French term *Terrain Crétacé* (Cretaceous System) in 1822 to refer to these rocks (*creta* is Latin for "chalk").

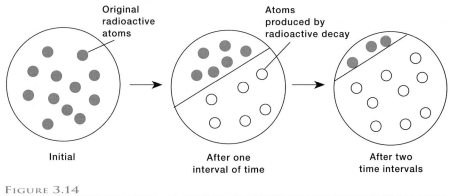

FIGURE 3.14

The slow decay of radioactive atoms provides a radioactive clock for measuring geologic time in millions of years.

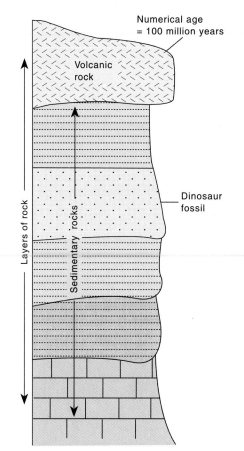

FIGURE 3.15

A numerical age from a volcanic rock only approximates the age of dinosaur fossils in nearby sediments. In this example, the volcanic rock yields a numerical age of 100 million years. Because the volcanic rock is above the layer with dinosaur bones, the principle of superposition indicates the bones must be older than 100 million years.

The Cretaceous Period is the interval of geologic time between the Jurassic and Tertiary, 145 to 65 million years ago (see figure 3.13). It has traditionally been divided only into Early and Late time intervals, but during the last 20 years a Middle Cretaceous time interval also has been distinguished. Dinosaurs are evident in rocks of Cretaceous age on all the world's continents. They became extinct at the end of the Cretaceous.

NUMERICAL AGES

The geologic time scale used here (see figure 3.13) includes not just the names of the eras, periods, and epochs, but also assigns numerical ages, in millions of years, to their boundaries. How are these numerical ages calculated?

Before the discovery of radioactivity, calculating numerical ages for events in geologic history was little more than guesswork. But radioactivity, the spontaneous decay or falling apart of some types of atoms, provides a natural clock for estimating numerical geologic ages, because the rate of decay is constant for a given type of atom (figure 3.14). Geologists can use this **radioactive clock** to determine the numerical ages of rocks, provided that the rate of decay is known for the radioactive atoms and that the rock contains a known quantity of such atoms.

In laboratories, geochemists have calculated with great precision the rates at which radioactive atoms decay. Some of these rates are very slow and therefore great precision is needed in the laboratory to calculate them. For example, the rate of decay of uranium-238 is so slow that it takes 4.5 billion years for half the uranium atoms in a sample to decay. Calculating the amount of decay of uranium atoms by measuring the product of the decay, which is lead-206, in a rock from the age of dinosaurs involves measuring a very small amount. Avoiding errors in measurement is difficult; sometimes mistakes are made, and incorrect numerical ages are calculated.

These problems, however, do not prevent the best laboratories from calculating accurate numerical ages. Instead, what poses the largest problem for a numerical time scale is that most rocks, indeed nearly all sedimentary rocks, do not contain enough decaying radioactive atoms. Sufficient quantities of these types of atoms are found almost exclusively in igneous rocks. Because igneous rocks do not usually contain fossils, the usual way to calculate a numerical age for a fossil is to find an igneous rock layer close to the sedimentary rock that contains fossils. Ideally, sheets of lava above and below a layer of sedimentary rock containing dinosaur fossils will yield numerical ages bracketing the age of the fossils (figure 3.15). But this does not happen often, and paleontologists can only estimate the numerical age of a dinosaur fossil by evaluating its proximity to the nearest rocks yielding a numerical age.

Such evaluation relies on several lines of evidence used in stratigraphic correlation. But the fact remains that we cannot assign precise numerical ages to all dinosaur fossils, and we may never be able to do so. This is why we continue to use the divisions of the relative geologic time scale, supplemented by the best numerical-age estimates available, when discussing the when and how fast.

COLLECTING DINOSAUR FOSSILS

Dinosaur fossils occur in Mesozoic sedimentary rocks formed in nonmarine environments. So, the search for dinosaur fossils focuses on these rocks. Paleontologists will look at such rocks, relying in part on the locations of previously discovered dinosaur fossils and in part on sheer luck to find dinosaur fossils.

Once the dinosaur fossil is found, if it is small enough and sufficiently solid it may be collected by simply picking it up (if it is on the surface) or digging it right out of the rock. But most dinosaur fossils are so large and/or fragile that they must be encased in a plaster jacket to be collected. This is done by carefully digging around the fossil (figure 3.16), covering it with paper (so the plaster does not adhere directly to the fossil) and then wrapping the fossil with strips of burlap soaked in wet plaster. When the wet plaster hardens, it forms a solid case that protects the fossil from damage during transport to the laboratory

In the laboratory, technicians remove the plaster jacket and clean the rock from the dinosaur fossil. This process of preparation has to be undertaken with great care and precision, so as to not damage the fossil. Often the cleaned dinosaur fossil needs further stabilization and is coated with shellac-like hardeners. Complete preparation of a dinosaur fossil may take months or years!

After preparation, the dinosaur fossil is ready for scientific study and display. Paleontologists and technicians at museums and universities worldwide undertake the collecting, preparation, and study of dinosaur fossils.

FIGURE 3.16

Excavating a dinosaur takes much care, patience, and hard work.

SUMMARY

1. Fossils are evidence of past life. Dinosaur fossils are not only bones but include fossilized footprints, eggs, skin impressions, stomach stones, and feces.

2. Dinosaur bones were almost always mineralized as they were fossilized, a process believed to have taken at least 10,000 years.

3. Taphonomy is the study of the processes that intervened between the life of a dinosaur and the fossils of dinosaurs we collect and study. Taphonomy particularly concerns the information lost via these processes.

4. Dinosaur fossils are preserved almost exclusively in sedimentary rocks formed on the continents by rivers, lakes, and deltas.

5. Geologic time is measured by two time scales, a relative one and a numerical one.

6. On the relative time scale, dinosaurs lived during the Mesozoic Era, from the Late Triassic Period through the entire Jurassic and Cretaceous Periods, until their extinction at the end of the Cretaceous.

7. On the numerical time scale, dinosaurs lived about 225 to 65 million years ago.

8. The numerical time scale is based primarily on the decay of radioactive atoms found in sufficient quantity, with few exceptions, in igneous rocks.

9. Because dinosaur fossils are not found in igneous rocks, numerical ages for dinosaurs are estimates with varying degrees of accuracy. This is why most statements about the ages of dinosaurs employ the relative time scale.

KEY TERMS

biostratigraphy
calcium phosphate
Cenozoic Era
coprolite
Cretaceous Period
deltaic
eolian
fluvial
fossil
gastrolith

igneous rock
Jurassic Period
lacustrine
marine
Mesozoic Era
metamorphic rock
mineralization
numerical time scale
Paleozoic Era
principle of biostratigraphic correlation

principle of superposition
radioactive clock
relative time scale
sedimentary (depositional) environment
sedimentary rock
strata
taphonomy
trace fossil
Triassic Period

REVIEW QUESTIONS

1. What types of dinosaur fossils can paleontologists collect and study?

2. How does bone fossilize? How long might fossilization take?

3. What taphonomic processes intervene between a living dinosaur and its fossils? What effect do they have on the information available to paleontologists?

4. What types of rocks and what types of sedimentary environments contain most dinosaur fossils? Why are few fossils found in igneous and metamorphic rocks?

5. Compare and contrast the relative and the numerical geologic time scales.

6. Why can't we assign precise numerical ages to all dinosaur fossils?

7. When, in terms of the relative and the numerical time scales, did dinosaurs live?

FURTHER READING

Berry, W. B. N. 1987. *Growth of a Prehistoric Time Scale*. Palo Alto, California: Blackwell Scientific Publications. 202 pp. (This book reviews the history of the relative geologic time scale and the principles behind it.)

Prothero, D. R. 1990. *Interpreting the Stratigraphic Record*. New York: W.H. Freeman & Company. 410 pp. (An intermediate-level college textbook that provides an introduction to stratigraphic principles and sedimentary environments.)

Selley, R. C. 1976. *Ancient Sedimentary Environments*. Ithaca, New York: Cornell University Press. 237 pp. (An excellent overview of sedimentary environments.)

Shipman, P. 1981. *Life History of a Fossil: An Introduction to Taphonomy and Paleoecology*. Cambridge, Massachusetts: Harvard University Press. 222 pp. (A good overview of the concepts and methods of taphonomy.)

Stanley, S. M. 1989. *Earth and Life Through Time*. New York: W.H. Freeman & Company. (An introductory-level college textbook that provides an overview of fossils and the history of life.)

A Primer of Dinosaur Anatomy

To understand dinosaurs, we must have some familiarity with their anatomy. In this text, we mean skeletal anatomy. A dinosaur skeleton is a complex piece of machinery consisting of more than 300 separate bones, each with its own distinctive features. It is from these bones that paleontologists identify different types of dinosaurs and glean much of what we know about them. In this chapter, we review the salient features of dinosaur skeletons and introduce the anatomical terms used throughout this book.

Posture and Orientation

Many dinosaurs were **bipeds,** which means they habitually walked on their hind limbs, as do living humans (figure 4.1). Other dinosaurs were **quadrupeds,** habitual walkers on all four limbs, like living horses, cats, and dogs (figure 4.1). Some dinosaurs walked both ways, sometimes on the hind limbs and at other times on all fours. Such dinosaurs were **facultative bipeds** (figure 4.1) or **facultative quadrupeds.** Some dinosaurs were facultative bipeds because they walked mostly on all fours, but occasionally on their hind limbs, like living bears. Other dinosaurs were facultative quadrupeds because they walked on hind limbs most of the time and occasionally on all fours, like some living kangaroos.

Whether a dinosaur skeleton belonged to a quadruped, biped, or something in between, the terms we use to orient ourselves to it are the same (figure 4.2). The direction toward the head is termed **anterior,** and the opposite direction is **posterior.** Paleontologists speak of the forelimbs as anterior to the hind limbs and the tail as posterior to the back. The belly side of a dinosaur is the **ventral** side, and the back side is **dorsal.** Thus, when we look at a dinosaur skull, the lower jaw is ventral to the eyes, and the nostrils are dorsal to the mouth. Indeed, the top and the bottom sides of a dinosaur skull are referred to as the dorsal and ventral sides, respectively.

In any dinosaur, the **axial** portion of the skeleton is the skull, backbone, and tail. In a quadrupedal dinosaur, down and up from the axial skeleton, of course, are ventral and dorsal. But in bipedal dinosaurs that held the body nearly upright, especially the front half of the body (such as *Tyrannosaurus rex*), dorsal points backward and ventral points forward, as in humans. If you are confused when locating dorsal and ventral on a bipedal dinosaur, imagine the animal as a quadruped.

From a horizontal perspective, the direction away from the midline of the body is called **lateral.** The opposite direction, toward the midline of the body, is **medial.** Thus, the lungs of a dinosaur are medial to its ribs, and the shoulder blade is lateral to the ribs.

Facultative quadruped

Facultative biped

Quadruped

Biped

FIGURE 4.1

Bipeds walk habitually on their hind limbs and quadrupeds walk on all four limbs. Facultative bipeds and facultative quadrupeds walk part of the time on the hind limbs and part of the time on all fours.

© Mark Hallett

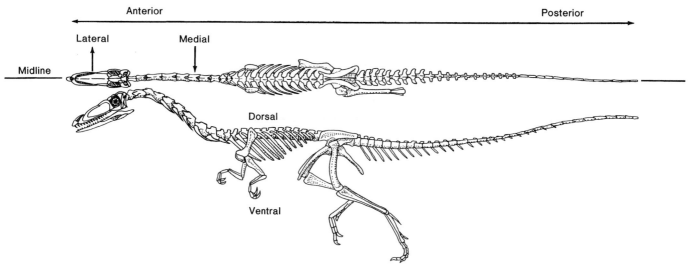

Anterior

Posterior

Lateral

Medial

Midline

Dorsal

Ventral

FIGURE 4.2

Dorsal, ventral, anterior, posterior, lateral, and medial are important terms of orientation in the skeletal anatomy of dinosaurs.

When we speak of dinosaur limbs, however, different terms are used. Those limb segments closer to the body are **proximal** to those farther away. And those limb segments farther from the body are **distal** to those closer to the body. So, the knee is proximal with respect to the ankle and, conversely, the ankle is distal with respect to the knee (figure 4.3).

Now we can orient ourselves to any dinosaur skeleton. We can look at the anterior or posterior ends or the ventral, dorsal, or lateral sides. Furthermore, we can locate in a general way any bone with respect to another. A bone is either ventral, dorsal, anterior, posterior, lateral, or medial (or more than one of these) with respect to another bone. And, in the limbs, a segment is either proximal or distal to another segment.

The posture of dinosaurs was characteristically **upright** (erect). This means the limbs were held directly under the body, as are our hind limbs and the limbs of our pet dogs and cats and most other mammals. This contrasts with the **sprawling posture** of most reptiles, in which the limbs are held out to the side so that their proximal bones are horizontal or nearly horizontal to the ground (see figure 1.2). Some dinosaurs, however, may have held the forelimbs in a semi-sprawling posture intermediate between the upright and sprawling postures.

SKULL, LOWER JAW, AND TEETH

A dinosaur skeleton consists of a **skull,** or cranium, lower jaw, or **mandible,** and the remaining bones, which are called the **postcrania.** The skull of a dinosaur (figure 4.4) is an intricate structure of more than 30 individual bones. These bones are connected to each other along **sutures.** A sutural connection between two bones is a relatively solid connection that allows little or no movement between the two bones. But many dinosaurs had joints between various bones in their skulls that allowed the bones to move. The skulls of these dinosaurs are referred to as **kinetic** (figure 4.5).

Learning the names and locations of all the bones in a dinosaur skull and mandible is not necessary in order to read this book. But a few key bones should be learned. These bones include the following: (1) the **premaxillary,** the bone at the

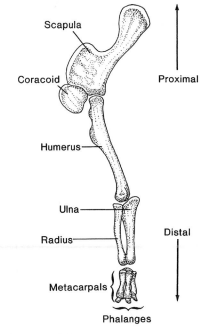

FIGURE 4.3

Limb segments farther away from the body are distal to those closer (proximal) to the body.

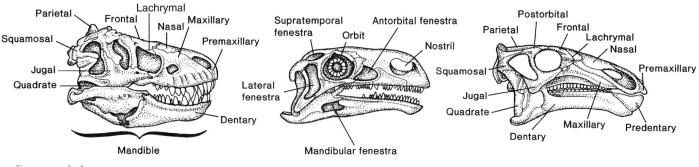

FIGURE 4.4

The skull of a dinosaur consists of more than 30 bones, most or all of which are tightly sutured to each other.

FIGURE 4.5

Kinetic skulls, like those of some snakes, have
joints that allow skull bones to move past
each other.

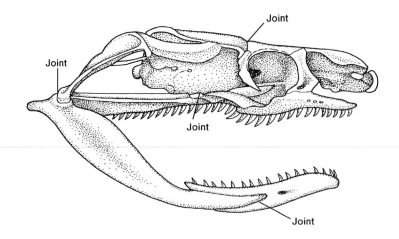

front of the upper jaw, which in some dinosaurs bears teeth; (2) the **maxillary,** the
upper jaw bone behind the premaxillary that bears the upper cheek teeth; (3) the
predentary, the bone in the front of the lower jaw, present in some dinosaurs; (4) the
dentary, the principal bone of the lower jaw, which bears the lower cheek teeth;
(5) the **jugal,** or the "cheekbone"; (6) the **parietals** and **squamosals,** two paired bones
near the back of the skull; (7) the **frontals** and **nasals,** two paired bones near the
front of the skull; (8) the **lachrymals,** small bones in front of the eye sockets; (9)
the **quadrates,** the principal bones of the upper jaw joints; and (10) the **occipital
condyle,** the bony knob at which the skull connects to the backbone.

In addition to the names of the individual bones, paleontologists use specific terms to refer to different regions of the dinosaur skull and mandible. The portion of the skull in front of the eyes is termed the **rostrum** or face; the eye socket is
the **orbit;** and the region behind the orbit along the side of the skull is the **temporal** region of the skull. The portion of the skull that encloses the brain is the
braincase. The bones outside of the braincase are **dermal bones.** Openings in these
dermal bones in a dinosaur skull are the **temporal fenestrae** (from the Latin word
for "window"), a lower one termed the **lateral temporal fenestra** and an upper one,
the **supratemporal fenestra.** Note that an opening in the mandible is a **mandibular fenestra,** and an opening in the rostrum in front of the orbit is an **antorbital** (literally "in front of the orbit") **fenestra.** The top of the skull is termed the **skull roof,**
and the area around the nostrils **(nasal cavity)** is the **nasal region.** The top of the
mouth is the **palate,** and the lower jaw, as described, is often called the **mandible.**

All of the teeth in a dinosaur's mouth are referred to collectively as its **dentition.** Dinosaur teeth come in a variety of shapes and sizes (figure 4.6), but the portion of each tooth above the gumline is called the **crown.** When the teeth mesh
together we speak of **occlusion,** and the surfaces along which the teeth meet each
other are thus the **occlusal surfaces.** The crown of a dinosaur tooth may be covered with **lophs** (ridges) or **denticles** (small cusps). When many teeth are present
and are attached to (or overlap) each other, they form a **dental battery.**

BACKBONE

The backbone of a dinosaur is a **vertebral column** composed of numerous separate
bones called **vertebrae** (figure 4.7). Each dinosaur's vertebral column can be divided into four regions: **cervical** (neck), **dorsal** (back), **sacral** (hips), and **caudal** (tail).
The number of cervical vertebrae for most dinosaurs is 9 or 10, but hadrosaurs
have as many as 15 and some sauropods have as many as 19 cervical vertebrae.
Sauropods have an increased number of cervical vertebrae in part at the expense

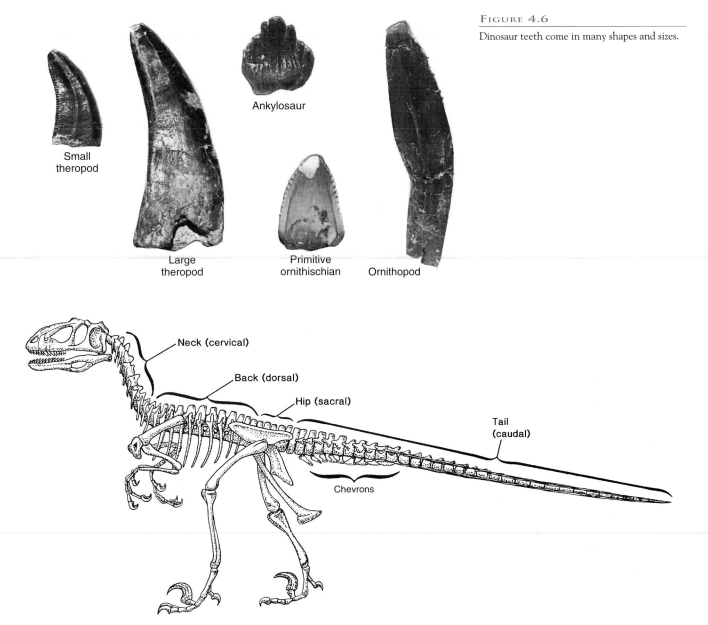

FIGURE 4.6

Dinosaur teeth come in many shapes and sizes.

Small theropod

Ankylosaur

Large theropod

Primitive ornithischian

Ornithopod

Neck (cervical)

Back (dorsal)

Hip (sacral)

Tail (caudal)

Chevrons

FIGURE 4.7

The vertebral column, composed of many individual vertebrae, can be divided into four regions.

of their dorsal vertebrae, which are as few as 9. Most dinosaurs have 15 to 17 dorsal vertebrae, and 3 to 5 sacral vertebrae make up the **sacrum.** But ceratopsians have as many as 10 sacrals. The number of caudal vertebrae ranges from as few as 35 to as many as 82 (in the sauropod *Apatosaurus*).

Each vertebra has a spool-shaped body along its ventral side, the **centrum** (plural: **centra**). Dorsal to the centrum is the **neural arch,** which covered the spinal cord (it ran through a canal between the centrum and the neural arch). The thin rod or blade of bone that projects dorsally from the neural arch is the **neural spine.** Ventral to the centrum of the caudal vertebrae of some dinosaurs is another arch-like structure, the **chevron.** The centra meet each other front to back, and bony ridges link the neural arches with each other, thereby producing an **articulated** (connected) vertebral column.

Separate ribs attach to the cervical and dorsal vertebrae of dinosaurs. Some dinosaurs also had rib-like bones, the **gastralia,** covering their bellies.

FORELIMB

The forelimb skeleton of a dinosaur (figure 4.8) attaches to the body at the **shoulder girdle.** The largest and most prominent bone of the shoulder girdle is the **scapula.** A smaller bone is the **coracoid.** The shoulder girdle in dinosaurs, like ourselves, is held near the front end of the rib cage by muscles and other tissues. Some dinosaurs also had a **clavicle** (collarbone) connecting the scapula to the **sternum,** a row of bones on the ventral midline of the dinosaur.

The shoulder joint of a dinosaur is the point of articulation between the scapula and the single bone of the upper arm, the **humerus.** At the elbow joint, the humerus articulates with the two bones of the lower arm, the **radius** and the **ulna.**

At the wrist joint, the radius and ulna meet the **carpals,** the separate bones of the wrist. Distally, the carpals meet the **metacarpals,** which, in turn, meet the bones of the fingers, the **phalanges** (singular: **phalanx**). Pointed terminal (distalmost) phalanges usually bore **claws,** whereas flattened terminal phalanges bore **hooves** or hoof-like coverings.

HIND LIMB

The hind limb of a dinosaur (figure 4.9) attaches to the body at the **pelvis.** The dinosaur pelvis consists of three bones on each side of the body: the **ilium, ischium,** and **pubis** (plural: ilia, ischia, and pubes). Differences in the shapes of these bones, especially in the shape of the pubis, are extremely important in the classification of dinosaurs.

The dinosaur pelvis is securely sutured along the medial surface of the ilia to the sacral vertebrae. The single bone of the upper leg, the **femur,** fits into a socket, called the **acetabulum,** at the junction of the three pelvic bones. Distally, the femur articulates with the **tibia.** The lower leg of a dinosaur also has another smaller bone, the **fibula,** which attaches to the tibia.

The tibia and fibula articulate distally with the bones of the ankle, the **tarsals.** Two tarsals are important to understanding the origin of dinosaurs. They are the most proximal tarsals, the **astragalus** and **calcaneum** (see figure 4.9).

Distally, the tarsals articulate with the **metatarsals,** which, in turn, articulate with the toe bones, the **phalanges.** As in the forelimb, the phalanges of the hind limb may have borne claws, hooves, or hoof-like coverings depending on their shape. Fingers and toes of dinosaurs are usually referred to by a single term, **digits.**

STRUCTURE AND FUNCTION

This book makes many statements about the behavior of dinosaurs. Some dinosaurs are identified as quadrupeds, others as bipeds. We distinguish plant-eating and meat-eating dinosaurs. Differing ideas about the forelimb postures of some dinosaurs are also discussed.

These types of statements reflect the relationship between a particular structure and its **function.** This relationship is one of the foundations of paleontology. The size and shape of a single bone, of several bones, or of an entire skeleton depend on, as well as determine, the function of that structure. This is because the skeleton of a dinosaur is the framework to which the muscles were attached and upon which the other soft tissues were hung. How the muscles moved largely depended on the skeleton to which they were attached. And the shape, size, and arrangement of the other soft tissues—internal organs, blood vessels, etc.—was very much influenced by the skeleton around them. So, it is possible to examine a skeleton and make some inferences about the dinosaur's muscles and other soft tissues (figure 4.10). This in turn permits an understanding of the appearance and behavior of the dinosaur.

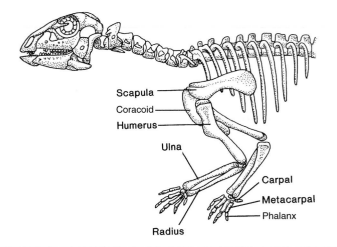

FIGURE 4.8

The forelimb skeleton of a dinosaur extends from the shoulder girdle to the phalanges.

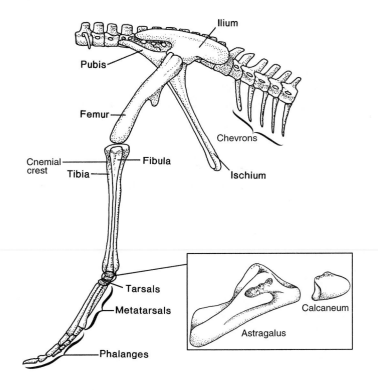

FIGURE 4.9

The hind-limb skeleton of a dinosaur extends from the pelvis to the phalanges.

Identification of dinosaurs as bipeds, quadrupeds, or something in between earlier in this chapter and throughout this book provides a good example of the inference of function from structure. Among living animals, bipeds share much larger and more massive (hence stronger) hind-limb skeletons. This makes sense mechanically because the hind limbs of a biped must propel and support its entire weight. In contrast, living quadrupeds have more nearly equally-sized forelimbs and hind limbs. Furthermore, the structure of the hips and vertebral columns of living bipeds and quadrupeds differ because of their very different postures while locomoting.

We can look for such structures in dinosaur skeletons as a key to their postures, or more easily just look at relative limb sizes. A clear and easy inference of function from structure can be made by looking at the skeleton of *Tyrannosaurus* (see figure 6.8). Its tiny forelimbs and massive hind limbs indicate bipedality. The more nearly equal-sized forelimbs and hind limbs of *Diplodocus* (see figure 7.8), however, indicate quadrupedality.

A Primer of Dinosaur Anatomy   **39**

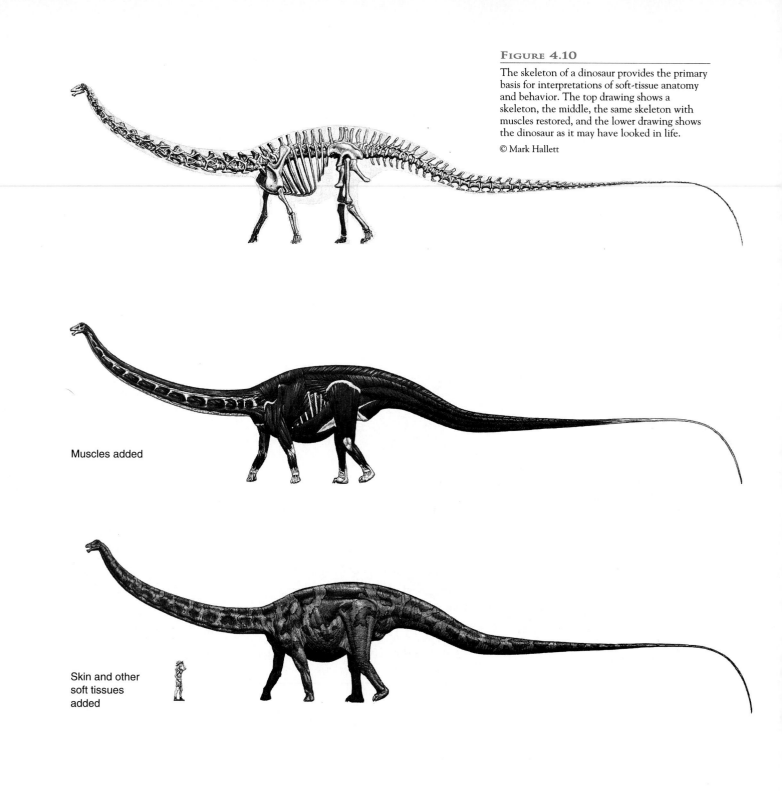

FIGURE 4.10

The skeleton of a dinosaur provides the primary basis for interpretations of soft-tissue anatomy and behavior. The top drawing shows a skeleton, the middle, the same skeleton with muscles restored, and the lower drawing shows the dinosaur as it may have looked in life.

© Mark Hallett

Muscles added

Skin and other soft tissues added

KEY TERMS

acetabulum
anterior
antorbital fenestra
articulated
astragalus
axial
biped
braincase
calcaneum
carpals
caudal
centrum (centra)
cervical
chevron
clavicle
claws
coracoid
crown
dental battery
dentary
denticle
dentition
dermal bones
digit
distal
dorsal
facultative biped
facultative quadruped
femur
fibula

frontals
function
gastralia
hooves
humerus
ilium
ischium
jugal
kinetic
lachrymals
lateral
lateral temporal fenestra
loph
mandible
mandibular fenestra
maxillary
medial
metacarpals
metatarsals
nasal cavity
nasal region
nasals
neural arch
neural spine
occipital condyle
occlusal surface
occlusion
orbit
palate
parietal
pelvis

phalanges (phalanx)
postcrania
posterior
predentary
premaxillary
proximal
pubis
quadrates
quadruped
radius
rostrum
sacral
sacrum
scapula
shoulder girdle
skull
skull roof
sprawling posture
squamosal
sternum
supratemporal fenestra
suture
tarsals
temporal
temporal fenestra
tibia
ulna
upright posture
ventral
vertebrae
vertebral column

REVIEW QUESTIONS

1. Orient yourself with respect to a dinosaur skeleton. Relative to the femur, where are the humerus, the maxillary, the tibia, and a caudal vertebra?

2. Compare the segments of the forelimb and hind-limb skeletons and note any similarities and differences.

3. What is the general relationship between skeletal structure and function?

FURTHER READING

Hildebrand, M. 1982. *Analysis of Vertebrate Structure* (second edition). New York: Wiley. 428 pp. (An introductory-level college text on the inference of function from structure.)

Hildebrand, M., Bramble, D. M., Liem, K. F., and Wake, D. B. 1985. *Functional Vertebrate Morphology.* Cambridge, Massachusetts: Harvard University Press. 430 pp. (An intermediate-level college text that examines all aspects of the relationship between vertebrate structure and function.)

Romer, A. S. 1956. *Osteology of the Reptiles.* Chicago: University of Chicago Press. 772 pp. (A detailed, technical review of all aspects of the skeletons of reptiles, including those of the dinosaurs.)

Romer, A. S. and Parsons, T. A. 1977. *The Vertebrate Body* (fifth edition). Philadelphia: W.B. Saunders Company. 624 pp. (A thorough review, in introductory textbook form, of all aspects of vertebrate anatomy, including two chapters on the skull and the skeleton.)

THE ORIGIN OF
DINOSAURS

The oldest dinosaur fossils are of Late Triassic age, about 225 million years old. These fossils, and those of other Triassic reptiles closely related to dinosaurs, provide paleontologists with a relatively good understanding of the origin of dinosaurs. This understanding, however, is far from complete, and the exact details of dinosaur origins remain to be discovered. In this chapter, we explore the relationships of dinosaurs to other reptiles and review the current understanding of the origin of dinosaurs.

DINOSAURS AND REPTILES

For many years scientists have used the word **reptile** to refer to living turtles, snakes, lizards, and crocodilians, as well as to their fossil relatives. *Reptile* traditionally referred to a tetrapod (four-legged vertebrate) with scaly skin that reproduces by laying an amniotic egg. An **amniotic egg** (figure 5.1) is usually a hard-shelled egg (some have leathery shells), such as the chicken egg we are most familiar with. More precisely, it is an egg in which the developing embryo is almost totally surrounded by a liquid-filled cavity that is enclosed by the amnion. This egg can be laid on dry land, unlike the eggs of fishes and amphibians, which must be laid in water or in a very moist place. The appearance of the amniotic egg freed reptiles from the dependence on water that characterizes the amphibians. As added evidence of that freedom, we see in reptiles a much more solidly connected vertebral column and more powerful limb skeletons than we do in amphibians (figure 5.2). Thus, the amniotic egg and skeletal modifications for terrestrial locomotion are the key evolutionary novelties that distinguish the reptiles from their ancestors among the amphibians.

Viewed cladistically, we can thus identify the origin of reptiles as a single clade or monophyletic group. But most of the key features of reptiles are also seen in their descendants, which we call birds and mammals. This means that the word *reptile* refers to a paraphyletic group unless we include birds and mammals in that group. Paraphyletic groups are clades that do not include all of their terminal branches (figure 5.3). They are only portions of clades and are avoided by most cladists.

There are several ways to deal with this cladistic problem. One way is to abandon the term *reptile* and use the term *amniote* to refer to what were formerly termed reptiles, and their descendants, the birds and mammals. Another way, and the one employed here, is to continue in the interest of easy communication to use *reptile* as a term to refer to all amniotes except birds and mammals. This use of *reptile* identifies dinosaurs as reptiles. Some paleontologists, however, prefer recognizing birds and dinosaurs as a group separate from reptiles, which they name Dinosauria

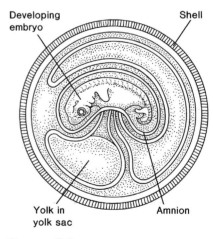

Developing embryo   Shell

Yolk in yolk sac   Amnion

FIGURE 5.1

The amniotic egg does not need to be laid in water, which freed reptiles of their dependence on water, a characteristic of their ancestors, the amphibians.

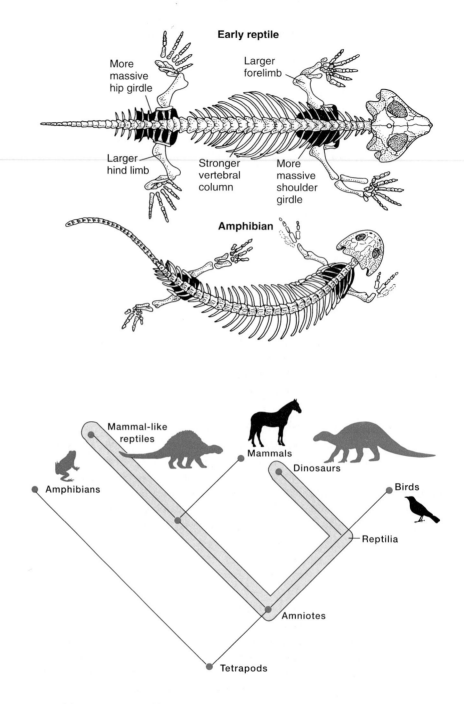

FIGURE 5.2

The skeleton of an early reptile differs from that of an amphibian principally in the modification of the limbs and girdles to support the reptile in fully terrestrial locomotion.

Early reptile

More massive hip girdle

Larger forelimb

Larger hind limb

Stronger vertebral column

More massive shoulder girdle

Amphibian

FIGURE 5.3

The cladogram of the amniotes indicates that Reptilia is only part of a clade because it does not include the descendants of reptiles, the birds, and mammals. In cladistic terms, Reptilia is a paraphyletic group.

Mammal-like reptiles

Mammals

Dinosaurs

Amphibians

Birds

Reptilia

Amniotes

Tetrapods

or Aves (the name normally applied only to birds). Because there is abundant evidence that dinosaurs laid amniotic eggs, and dinosaur skeletons show extensive modifications for terrestrial locomotion, this book classifies them as reptiles.

DINOSAURS AS DIAPSIDS

Reptiles have long been classified into four groups based on the pattern of openings in the skull roof behind the orbits (figure 5.4). The idea of a skull roof having openings or holes behind the eyes may strike you as strange. This is because our skull roof

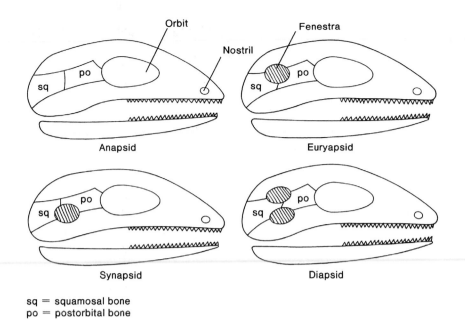

Orbit

Fenestra

Nostril

po

sq

Anapsid

po

sq

Euryapsid

po

sq

Synapsid

po

sq

Diapsid

sq = squamosal bone
po = postorbital bone

FIGURE 5.4

Four groups of reptiles can be recognized based on the number and position of temporal fenestrae.

Dermal
skull
roof

Braincase
(under dermal skull roof)

FIGURE 5.5

The braincase of a reptile, such as the turtle shown here, is hidden within a second wall of bone, the dermal skull roof.

behind the eyes seems to be a solid wall of bone surrounding our extremely large brains. We actually have one small opening, behind the eye, but it is not obvious. In contrast, reptilian brains are relatively smaller and are contained in a solid braincase. This braincase is inside of a second wall of bone that contains the openings characteristic of different reptile groups (figure 5.5).

The most primitive reptiles had no openings in the wall of dermal bone behind the eyes. These reptiles are called **anapsids** (*an*—"without"; *apsis*—"opening"), and turtles today have an anapsid skull structure. Other reptiles evolved one or more pairs of openings (see figure 5.4).

The development of these openings, the **temporal fenestrae,** may be attributed to two things. The first is the concentration of mechanical stress in the skull. Experiments have shown that bone grows more thickly in stressed areas of the skull and other bones, and between such areas bone is thin or absent. The second is the distribution of the muscle attachments. Muscles can be more strongly anchored to ridges and edges of bone than to flat surfaces. The stresses created by chewing and the attachment of chewing muscles to the skull determined the number and position of the temporal fenestrae.

Dinosaurs have two temporal fenestrae on each side of their skulls and thus belong to the group of reptiles called Diapsida. All living reptiles, except turtles, also are **diapsids.** Euryapsids include two groups of Mesozoic marine reptiles, the very fish-like ichthyosaurs and the long-necked plesiosaurs. Synapsids encompass the mammal-like reptiles, which include the ancestors of mammals, as well as the pelycosaur *Dimetrodon* (see figure 1.1), a reptile often mistaken for a dinosaur.

The Origin of Dinosaurs   **45**

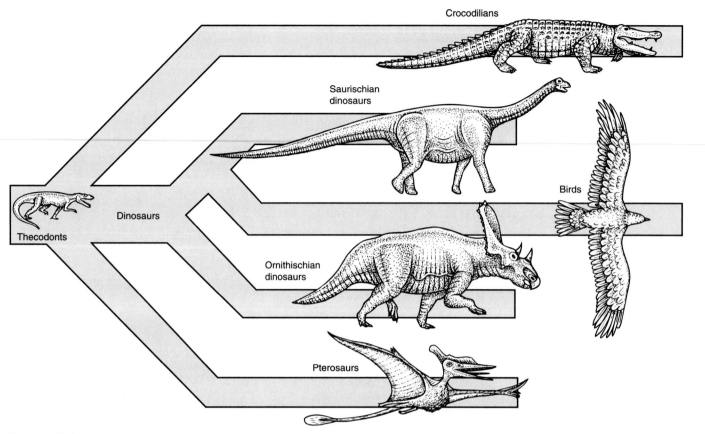

Crocodilians

Saurischian
dinosaurs

Birds

Thecodonts

Dinosaurs

Ornithischian
dinosaurs

Pterosaurs

FIGURE 5.6

The archosaurs, other than a few primitive types not considered here, consist of four groups: the thecodonts, crocodiles, pterosaurs, and dinosaurs.

DINOSAURS AS ARCHOSAURS

The diapsid reptiles consist of two great groups, the **lepidosaurs** and the **archosaurs,** which diverged from each other during the Permian Period, more than 250 million years ago. Living lizards and snakes and their ancestors are lepidosaurs and are of no further concern to us in this book.

Archosaurs include the dinosaurs, a group called **thecodonts** (which includes the immediate ancestors of dinosaurs), and two groups of close dinosaur relatives, the pterosaurs (flying reptiles) and the **crocodilians** (figure 5.6). Key evolutionary novelties among archosaurs that distinguish most of them from lepidosaurs include a fenestra in front of the orbit, a fenestra in the mandible, laterally compressed, serrated teeth, no teeth on the palate, and features of the limb skeleton that indicate a semi-upright or upright limb posture.

Among the archosaurs, crocodilians first appeared in the Late Triassic and survive today. **Pterosaurs** are often included with the dinosaurs in popular books. But they are a distinct group of archosaurs with a fascinating and complicated evolutionary history that took place at the same time as the dinosaurs, during the Late Triassic–Late Cretaceous (figure 5.7). The ancestry of dinosaurs, which are specialized archosaurs, must be sought among the thecodonts.

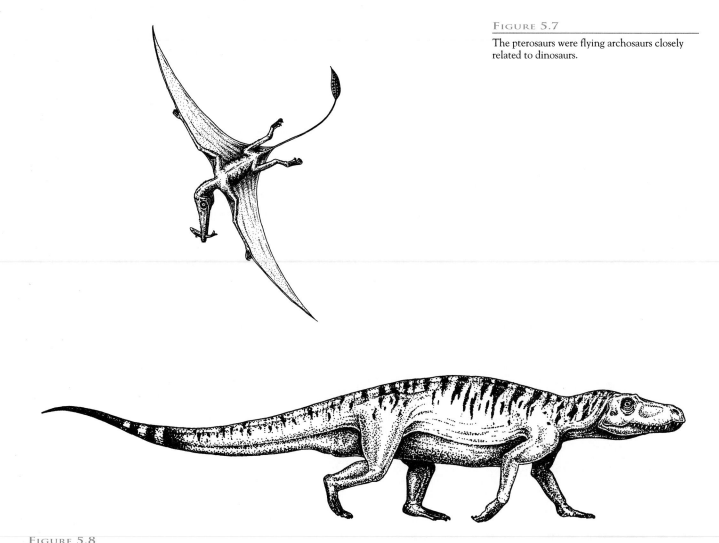

FIGURE 5.8

Thecodonts were very successful during the Triassic and include one of the largest land-living predators of the Late Triassic, *Postosuchus*.

THE THECODONT ANCESTRY OF DINOSAURS

Thecodonts form a paraphyletic grade, not a clade, of archosaurs. This is because thecodonts gave rise to crocodiles, dinosaurs, and pterosaurs. Thecodonts were very diverse and successful during the Triassic (figure 5.8). In fact, Triassic archosaurs that were not crocodiles, dinosaurs, or pterosaurs are classified as thecodonts. Unfortunately, there is no currently accepted phylogeny or classification of the thecodonts.

Those interpreting thecodont phylogeny and dinosaur ancestry have relied heavily on analysis of ankle structures. There are two reasons for this. First, the bones of the ankle are very compact and dense, and thus are usually well preserved and common as fossils. Second, and more important, the structure of thecodont and dinosaur ankles provides us with insight into how these animals walked. This is

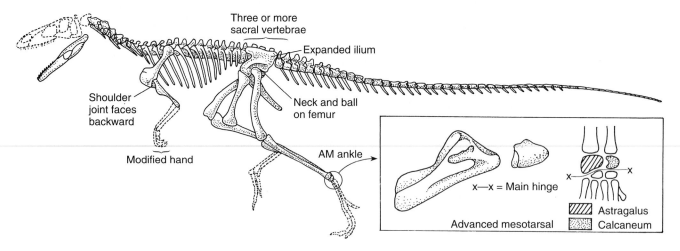

FIGURE 5.9

Several evolutionary novelties—most associated with an upright posture—distinguish dinosaurs from other archosaurs.

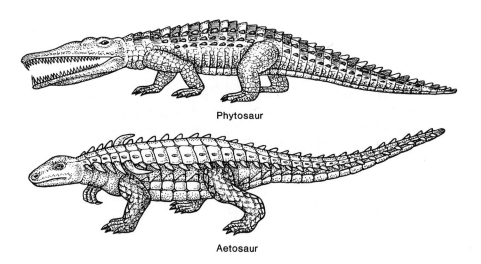

Phytosaur

Aetosaur

FIGURE 5.10

Aetosaurs and phytosaurs were thecodonts whose CN (crocodile normal) ankle removed them from the ancestry of dinosaurs. They are more closely related to crocodilians.

significant because the origin of dinosaurs began, in one important sense, with the evolution of archosaurs having an upright posture from those having a semi-upright (sprawling) posture.

Skeletal features indicative of an upright posture thus are among those that paleontologists identify as evolutionary novelties of the dinosaurs (figure 5.9). A special type of ankle structure, called the **advanced mesotarsal (AM) ankle,** is one of these evolutionary novelties. In the AM ankle, the astragalus is much larger than the calcaneum, and both bones are rigidly attached to each other and to the tibia. Because of this, the AM ankle has a single hinge between the calcaneum-astragalus and the rest of the foot. This hinge allows little twisting of the ankle when walking. Instead, the foot below the AM ankle swings backwards and forwards in a straight line to enable speedy, upright walking and running.

The AM ankle of dinosaurs contrasts with the more crocodile-like ankles of thecodonts. These ankles have joints that allow them to twist while walking. This twisting is normal when walking with a sprawling posture, because it helps the entire foot to stabilize slowly as it touches the ground. Most thecodonts, including the heavily armored, plant-eating **aetosaurs,** and the crocodile-like **phytosaurs** (figure 5.10), walked with a sprawling posture.

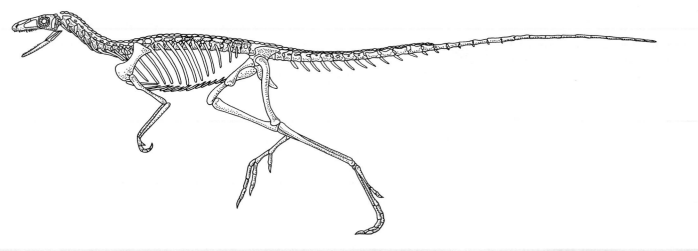

FIGURE 5.11

Half-meter-long *Lagosuchus* from the Middle Triassic of Argentina best approximates the dinosaur ancestor.

The shapes of the dinosaur pelvis and femur also contrast with the shapes of those bones in thecodonts. Their shapes indicate that dinosaurs held the hind limb upright and directly under the body.

To identify a possible ancestor—or an animal closely related to that ancestor—paleontologists look to small, predatory thecodonts with limb structures that indicate they walked with a nearly upright posture. This would have been a posture intermediate between the sprawling posture of other thecodonts, such as phytosaurs and aetosaurs (see figure 5.10), and the fully upright posture of the dinosaurs.

Thecodonts with these modifications were the **ornithosuchids** and an animal named ***Lagosuchus.*** Ornithosuchids were 1 to 3 meters long, facultatively bipedal predators from the Triassic of Argentina and Scotland. They were very dinosaur-like thecodonts, as was *Lagosuchus* from the Middle Triassic of Argentina. Indeed, the anatomy and geological age of *Lagosuchus* (figure 5.11) are as close to those of a suitable ancestor of dinosaurs as in any known thecodont.

PHYLOGENY OF DINOSAURS

Dinosaurs appear suddenly in the Late Triassic fossil record (box 5.1). These diapsid archosaur reptiles were distinguished primarily by skeletal features that indicated an upright posture. Their ancestry lay among advanced thecodonts, and *Lagosuchus* best approximates that ancestry.

In the more than 150 years since dinosaurs were first recognized, many dinosaur phylogenies have been proposed. Recent studies of dinosaur phylogeny employ the methods of cladistics discussed in Chapter 2, and the phylogeny used in this book is cladistic, too (figure 5.12).

For many years, paleontologists viewed dinosaurs as a polyphyletic group of two or more distinct clades that evolved from different groups of thecodonts. But now it is generally agreed that dinosaurs are a monophyletic, single clade united by evolutionary novelties that include three or more sacral vertebrae, a shoulder joint

BOX 5.1

WHICH DINOSAUR WAS THE OLDEST?

Dinosaurs of Late Triassic age are known from the United States, Canada, Brazil, Argentina, Morocco, South Africa, Lesotho, Great Britain, and Germany. But the idea has long persisted that of the Late Triassic dinosaurs the oldest is either **Staurikosaurus** from Brazil or **Herrerasaurus** from Argentina. A recent reevaluation of the ages of these dinosaurs, however, has indicated that they are of the same age and that equally old, or slightly older, dinosaurs are also known from the western United States, Morocco, and India. This means that dinosaurs appeared almost simultaneously (within our current level of geologic-time resolution) over a broad geographic area during the Late Triassic.

Late Triassic tetrapod faunas are of two types—aquatic and terrestrial. The aquatic faunas are dominated by fossils of large amphibians and phytosaurs, a group of crocodile-like thecodonts. The terrestrial faunas lack phytosaurs and amphibians, and instead are dominated by rhynchosaurs, a group of plant-eating primitive diapsids, and traversodontids, a group of plant-eating, mammal-like reptiles. Comparing aquatic and terrestrial Late Triassic faunas with each other in order to decide whether they are of the same age is somewhat difficult. Fortunately, enough animals are found in both aquatic and terrestrial faunas to make their age relationships reasonably clear.

We can thus identify three aquatic faunas—from the United States, Morocco, and India—and two terrestrial faunas—from Brazil and Argentina—as being of about the same age, 225 million years old. These are the oldest Triassic faunas that contain dinosaur fossils (box figure 5.1). Thus, there is a nearly simultaneous first record of dinosaur fossils across a broad expanse of the Late Triassic landscape. Furthermore, even at their first appearance, a wide variety of dinosaurs, perhaps as many as 20 different genera, can already be distinguished. This probably means that the origin of dinosaurs actually took place well before 225 million years ago.

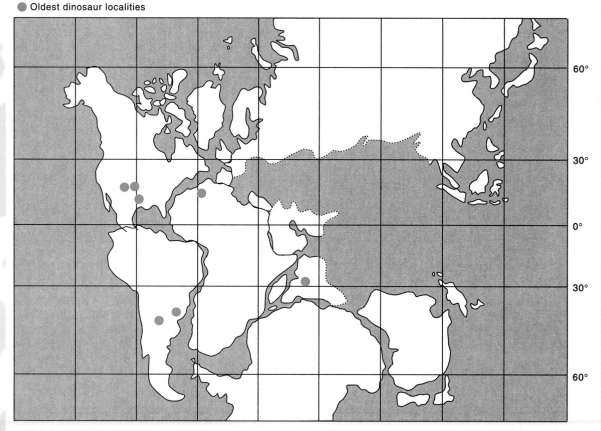

● Oldest dinosaur localities

Triassic continental configuration due to continental drift

BOX FIGURE 5.1

The oldest Triassic dinosaurs are from Argentina, Brazil, the western United States, India, and Morocco. Note that because of continental drift, all the continents were united into one supercontinent called Pangaea during the Late Triassic.

FIGURE 5.12

This phylogeny of the major groups of dinosaurs is employed in this book.

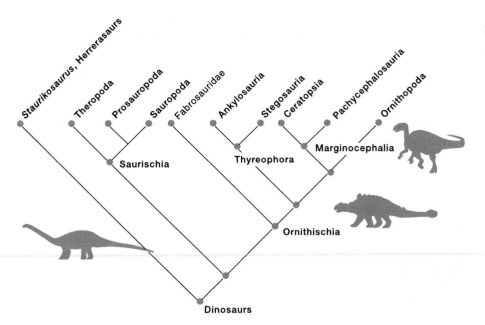

that faces backward, three or fewer phalanges in the fourth digit of the hand, a distinct neck and ball offset from the shaft of the femur to articulate with the open hip socket, and an expanded ilium. These and other features distinguish all dinosaurs from their closest relatives among the thecodonts.

Dinosaurs were long ago divided into two groups by British paleontologist Harry G. Seeley. The two groups, **Saurischia** ("lizard hips") and **Ornithischia** ("bird hips"), were distinguished primarily on the basis of their pelvic structure (figure 5.13). In the pelvis of saurischian dinosaurs the three pelvic bones radiate in different directions from the hip socket **(acetabulum),** as in most other reptiles. In the pelvis of ornithischian dinosaurs the pubis is parallel to the ischium, a feature seen also in birds (figure 5.13).

Despite resemblance of the dinosaur pelvis to that of either a living lizard or a living bird, it had many distinctive features. These included an opening in the acetabulum below a lip of bone against which the femur pressed, and an elongated pubis and ischium that hung down between the legs.

Recent cladistic analysis has upheld a twofold division of all but a few dinosaurs including *Staurikosaurus* and the herrerasaurs, into the two clades, Saurischia and Ornithischia (see figure 5.12). Indeed, a number of other evolutionary novelties distinguish these two dinosaurian clades. These include the presence of a toothless predentary bone in the lower jaw and ossified (bone-like) tendons in the backs and tails, both distinctive features of ornithischians (figure 5.14).

FIGURE 5.13

The two major groups of dinosaurs, Saurischia and Ornithischia, are distinguished primarily by differences in pelvic structure.

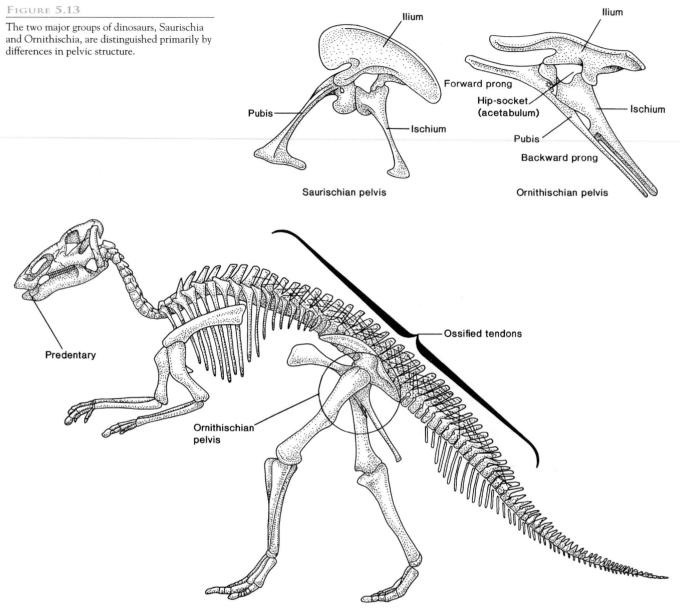

FIGURE 5.14

The predentary bone and ossified tendons along the vertebral column of ornithischians are two features, in addition to pelvic structure, that distinguish them from saurischians.

Saurischia itself consists of two clades, the **Theropoda** and **Sauropodomorpha.** The evolutionary novelties of these clades are discussed in Chapters 6 and 7, respectively. *Staurikosaurus* and the herrerasaurs were neither saurischians nor ornithischians because they lacked the evolutionary novelties that unite the saurischians and ornithischians into a clade.

The most primitive ornithischians were the fabrosaurs. They lacked the evolutionary novelties of other ornithischians, especially the spout-shaped front end of the lower jaw and the well-defined fenestra in front of the eye. **Thyreophoran** ("shield-bearers") dinosaurs are united principally by distinctive body armor (see Chapter 9), whereas the incipient frill (backward-projecting shelf of bone) present on the skulls of both **ceratopsians** and **pachycephalosaurs** is considered to be the principal reason for their close relationship as **Marginocephalia** (see Chapter 10). The evolutionary novelties of the **Ornithopoda** are discussed in Chapter 8.

The phylogeny of the ornithischian groups of dinosaurs is not yet agreed on by paleontologists, but most phylogenies agree on the close relationships between **stegosaurs** and **ankylosaurs** and between ceratopsians and pachycephalosaurs. They disagree primarily on how these groups relate to ornithopods and on the composition of the ornithopods. The phylogeny employed here (see figure 5.12) recognizes ornithopods as close relatives of marginocephalians because of several shared evolutionary novelties, including a gap between teeth in the premaxillary and the maxillary, five or fewer premaxillary teeth, unequal layers of enamel on the teeth, and the absence of a bony lip above the acetabulum.

A classification of the major groups of dinosaurs (figure 5.15) can be derived from the dinosaur phylogeny presented here . What rank in the Linnaean hierarchy each group is assigned is somewhat arbitrary, but the suggestion of one recent scientist who views the major groups at the branch tips of the cladogram—theropods, sauropodomorphs, etc.—as orders, is followed in this book.

More interesting, perhaps, than turning the cladogram into a classification, is to read it as a roadmap of the important milestones in dinosaur evolution (figure 5.16). Thus, from an as-yet-undiscovered ancestor (see box 5.1), the primitive *Staurikosaurus*–herrerasaur clade diverged from the clade of other dinosaurs by the Late Triassic. Also by the end of the Triassic, saurischian and ornithischian clades had diverged from an unknown common ancestor. And during the Late Triassic the two major saurischian clades—theropods and sauropodomorphs—must also have diverged. Clearly, much happened in the origin and evolution of dinosaurs just before and during the Late Triassic. Major events in ornithischian evolution seem to have taken place a bit later, with basal thyreophorans and ornithopods not appearing until the Early Jurassic. The ankylosaur–stegosaur split in the thyreophorans took place by Middle Jurassic time, whereas marginocephalians apparently did not diverge from ornithopods until the Cretaceous.

THE OLDEST DINOSAURS

Some Triassic–Early Jurassic dinosaurs can be assigned to the Theropoda (see Chapter 6), but others lacked the evolutionary novelties of theropods, sauropods, ornithopods, thyreophorans, or marginocephalians. Most of these primitive dinosaurs are known only from a few bones or isolated teeth. So it is difficult to gain a complete picture of them and their phylogenetic relationships to other dinosaurs (box 5.2). Two of these dinosaurs, *Staurikosaurus* and *Lesothosaurus,* are known well enough to give us some idea of the diversity of the most primitive dinosaurs.

Staurikosaurus is the best known from an incomplete skeleton from the Upper Triassic of Brazil (figure 5.17). This dinosaur was about 2 meters long with very long, slender hind limbs, apparently a biped and a fast runner. The head was relatively large and had numerous blade-like teeth, suggesting that *Staurikosaurus* was a meat eater. The pelvis was saurischian-like but differed from that of saurischians in having a well-developed hip socket (acetabulum) on the ilium.

Staurikosaurus-like fossils are also known from Argentina and the western United States. Closely related primitive dinosaurs are *Eoraptor* and the herrerasaurs, typified by *Herrerasaurus,* from the Upper Triassic of Argentina. Paleontologists regard *Eoraptor, Staurikosaurus,* and *Herrerasaurus* as representatives of early clades of primitive, saurischian-like dinosaurs.

The most primitive, plant-eating dinosaurs can be assigned to the Ornithischia. Triassic–Early Jurassic ornithischians of this type are often called **fabrosaurids** and include *Pisanosaurus* from Argentina and *Technosaurus* from the United States. However, these two dinosaurs are known from very few bones, so we will examine **Lesothosaurus** (formerly called **Fabrosaurus**) from the Lower Jurassic of Lesotho as a typical fabrosaur.

Staurikosaurus, Herrerasaurs

Superorder Saurischia
  Order Theropoda
  Order Sauropodomorpha
    Suborder Prosauropoda
    Suborder Sauropoda
Superorder Ornithischia
  Order Ankylosauria
  Order Stegosauria
  Order Ceratopsia
  Order Pachycephalosauria
  Order Ornithopoda

FIGURE 5.15

This classification of dinosaurs is based on the phylogeny in figure 5.12.

BOX 5.2

ISOLATED TEETH VS. SKULLS AND SKELETONS

The Late Triassic fossil record of the earliest dinosaurs includes relatively few complete skeletons, but many isolated bones and teeth. Recent attempts to interpret these fragmentary fossils has led to some disagreement among paleontologists.

Some paleontologists believe that isolated teeth provide a good basis for distinguishing different types of early dinosaurs. According to them, at least 20 different dinosaur tooth types are known from the Late Triassic, and each deserves recognition as a distinct dinosaur genus. One of the latest tooth types to be recognized is *Revueltosaurus*, a name coined for fabrosaur teeth from the Upper Triassic of New Mexico and Arizona (box figure 5.2).

An alternative point of view, held by other paleontologists, is that teeth alone are not sufficient to distinguish Late Triassic dinosaurs. These paleontologists argue that tooth shape varies within a single dinosaur jaw, and that we don't have enough complete Late Triassic dinosaur jaws to understand that variation. It is thus very risky to recognize distinct dinosaurs by their teeth alone, because several distinct tooth types might come from a single dinosaur jaw.

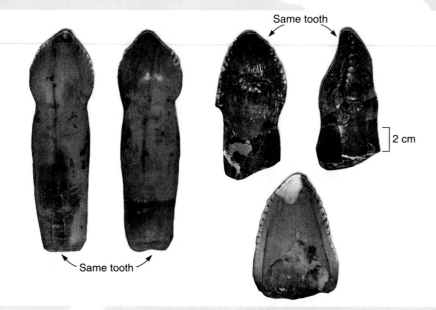

Same tooth

Same tooth

2 cm

BOX FIGURE 5.2

These fabrosaur teeth from the Upper Triassic of New Mexico have been named *Revueltosaurus*.

This argument might seem so strong that nobody would try to recognize distinct types of Late Triassic dinosaurs based on isolated teeth. But, in fact we don't have enough Late Triassic dinosaur jaws to understand tooth variation, and what jaws we have do not show sufficient variation in tooth shape in a single jaw to encompass many of the types of isolated Late Triassic dinosaur teeth. The paleontologists who use isolated teeth to recognize dinosaurs, and their critics, are at a standstill pending the discovery of more complete jaws of Late Triassic dinosaurs.

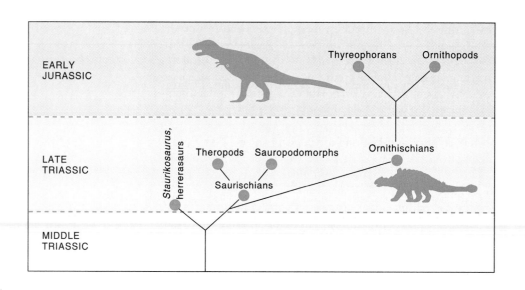

FIGURE 5.16

Much divergence took place in the early evolution of dinosaurs during the Late Triassic and Early Jurassic.

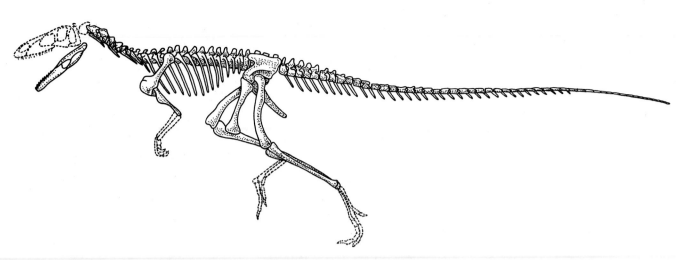

FIGURE 5.17

Two-meter-long *Staurikosaurus* from the Upper Triassic of Brazil was one of the most primitive dinosaurs. It cannot be assigned to either the Saurischia or the Ornithischia.

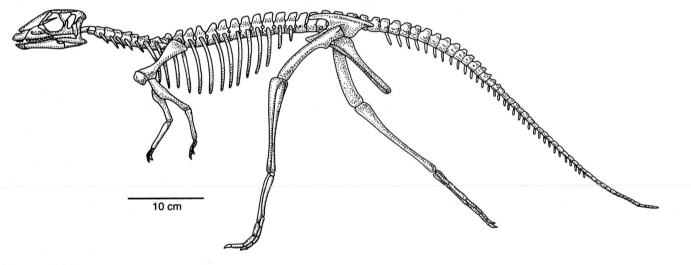

10 cm

FIGURE 5.18

Lesothosaurus from the Lower Jurassic of Lesotho was a fabrosaur and one of the most primitive ornithischians.

Lesothosaurus (figure 5.18) was a small dinosaur (90 centimeters long) known from several skulls and skeletons. The skull was short and high, with very large eyes and numerous slender, leaf-shaped cheek teeth that clearly were those of a plant eater. A pocket on the side of the skull in front of the eye may have contained a salt gland.

The neck of *Lesothosaurus* was long and flexible, the back was long, the tail was very long, and the slender hind limbs were much longer than the forelimbs. The limbs were those of an agile biped that probably plucked vegetation with its front teeth and hands. *Lesothosaurus* had the proportions of primitive ornithopods, such as the heterodontosaurids (see Chapter 8), so some paleontologists include the fabrosaurs with the ornithopods. But fabrosaurs lacked the evolutionary novelties diagnostic of ornithopods, although they did have some features (predentary bone and pelvis) characteristic of ornithischians. Here, fabrosaurs are regarded as primitive ornithischians.

SUMMARY

1. Reptile is a term that refers to tetrapods that lay an amniotic egg, have limb skeletons modified for fully terrestrial locomotion, and are ancestral to birds and mammals.

2. Dinosaurs are reptiles because they laid amniotic eggs and had limb skeletons adapted to terrestrial locomotion.

3. Reptiles are classified into four groups based on the number and position of openings (temporal fenestrae) in the skull roof behind the orbits.

4. Dinosaurs are diapsids because they had two temporal fenestrae on each side of their skull.

5. Diapsids consist of two groups, the lepidosaurs (lizards, snakes, and their ancestors) and the archosaurs (thecodonts, crocodilians, pterosaurs, and dinosaurs).

6. The ancestry of dinosaurs lies among the thecodonts. Key to deciphering this ancestry is ankle structure and other skeletal features that indicate the evolution of upright dinosaurs from semi-upright thecodonts.

7. Dinosaurs appeared suddenly during the Late Triassic over a geographically wide area. They were the descendants of *Lagosuchus*-like thecodonts.

8. The earliest dinosaurs include *Eoraptor, Staurikosaurus* and herrerasaurs, close relatives of the Saurischia, and theropods and very primitive ornithischians, the fabrosaurs.

KEY TERMS

acetabulum
advanced mesotarsal (AM) ankle
aetosaurs
amniotic egg
anapsid
Ankylosauria
archosaur
Ceratopsia
crocodilian
diapsid
fabrosaurids

Fabrosaurus
Herrerasaurus
Lagosuchus
lepidosaur
Lesothosaurus
Marginocephalia
Ornithischia
Ornithopoda
ornithosuchids
Pachycephalosauria
phytosaurs

pterosaur
reptile
Saurischia
Sauropodomorpha
Staurikosaurus
Stegosauria
temporal fenestrae
thecodont
Theropoda
Thyreophora

REVIEW QUESTIONS

1. Explain why dinosaurs can be called a group of archosaurian diapsid reptiles.

2. Why are cladists not satisfied with groups of animals like reptiles and thecodonts?

3. How do the ankle structures of archosaurs provide a key to their phylogenetic relationships?

4. What features distinguish saurischian from ornithischian dinosaurs?

5. Summarize briefly the when, where, and from what of dinosaur origins.

6. How do two of the earliest dinosaurs, *Staurikosaurus* and *Lesothosaurus*, differ from each other?

FURTHER READING

Bakker, R. T. and Galton, P. M. 1974. Dinosaur monophyly and a new class of vertebrates. *Nature*, vol. 248, pp. 169–72. (A provocative article that argues for recognition of dinosaurs as a distinct class of vertebrates that includes birds.)

Benton, M. J. 1988. The origins of the dinosaurs. *Modern Geology*, vol. 13, pp. 41–56. (A very readable overview of dinosaur origins.)

Benton, M. J. 1990. Origin and interrelationships of dinosaurs; in Weishampel, D. B., Dodson, P., and Osmólska, H., eds., *The Dinosauria*. Berkeley: University of California Press, pp. 11–30. (A comprehensive technical review of dinosaur origins and cladistic phylogenies of dinosaurs.)

Charig, A. J. 1972. The evolution of the archosaur pelvis and hind limb: An explanation in functional terms; in Joysey, K. A. and Kemp, T. S., eds., *Studies in Vertebrate Evolution*. New York: Winchester, pp. 121–55. (A technical analysis of the functional morphology of the evolution of the archosaur pelvis and hind limb.)

Cruickshank, A. R. I. and Benton, M. J. 1985. Archosaur ankles and the relationships of the thecodontian and dinosaurian reptiles. *Nature*, vol. 317, pp. 715–17. (A technical analysis of the origin of the advanced mesotarsal ankle of dinosaurs.)

Hunt, A. P. 1991. The early diversification pattern of dinosaurs in the Late Triassic. *Modern Geology*, vol. 16, pp. 43–60. (A review of the ages, distribution, and environments of the earliest dinosaurs.)

Lucas, S. G., Hunt, A. P., and Long, R. A. 1992. The oldest dinosaurs. *Naturwissenschaften*, vol. 79, pp. 171–72. (A brief article on the age of the oldest dinosaurs.)

Sereno, P. C. 1991. Basal archosaurs: Phylogenetic relationships and functional implications. *Society of Vertebrate Paleontology Memoir 2*, 53 pp. (A new look at archosaur cladistics that challenges some of the consensus views presented in this chapter.)

Sereno, P. C., Forester, C. A., Rogers, R. R., and Monetta, A. M. 1993. Primitive dinosaur skeleton from Argentina and the early evolution of Dinosauria. *Nature*, vol. 361, pp. 64–66. (Describes one of the most primitive dinosaurs, *Eoraptor*.)

PREDATORY DINOSAURS

Most predatory, or meat-eating dinosaurs belong to one group, **Theropoda** "beast foot" (box 6.1). The theropod dinosaurs spanned the entire duration of dinosaurs, from the Late Triassic until the end of the Cretaceous. They include animals that ranged in size from the chicken-sized *Compsognathus* to one of the largest land-living predators of all time, *Tyrannosaurus rex*. Throughout most of their long history, theropods were a diverse and successful group of dinosaurs.

In this chapter we examine the main types of theropods and discuss their behavior and evolution. But before doing this we need to consider some of the problems associated with the fossil record of theropods and how they affect our view of the evolution of these dinosaurs.

THEROPOD FOSSILS AND PHYLOGENY

Although theropod fossils have an extremely long distribution in time (Late Triassic–Late Cretaceous) and are known from all the continents, most of the fossils are frustratingly incomplete. A large number of theropods have been named from isolated bones, and much of what we know about theropods for significant intervals of Mesozoic time and over wide geographic areas is based on such fossils. Because deciphering the phylogenetic relationships of theropods requires complete skulls and skeletons, the incomplete fossil record of many theropods makes it difficult to fit them into a coherent theropod phylogeny.

The oldest widely accepted scheme of theropod phylogeny recognized two clades. According to this scheme, the very large theropods with short necks and small forelimbs, the **carnosaurs** (literally "meat lizards"), diverged early from the smaller, long-necked theropods having large forelimbs, the **coelurosaurs** (literally, "hollow tailed lizards"). This view of theropod phylogeny, however, has recently been modified to recognize a group of primitive theropods that are neither carnosaurs nor coelurosaurs (figure 6.1). These primitive theropods, the **ceratosaurs** (literally "horned lizards"), represent a third branch in the evolution of theropods, a clade that diverged early from the clade that later branched into carnosaurs and coelurosaurs. The clade that led to the carnosaurs and coelurosaurs is referred to as the tetanuran theropods. The ancestry of birds lies among the tetanurans and is discussed in Chapter 16.

Although the picture of theropod phylogeny presented here (see figure 6.1) seems neat and clear, ongoing debate about the phylogeny of theropods makes it one of the least agreed-upon phylogenies among the dinosaurs. In part, this is because different paleontologists place greater emphasis on different features as significant

BOX 6.1

WHAT'S IN A NAME?

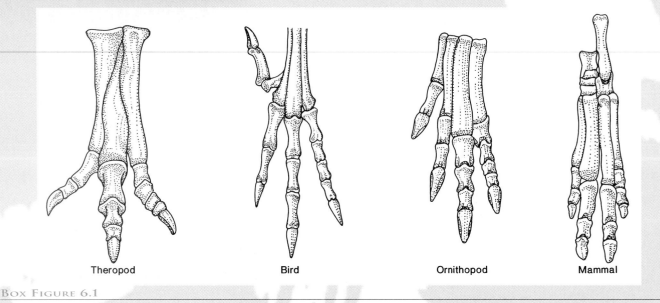

BOX FIGURE 6.1
Theropod feet were bird-like, whereas ornithopod feet were mammal-like.

The Latinized names paleontologists give to extinct animals usually make some sort of sense. They typically either describe some feature or attribute of the animal, make reference to the place where its fossils were found, or honor another paleontologist. Some names are very colorful, like *Tyrannosaurus rex*, the "king of the tyrant lizards." Other names are rather pedestrian, like *Allosaurus*, the "different lizard."

The name applied to all meat-eating dinosaurs is Theropoda, from the Greek *therios*, meaning "beast" and *podos*, meaning "foot." Although *therios* literally means "beast," it usually refers to mammals, so the name Theropoda also means "mammal foot." Yale paleontologist O. C. Marsh coined the name Theropoda for the meat-eating dinosaurs in 1881. Ten years earlier, Marsh had coined the name Ornithopoda ("bird foot"), and in 1878 he introduced the name Sauropoda ("lizard foot"). Indeed, 1882 was a milestone in

the history of dinosaur studies, for in that year Marsh published a comprehensive classification of dinosaurs. He divided them into theropods, ornithopods, sauropods, and stegosaurs ("plated lizards"). Marsh also considered the Hallopoda ("leaping foot") to be possible dinosaurs, but they are now thought to be crocodiles.

Clearly, Marsh relied heavily on foot structure as a guide to classifying dinosaurs. In the feet of the dinosaurs he called sauropods, Marsh saw resemblances to the feet of living lizards, hence the name "lizard foot."

But what similarities in the feet of meat-eating dinosaurs and mammals did Marsh see? And, given the very bird-like feet of these dinosaurs, why didn't Marsh name them Ornithopoda? Furthermore, why did Marsh assign the name Ornithopoda to dinosaurs with feet that were more mammal-like than bird-like (box figure 6.1)?

No clear answer to these questions can be found in Marsh's writings, which do, however, make it clear that he knew the meanings of the words theropod and ornithopod. The best guess is that Marsh goofed when he introduced the names ornithopod, and later, theropod, applying them in reverse order from what had been his original intention. The result is that the bird-footed dinosaurs are not called ornithopods, but, nonsensically, they are the theropods. Conversely, the name ornithopod is applied to dinosaurs with rather mammal-like feet.

Marsh was a very famous paleontologist whose knowledge of dinosaurs was immense. So his names for two major groups of dinosaurs, Theropoda and Ornithopoda, were accepted and used by paleontologists worldwide. They continue to be used to this day, despite the fact that neither name quite makes sense.

evolutionary novelties in theropod evolution. For example, the ceratosaurs include **Dilophosaurus** and **Ceratosaurus,** two large (6 meters long) theropods that possessed the fused hind-limb skeletal elements here judged to be significant evolutionary novelties of the Ceratosauria. Some paleontologists, however, include *Dilophosaurus*

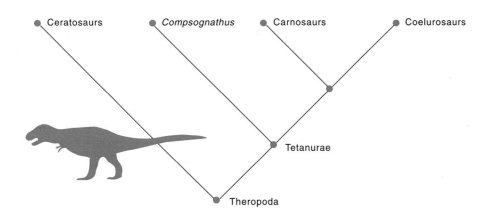

FIGURE 6.1

The phylogeny of theropods currently accepted by most paleontologists identifies ceratosaurs as an early side branch from the main line of tetanuran evolution, which split into carnosaurs and coelurosaurs.

and *Ceratosaurus* among the carnosaurs because of their large size, short necks, and other features stressed by the paleontologists as key carnosaur features. These disagreements cannot be readily resolved at present because so many theropods are known from such incomplete fossils. It is sufficient to say that several alternative views of theropod phylogeny are plausible, and the one presented here represents a consensus of most paleontologists.

WHAT IS A THEROPOD?

Because theropods comprise most of the meat-eating dinosaurs, it might seem sufficient to identify theropods by the skeletal features, especially the teeth, that were involved in acquiring and processing animal food. It is important to remember, however, that many of the most primitive dinosaurs were also meat eaters (see Chapter 5). Indeed, meat eating is the primitive condition for all non-dinosaurian archosaurs. Thus, to identify theropods specifically, we must distinguish them from the primitive meat-eating dinosaurs and from other meat-eating archosaurs.

There are at least 20 evolutionary novelties that distinguish theropods from other dinosaurs. Most of these novelties reflect more specialized structures for meat eating than were present in the primitive, meat-eating dinosaurs. They also reflect the fact that theropods were highly specialized runners and predators. These novelties include broad exposure of the lachrymal bone on the skull roof, a sacrum comprising at least five vertebrae, a clawed hand, a bowed femur, and a hind foot that was compact, narrow, and long, with three functional digits and the first digit separated from the rest of the foot (figure 6.2). These novelties and others distinguish theropods from other dinosaurs. Combining these novelties with the primitive features inherited from their nontheropod ancestors gives us an overall picture of theropods as remarkable predators.

The teeth of all but a few theropods were relatively large, curved, compressed, and serrated. The mouth bore numerous such teeth, which were held in the jaw by a ligament (figure 6.3). The relatively large eyes suggest that theropods located their prey visually. Theropods had the largest and most sophisticated brains of any known dinosaurs (see Chapter 15). Indeed, the brains of the more advanced theropods were very bird-like and suggest that at least some theropods may have been very sophisticated behaviorally.

The slicing teeth of theropods were set in a lightly built skull in which many of the bones were loosely joined to each other. Even the bones of the theropod lower jaw were not tightly sutured to each other (see figure 6.3). The loose joints probably helped the skull compensate for the shocks it encountered when the theropod grabbed and chewed its prey.

The theropod skull was attached to the neck at a highly mobile joint. This joint allowed rapid and precise movement of the head, and its presence further supports the idea that theropods were highly sophisticated visual hunters. Today, birds have the same type of head-neck joint as did their theropod ancestors.

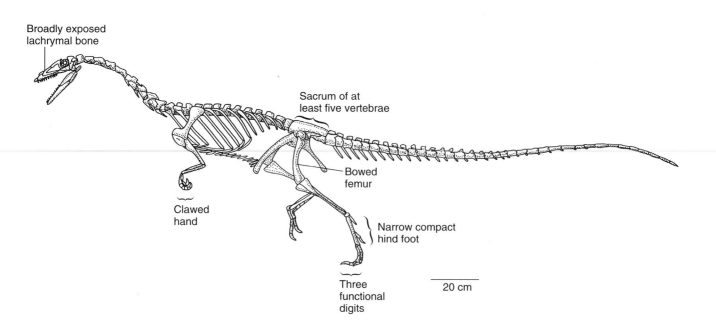

Broadly exposed
lachrymal bone

Sacrum of at
least five vertebrae

Bowed
femur

Clawed
hand

Narrow compact
hind foot

Three
functional
digits

20 cm

FIGURE 6.2

Typical features of theropods are well illustrated by this skeleton of one of the earliest theropods, Late Triassic *Coelophysis*.

FIGURE 6.3

This skull of *Albertosaurus* shows typical features of theropods.

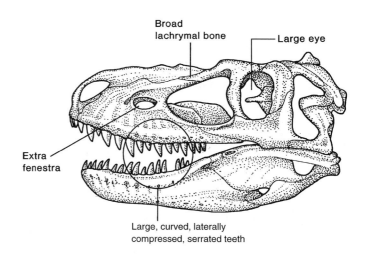

Broad
lachrymal bone

Large eye

Extra
fenestra

Large, curved, laterally
compressed, serrated teeth

We also see many distinctive features designed for predation in the postcranial skeletons of theropods. Thus, the hands of most theropods (see figure 6.16) had only three digits, one of which (the first digit) was offset from the other two. This digit, like our thumb, may have allowed the theropod hand to grasp. On all three digits of the theropod hand, the next-to-last phalanges were elongated, to extend the reach, and the tips of the digits were long, laterally compressed, and bore curved claws.

Theropod hands clearly were not used for walking. So theropods were obligate bipeds, and their vertebral columns and hind limbs were modified accordingly. At least five vertebrae made up the theropod sacrum to provide greater rigidity at the attachment point of the powerful hind limbs and backbone. The pelvis was very large and provided considerable space for the attachment of the large hip muscles. The femur was distinctly bowed downward, and the hind foot was elongate and symmetrical around the middle digit. Indeed, the theropod hind foot was the very compact foot of a fast runner and was strikingly bird-like.

The theropod tail changed about midway from being flexible proximally to being stiff distally. A similar type of tail is still present in living birds. The rigid distal portion could have been used by theropods as a stabilizer while running.

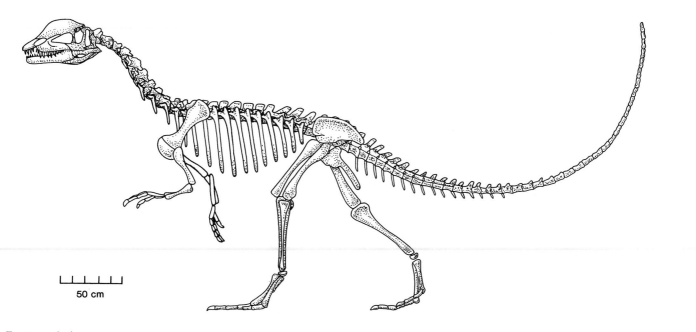

FIGURE 6.4

Dilophosaurus from the Lower Jurassic of Arizona was a typical ceratosaur.

A final typical theropod feature was hollow bones. This lightened the theropod skeleton and also increased the strength of the bones to resist bending. Hollow bones evolved in theropods as an aid to rapid, terrestrial locomotion, but later aided their descendants, the birds, in flight.

CERATOSAURS

The ceratosaurs were primitive theropods, among which were the earliest theropods as well as many of Jurassic age. Indeed, some of the oldest dinosaurs of Late Triassic age were ceratosaurs. Although ceratosaurs appeared early in the evolution of dinosaurs, they were already highly specialized meat eaters during the Late Triassic. Most of their specialization is seen in their key evolutionary novelties. Many of these novelties involve the fusion of skeletal elements in the hind limb. This gave ceratosaurs a very strong hind-limb skeleton well adapted to fast running while maintaining a very narrow gait. Thus, in ceratosaurs the sacrum was totally fused, and it was fused to the ilium. Much fusion of bones also took place in the ankles and feet of adult ceratosaurs (figure 6.4). Other ceratosaur novelties included a gap between the premaxillary and maxillary bones of the skull, into which fitted a large tooth anchored in the dentary bone of the lower jaw. Ironically, the only ceratosaur that lacked this feature was *Ceratosaurus* itself.

Another distinctive ceratosaur feature is the marked **sexual dimorphism** (differences between presumed males and females) seen in adult skeletons. In skeletons of a given type of ceratosaur, there seems to have been a "female" form with a longer skull and neck, thicker and more robust limbs, and very large muscle attachment sites. The "male" form, in contrast, had a juvenile-like skeleton with a shorter skull and neck and slender limbs. Further adding to the characteristic sexual dimorphism of ceratosaurs were the crests on the skulls of some of these dinosaurs. These were made of very thin bone (see figure 6.4) and presumably functioned in display, probably by males.

Ceratosaurs are some of the best-known theropods, and include Late Triassic **Coelophysis** (formerly called **Rioarribasaurus**) and Early Jurassic **Syntarsus.** A typical ceratosaur is *Dilophosaurus* (see figure 6.4) from the Lower Jurassic of Arizona. This large (6 meters long) ceratosaur displayed many typical theropod features, such as a large head full of long, blade-like teeth, a large antorbital fenestra, and a thick and powerful lower jaw. The neck and tail were long, and the forelimb was much shorter than the hind limb.

However, like other ceratosaurs, *Dilophosaurus* had many fused bones in the hind limb. It also had the distinct gap between the premaxillary and maxillary bones in the skull; and the hand had four fingers, the first three of which bore claws. The two thin, bony crests on the skull of *Dilophosaurus* are the basis of its name, which means "two-crested lizard."

About seven genera of ceratosaurs are known from the Upper Triassic-Upper Jurassic of western Europe, the United States, and southern Africa. However, a possible Late Cretaceous ceratosaur, *Xenotarsosaurus,* is known from fragmentary fossils collected in South America. Although ceratosaurs were the first theropods, they do not appear to have been particularly diverse. Nevertheless, the crests on the skulls of some ceratosaurs suggest that they may have had some sort of sophisticated social behavior based on visual display.

TETANURAE

The strange name **Tetanurae** ("fused tails") is applied by paleontologists to the non-ceratosaurian theropods (see figure 6.1). These theropods were much more bird-like than the ceratosaurs. Indeed, the ancestry of birds lies among the tetanuran theropods as seen in their many bird-like evolutionary novelties, such as the reduction of dentition so that all the teeth were in front of the orbit. No fang-like tooth was present in the dentary, and there was no corresponding notch to receive the tooth between the premaxillary and the maxillary. A second fenestra opened in front of the eye, further lightening the skull, and the structure of the hind limb was modified to produce an even faster runner. The hip and thigh were structured to shift the insertions of the leg-moving muscles upward, which shortened them, so that when they were contracted, they produced quick movements of the hind limb.

Many advanced tetanuran theropods had an expanded distal end to their pubis, which exaggerated the size of the typical theropod pubic "boot." This anchored large abdominal muscles needed to produce a spring-like motion of the vertebral column during running. This motion was created by flexing the body of the theropod over the rigid sacrum.

Two great groups of tetanuran theropods can be recognized: the carnosaurs and the coelurosaurs. However, not all tetanuran theropods fit into one or the other of these groups (box 6.2)

CARNOSAURS

Carnosaurian theropods include the largest meat-eating animals to have lived on land. All carnosaurs were 5 meters or more in length and had large heads, short, powerful necks, very short forelimbs, massive hind limbs, and long tails. The largest and most famous carnosaur is *Tyrannosaurus rex* which was 14 meters long and had a head 1.3 meters long that bore serrated, blade-like teeth as much as 20 centimeters long.

Most carnosaurs are readily distinguished from other theropods by a number of skeletal features. These include an opening (foramen) in the lachrymal bone, low spines on the vertebrae in the shoulder region, prongs on the chevrons, and an upwardly inclined head of the femur. Although carnosaur fossils are known from rocks as old as Middle Jurassic, their fossil record is mostly fragmentary prior to the Late Cretaceous. Two principal families of carnosaurs, the **Allosauridae** and the **Tyrannosauridae,** are recognized.

BOX 6.2

COMPSOGNATHUS: A CLASSIFICATORY CONUNDRUM

The advanced, tetanuran theropods belong to two groups: carnosaurs and coelurosaurs. But this does not mean that all tetanurans can be assigned to one group or the other. *Compsognathus* ("delicate jaw") is a case in point.

This small dinosaur is known only from two virtually complete skeletons from the Upper Jurassic of western Europe. The better of the two specimens (box figure 6.2) is exquisitely preserved on lithographic limestone collected near Solenhofen in Bavaria, southern Germany. In fact, this skeleton of *Compsognathus* was one of the first complete dinosaur skeletons ever described.

This skeleton is of a small theropod only 70 centimeters long. Its small size, large eyes, and relatively large head suggest it belonged to an immature theropod. Indeed, the second skeleton of *Compsognathus*, from France, is about 50 percent larger than the German specimen.

Compsognathus had the typical proportions of a small tetanuran. It was lightly built and had a long neck, long tail, and short forelimbs that were only 37 percent of the length of the large hind limbs. It also displayed typical tetanuran evolutionary novelties, such as all teeth in the skull and lower jaws in front of the orbit, a hand lacking a fourth finger, and a pubis with a distinct "boot." But the evolutionary novelties of neither carnosaurs nor coelurosaurs are present in *Compsognathus*. So *Compsognathus* is regarded as the most primitive tetanuran (see figure 6.1).

Perhaps one of the most interesting features of *Compsognathus* is that the

30 mm

BOX FIGURE 6.2

The skeleton of *Compsognathus* from Germany is articulated and nearly complete.

From John H. Ostrom, "The Osteology of *Compsognathus longipes* Wagner " in Zitteliana, 4:73–118, August 1978. Copyright © 1978 Bayerische Staatssammlung für Paläontologie und historische Geologie, Munich, Germany. Reprinted by permission.

German specimen preserved its last meal. Inside the abdomen of the skeleton is most of the skeleton of an extinct lizard, *Bavarisaurus*. It was originally identified as an embryo of *Compsognathus* and was presented as evidence that the small theropod gave live birth. Closer examination of the skeleton in the *Compsognathus* abdomen, however, now convinces paleontologists that just before the dinosaur died, it caught and ate a small lizard.

ALLOSAURIDAE

Carnosaurs of Early Jurassic to Early Cretaceous age that are well enough known to be assigned to a family are allosaurids. Some key evolutionary novelties of Allosauridae are the evenly rounded face, the medially flattened tip of the lower jaw, and the upper tooth sockets that extend all the way to the back of the face.

Allosaurus (figure 6.5) is the best known and the archetypal allosaurid. It displays all the typical carnosaurian body proportions. A unique feature of *Allosaurus* was its lightly constructed skull, which had a distinctive roughened ridge just above

Predatory Dinosaurs 65

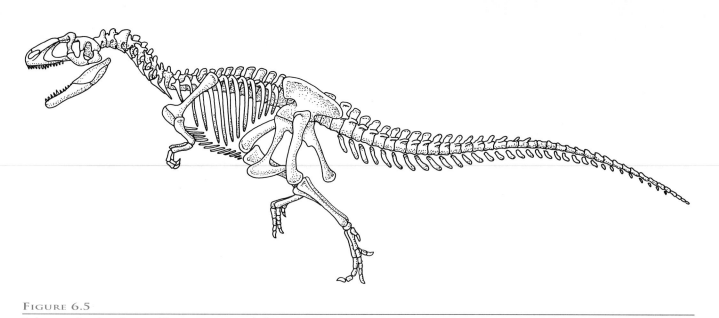

FIGURE 6.5

Eight-meter-long Late Jurassic *Allosaurus* was a typical allosaurid carnosaur.

and in front of the orbit. *Allosaurus* is best known from the remains of at least 44 specimens collected at the Cleveland-Lloyd dinosaur quarry in eastern Utah (figure 6.6).

The oldest allosaurid is *Piatnitzkysaurus*, known from an almost complete skeleton collected in the Middle Jurassic of Argentina. Well-known Late Jurassic allosaurids include *Allosaurus* from the western United States and eastern Africa and *Szechuanosaurus* (figure 6.7) from southern China. Allosaurids of Early Cretaceous age are known from the United States, China, and Russia. The best known is *Acrocanthosaurus*, from the Lower Cretaceous of the United States. Allosaurids apparently were never very diverse, but they were the dominant theropods of the Late Jurassic-Early Cretaceous.

TYRANNOSAURIDAE

Tyrannosaurids are known only from fossils collected in Upper Cretaceous deposits of Asia and western North America. The best-known genera are *Albertosaurus*, *Daspletosaurus*, *Nanotyrannus*, and *Tyrannosaurus* from North America and *Tarbosaurus* from Asia (*Tyrannosaurus* is also known from Asia). Evolutionary novelties of tyrannosaurids include the D-shaped cross sections of the teeth in the premaxillary, an opening in the jugal bone of the skull, and very small forelimbs, each of which had only two functional fingers (figure 6.8).

The archetypal tyrannosaurid is ***Tyrannosaurus*** (see figure 6.8), the largest (14 meters long) land-living meat eater of all time. Its massive head was supported by a short thick neck, and its short thick abdomen projected forward from a massive pelvis supported by huge, pillar-like limbs. The long heavy tail acted to counterbalance the body during running. The tiny forelimbs make a curious impression; their function is not clear. Other tyrannosaurids were, in many ways, slightly abbreviated, more primitive versions of *Tyrannosaurus*.

During the Late Cretaceous in Asia and western North America, tyrannosaurids were moderately diverse and successful predators. They include some of the last dinosaurs.

This map shows some of the scattered bones at the Cleveland-Lloyd dinosaur quarry in Utah, where the remains of at least 44 individuals of *Allosaurus* were collected.

From James H. Madsen, Jr., "*Allosaurus fragilis: A Revised Osteology*," *Utah Geological and Mineral Survey, Bulletin 109*, August 1976, map of the Cleveland-Lloyd dinosaur quarry in east central Utah. Copyright © 1976 James H. Madsen, Jr. Reprinted by permission.

FIGURE 6.7

Szechuanosaurus was a well-known allosaurid from the Upper Jurassic of China.

Photograph by Li Jianjun

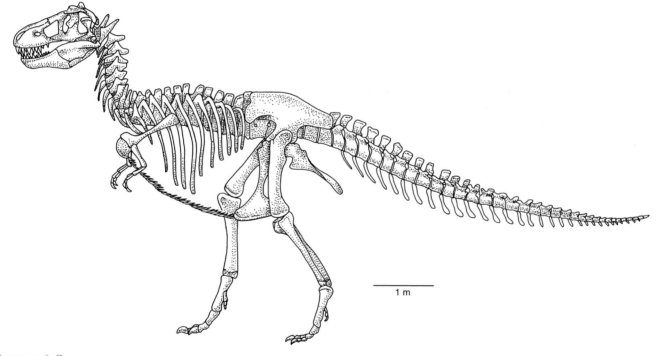

1 m

FIGURE 6.8

Late Cretaceous *Tyrannosaurus* was a typical tyrannosaurid carnosaur.

OTHER CARNOSAURS

A variety of family names exist for carnosaurs that seem to be neither allosaurids nor tyrannosaurids. Most of these carnosaurs are not known from very complete skeletal material. Two of the best known are *Megalosaurus* and *Spinosaurus*.

    Megalosaurus (figure 6.9), from the Lower and Middle Jurassic of Great Britain and France, is known from skull fragments, lower jaws, teeth, and various postcranial bones. Described by the British naturalist William Buckland in 1824, *Megalosaurus* was the first dinosaur to receive a scientific name. It is estimated to have been about 9 meters long and shared many *Allosaurus* features.

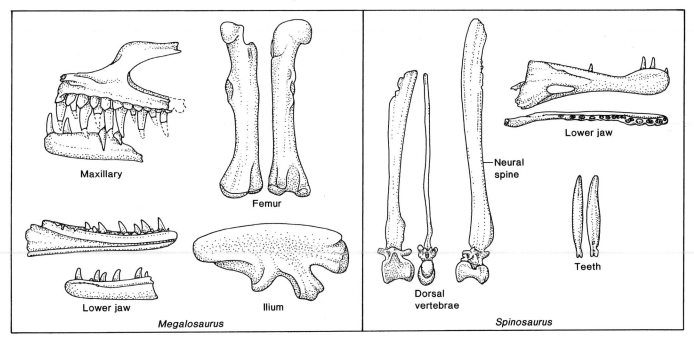

FIGURE 6.9

Megalosaurus and *Spinosaurus* were two carnosaurs that cannot be assigned to either the Allosauridae or the Tyrannosauridae.

Spinosaurus (see figure 6.9), from the Lower Cretaceous of Egypt, is a truly unusual theropod. Known from jaw fragments, teeth, vertebrae, and part of the hind limb, *Spinosaurus* had neural spines 1.8 meters long on its back that formed a "sail" reminiscent of that of *Dimetrodon*, a Permian reptile often mistakenly thought to be a dinosaur. Whether or not *Spinosaurus* is a carnosaur is not even clear. For example, its teeth lacked the serrations characteristic of carnosaur teeth. Much more will need to be discovered of *Spinosaurus* and many other poorly known large theropods before their phylogenetic relationships are clear.

CARNOSAUR BEHAVIOR

Few dinosaurs are as well known to the public as carnosaurs. These huge meat eaters have been the subject of much analysis and speculation about their behavior. To review briefly the behavior of carnosaurs, let's begin with well-supported inferences and then proceed to more speculative ideas.

Carnosaur skeletons identify them as obligate bipeds that ate meat. Mechanical considerations indicate that carnosaurs ran with the body extended forward, nearly horizontal, pivoted at the pelvis, with the long tail held out also nearly horizontal, acting as a counterbalance. When the neck vertebrae of carnosaurs are properly articulated, they form a swan-like curve. We thus arrive at a much different posture for carnosaurs than the classic posture, in which the body was held upright and the tail dragged on the ground (figure 6.10).

The numerous sharp, serrated teeth and the skull structure of carnosaurs identify them as meat eaters. Some have suggested that carnosaurs were scavengers, not predators. This idea stems from the observation that most carnosaur teeth are not heavily worn, suggesting that these dinosaurs fed on soft flesh from rotting carcasses. Yet some carnosaurs do show extensive tooth wear and even had teeth that were broken and subsequently worn. Also, there is reason to question whether enough rotting carcasses would have been lying around the Late Cretaceous landscapes to feed such large dinosaurs as tyrannosaurids if they were exclusively scavengers. On the whole, the teeth and skulls of carnosaurs are more consistent with

FIGURE 6.10

The classic (top) and modern (bottom) postures of *Tyrannosaurus* well demonstrate our changing ideas about carnosaur posture and locomotion.

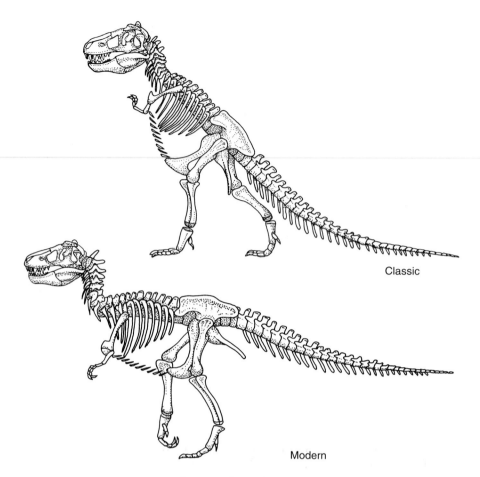

Classic

Modern

them having been predators, rather than principally scavengers. But let's not forget that today most predators will feed from a carcass killed by another animal, so some scavenging by carnosaurs was quite likely.

How fast carnosaurs could run has also been debated. Speeds as high as 70 kilometers per hour have been suggested for *Tyrannosaurus rex*. These estimates were made by simply scaling a smaller running dinosaur until it was as large as a *Tyrannosaurus*. In fact, maximum speed in living animals seems to peak in those that weigh 50 to 100 kilograms. Larger animals are not proportionately faster than smaller animals. This means that carnosaurs, with their long strides, were probably fast runners, certainly as fast or faster than their prey, but just how fast is difficult to estimate.

As running, bipedal predators, how did carnosaurs hunt? Here, we enter the realm of speculation, although some interesting suggestions have been made. One is that relatively small carnosaurs, such as *Allosaurus*, when hunting large prey such as sauropods, hunted in packs, as wild dogs do today. An *Allosaurus* attack on a sauropod may be documented (scavenging is an alternative explanation) by a skeleton of *Apatosaurus* in which some of the caudal vertebrae were bitten off. The bite marks match the tooth spacing of *Allosaurus*, and broken teeth of *Allosaurus* were associated with the sauropod fossil. Pack hunting by smaller carnosaurs attacking large prey seems necessary if such comparatively small predators were to take much larger prey.

An ambush style of predation has been suggested for the larger tyrannosaurids. This is analogous to the great white shark that attacks its victim from behind and below, inflicts a terrible wound and then retreats and waits until its victim either goes into shock or bleeds to death. Such a strategy as employed by large carnosaurs was appropriately dubbed the **"land shark"** mode of hunting.

Another slightly different view sees large carnosaurs as the big cats (lions and tigers) of the Mesozoic. This view suggests that large carnosaurs either ran down or ambushed their victims, delivering a single (when possible) killing blow with their huge, tooth-filled jaws.

It is important to emphasize that these different ideas about how carnosaurs hunted are speculation. But it is certain that carnosaurs were fast, bipedal predators that surely struck terror in the hearts of any animal they chose to pursue.

Coelurosaurs

The most bird-like tetanurans were the coelurosaurs, among which were the ancestors of birds. Their key evolutionary novelties include an extra fenestra in the palate, elongate forelimbs more than 50 percent as long as the hind limbs, and a long, slender hand with long second and third digits.

Coelurosaurs were mainly a Cretaceous group, known principally from Asia and western North America. Several different phylogenies of coelurosaurs have been proposed, so there is a variety of classifications of the many theropods assigned to Coelurosauria. Here we contrast two rather different groups of coelurosaurs—the ornithomimosaurids and the dromaeosaurids—and then discuss some of the other, lesser-known coelurosaurs.

Ornithomimosauridae

The best known and only truly abundant coelurosaurs are the "bird-mimic lizards," the **ornithomimosaurids.** Known only from the Upper Cretaceous of Asia and western North America, the ornithomimosaurs strongly resemble modern flightless birds such as emus and ostriches, having small heads, long necks, and long legs (figure 6.11). But their long arms with clawed hands and their long, bony tails are the two most obvious features that distinguish them from birds.

Evolutionary novelties that distinguish ornithomimosaurids from other coelurosaurs include the lightly built skull with very large orbits and a shallow snout, the lack of teeth (a horny bill covered much of the jaws), and the long neck, which accounts for about 40 percent of the length of the vertebral column in front of the sacrum. *Struthiomimus* (figure 6.12), from the Upper Cretaceous of western Canada, was a typical ornithomimosaur and possessed these evolutionary novelties. Other features of *Struthiomimus* characterize a broader group of coelurosaurs. These include the very flexible joints in this dinosaur's long neck, which conferred great mobility. The ventral part of the abdomen was protected by belly ribs (gastralia), and deep scars on the spines of the dorsal vertebrae suggest the presence of powerful ligaments along the back. Such ligaments and the gastralia would have produced a very rigid abdomen that was held forward and nearly horizontal as the dinosaur ran. Large attachment sites for muscles on the distal caudal vertebrae would have helped to hold the tail rigid as a counterbalance.

The forelimbs of *Struthiomimus* were extremely long and slender, about 50 percent the length of the hind limbs. The long slender hands had three functional fingers that bore long, pointed, but only slightly curved, claws. The long, slender hind limbs had three functional toes as well, but they bore flattened claws.

The anatomy of *Struthiomimus* and other ornithomimosaurids strongly suggests that they were fast ground runners, perhaps as swift as living, similarly proportioned ostriches, which achieve top speeds of 50 kilometers per hour. Their diet, however, is less clearly interpreted from their toothless, beak-like mouths. Most paleontologists view ornithomimosaurids as omnivores that had a mixed diet of plants and animals.

FIGURE 6.11

Ornithomimosaurids were very similar in overall body shape and proportions to living ostriches.

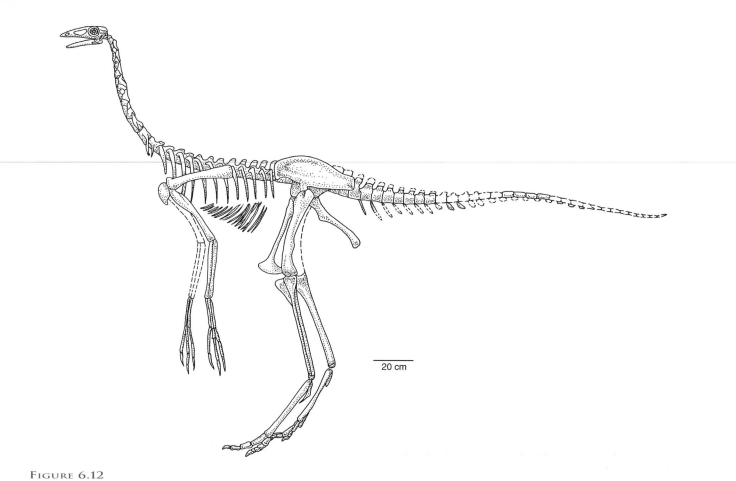

FIGURE 6.12

Late Cretaceous *Struthiomimus* was a typical ornithomimosaurid.

DROMAEOSAURIDAE

Unlike the ornithomimosaurid lifestyle, the meat-eating lifestyle of **dromaeosaurids** is easy to deduce from their skulls. Typical evolutionary novelties of these coelurosaurs include a relatively large head, which bore numerous teeth serrated on both edges; relatively long forelimbs with elongate, three-fingered hands; a pelvis with a posteriorly directed pubis; a tail with ossified tendons; and hind feet with an enormous claw on digit two, which compelled the dinosaur to walk on just two toes of each hind foot.

Dromaeosaurids are known from the Lower and Upper Cretaceous of western North America and the Upper Cretaceous of Asia. *Velociraptor* from Asia is well known to the public thanks to the movie *Jurassic Park*. **Deinonychus** ("terrible claw," figure 6.13) from the Lower Cretaceous of Wyoming and Montana, is one of the best-known and characteristic dromaeosaurids. This rather large (3 to 3.3 meters long) dromaeosaurid displays the diagnostic features of this group of dinosaurs well. Note especially the large skull full of serrated teeth, the backward-directed pubis, stiffened tail, and the huge claws on the second toes of the hind feet. Aside from these specializations, much of the anatomy of *Deinonychus* was typically theropod.

A quick examination of the skeleton of *Deinonychus* convincingly demonstrates it was a habitual biped. How the dinosaur might have used the huge, curved claws on its hind feet, however, is puzzling. The only way to use these claws, of course, would have been to have one or both hind feet off the ground, stabbing the prey. To do so would have required great agility and balance, aided in part by the stiff counterbalancing tail. The skeleton of *Deinonychus* was clearly that of a very active, bipedal predator.

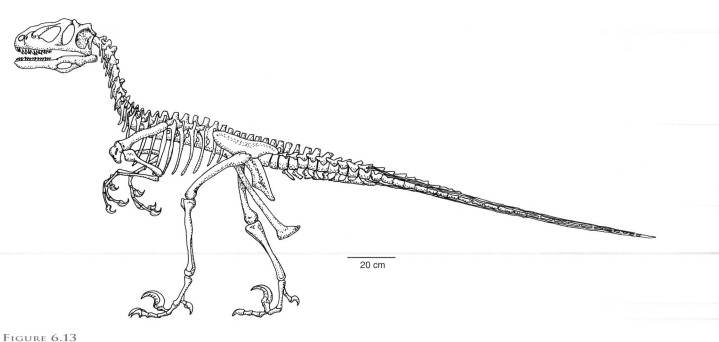

FIGURE 6.13

Early Cretaceous *Deinonychus* was a typical dromaeosaurid.

OTHER COELUROSAURS

Other coelurosaurs are much more rare and less completely known than ornithomimosaurids and dromaeosaurids. These poorly known coelurosaurs comprise four or more distinct types.

The best known of these are the **oviraptorosaurs,** rare coelurosaurs from the Upper Cretaceous of Asia and western North America, which are usually considered to be close relatives of ornithomimosaurids. Unique features of oviraptorosaurs include their toothless jaws, very large fenestrae in the mandible, short snouts, very deep and strong lower jaws, crest of sponge-like bone on the tip of the snout (possibly for display) and fused collarbones (clavicles), similar to the wishbones of birds.

Oviraptor (figure 6.14) from the Upper Cretaceous of Mongolia was a characteristic oviraptorosaur. This 2-meter-long coelurosaur had large claws on the hands and slender hind limbs. Its resemblance to an ornithomimosaurid is striking. However, unlike ornithomimosaurids, *Oviraptor* had a skull and jaws designed to crush tough food items. At first, paleontologists thought *Oviraptor* ate the eggs of other dinosaurs; hence its name, which means "egg stealer." But now it is believed that oviraptorosaurs primarily ate the freshwater clams that are common fossils in the lake-margin deposits where most oviraptorosaur fossils are found.

The second group of rare coelurosaurs is the **troodontids.** These coelurosaurs, best known from *Saurornithoides* (figure 6.15) from the Upper Cretaceous of Asia, are often considered closely related to dromaeosaurids. Evolutionary novelties of the troodontids include a long skull with a narrow snout, large braincase (troodontids have the largest brains relative to body size of any dinosaur), and inflated bony casing for the middle ear. The teeth of troodontids were small and numerous (as many as 35 in the lower jaw), and many were serrated along their posterior edges. Troodontids had ankle bones fused to each other and to the tibia, and small claws on the second digits of their hind feet.

Other features that distinguish *Saurornithoides* and other troodontids include their extremely large eyes and possible stereoscopic vision. Like dromaeosaurids, troodontids were agile bipedal predators. The earliest-known troodontids are from

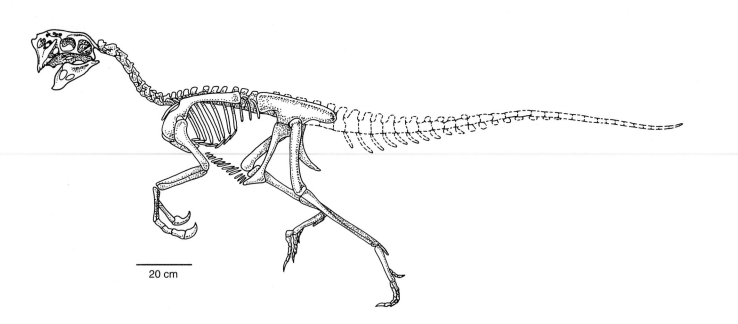

FIGURE 6.14

Late Cretaceous *Oviraptor* was a typical oviraptorosaur.

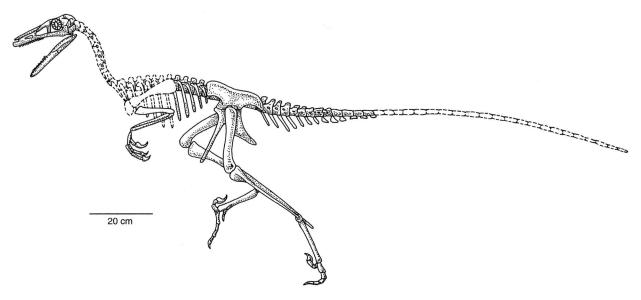

FIGURE 6.15

Late Cretaceous *Saurornithoides* was a typical troodontid.

the Lower Cretaceous of Asia, but they are best (though still poorly) known from the Upper Cretaceous of Asia and western North America. A few fragmentary fossils from the Upper Cretaceous of Romania may also be of troodontids.

The third, poorly known coelurosaur group, is the **elmisaurids.** Nothing is known of these dinosaurs except limb bones that indicate they had large feet and slender hands with raptorial claws. A typical elmisaurid is **Chirostenotes** ("slender hand") from the Upper Cretaceous of Canada (figure 6.16). Other elmisaurids are also known from the Upper Cretaceous of Canada and Asia. Elmisaurids probably are close relatives of oviraptorosaurs, which they resemble in many features.

A fourth group of poorly known coelurosaurs are the segnosaurs. These dinosaurs are rare as fossils and known only from the Cretaceous of Asia. *Therizinosaurus* is the most striking segnosaur. It is known from huge forelimbs found in the Upper Cretaceous of Mongolia that include claws as long as 28 centimeters! Recently discovered *Alxasaurus* (figure 6.17) from the Lower Cretaceous of China is the best known segnosaur. This nearly 4-meter-long theropod had 1-meter-long forelimbs with huge claws, somewhat longer hind limbs, and a short tail and weighed an estimated 400 kilograms. Various features suggest *Alxasaurus* was a tentanuran, but its small head, blunt beak, prosauropod-like teeth, and large size indicate that it, like other segnosaurs, probably ate plants. Segnosaurs may have used the large, clawed hands to grasp and tear vegetation.

THEROPOD EVOLUTION

Theropod dinosaurs appeared as highly specialized, running predators almost at the outset of dinosaur evolution. The first theropods, the ceratosaurs, were an early evolutionary sideline that comprised fast, small to large (2 to 14 meters long) bipedal predators that persisted through at least the Jurassic.

Another lineage, the "main line" of theropod evolution, led by Jurassic time through small, *Compsognathus*-like theropods to the advanced tetanurans. This bird-like theropod clade split by Middle Jurassic time into two distinct clades, the large carnosaurs and the small coelurosaurs.

Carnosaurs of the Middle Jurassic through Early Cretaceous were mostly allosaurids. By Late Cretaceous time, the largest meat-eating land animals of earth history, the tyrannosaurids, appeared, but their exact origin is obscure. Coelurosaurs, in contrast, were a mostly Cretaceous group whose evolution may have been largely restricted to Asia and western North America. Their exact origin is also obscure.

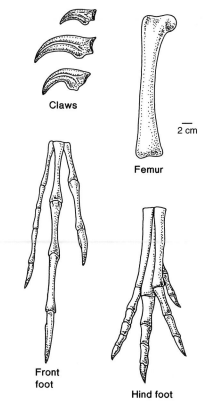

Claws

Femur

2 cm

Front foot

Hind foot

FIGURE 6.16

These limb bones are from the best-known elmisaurid, Late Cretaceous *Chirostenotes*.

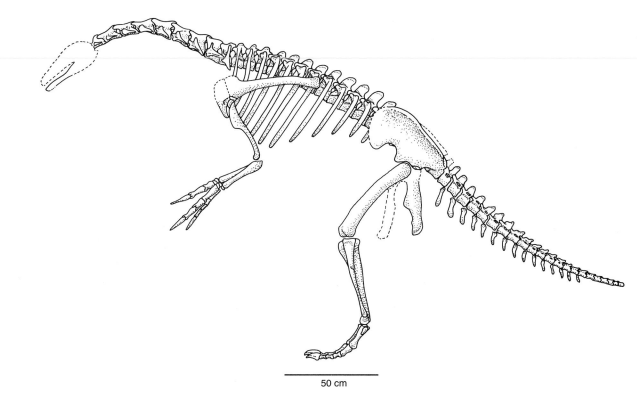

50 cm

FIGURE 6.17

This incomplete skeleton of *Alxasaurus* from the Lower Cretaceous of China is the most complete specimen known of a segnosaur.

SUMMARY

1. Most predatory dinosaurs were theropods.

2. Theropod phylogeny is not as clear as the phylogeny of some other dinosaur groups largely because of the fragmentary nature of most theropod fossils.

3. Nevertheless, theropods can be distinguished from other dinosaurs by many skeletal features, most of which identify them as bird-like, bipedal cursors. Theropods include the ancestors of birds.

4. The most primitive theropods were the Late Triassic-Late Jurassic ceratosaurs distinguished primarily by the fusion of bones in their hind limbs.

5. The very bird-like tetanurans were advanced theropods.

6. The carnosaurs were large tetanurans having huge skulls and short forelimbs, among other features.

7. Carnosaurs of the Middle Jurassic through Early Cretaceous were mostly allosaurids. The tyrannosaurids, the largest meat-eating land animals of all time, were advanced, extremely large carnosaurs of the Late Cretaceous.

8. The coelurosaurs were small tetanurans having small skulls and long forelimbs, among other features.

9. Coelurosaurs are known almost exclusively from the Cretaceous of Asia and western North America and consist of ornithomimosaurids, dromaeosaurids, troodontids, oviraptorosaurs, elmisaurids, and segnosaurs.

KEY TERMS

Allosauridae
Allosaurus
carnosaur
ceratosaur
Ceratosaurus
Chirostenotes
Coelophysis
coelurosaur

Deinonychus
Dilophosaurus
Dromaeosauridae
elmisaurid
"land shark"
Ornithomimosauridae
Oviraptor
oviraptorosaur
Rioarribasaurus

Saurornithoides
sexual dimorphism
Struthiomimus
Syntarsus
Tetanurae
Theropoda
troodontid
Tyrannosauridae
Tyrannosaurus

REVIEW QUESTIONS

1. What features are diagnostic of theropods and what types of behavior can we infer from these features?

2. What relationship exists between the theropod fossil record and our understanding of theropod phylogeny?

3. What are the bird-like features of theropods?

4. How are ceratosaurs distinguished from other theropods and what is the significance of their distinctive features?

5. How did tetanurans hunt?

6. Draw an evolutionary tree of the coelurosaurs. Where would you place the origin of birds on this tree?

7. Compare and contrast the anatomy and behavior of *Struthiomimus* and *Saurornithoides*.

FURTHER READING

Horner, J. R. and Lessem, D. 1993. *The Complete T. rex*. New Youk: Simon & Schuster Inc. 239 pp. (Everything you need to know about *T. rex*.)

Madsen, J. H., Jr. 1976. *Allosaurus fragilis*: A revised osteology. *Utah Geological and Mineralogical Survey, Bulletin 109*, 163 pp. (A detailed, technical, and extensive bone-by-bone description of *Allosaurus*.)

Ostrom, J. H. 1969. Osteology of *Deinonychus antirrhopus*, an unusual theropod from the Lower Cretaceous of Montana: *Peabody Museum of Natural History, Yale University, Bulletin 30*, 165 pp. (A comprehensive, technical description of the anatomy, behavior, and relationships of *Deinonychus*.)

Ostrom, J. H. 1978. The osteology of *Compsognathus longipes* Wagner. *Zitteliana [Abhandlungen der Bayerischen Staatssammlung für Paläontologie und historische Geologie]*, vol. 4, pp. 73–118. (A comprehensive, technical description of the anatomy, behavior, and relationships of *Compsognathus*.)

Paul, G. S. 1988. *Predatory Dinosaurs of the World*. New York: Simon & Schuster Inc. 564 pp. (A complete review of the predatory dinosaurs that presents many controversial ideas.)

Russell, D. A. and Dong, Z. 1993. The affinities of a new theropod from the Alxa Desert, Inner Mongolia, People's Republic of China. *Canadian Journal of Earth Sciences*, vol. 30, pp. 2107–27. (New fossils from China clarify the relationships of segnosaurs.)

Weishampel, D. B., Dodson, P., and Osmólska, H. 1990. *The Dinosauria*. Berkeley: University of California Press, 733 pp. (Chapters 5–14, pp. 148–317 present a detailed technical review of all the predatory dinosaurs.)

SAUROPODOMORPHS

ew animals are more awe inspiring than the largest land animals of all time, the sauropod dinosaurs. Their anatomy, classification, lifestyle, and evolution are the focus of this chapter, which begins with a consideration of their closest relatives, the prosauropod dinosaurs.

The prosauropods and the sauropods constitute a group of dinosaurs with the ungainly name **Sauropodomorpha.** Evolutionary novelties that distinguish them from other dinosaurs include having heads that were very small relative to their bodies, spatulate teeth, at least 10 elongated vertebrae in relatively long necks, short feet and very large claws on the first digits of their forefeet. Sauropodomorphs span the entire age of dinosaurs, from the Late Triassic until the end of the Cretaceous. They were one of the most successful groups of plant-eating dinosaurs, as well as nature's most amazing experiment in animal gigantism.

PROSAUROPODS

Prosauropods represent one of the first evolutionary diversifications of plant-eating dinosaurs. Known as fossils from all the continents except Antarctica (figure 7.1),

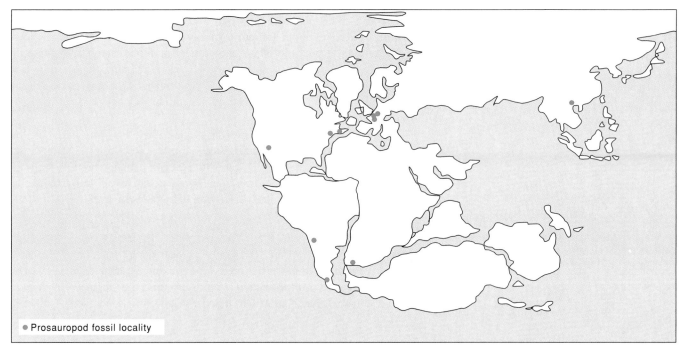

● Prosauropod fossil locality

FIGURE 7.1

This map of the Early Jurassic world showing the occurrences of some well-known prosauropods indicates their nearly worldwide distribution during the Early Jurassic.

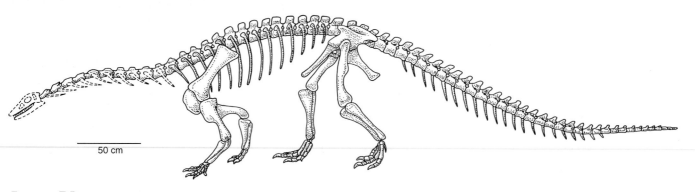

FIGURE 7.2

Riojasaurus, an 11-meter-long prosauropod from the Upper Triassic of Argentina, may best approximate the ancestry of sauropods.

FIGURE 7.3

Although some paleontologists see prosauropods as the ancestors of sauropods, the two groups are best regarded as close relatives derived from an as yet undiscovered ancestor.

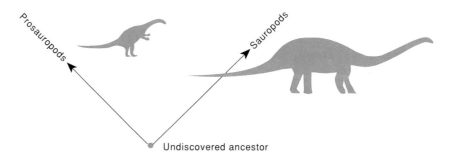

they range in age from Late Triassic to Early Jurassic and so include some of the oldest dinosaurs. Prosauropods were sauropod-like in general build, though much smaller and more slender.

Prosauropods were usually considered ancestral to sauropods (hence their name). Indeed, some paleontologists believed the "missing link" between the two groups was provided by prosauropods such as *Vulcanodon* from the Lower Jurassic of southern Africa and **Riojasaurus** (figure 7.2) from the Upper Triassic of Argentina. But all prosauropods, including these two types, had some features in their skeletons, such as the small size of the fifth digit of the hind foot (an evolutionary novelty), whose existence would require a highly unlikely reversal in evolution if prosauropods were the ancestors of sauropods. Sauropods had large fifth digits as did, presumably, the ancestors of prosauropods. Therefore, paleontologists now favor the view that prosauropods were the closest relatives, but not the ancestors, of sauropods, and that both groups derived from a common ancestor as yet undiscovered (figure 7.3).

Typical prosauropods include the massive, heavily built 11-meter-long *Riojasaurus* from Argentina, lightly built *Anchisaurus* from the eastern United States, and *Yunnanosaurus* from southern China, with its chisel-shaped teeth reminiscent of those of some later sauropods. *Plateosaurus* is a particularly well-known and characteristic prosauropod from the Late Triassic of western Europe.

THE GENUS *PLATEOSAURUS*

Most prosauropods are classed in the family **Anchisauridae,** named for *Anchisaurus* from the Lower Jurassic of eastern North America and South Africa. One of the best-known anchisaurids is **Plateosaurus** (figure 7.4) from the Upper Triassic of western Europe (Germany, France, and Switzerland). Mass death assemblages of this large

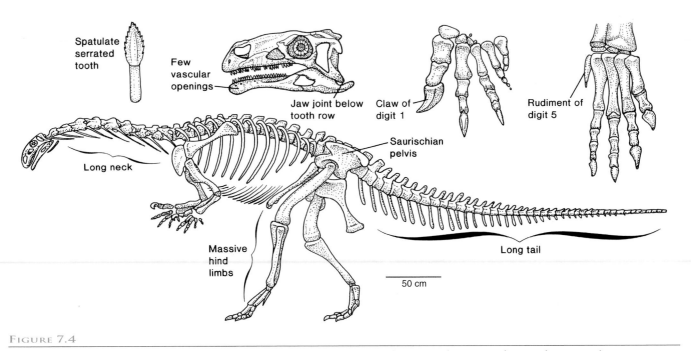

Spatulate serrated tooth

Few vascular openings

Jaw joint below tooth row

Claw of digit 1

Rudiment of digit 5

Saurischian pelvis

Long neck

Massive hind limbs

Long tail

50 cm

FIGURE 7.4

The skeleton of 6–8-meter-long *Plateosaurus* from the Upper Triassic of western Europe shows many characteristic features of prosauropods.

(6 to 8 meters body length) prosauropod are known from Trössingen in Germany, where the animals may have been killed and their skeletons accumulated by mud slides. The complete skeletons of *Plateosaurus* from Trössingen give us a remarkable knowledge of this early prosauropod.

Salient features of the skeleton of *Plateosaurus* include its large size and robustness, the numerous coarsely serrated teeth, and the jaw joint below the level of the teeth. Its small head was attached to a long neck followed by a long back and tail, proportions characteristic of prosauropods. The pelvis was typically saurischian and anchored massive hind limbs. The first finger of the hand bore a very large claw, and the fourth and fifth digits of the hind foot were small and must not have borne much weight when the animal walked.

PROSAUROPOD LIFESTYLES

Prosauropods are often restored as bipedal animals (see figure 7.4), but their footprints (figure 7.5) indicate that they usually walked quadrupedally. Indeed, the forelimbs of prosauropods were at least two-thirds the length of their hind limbs as in the later diplodocid sauropods, which are generally considered to have been obligatory quadrupeds. The first digit of the hand was much larger than the others and bore a huge claw, and that digit must have been held clear of the ground while walking. There is little doubt that prosauropods could rear up on their hind limbs to reach vegetation in tall trees, which is consistent with the evidence that prosauropods were herbivores. A large number of features suggest prosauropods ate plants:

1. Their long necks would have extended their vertical feeding range so that they could have cropped vegetation from tall trees as do living giraffes.

2. As in ornithischians, cheeks were present so food could be retained in the mouth as it was chewed by the jaws and dentition. A recessed ridge, diagonally inclined on the outside of the jaw, is evidence of this, as are the few, very large vascular foramina (canals for blood vessels) on the outside of the jaw.

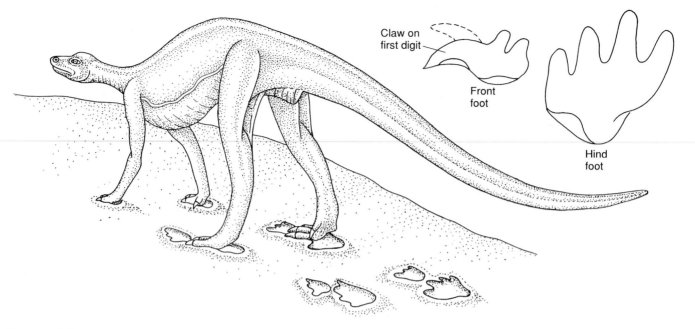

FIGURE 7.5

Prosauropod footprints like these indicate that prosauropods did sometimes walk on all fours as in the restoration of *Massospondylus* walking up a sand dune. Note the impression of the large claw in the first digit of the hand.

3. The jaw hinge is below the line of the upper tooth row as in plant-eating ornithischians.

4. The offset of the jaws of prosauropods ranges from small to large. This offset allows the tooth rows to be almost parallel so that contact would have occurred nearly simultaneously along their entire length during chewing, as in many living plant-eating mammals.

5. The spatulate teeth of prosauropods had about 20 coarse serrations per tooth that are set at an angle of about 45° to their cutting edge. They bear an uncanny resemblance to the teeth of the living *Iguana*, a plant-eating lizard.

6. A mass of small stones (gastric mill or gizzard) found in the stomach region of a skeleton of the African prosauropod *Massospondylus* may have been used to crush swallowed vegetation.

THE GENUS MUSSAURUS

No review of prosauropods would be complete without mentioning **Mussaurus** ("mouse lizard"), which was described during the late 1970s from a tiny skeleton and associated eggs from the Upper Triassic of southern Argentina. The total body length of *Mussaurus* was about 20 centimeters. Clearly, this tiny baby dinosaur, which could have stood in the palm of your hand, is a hatchling prosauropod. It may have been a juvenile of *Coloradisaurus*, a prosauropod dinosaur from the same locality known only from adult bones. The discovery of *Mussaurus* not only brought the world one of its smallest dinosaurs, but also demonstrated that prosauropods, like sauropods, laid eggs.

PROSAUROPOD EVOLUTION

Prosauropods were among the first dinosaurs to appear during the Late Triassic. They rapidly achieved a worldwide distribution and were among the largest and most successful plant-eating vertebrates of the Late Triassic and Early Jurassic. The great

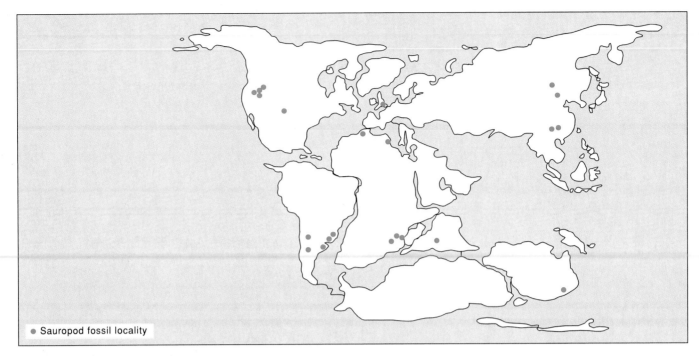

FIGURE 7.6

Sauropod dinosaurs were the largest and among the most successful plant-eating vertebrates of the Jurassic and Cretaceous. Their fossils are known from all of the continents except Antarctica.

similarity of prosauropods such as *Ammosaurus* from North America and *Lufengosaurus* from southern China suggests that by the Early Jurassic, environments favorable to prosauropods were present across the continents. The extinction of prosauropods at the end of the Early Jurassic marks the first significant disappearance of a group of dinosaurs. It coincides with the appearance of sauropod dinosaurs as well as other large plant eaters, the stegosaurs and ankylosaurs. It is tempting to believe that prosauropods were replaced by these larger herbivores.

SAUROPODS

These gigantic quadrupedal herbivores include the largest land animals of all time, behemoths that weighed as much as 55 tons and attained body lengths of more than 40 meters. Evolutionary novelties of sauropods include their gigantic size, long necks and tails, tiny heads and dorsally located nostrils, among other features. *Brontosaurus*, correctly called *Apatosaurus*, is the **sauropod** most familiar to the general public followed by *Diplodocus* and *Brachiosaurus*. Paleontologists recognize as many as 75 genera of sauropods, although most of them are not known from complete skeletons.

The oldest-known sauropods are of Early Jurassic age, and the group persisted until the extinction of all the dinosaurs at the end of the Cretaceous, with a worldwide distribution (figure 7.6). In terms of size and diversity, the zenith of sauropod evolution occurred during the Jurassic-Cretaceous transition. At that time, at least two very distinct types of sauropods coexisted, the diplodocids and camarasaurids, which are distinguished by features of their skulls, vertebrae (box 7.1), and limbs.

DIPLODOCIDAE

The two sauropod types of the Jurassic-Cretaceous transition are most easily distinguished by their skulls (figure 7.7). **Diplodocid** skulls were long and slender with elongate muzzles. The jaws bore slender, peg-like teeth confined to the front of the mouth. The nostrils were on top of the skull in front of and above the orbits.

BOX 7.1

SAUROPOD VERTEBRAE: KEY TO CLASSIFICATION

The skulls of sauropods were small and weakly connected to their vertebral columns. Because of this they were easily detached and lost after death, thus it is the norm to find sauropod skeletons without skulls (see box 7.2, The *Brontosaurus* Business). Indeed, the skulls of many sauropod taxa are not known. This has forced paleontologists to rely on other aspects of the skeletons of sauropods, especially their vertebrae, to classify them. Fortunately, sauropod vertebrae were intricate structures that varied significantly from sauropod to sauropod, and may offer a useful basis for the classification of these giants.

The basic sauropod vertebra (box figure 7.1A), like that of most vertebrates, consists of a **centrum** beneath a **neural arch.** The centrum is the body of the vertebra and provides a site of attachment for muscles that support the body. The connected centra together comprised the flexible rod upon which the body of the dinosaur was hung. The centrum also supports the neural arch, a complex structure that encloses the spinal cord and sends out bony struts to which the ribs and other vertebrae are attached. The top of the neural arch is a flange of bone called the neural spine, another site of attachment for tendons, muscles, and ligaments, especially in the shoulder and hip regions.

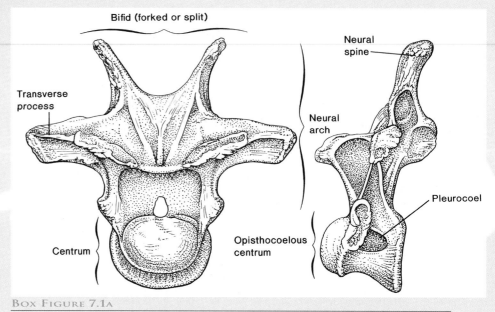

BOX FIGURE 7.1A

Sauropod vertebrae, such as this dorsal vertebra of *Apatosaurus*, present a variety of features that can be used in sauropod classification.

As stated in Chapter 4, the vertebral column of all dinosaurs, including sauropods (and most other vertebrates), can be divided into four regions: cervical (neck), dorsal (back), sacral (hip), and caudal (tail). In addition, the shapes of the surfaces at which the centra meet each other (articulate) have descriptive names. In sauropods, the centra meet at ball-and-socket joints (box figure 7.1B). In a single centrum, if the cup is anterior and the ball is posterior, the vertebra is termed **procoelous,** from the Greek words *pro,* meaning "before" and *koilus* (*coelos*), meaning "hollow" or "cavity." If the situation is reversed—cup posterior and

Diplodocid bodies (figure 7. 8) were long and relatively lightly built, and they include the longest (up to 44 meters long) though not necessarily the heaviest dinosaurs. A 27-meter-long **Diplodocus** would have weighed about 10 tons, considerably less than the shorter, 50-ton *Brachiosaurus*. The necks of diplodocids were extremely long with an increased number of vertebrae at the expense of those in the back. This culminated in the neck of **Mamenchisaurus,** from the Jurassic of China, which had 19 vertebrae but only 12 in the back (figure 7.9). The neck vertebrae of diplodocids had unusually short ribs, and their neural spines were marked by a deep, V-shaped groove, as were those of the anterior dorsal vertebrae. At least one pulley-like muscle or tendon may have occupied this groove as part of the neck- and head-lifting musculature. The spines of the vertebrae in the hip region were high, and the chevrons of the tail were modified considerably from the type of chevron characteristic of earlier sauropods. Instead of projecting downward as simple spines, the chevrons of diplodocids were modified with fore and aft expansions

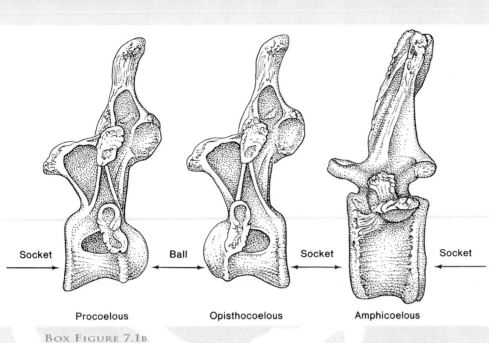

Socket → Procoelous

Ball ← → Opisthocoelous → Socket

Socket ← Amphicoelous → Socket

BOX FIGURE 7.1B

Sauropod vertebrae are procoelous, opistocoelous, or amphicoelous, depending on the arrangement of the ball-and-socket joints of the centra.

ball anterior—the vertebra is termed **opisthocoelous** (*opisthen* is Greek for "behind"). Vertebrae bounded by two cavities are called **amphicoelous** (*amphi* is Greek for "double"). Indeed, one sauropod genus, *Amphicoelias*, takes its name from the amphicoelous nature of some of its vertebral centra.

The centra of many sauropod dinosaurs, particularly in the cervical region, were a lightly built framework of delicate struts and buttresses bounding deep cavities, especially along the sides of the centra (see box figure 7.1A). Such cavities are called **pleurocoels** (*pleura* is the Greek word for "side," thus "side cavities"). Through evolution, the solid, spool-like vertebrae of sauropod ancestors were greatly modified by removing bone so that the vertebrae became much lighter. The

development of pleurocoels may thus have helped lighten an otherwise inordinately heavy structure in a very big animal already fighting a tremendous battle against gravity during its day-to-day activities. Some paleontologists have also suggested that the pleurocoelous vertebrae may have been invested with air sacs that functioned in a fashion similar to the air sacs that modern birds have in their bones, which help to lighten them and make their respiration more efficient. Another suggestion is that the pleurocoels were sites of glycogen (from glucose, a natural sugar) storage. These ideas are interesting speculation, but difficult to evaluate from just the structure of the vertebrae alone. What is certain is that the vertebrae were lightened considerably by the presence of pleurocoels.

The caudal vertebrae of sauropods had chevron bones to which muscles attached on their undersides that surrounded and protected blood vessels for the tail (see figure 7.10). The shape of these **chevrons,** the shapes and lengths of the neural spines, and whether or not various vertebrae are procoelous, opisthocoelous or amphicoelous, are important features used to classify sauropods. Thus, for example, the titanosaurid sauropods are identified almost exclusively on the basis of their procoelous caudal vertebrae, which differ from the caudals of other sauropods.

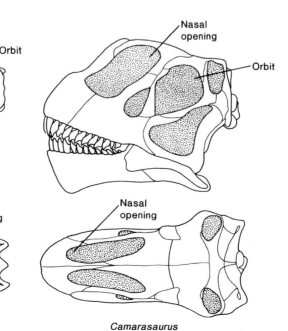

Nasal opening

Orbit

Nasal opening

Orbit

Nasal opening

Nasal opening

Diplodocus

Camarasaurus

FIGURE 7.7

Diplodocid and camarasaurid sauropods can most easily be distinguished by features of their skulls.

From W. P. Coombs, Jr., "Sauropod Habits and Habitats" in *Palaeogeography, Palaeoclimatology, Palaeoecology,* 17:1–33. Copyright © 1975 Elsevier Science Publishers, Amsterdam, Netherlands. Reprinted by permission.

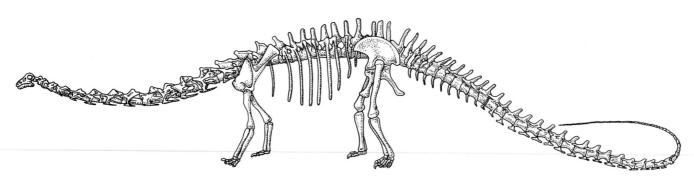

FIGURE 7.8

An adult *Diplodocus* was a 27-meter-long, lightly built sauropod, characteristic of the diplodocids.

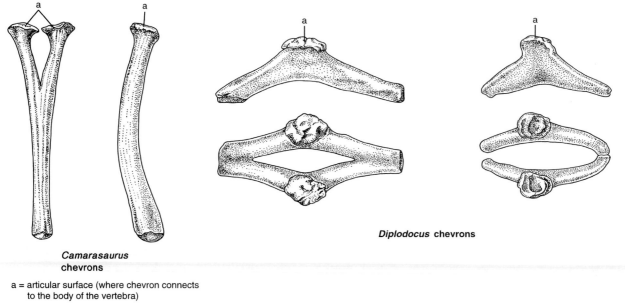

FIGURE 7.9

The development of an extremely long neck in the evolution of diplodocid sauropods culminated in 22-meter-long *Mamenchisaurus* from China.
© Mark Hallett

a

a

a

a

Diplodocus chevrons

Camarasaurus
chevrons

a = articular surface (where chevron connects
to the body of the vertebra)

FIGURE 7.10

The normal chevrons of sauropod dinosaurs were shaped like "tuning forks" of bone directed downward. Those of diplodocids were modified to have fore-and-aft expansions that, in some posterior caudal vertebrae, became rod-like extensions.

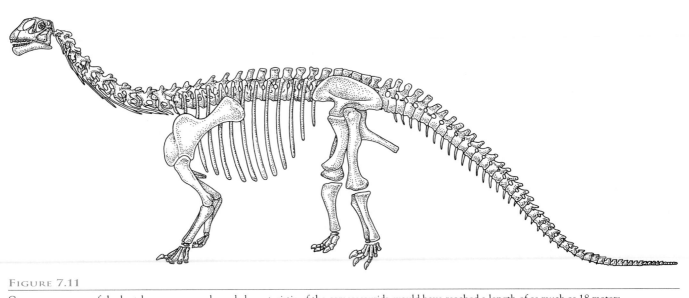

FIGURE 7.11

Camarasaurus, one of the best-known sauropods, and characteristic of the camarasaurids, would have reached a length of as much as 18 meters.

into parallel rods (figure 7.10). The tails of diplodocids were very long and made up of at least 80 vertebrae. The last 30 to 40 of these vertebrae were little more than elongate rods that formed what has been called a "whiplash."

The limbs of diplodocids were relatively slender, and their rib cages were deep and narrow. The forelimbs were relatively short for sauropods, with a typical humerus-to-femur ratio of 0.66. The numbers of bones in the wrist and ankle were reduced; only one or two remained in the wrist and one (astragalus) in the ankle. Apparently, both the wrist and the ankle were heavily invested with cartilage, which absorbed the stresses produced by so heavy a creature.

Diplodocus (see figure 7.8), of course, is the typical and best-known diplodocid. Its fossils are known from Jurassic-Cretaceous transition deposits in the western United States, as are those of the closely related diplodocid, *Barosaurus*. *Barosaurus* has also been reported from eastern Africa. It had much longer neck vertebrae and a shorter tail than *Diplodocus*.

Perhaps the most famous diplodocid is **Apatosaurus,** which we also know as **Brontosaurus** (box 7.2). *Apatosaurus* was one of the bulkiest diplodocids, with robust limb bones, heavy cervical ribs, and a single bone in its wrist. Huge diplodocids, called *Supersaurus* and *Seismosaurus*, are also known from the western United States. They were the longest land animals of all time and among the heaviest.

CAMARASAURIDAE

Camarasaurus is the best-known sauropod (figure 7.11), and along with its close relatives, is a remarkable contrast to the diplodocids. The most obvious difference is in the skulls (see figure 7.7). That of the **camarasaurid** was short and heavy with a blunt snout. The jaws bore relatively large, spoon-shaped (spatulate) teeth along their entire length. The nostrils were large and located on the sides of the skull just in front of the eyes.

The camarasaurid body was solidly built but neither exceptionally long nor overly heavy. There were only 12 neck vertebrae (the primitive number for sauropods), and a U-shaped trough in the neural spines extended along the first four dorsal vertebrae. The spines of the sacral vertebrae were lower and thicker than in diplodocids. In the neck and back vertebrae, the pleurocoels were very extensive. The tail chevrons were of the standard sauropod type.

BOX 7.2

THE *BRONTOSAURUS* BUSINESS

*B*rontosaurus stands out as one of the most popular names for a dinosaur. Yet few grade school children shrink from pointing out that *Brontosaurus* is not the technically correct name for this sauropod; *Apatosaurus* is. This is because since 1903 scientists have agreed that *Apatosaurus,* named by Yale paleontologist O. C. Marsh in 1877, and *Brontosaurus,* also named by Marsh, but in 1879, represent the same kind of sauropod dinosaur. When more than one name exists for the same genus, the internationally accepted rules for naming animals, living and extinct, force paleontologists to use the earliest proposed name. The younger name, in this case *Brontosaurus,* is then branded a "synonym" and abandoned.

Marsh's research also lies at the crux of another aspect of the *Brontosaurus* business, the question of what type of head this sauropod had. In 1883, Marsh produced the first reconstruction of a sauropod dinosaur, that of *Brontosaurus excelsus* (box figure 7.2). In so doing, he relied primarily on a fairly complete skeleton from a dinosaur quarry at Como Bluff, Wyoming. But this skeleton lacked a head. To complete his reconstruction Marsh had to guess which type of head, from among the sauropod heads known to him, belonged to *Brontosaurus.*

Unfortunately, he guessed incorrectly when he based the head in the reconstruction on two incomplete detached skulls, one from a dinosaur quarry east of Como Bluff and another from Garden Park, Colorado. Hence *Brontosaurus* was presented to the public with a *Camarasaurus*-like skull, one with large, spatulate teeth.

More than a decade after Marsh's death, between the years 1909 and 1915, the Carnegie Museum began to excavate the famous dinosaur quarry near Jensen, Utah now known as Dinosaur National Monument. The most complete *Apatosaurus* known was one of the fruits of their labors, but even it did not have a head connected to the vertebral column. In 1916, this skeleton was named *Apatosaurus louisae* by W. J. Holland, the director of the Carnegie Museum, after Louise Carnegie, wife of the museum's patron, Andrew Carnegie. The *Apatosaurus louisae* skeleton was found lying on top of another smaller, headless *Apatosaurus* skeleton. Nearby lay part of the skeleton of a third sauropod thought to be a *Diplodocus.* Also among those bodies was a *Diplodocus*-like skull. Holland thought this skull was too large to belong to the supposed *Diplodocus* skeleton or to

the smaller *Apatosaurus.* In his mind, it made sense to attach it to the skeleton of *Apatosaurus louisae.* Thus, Holland reasoned, Marsh had guessed wrong.

The skeleton of *Apatosaurus louisae* was mounted at the Carnegie Museum, and Holland planned to place the *Diplodocus*-like skull on it. But Henry Fairfield Osborn, one of the most eminent vertebrate paleontologists of the time, believed that Marsh was right and "convinced" Holland not to do so. Or did he? Holland left the *Apatosaurus louisae* skeleton on display without a head for more than 20 years. Only after Holland's death in 1932 was a head placed on the skeleton—a copy of the *Camarasaurus*-like skull originally chosen by Marsh!

Holland, as the saying goes, must have rolled over in his grave. But in the late 1970s he was vindicated. Further preparation of the skeletons from the Utah quarry showed that the skeleton Holland thought was a *Diplodocus* was actually another *Apatosaurus.* Three *Apatosaurus* skeletons in the same quarry with a *Diplodocus*-like skull provides very strong evidence that the skull belonged to *Apatosaurus* too. Indeed, modern studies of sauropods have listed numerous similarities shared by the skeletons of

---

Camarasaurid limbs were stout, and the typical humerus-to-femur ratio was .70 or more. So, the forelimbs were relatively longer than in diplodocids. The wrist and ankles each had two bones, and the forefoot was elongated. Besides *Camarasaurus,* the best-known camarasaurids are its compatriot *Haplocanthosaurus* from the Jurassic-Cretaceous transition of the western United States, the Chinese Late Jurassic *Euhelopus,* and the Mongolian Late Cretaceous *Opisthocoelicaudia.*

OTHER SAUROPODS

If we examined only their teeth, all sauropods would be assigned to the diplodocids (those with rod-like teeth) or camarasaurids (those with spatulate teeth). But once we begin to examine other features, especially the vertebrae, a more complex classification of sauropods emerges. Currently, paleontologists recognize five or six families of sauropods, including the diplodocids and camarasaurids just discussed.

The best-known of these other sauropod families are the **brachiosaurids,** typified by one of the heaviest land animals of all time, ***Brachiosaurus*** (figure 7.12). In features of the skull and the teeth, *Brachiosaurus* most resembled camarasaurids. But

1 m

O. C. Marsh's classic reconstruction of the
skeleton of *Apatosaurus* included a
Camarasaurus-like head. Only 75 years later was
the correct, *Diplodocus*-like skull (right) placed
on the body of *Apatosaurus*.
(*top*) From John H. Ostrom, Peabody Museum of
Natural History, and U.S. Geological Survey.
Reprinted by permission of John H. Ostrom.

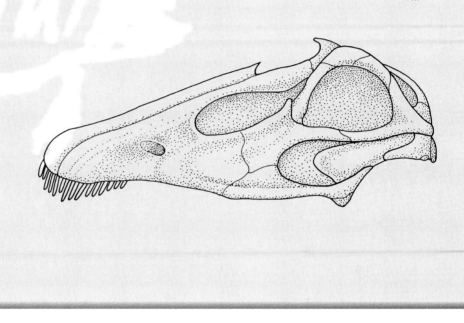

Diplodocus and *Apatosaurus*, making it no
surprise that their skulls would also be
similar. The *Camarasaurus*-like skulls that
sat on the necks of *Apatosaurus* skeletons
for nearly 100 years came off and were
replaced by *Diplodocus*-like skulls with rod-
shaped teeth. There ends the *Brontosaurus*
business—except that we still don't know
for certain what the lower jaw of
Apatosaurus looked like!

in *Brachiosaurus* the forelimb was relatively long—the humerus-to-femur ratio was
greater than 1.0. Thus, the shoulders of *Brachiosaurus* were higher than its hips.
Although there were only 13 neck vertebrae and 11 to 12 vertebrae in the back, those
of the neck were elongate, resulting in a very long neck. The neural spines were all
undivided, and those in the sacral region were low. Although there were about 50
vertebrae in the tail, each vertebra was short, which made for a relatively short tail.
The chevrons were simple, and the hand bore a very short claw on its first digit.
Brachiosaurus from the Jurassic-Cretaceous transition of the western United States,
Tanzania, and Portugal, was not even as long as *Apatosaurus* (only 17 meters), but it
was at least twice as heavy and could raise its head 12 meters off the ground.

Another well-known group of sauropods are the primarily Early and Middle
Jurassic **cetiosaurids.** Among the best-known cetiosaurids are the Chinese genera
Shunosaurus and *Datousaurus,* described from the Zigong dinosaur quarry in the
Middle Jurassic of Sichuan Province. These were relatively small sauropods;
Datousaurus, the longer of the two, was "only" 12 meters long. Their skulls were
rather similar to those of camarasaurids, but had longer muzzles. The numerous

FIGURE 7.12

Brachiosaurus was the heaviest land animal of all time, weighing as much as 55 tons and measuring 22 meters from snout to tail tip.

Courtesy Museum Für Naturkunde, Berlin

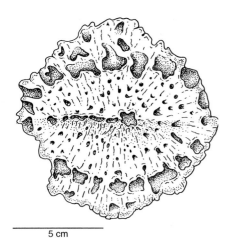

5 cm

FIGURE 7.13

Armor plates like this one adorned the back of the titanosaurid *Saltasaurus* and may have characterized all titanosaurids.

teeth were slender, but had small, spoon-shaped crowns and were thus intermediate in structure between those of diplodocids and those of camarasaurids. There were 12 cervical vertebrae and 13 in the back. The neck vertebrae were short and lacked much development of pleurocoels. The neural spines were not divided, and there were three bones in the wrist and two in the ankle. The humerus-to-femur ratio was about 0.66, the same as in diplodocids. The chevrons were forked, and in *Shunosaurus* there was even a club at the end of the tail!

The fifth well-established sauropod family is the Titanosauridae. These sauropods are identified by their procoelous tail vertebrae and the large number (six) of vertebrae in the sacrum. One **titanosaurid**—*Saltasaurus* from the Cretaceous of Argentina—had body armor (figure 7.13). So it is reasonable to assume that other titanosaurids also may have been armored. But because relatively complete skeletons of titanosaurids are rare, this is far from certain. Most titanosaurids are of Cretaceous age and come from Argentina (*Antarctosaurus, Saltasaurus*), India (*Titanosaurus*) and other parts of the Mesozoic southern supercontinent called Gondwana.

In North America, the last-known sauropod of the Late Cretaceous is **Alamosaurus**. This fairly large titanosaurid is known only from a few teeth (of the diplodocid type), a shoulder blade and forelimb, some pelvic bones, a femur, a few

BOX 7.3

THE SAUROPOD HIATUS

It is a curious fact that sauropod dinosaurs have a temporally disjunct distribution in the western United States during the Cretaceous. In Lower Cretaceous strata, sauropod bones and footprints are found in Wyoming, Texas, Oklahoma, and Arkansas. Thereafter, sauropod fossils are absent for about 30 million years, reappearing solely in the form of the titanosaurid *Alamosaurus*, in the uppermost Cretaceous deposits of Texas, New Mexico, Utah, and Wyoming. Two explanations have been offered to explain this 30-million-year absence, the **sauropod hiatus.**

The first explanation is that sauropods were not absent in western North America during the hiatus, but were actually there all along. The environments the sauropods lived in during the hiatus either are not preserved in the rock record or have not yet been sampled by paleontologists. So, sauropods did live in the western United States during the hiatus, but their remains either were not fossilized or are yet to be discovered.

The second explanation posits the extinction of sauropods in western North America at the end of the Early Cretaceous, about 100 million years ago.

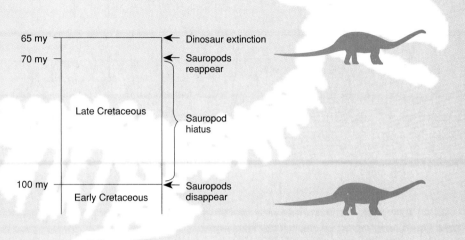

BOX FIGURE 7.3

The sauropod hiatus lasted 30 million years.

Thirty million years later, *Alamosaurus* arrived from elsewhere, probably South America, where sauropods prospered throughout the Cretaceous.

The balance of evidence favors the second explanation. Particularly important is the fact that there are some very well-known dinosaur faunas in the western United States during the 30-million-year-long hiatus, representing a variety of environments from which no trace of a sauropod fossil is known. Also significant is the fact that the last North American sauropod, *Alamosaurus*, is a titanosaurid closely related to South American Cretaceous sauropods. Although it does seem reasonable to believe that, in the western United States, sauropods became extinct at the end of the Early Cretaceous and invaded 30 million years later (box figure 7.3), the reasons for their extinction and subsequent invasion remain unknown.

dorsal vertebrae and a tail, yet it is one of the better-known titanosaurids. It almost certainly emigrated into North America from South America at about the end of the Cretaceous (box 7.3).

HOW LARGE WAS THE LARGEST?

Recent discoveries of huge sauropods have pushed up the known limits of body size in terrestrial vertebrates and raised the question of which was the largest sauropod. When using the word large, however, it is important to distinguish between weight (body mass) and length. As the previous discussion indicates, the longest sauropods were relatively lightly built and thus generally weighed less than the shorter, more robust sauropods like *Brachiosaurus*.

Some recent candidates for the award for largest are *Ultrasauros*, *Supersaurus*, and *Seismosaurus*. **Ultrasauros** is a name formally applied to a gigantic crushed vertebra from Jurassic-Cretaceous transition beds in western Colorado. It is now considered by many paleontologists to be a synonym of *Brachiosaurus*. Claims of weights as high as 190 tons for *Ultrasauros* clearly were exaggerated, and a weight estimate for these largest brachiosaurs of 45 to 55 tons is much more reasonable. At this estimate, *Brachiosaurus* was the heaviest sauropod.

A huge sauropod shoulder blade from Colorado has been referred to as *Supersaurus* (figure 7.14) and was originally thought to be a brachiosaur. Closer examination, though, reveals it to be more similar to the shoulder blade of *Diplodocus*. If it is a gigantic sauropod with *Diplodocus*-like proportions, then a weight estimate as high as 50 tons and a length estimate of 42 meters is not unreasonable. *Supersaurus* thus stands out as the longest sauropod and among the heaviest.

Portions of the tail, back, pelvis, and hind limb of an enormous diplodocid still being excavated in the Upper Jurassic of northern New Mexico have been identified as **Seismosaurus.** Length estimates as long as 58 meters have been made for *Seismosaurus*, but do not stand up to critical scrutiny. Very recent estimates of a 60-meter-long, 150-ton *Amphicoelias* are based on fragmentary material, so they may not be accurate.

At present, the reliable upper limits of known sauropod size are 55 tons for an extremely heavy *Brachiosaurus* and 42 meters long for a very elongate diplodocid, *Supersaurus*. To put these estimates into perspective, note that living African elephants weigh 5 to 7.5 tons and are 5 to 7.5 meters long (figure 7.15).

SAUROPOD LIFESTYLES

The enormous size and the unusual body shape (especially the long neck and miniscule head) of sauropod dinosaurs have led to much speculation about their way of life. Particularly significant topics for discussion are sauropod diet, metabolism, locomotion, habitat preferences, and reproduction, as well as evidence of social behavior among sauropods.

Diet

Both types of sauropod teeth—the peg-like teeth of diplodocids and the spatulate teeth of camarasaurids—appear to have been well suited to cropping vegetation in much the same way that a living horse uses its incisors (figure 7.16). Some sauro-

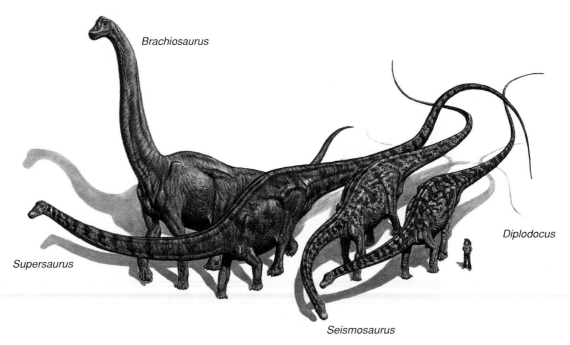

Brachiosaurus

Diplodocus

Supersaurus

Seismosaurus

FIGURE 7.15

Brachiosaurus at 55 tons was the heaviest dinosaur, and *Supersaurus* at 42 meters long was the longest dinosaur. Both would have dwarfed a living African elephant.

© Mark Hallett

pod teeth found are worn, but sauropods clearly had no grinding or shearing teeth for smashing and pulverizing vegetation as did the dental batteries of duck-bill dinosaurs, or do the premolars and molars of living horses. Sauropods must have swallowed the vegetation with little chewing, relying on chemical or bacterial mechanisms in the gut to break it down. Polished stones found with some sauropod skeletons have been identified as gizzard stones. This suggests sauropods may have used a gastric mill to help grind the vegetation they ate.

Some paleontologists have argued that the rod-like teeth of the diplodocids were used as a sieve to collect algae and invertebrates. This is plausible, though it would necessitate an incredible supply of algae and invertebrates to feed the diplodocids. Sauropod cropping of different kinds of plants, which were quickly swallowed and broken down in the gut chemically or bacterially while being ground by a gastric mill, seems most plausible. Assuming modern nutritional values for vegetation of the Mesozoic, it has been estimated that a 29-ton sauropod would have had to eat 50 kilograms of vegetation each day!

Metabolism

The 50-kilogram-per-day calculation is based on the notion that sauropods had metabolic rates comparable to those of living reptiles. Of course, if they had higher metabolic rates like those of living mammals, they would have had to eat more. There is no conclusive evidence, however, that this was so (see Chapter 15), and it is reasonable to conclude that they had an ectothermic ("cold-blooded") reptilian metabolism, with one important difference. This difference is evident considering the great bulk of sauropods; their massiveness would have made them into what physiologists term inertial homeotherms (also called gigantotherms). In other words, sauropods would have maintained an essentially constant body temperature (homeothermy) because of the resistance to heat transference inherent in their

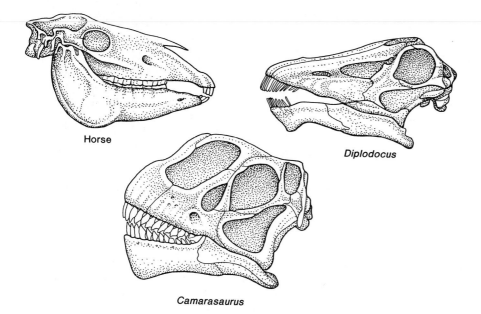

Horse

Diplodocus

Camarasaurus

FIGURE 7.16

The teeth of sauropods probably functioned like the incisors of a living horse, and were used to crop vegetation.

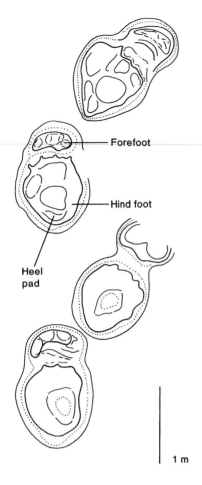

FIGURE 7.17

Sauropod footprints like these from Morocco indicate that sauropods walked on all fours and that their heels were supported by thick, fleshy pads as are the heels of living elephants.

FIGURE 7.18

Classic reconstructions of sauropods such as this one (drawn by paleontologist E. D. Cope and published in 1897) show them submerged in water. Paleontologists now envision sauropods as tree-top browsers that spent most of their lives on dry land.

large mass (thermal inertia). Thus, by virtue of its size alone, once it reached its ideal body temperature, a sauropod would have retained that temperature much longer than a smaller animal. Of course it would also have taken much longer to reach that temperature in the first place!

Locomotion and Habitat Preferences

The nearly equal length of the fore and hind limbs, the thick, solid limb bones, the massive pelvic and shoulder girdles, and the short broad feet of sauropods indicate that they were obligatory quadrupeds. Sauropod foot structure indicates that they walked on the tips of their front toes with their hind-foot heels resting on large pads similar to living elephants. Sauropod footprints confirm these conclusions (figure 7.17). The limb structure of sauropods is what anatomists term **graviportal,** meaning designed to bear great weight on land.

The oldest notion about sauropod lifestyles is that they were aquatic. For nearly a century paleontologists believed that sauropod limbs were not strong enough to support their bulky bodies, that the "weak" teeth of sauropods could only be used to eat soft, aquatic vegetation, and that the nostrils on the tops of some sauropod skulls functioned as snorkels, allowing the animal to breathe while most of the head was submerged. The image of a sauropod dinosaur standing in deep water, its head emerging like the periscope of a submarine (figure 7.18), is classic. Indeed, one paleontologist even went so far as to conclude that the differing neck lengths and limb proportions indicated habitation of different depths of water. According to this scheme, *Brachiosaurus* lived in water depths of about 8 meters, *Diplodocus* in depths of 4 to 5 meters and *Apatosaurus* in shallow depths of 2 to 3 meters.

A modern view of sauropod habitat preferences has resulted from a reappraisal of sauropod anatomy. This reappraisal demonstrates that there is little, if any, evidence to support the idea of aquatic sauropods. Indeed, it has been estimated that water pressure would have prevented expansion and contraction of a sauropod's lungs if the dinosaur were submerged. The massive limbs of sauropods could certainly have supported their huge bodies; the graviportal limb skeletons of sauropods seem to have been designed to do just that. The teeth of sauropods were as robust as a horse's incisors and could easily have cropped tough vegetation. And the nostrils on top of some sauropod heads were remarkably like those of living tapirs, land-living mammals that have a short trunk (proboscis) like a miniature version of an elephant's trunk. The nostrils far back on a tapir's skull are an outgrowth of the presence of a proboscis. Perhaps some sauropods, especially the diplodocids, had a tapir-like proboscis. The evidence thus seems to support a view of sauropods as land-living tree-top browsers analogous to living giraffes and elephants.

Reproduction

Like prosauropods, sauropod dinosaurs were egg layers. The most direct evidence for this comes from Aix-en-Provence, France where numerous eggs with bumpy shell textures, as much as 25 centimeters long, have been attributed to the titanosaurid *Hypselosaurus*. Some paleontologists have questioned whether an animal as heavy as an adult, female sauropod could have laid a clutch of eggs without crushing them. But at Aix-en-Provence, the eggs were arranged in a line, suggesting that they were laid while the female sauropod was walking.

Social Behavior

Although discussed at greater length in Chapter 14, it is appropriate to mention the circumstantial evidence of social behavior in sauropods. Many of the great dinosaur quarries of the Jurassic-Cretaceous transition, such as those at Como Bluff, Wyoming, are populated mostly by sauropod skeletons. These mass-death assemblages of sauropods may indicate group (gregarious) behavior, but some of the dinosaur quarries, such as the one at Dinosaur National Monument, Utah, are populated mostly by river-transported carcasses that accumulated in sand banks. The evidence of group behavior among sauropods provided by the mass-death assemblages is thus not totally convincing.

Sauropod trackways also support to some extent the notion of gregarious behavior among sauropods. For example, Early Cretaceous footprints from near Glen Rose, Texas (figure 7.19) seem to document a group of sauropods walking together in the same direction. But to call this group a herd, which implies a complex social structure, may be overly generous. Not only is there no unequivocal evidence that all those sauropods walked together at one time, the distribution of track sizes, which would indicate the presence and number of sauropods of different ages, is scattered, and does not imply that any orderly movement of young and old was involved.

The evidence supporting sauropod group behavior is at best circumstantial. Mass-death assemblages and multiple trackways suggest some sort of group behavior among sauropods, but little else can be concluded at present.

SAUROPOD EVOLUTION

Sauropod dinosaurs evolved from a prosauropod-like ancestry at about the end of the Triassic or the beginning of the Jurassic. Although no known prosauropod is a strong candidate for sauropod ancestry (unless evolutionary reversals are accepted), *Riojasaurus* from the Late Triassic of Argentina or *Vulcanodon* from the Early Jurassic of southern Africa may best approximate that ancestor.

The oldest sauropods are of Early Jurassic age and include *Barapasaurus* from India and *Rhoetosaurus* from Australia. They and Middle Jurassic sauropods such as *Datousaurus* and *Shunosaurus* (China), *Cetiosaurus* (England), and *Patagosaurus* (Argentina), form a group of primitive sauropods nominally termed cetiosaurids. This "family" is clearly a grade level (not a clade) in the evolution of sauropods characterized by relatively small (up to 12 meters long), short-necked forms with *Camarasaurus*-like heads and teeth. It is interesting that these large animals appear

FIGURE 7.19

These sauropod trackways, from the Lower Cretaceous of Texas, are taken by some paleontologists as evidence of group behavior among sauropods.

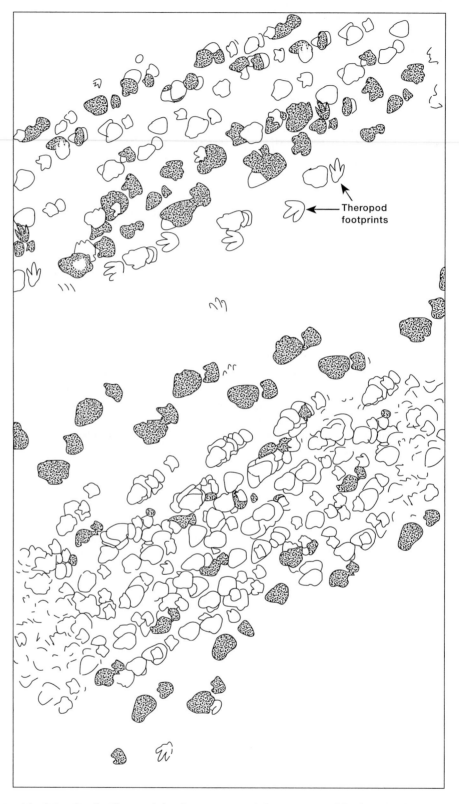

Theropod footprints

suddenly in the fossil record displaying most of the graviportal limb specializations we associate with sauropods. Their geographic distribution suggests a likely origin of sauropods in the southern supercontinent of Gondwana.

The zenith in size and diversity of sauropods was achieved during the Jurassic-Cretaceous transition. The terrestrial giants had a worldwide distribution by this time, and *Diplodocus, Brachiosaurus* and *Camarasaurus* well represent their structural diversity. In terms of size, diversity, and sheer abundance, sauropod dinosaurs were the dominant herbivores on land during the Jurassic-Cretaceous transition.

Sauropod fortunes seem to have waned during the Cretaceous when there were fewer and smaller animals. It is tempting to suggest that the rise of ornithopod dinosaurs, potential herbivorous competitors of sauropods, and the appearance and evolution of flowering plants during the Cretaceous, may have contributed to or resulted from the decline in the sauropods. Particularly significant is that most sauropod diversity during the Cretaceous was limited to the southern continents, where ornithopods were not so successful. The extinction of sauropods coincided with the extinction of the dinosaurs at the end of the Cretaceous. Though reduced in size, diversity, and numbers, sauropods can truly be said to have met the end with "their heads held high."

S U M M A R Y

1. Sauropodomorph dinosaurs comprise two closely related groups, prosauropods and sauropods, distinguished from other dinosaurs by having had small heads, spatulate teeth, long necks, short feet, and large claws on the first digits of their forefeet.

2. No known prosauropod is a suitable ancestor of sauropods, although *Riojasaurus* from the Upper Triassic of Argentina may best approximate that ancestry.

3. Prosauropods lived during the Late Triassic and Early Jurassic and so were some of the oldest dinosaurs, representing the first evolutionary diversification of plant-eating dinosaurs.

4. Sauropod dinosaurs first appeared in the Early Jurassic, and by the Late Jurassic at least two types were extant: diplodocids and camarasaurids, distinguished by a variety of skeletal features.

5. At least three other types (families) of sauropods can be recognized in the Jurassic-Cretaceous: brachiosaurids, cetiosaurids, and titanosaurids.

6. The heaviest known sauropod was *Brachiosaurus* at 50 to 55 tons, and the longest sauropod was *Supersaurus* at 42 meters.

7. Sauropods were plant eaters, egg layers, and inertial homeotherms. The long popular notion of aquatic sauropods has no evidence to support it. Sauropods had elephant-like limb structures and probably spent most of their time on dry land.

8. By the Jurassic-Cretaceous transition, sauropods had reached their evolutionary zenith in terms of size and diversity.

9. Sauropods were much less successful after the Jurassic, but did survive until the end of the Cretaceous.

K E Y   T E R M S

Alamosaurus
amphicoelous
Anchisauridae
Apatosaurus
brachiosaurid
Brachiosaurus
Brontosaurus
camarasaurid
Camarasaurus
centrum
cetiosaurid

chevrons
diplodocid
Diplodocus
graviportal
Hypselosaurus
Mamenchisaurus
Mussaurus
neural arch
opisthocoelous
Plateosaurus
pleurocoel

procoelous
prosauropod
Riojasaurus
sauropod
sauropod hiatus
sauropodomorph
Seismosaurus
Supersaurus
titanosaurid
Ultrasauros

REVIEW QUESTIONS

1. Why do most paleontologists exclude any known prosauropod from the ancestry of sauropods?

2. What characteristic features of prosauropods are exemplified by *Plateosaurus?*

3. What anatomical evidence supports the notion that prosauropods and sauropods were herbivores?

4. Distinguish diplodocid from camarasaurid sauropods.

5. What other families of sauropods are recognized by paleontologists and what are their salient characteristics?

6. Describe the vertebrae of sauropods and explain how they are relevant to sauropod classification.

7. How was the confusion about the name and the skull of *Brontosaurus* resolved?

8. Why did paleontologists believe sauropods were aquatic and why do they no longer hold this view?

9. Review the evolutionary history of the sauropodomorph dinosaurs.

FURTHER READING

Berman, D. S. and McIntosh, J. S. 1978. Skull and relationships of the Upper Jurassic sauropod *Apatosaurus* (Reptilia, Saurischia): *Bulletin of the Carnegie Museum of Natural History,* no. 8, 35 pp. (An in-depth technical description of the skull of *Apatosaurus* and related sauropods as well as an authoritative review of the "*Brontosaurus* business.")

Coombs, W. P., Jr. 1975. Sauropod habits and habitats. *Palaeogeography, Palaeoclimatology, Paleoecology* 17: 1–33. (A thorough review of the evidence for aquatic habits among sauropods that is the key article debunking this notion.)

Desmond, A. J. 1976. *The Hot-Blooded Dinosaurs.* New York: The Dial Press, 238 pp. (Chapter 5, pp. 100–133, recounts the history of ideas on sauropod behavior, habitat preferences, and the rise and demise of the idea of aquatic sauropods.)

Galton, P. M. 1990. Basal Sauropodomorpha—Prosauropoda; in Weishampel, D. B., Dodson, P., and Osmólska, H., eds., *The Dinosauria.* Berkeley: University of California Press, pp. 320–44. (A detailed technical review of the prosauropods.)

Lucas, S. G. and Hunt, A. P. 1989. *Alamosaurus* and the sauropod hiatus in the Cretaceous of the North American Western Interior. *Geological Society of America, Special Paper* 238: 75–85. (Develops and evaluates explanations for the sauropod hiatus.)

McIntosh, J. S. 1990. Sauropoda; in Weishampel, D. B., Dodson, P., and Osmólska, H., eds., *The Dinosauria.* Berkeley: University of California Press, pp. 345–401. (A detailed technical review of the sauropods.)

Ostrom, J. H. and McIntosh, J. S. 1966. *Marsh's Dinosaurs: the Collections from Como Bluff.* New Haven: Yale University Press, 388 pp. (A thorough review of the collections from one of the world's great Jurassic-Cretaceous dinosaur quarries including publication of 65 lithographs prepared for O. C. Marsh of *Diplodocus, Apatosaurus* and *Camarasaurus,* among others.)

ORNITHOPODS

rnithopods ("bird feet," see box 6.1) were bipedal or facultatively quadrupedal, ornithischian dinosaurs that lacked body armor. They first appeared during the Early Jurassic and were among the last dinosaurs to become extinct at the end of the Cretaceous. Ornithopods were thus one of the longest-lived dinosaur groups, and they were also one of the most diverse.

Five families of ornithopods have been recognized (figure 8.1), from the tiny heterodontosaurids to the enormous iguanodontids and their close relatives, who were the well-known duck-billed dinosaurs. Many features of the skull were evolutionary novelties of the ornithopods, including the "ventrally offset" premaxillary tooth row (it is "lower" than the maxillary tooth row), the elongate lateral process of the premaxillary, and the lower jaw joint located well below the level of the maxillary and lower tooth rows (figure 8.2). In this chapter, we review the anatomy and evolution of the five families of ornithopods.

HETERODONTOSAURIDAE

Heterodontosaurids are known only from the Lower Jurassic of southern Africa. These small (about 1 to 1.5 meters long) ornithopods had uniquely shaped cheek teeth (figure 8.3) that were chisel-shaped with tiny cusps (denticles) restricted to the apex of the crown. The name heterodontosaurid, which means "different-toothed lizard," is based on the canine-like teeth in the front of the mouth (see figure 8.2), which had a markedly different shape from the chisel-shaped cheek teeth.

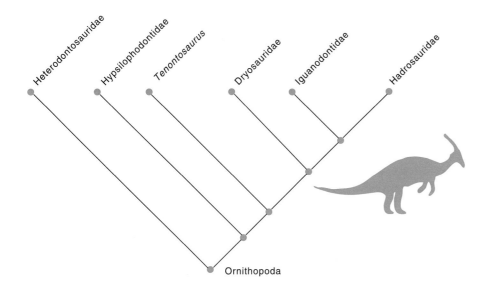

FIGURE 8.1

This cladogram of the ornithopods divides them into five families.

FIGURE 8.2

This skull of *Heterodontosaurus* well displays evolutionary novelties of ornithopods.

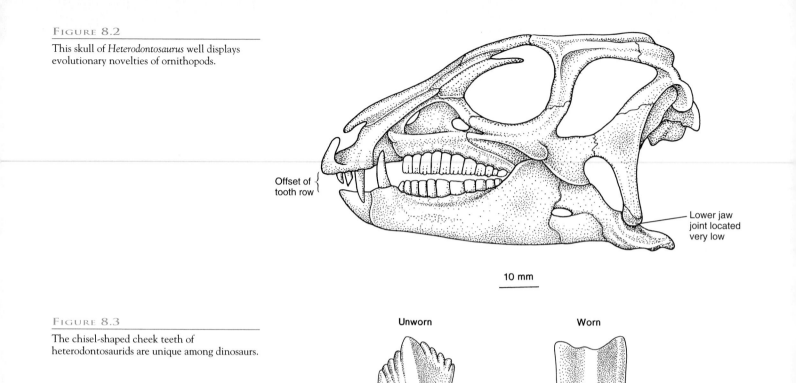

Offset of tooth row

Lower jaw joint located very low

10 mm

FIGURE 8.3

The chisel-shaped cheek teeth of heterodontosaurids are unique among dinosaurs.

Unworn

Worn

5 mm

Heterodontosaurus (figure 8.4) was a characteristic **heterodontosaurid.** This 1.2-meter-long dinosaur had short forelimbs and relatively long hind limbs, indicating it was a biped. The cheek teeth formed a **dental battery** set in massive lower jaws hinged to a solidly built skull. The teeth in this dental battery were usually heavily worn. The heavy wear and the chisel-shape of the teeth indicate this dinosaur was a plant eater. Paleontologists disagree about how *Heterodontosaurus* moved its jaws when chewing; either the lower jaw was moved backward and forward, or it was rotated against the upper jaw during closing of the mouth.

The long tail and short neck of *Heterodontosaurus* were features typical of primitive ornithischians. Ossified tendons were present only in the back region. A very bird-like feature of the hind-limb skeleton of *Heterodontosaurus* was the fusion of the tibia and fibula and their fusion to the tarsals. This fusion stabilized the lower leg and ankle and suggests that *Heterodontosaurus* was a fast runner. In contrast, the hands of *Heterodontosaurus* were stout and flexible; they may have been used to dig up or grasp vegetation.

Although *Heterodontosaurus* was a plant eater, it had large tusks near the front of its jaws (see figure 8.2). These were probably used for defense and display, as are the tusks of some living, large plant-eating mammals such as pigs. Some heterodontosaurid fossils lack these tusks, suggesting that they may have been a sexually dimorphic feature. Males presumably had tusks and females did not. The tusks may also have been used in feeding, helping the dinosaur to stab and tear vegetation.

Four different types of heterodontosaurids are known from the Lower Jurassic of southern Africa. But other than *Heterodontosaurus* and *Abrictosaurus*, they

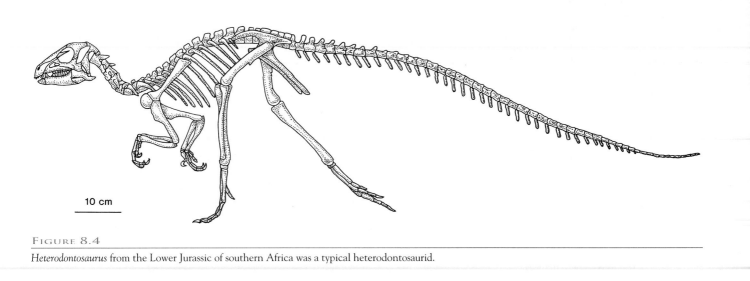

FIGURE 8.4

Heterodontosaurus from the Lower Jurassic of southern Africa was a typical heterodontosaurid.

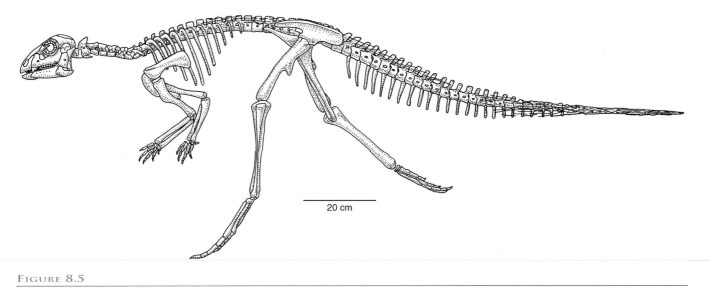

FIGURE 8.5

Early Cretaceous *Hypsilophodon* was a typical hypsilophodontid.

are known only from fragmentary fossils. The rocks in which heterodontosaurid fossils are collected were deposited in deserts and on arid alluvial fans. These primitive ornithischians were agile bipeds and, on occasion, quadrupedal diggers that browsed on vegetation low to the ground in relatively dry, sparsely vegetated country.

HYPSILOPHODONTIDAE

Hypsilophodontids were small- to medium-sized (2 to 4 meters long) bipedal ornithischians. Their fossils are known from the Middle Jurassic to Upper Cretaceous of North America, Europe, Asia, and Australia. Best known and typical of the hypsilophodontids is **Hypsilophodon** (figure 8.5).

The limb proportions of *Hypsilophodon* were those of a bipedal runner. The hind limbs were much longer than the forelimbs, and the distal segments of the hind limb, especially the ankle, were elongate. The long tail, stiffened by calcified tendons, would have counterbalanced the dinosaur while it ran. Although some paleontologists previously believed that *Hypsilophodon* was a tree-climbing dinosaur, its skeleton is much more that of a fast ground runner.

BOX 8.1

GRINDING: THE KEY TO HYPSILOPHODONTID SUCCESS

M any living mammals that eat plants grind their food by moving their lower jaws from side to side while chewing. This transverse movement of the lower jaw is achieved by arranging the jaw muscles and their points of attachment to pull the jaw laterally and medially. In tandem with teeth that provide flat surfaces for grinding and sharp edges for tearing, side-to-side movement of the lower jaw efficiently mills vegetation prior to swallowing.

Hypsilophodontid dinosaurs efficiently milled the vegetation they ate with a mechanism analogous to, but different from that of living mammals. First, instead of moving their lower jaws transversely, hypsilophodontids had a joint within their skulls that allowed their upper jaws to move sideways while chewing (box figure 8.1). This joint was essentially a diagonal hinge between the premaxillary, the upper jawbone at the front of the mouth, and the maxillary, the upper jawbone behind it. When the dinosaur closed its mouth, the teeth sheared past each other and the maxillary rotated slightly outwards while the lower jaw rotated inwards. Thus while the hypsilophodontid chomped on vegetation, the outwardly-rotating upper jaw produced a grinding movement.

Hypsilophodontids had broad, chisel-like teeth that locked together

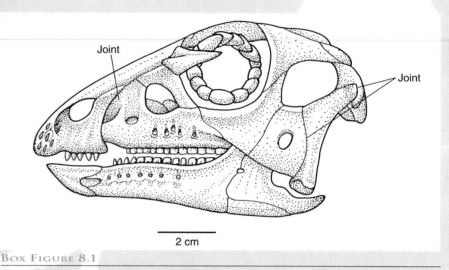

BOX FIGURE 8.1

The skull of *Hypsilophodon* had joints that allowed the upper jaws to rotate outward when the mouth was closed.

along their crowns to form a continuous, cutting edge. A cheek pouch was present alongside the teeth to catch and hold food while chewing. This sophisticated mechanism for milling vegetation of the hypsilophodontids was very different from the generalized teeth and jaws of primitive ornithischians such as the fabrosaurs (see Chapter 5), dinosaurs that were otherwise rather similar to the hypsilophodontids.

We should not be surprised that fabrosaurs were never very diverse and disappeared during the Early Jurassic. In contrast, hypsilophodontids were a diverse and widespread group of small, plant-eating dinosaurs from the Middle Jurassic through the Early Cretaceous, and a few survived to the Late Cretaceous. The hypsilophodontid mechanism of grinding vegetation must have been one of the keys to their survival.

The skull of *Hypsilophodon* resembled that of *Heterodontosaurus* but lacked the large tusks. The eyes were large, and a narrow, horny beak was present at the tip of both the upper and lower jaws. The massive jaws of *Hypsilophodon* supported a dental battery of interlocking cheek teeth that wore down to produce a continuous, inclined cutting edge (figure 8.6). Unlike heterodontosaurids, there was a hinge in the skull of *Hypsilophodon* that ran from near the front of the tooth row to nearly the jaw joint on the posterior corner of the skull. This hinge allowed the upper jaw to swing out as the dinosaur chewed (box 8.1).

Hypsilophodontids are extremely well known from complete skeletons and eggs. They first appeared during the Middle Jurassic in southern China where complete skeletons of the early hypsilophodontid *Xiaosaurus* have been discovered (figure 8.7). The zenith of hypsilophodontid diversity was during the Late Jurassic and Early Cretaceous when these small, bipedal herbivores lived in North America, Europe, Africa, Australia, and Antarctica. Only a few Late Cretaceous

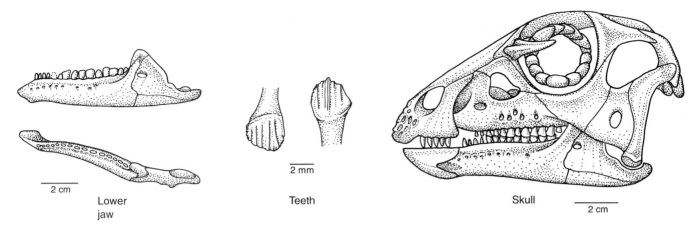

Lower
jaw

2 cm

Teeth

2 mm

Skull

2 cm

FIGURE 8.6

The dental battery of *Hypsilophodon* was used to grind vegetation.

FIGURE 8.7

Xiaosaurus, from the Middle Jurassic of China, is the oldest known hypsilophodontid.

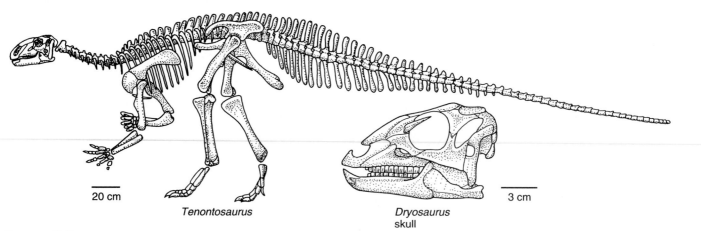

20 cm

Tenontosaurus

Dryosaurus
skull

3 cm

FIGURE 8.8

Early Cretaceous *Tenontosaurus* and *Dryosaurus* provide an evolutionary link between hypsilophodontids and iguanodontids.

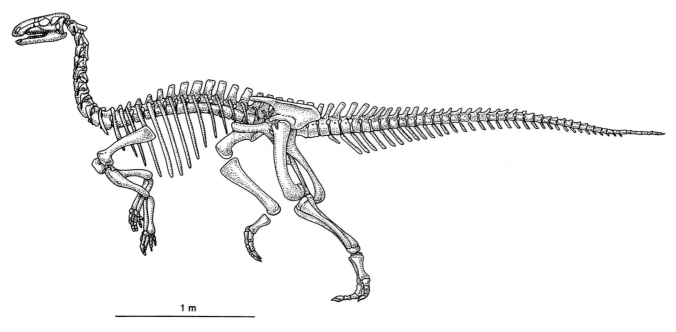

1 m

FIGURE 8.9

Late Jurassic and Early Cretaceous *Camptosaurus* is the oldest iguanodontid known from a complete skeleton.

hypsilophodontids are known, *Thescelosaurus, Orodromeus,* and *Parksosaurus* from western North America. Hypsilophodontid success was probably due in large part to their ability to grind vegetation.

Three dinosaurs closely related to hypsilophodontids are **Tenontosaurus** from the Lower Cretaceous of North America, **Dryosaurus** from the Upper Jurassic of North America and eastern Africa, and **Valdosaurus** from the Lower Cretaceous of Europe and Niger. These dinosaurs provide an evolutionary link between the small hypsilophodontids and the much larger iguanodontids (figure 8.8).

Tenontosaurus ranged in length from 1.5 to more than 7.5 meters. It resembled *Hypsilophodon,* yet lacked premaxillary teeth and had three instead of four phalanges in the third finger of the hand. In many ways, *Tenontosaurus* is an ideal transitional form between the small hypsilophodontids and the large iguanodontids.

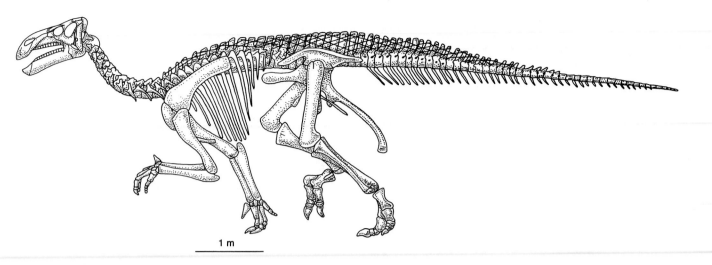

FIGURE 8.10

Early Cretaceous *Iguanodon* was a powerful quadrupedal walker.

Dryosaurus and *Valdosaurus* are usually placed in the family **Dryosauridae** distinct from Hypsilophodontidae and *Tenontosaurus*. Like *Tenontosaurus,* the dryosaurids lacked premaxillary teeth and have other skeletal features that mark them as transitional between the hypsilophodontids and iguanodontids.

IGUANODONTIDAE

Iguanodontids have a special place in the history of dinosaur studies because *Iguanodon* was one of the first dinosaurs to be described scientifically, by Gideon Mantell in 1825 (see Chapter 12). The iguanodontids were relatively large (*Iguanodon* was as much as 10 meters long), mostly bipedal herbivores, that lived principally during the Late Jurassic and Early Cretaceous.

All iguanodontids were large, heavily-built ornithopods, with heavy shoulders and forelimbs. The hind limbs were massive, and the feet were broad with hoof-like tips on their toes. A spike-like "thumb" was an evolutionary novelty of many iguanodontids. Their heads were large, and the horse-like snout ended in a broad, toothless beak.

Camptosaurus (figure 8.9) from the Upper Jurassic and Lower Cretaceous of North America and Europe is the oldest iguanodontid known from a complete skeleton. This relatively small iguanodontid, 5 to 7 meters long, did not have a fully developed "thumb" spike and had small hooves on the tips of all its toes. *Camptosaurus* had four digits in the hind foot, massive hind limbs, and limb proportions that suggest it was a facultative quadruped. The fused wrist bones provide strong evidence of stable hand walking. The neck of *Camptosaurus* was relatively long, and its head was relatively small for an iguanodontid. But it had the long, horse-like snout and broad, toothless beak characteristic of all iguanodontids.

Iguanodon (figure 8.10), best known from the Lower Cretaceous of Belgium (box 8.2), was a much larger and more specialized iguanodontid than *Camptosaurus*. Like *Camptosaurus,* it had massive hind limbs. But unlike *Camptosaurus, Iguanodon* had long forelimbs that were 70 to 80 percent as long as its hind limbs. The wrist bones of *Iguanodon* were fused, and the central three digits of the hand ended in hooves. The large conical "thumb" spike on the first digit must have been used as a defensive weapon, and the fifth digit was long and slender.

Iguanodon had a large head with a long snout, neck, and tail, and an extensive boxwork of ossified tendons that extended along the back from the shoulder region to the middle of the tail (see figure 8.10). The limb proportions and

BOX 8.2

AN *IGUANODON* GRAVEYARD AT BERNISSART

Bernissart is a small mining town in southwestern Belgium. In 1878, miners there discovered a crevice full of clay that cut across a bed of coal and was full of dinosaur bones. This crevice, at a depth of 322 meters, was excavated from 1878 until 1881. The fossils of 39 individuals of *Iguanodon,* many of them complete skeletons (box figure 8.2), were recovered, as were the fossils of many plants, fishes, and other reptiles. Bernissart thus stands as one of the greatest dinosaur localities on earth.

For many years, paleontologists thought a single catastrophe led to the accumulated *Iguanodon* skeletons at Bernissart. One popular image shows the dinosaurs falling off a cliff into the crevice which later filled with clay. Indeed, the "evidence" of a single catastrophe at Bernissart suggested to some paleontologists that *Iguanodon* lived in groups or herds.

Careful reexamination of the Bernissart *Iguanodon* by British paleontologist David Norman, however, indicates that the *Iguanodon* skeletons accumulated in groups on at least three different occasions. The skeletons were buried and fossilized in a marshy environment, but the precise cause of death of the dinosaurs remains uncertain. What is certain, though, is that a single catastrophe did not kill the Bernissart *Iguanodon,* so the accumulation of skeletons here does not necessarily indicate that *Iguanodon* lived in herds.

BOX FIGURE 8.2

This is a nineteenth century sketch of one of the many complete skeletons of *Iguanodon* from Bernissart as it was found in the rock.

modifications of the hands of *Iguanodon* suggest that it did much more quadrupedal walking than did *Camptosaurus* or the smaller ornithopods. It seems likely, however, that *Iguanodon* could rear up on its hind limbs and swing its spike-shaped thumb when attacked.

The skulls of iguanodontids varied greatly, but all had long snouts and toothless beaks. The long snouts contained many more teeth (as many as 29 in the maxillary of *Iguanodon*) than did the snouts of heterodontosaurids and hypsilophodontids. The iguanodontid beak was used to crop vegetation. The teeth were leaf shaped with long ridges on their sides and small cusps on the cutting edges and resembled the teeth of living iguanas, hence the name of the dinosaur family (see Chapter 12). Paleontologists are certain that iguanodontids were plant eaters.

The oldest iguanodontids are from the Upper Jurassic of North America and western Europe. *Camptosaurus* is the best known and is characteristic of the Late Jurassic iguanodontids. The zenith of iguanodontid diversity was during the Early-Middle Cretaceous, and their fossils are known from Europe, North America, Africa, Asia, and Australia. A particularly interesting iguanodontid from this time period is **Ouranosaurus** (figure 8.11) from Niger with its very distinctive head and long neural spines along its back. Clearly, iguanodontids were a diverse, widespread, and significant group of medium to large herbivorous dinosaurs of the Early and Middle Cretaceous world.

There was a marked decline of iguanodontids during the Late Cretaceous, probably because of the appearance of the hadrosaurids (see below). Only two types of possible Late Cretaceous iguanodontids are known, both from Europe.

HADROSAURIDAE

Hadrosaurids, popularly known as the duck-billed dinosaurs, first appeared during the Middle Cretaceous and thus were the last major group of ornithopods to evolve.

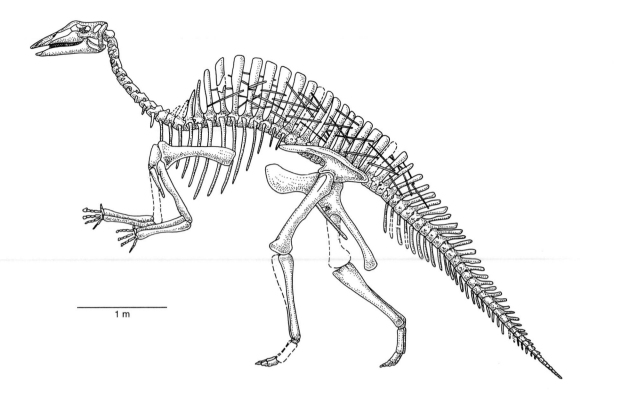

FIGURE 8.11

Ouranosaurus from the Middle Cretaceous of Niger was one of the most distinctive iguanodontids.

Their ancestry is uncertain, though much more is probably known about hadrosaurids than about any other single group of dinosaurs. Their outstanding fossil record includes many complete skeletons, eggs, footprints, and even two mummified individuals with skin intact.

The hadrosaurids (figure 8.12) were large ornithopods, 7 to 10 meters long, characterized by, among other features, their broad, toothless beaks, intricate dental batteries in which three or more replacement teeth existed for each tooth position (figure 8.13), and the loss of the first digit (thumb) on the hands. The jaws were deep and long, and the jaw muscles were evidently powerful. Like hypsilophodontids, hadrosaurids chomped their food and achieved a side-to-side motion of the jaws by slightly rotating the upper tooth rows outward when the mouth was closed.

Hadrosaurid teeth were arranged in dental batteries consisting of literally hundreds of teeth cemented together in each jaw (figure 8.13). The teeth thus formed washboard-like grinding surfaces that milled the vegetation cropped by the horny beak at the front of the mouth. The hadrosaurid jaw mechanism could process resistant, fibrous vegetation, and even twigs. Indeed, the two mummified hadrosaurids discovered in Alberta, Canada have stomachs full of conifer needles and twigs, seeds, and other tough plant debris.

The skeletons of hadrosaurids were very similar to those of iguanodontids but lacked thumbs, had a different-shaped pelvis, and had as many as 8 to 10 sacral vertebrae. There is little variation among the skeletons of different types of hadrosaurids, so identifying them is done almost exclusively by comparing their skulls.

Although the variation in skull types among hadrosaurids is astounding (figure 8.14), just two hadrosaurid subfamilies are generally recognized. **Hadrosaurines** are the more primitive subfamily and had rather flat skull roofs. They are sometimes called the "Roman-nosed" hadrosaurs after their large and long nasals, which often peaked near the posterior end of the nostrils (figure 8.14). *Edmontosaurus* (see figure 8.12) from the Upper Cretaceous of North America is a characteristic hadrosaurine.

FIGURE 8.12

Edmontosaurus, a hadrosaurine, and Parasaurolophus, a lambeosaurine, are representative hadrosaurids.

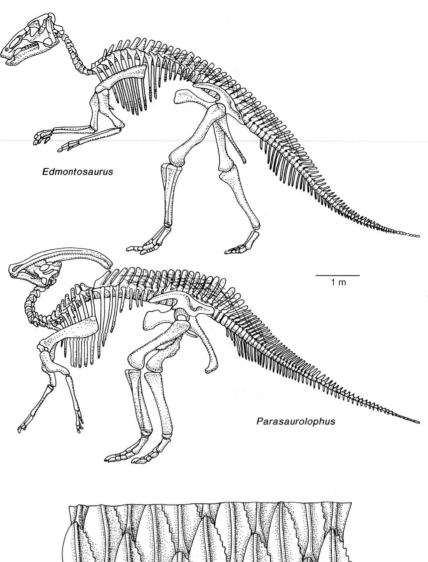

Edmontosaurus

1 m

Parasaurolophus

FIGURE 8.13

The complex dental batteries of hadrosaurids had three or more replacement teeth at each tooth position.

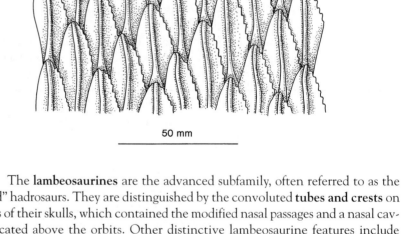

50 mm

The **lambeosaurines** are the advanced subfamily, often referred to as the "crested" hadrosaurs. They are distinguished by the convoluted **tubes and crests** on the tops of their skulls, which contained the modified nasal passages and a nasal cavity relocated above the orbits. Other distinctive lambeosaurine features include elongated neural spines on the vertebrae and relatively robust limbs. The varied crests and tubes on lambeosaurine heads may have served as visual display and probably acted as resonators to produce distinctive calls (box 8.3). Many of the differences in crest and tube size and shape reflect growth and sexual dimorphism (figure 8.15). *Parasaurolophus* (see figure 8.12) from the Upper Cretaceous of North America is a representative lambeosaurine.

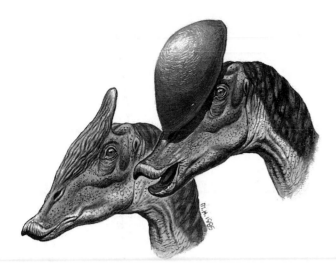

FIGURE 8.14

The flat skulls of hadrosaurines (left) contrast with the crested skulls of
lambeosaurines (right), among which there was great variety.

© Mark Hallett

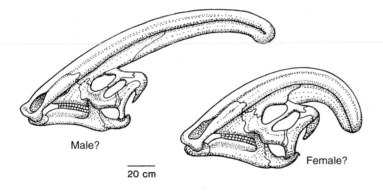

Male?

20 cm

Female?

FIGURE 8.15

The crests and tubes on the skulls of
lambeosaurines changed during growth and
were sexually dimorphic.

Most of the features of the hadrosaurid skeleton suggest that, like iguanodontids, they were powerful quadrupedal walkers also well suited to bipedal
locomotion. The hadrosaur mummies from Alberta, however, have flaps of skin
between their fingers that suggest a webbed hand. And, the tall, paddle-like tail of
hadrosaurids looks suited (though its flexibility was limited) to propelling the
dinosaurs in water. These features, and the fact that many hadrosaurids, including
complete, articulated skeletons, are found in rocks deposited in rivers, lakes, swamps,
and even the sea, have led some paleontologists to view hadrosaurids as aquatic
dinosaurs. It seems most likely, however, that hadrosaurids were very well suited to

BOX 8.3

A LAMBEOSAURINE SYMPHONY?

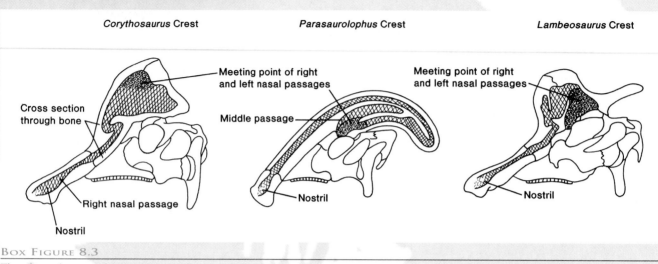

Corythosaurus Crest   *Parasaurolophus* Crest   *Lambeosaurus* Crest

BOX FIGURE 8.3

The tubes and crests on lambeosaurine skulls were hollow and connected to the nasal passages.

The crests and tubes on the heads of lambeosaurines (box figure 8.3) have elicited speculation about their function for decades. An early idea was that the crests and tubes allowed feeding underwater either by acting as snorkels (but no upward openings were present in the crests and tubes), as air storage tanks (but the volume of air that could be stored in the crests was very small relative to lung volume) or as "air locks" to prevent water from entering the lungs (although how this "air lock" would have worked is unclear). Other, more plausible suggestions are that the hollow spaces inside the tubes and crests provided space for glands or, by increasing the surface area for tissue inside the nasal cavity, warmed and moistened

inhaled air and improved the sense of smell. Another recent suggestion is that the tubes and crests were used to deflect foliage when lambeosaurines crashed through dense forests.

These plausible functions of the crests and tubes do not exclude what may have been their most important function—as signalling devices. This signalling would have been both visual and auditory. The fact that particular shapes of crests and tubes were specific to particular types of lambeosaurines, and that males and females of a specific type of lambeosaurine had different sizes and shapes of crests, strongly supports their identification as visual signalling devices. Distinctive-looking tubes and crests thus

allowed lambeosaurines to recognize members of their own species and to distinguish males from females.

Another kind of display was also possible with the lambeosaurine crests and tubes because they were hollow and connected to the air passages. Such hollow structures could have acted as **resonating chambers,** with differently shaped tubes and crests producing distinctive sounds like the differently shaped wind instruments of a symphony orchestra. So not only could lambeosaurines identify each other visually by their crests and tubes, they could recognize each other and signal with distinctive sounds. The Late Cretaceous landscapes they inhabited must have been noisy places!

living on dry land and may have entered water only for defense or feeding. Much more has been suggested about hadrosaurid behavior, especially based on their nests of eggs, and is discussed in Chapter 14.

Hadrosaurids first appeared in Asia and North America during the Middle Cretaceous. By the Late Cretaceous, they had spread to North America, Asia, Europe, and South America, though they were most diverse and abundant in Asia and North America. Hadrosaurids lived in a variety of habitats, from inland floodplains to coastal swamps and jungles. In the New World, their distribution

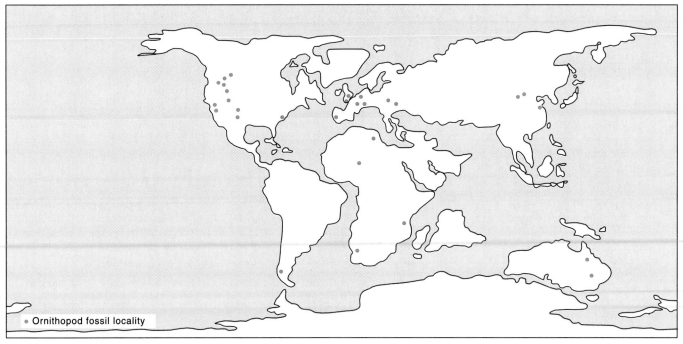

- Ornithopod fossil locality

FIGURE 8.16

Ornithopods had a nearly worldwide distribution during the Late Jurassic through Late Cretaceous.

extended from Alaska to Argentina. Hadrosaurids were among the dominant plant-eating dinosaurs of the Late Cretaceous and were among the last dinosaurs to become extinct.

EVOLUTION OF THE ORNITHOPODS

As mentioned at the beginning of this chapter, the ornithopods were one of the most long-lived and diverse groups of dinosaurs. They first appeared during the Early Jurassic as small, bipedal heterodontosaurids that roamed the dry countryside of southern Africa. But the heterodontosaurids already had a dental battery that allowed more effective milling of vegetation than the simpler and less numerous teeth of other dinosaurian herbivores. The dental battery was a hallmark of most ornithopods and one of the keys to their great success.

By the Late Jurassic, it would have been virtually impossible to visit any place on earth without encountering an ornithopod dinosaur (figure 8.16). Small hypsilophodontids, medium-sized dryosaurids, and large iguanodontids were very diverse and abundant plant-eating dinosaurs of the Late Jurassic through Early Cretaceous and had an essentially worldwide distribution.

From an iguanodontid-like ancestor the hadrosaurids arose by Middle Cretaceous time. Their first appearance coincided with a marked decline in the types and numbers of hypsilophodontids and iguanodontids. It is thus tempting to believe that hadrosaurids contributed to the demise of their more primitive relatives. Hadrosaurids were extremely diverse and abundant during the Late Cretaceous, and inhabited a variety of environments until their own demise 65 million years ago.

SUMMARY

1. Ornithopods were bipedal or facultatively quadrupedal ornithischian dinosaurs that lived from the Early Jurassic to the Late Cretaceous.

2. Heterodontosaurids were the first ornithopods and were small, bipedal dinosaurs with unique, chisel-like teeth. They are known only from the Lower Jurassic of southern Africa.

3. Hypsilophodontids were small, bipedal ornithopods that were especially diverse and widespread during the Late Jurassic and Early Cretaceous.

4. Hypsilophodontid success may have been based in part on their ability, via hinges in the skull, to move their dental batteries sideways in order to grind vegetation.

5. *Tenontosaurus* and dryosaurids were medium-to-large hypsilophodontid-like ornithopods of the Late Jurassic and Early Cretaceous that provide a possible evolutionary link between the small hypsilophodontids and the large iguanodontids.

6. The iguanodontids were large, facultatively bipedal ornithopods that were particularly successful during the Late Jurassic and Early Cretaceous.

7. Hadrosaurids, the duck-billed dinosaurs, first appeared during the Middle Cretaceous and were diverse and abundant during the Late Cretaceous, especially in Asia and North America.

8. The appearance of hadrosaurids nearly coincides with the decline of hypsilophodontids and iguanodontids.

9. Hadrosaurids encompass two subfamilies, the hadrosaurines with flat skulls and the lambeosaurines with skulls bearing dorsal tubes or crests.

10. The hollow tubes and crests on lambeosaurine skulls were most likely signalling devices used for both display and as resonating chambers to produce distinctive sounds.

11. Hadrosaurids were powerful quadrupedal walkers that may also have been amphibious.

KEY TERMS

Camptosaurus
dental battery
Dryosauridae
Dryosaurus
Edmontosaurus
Hadrosauridae
Hadrosaurinae

Heterodontosauridae
Heterodontosaurus
Hypsilophodon
Hypsilophodontidae
Iguanodontidae
Lambeosaurinae
ornithopod

Ouranosaurus
Parasaurolophus
resonating chamber
Tenontosaurus
tubes and crests
Valdosaurus

REVIEW QUESTIONS

1. What are the distinctive features of ornithopods?

2. To what feature(s) might you attribute the success of ornithopods?

3. How did hypsilophodontids differ from heterodontosaurids, and how might these differences explain the greater success of hypsilophodontids?

4. How did hadrosaurids resemble and differ from hypsilophodontids?

5. What features of the skeletons of different groups of ornithopods identify them as either bipeds or facultative bipeds?

6. What defensive strategies did ornithopods employ? What anatomical evidence supports your conclusions?

7. How do the jaw, tooth, and skull structures of the various ornithopod families differ from each other? Is a progression in the evolution of chewing mechanisms evident among the ornithopods?

8. Why do paleontologists think the crests and tubes of lambeosaurines functioned as signalling devices?

FURTHER READING

Norman, D. B. and Weishampel, D. B. 1990. Iguanodontidae and related ornithopods; in Weishampel, D. B., Dodson, P., and Osmólska, H., eds., *The Dinosauria*. Berkeley: University of California Press, pp. 510–33. (A detailed technical review of iguanodontids and closely related taxa.)

Sues, H-D. and Norman, D. B. 1990. Hypsilophodontidae, *Tenontosaurus*, Dryosauridae; in Weishampel, D. B., Dodson, P., and Osmólska, H., eds., *The Dinosauria*. Berkeley: University of California Press, pp. 498–509. (A detailed, technical review of hypsilophodontids and closely related taxa.)

Weishampel, D. B. 1981. Acoustical analysis of potential vocalization in lambeosaurine dinosaurs (Reptilia: Ornithischia): *Paleobiology*, v. 7, pp. 252–61. (A technical analysis of the acoustical properties of lambeosaur cranial crests.)

Weishampel, D. B. 1984. Evolution of jaw mechanisms in ornithopod dinosaurs: *Advances in Anatomy, Embryology and Cell Biology*, v. 87, 110 pp. (A detailed examination of the skulls and teeth of ornithopods.)

Weishampel, D. B. and Heinrich, R. E. 1992. Systematics of Hypsilophodontidae and basal Iguanodontia (Dinosauria: Ornithopoda): *Historical Biology*, v. 6, pp. 159–184. (Analyzes the phylogeny of hypsilophodontids and allied forms.)

Weishampel, D. B. and Horner, J. R. 1990. Hadrosauridae; in Weishampel, D. B., Dodson, P., and Osmólska, H., eds., *The Dinosauria*. Berkeley: University of California Press, pp. 534–61. (A detailed technical review of the hadrosaurids.)

Weishampel, D. B. and Witmer, L. M. 1990. Heterodontosauridae; in Weishampel, D. B., Dodson, P., and Osmólska, H., eds., *The Dinosauria*. Berkeley: University of California Press, pp. 486–97. (A detailed technical review of the heterodontosaurids.)

STEGOSAURS AND ANKYLOSAURS

Stegosaurus is one of the most familiar dinosaurs, and the armadillo-like Ankylosaurus is one of the most unusual. Paleontologists now consider the stegosaurs (plated dinosaurs) and ankylosaurs (armored dinosaurs) to be closely related and have united them in a group with the unfamiliar name **Thyreophora** (figure 9.1), the "shield bearers." Thyreophorans were a diverse group of armored, primarily quadrupedal ornithischians of Jurassic and Cretaceous age with a virtually worldwide distribution. The key evolutionary novelty of thyreophorans is the presence of one or more rows of **armor plates** in the skin above or alongside the vertebral column. In this chapter, we review the anatomy and evolution of thyreophoran dinosaurs.

PRIMITIVE THYREOPHORANS

Not all thyreophorans can be assigned to the stegosaurs or the ankylosaurs. The most primitive of the thyreophorans are also among the most primitive ornithischians. Two of these dinosaurs—**Scutellosaurus** and *Scelidosaurus*—provide us with a look at the early diversity of the Thyreophora.

Scutellosaurus (figure 9.2) was a relatively small (about 1.2 meters long) generalized ornithischian. It had a relatively small skull and jaws, cheek teeth positioned on the jaw margins, a short neck, hind limbs only slightly longer than the forelimbs, and a long tail. These are primitive ornithischian characteristics and explain why

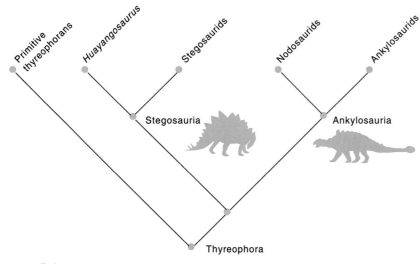

FIGURE 9.1

Thyreophoran dinosaurs include the stegosaurs, the ankylosaurs, and some primitive forms as shown in this cladogram.

115

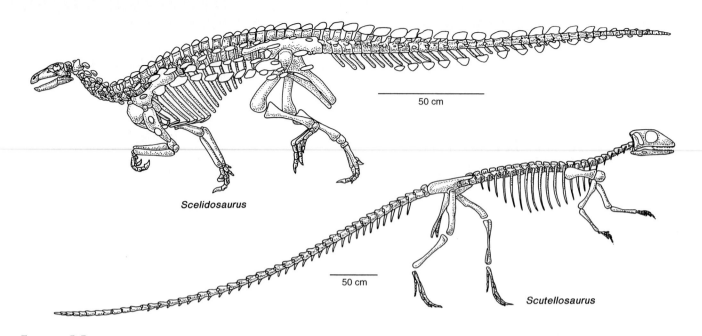

FIGURE 9.2

Early Jurassic *Scutellosaurus* and *Scelidosaurus* were primitive Jurassic thyreophorans that lacked the evolutionary novelties of either stegosaurs or ankylosaurs.

FIGURE 9.3

The armor plates of *Scutellosaurus* were characteristically thyreophoran—they were keeled dorsally and excavated ventrally.

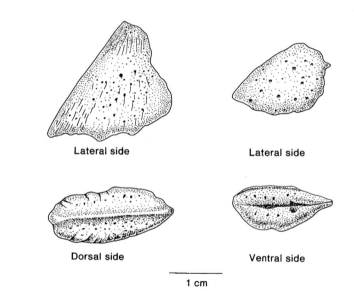

some paleontologists consider *Scutellosaurus* to be closely related to primitive ornithischian dinosaurs like *Lesothosaurus*. However, *Scutellosaurus* had an extensive body covering of bony plates set in the skin (figure 9.3), which is an evolutionary novelty of thyreophorans justifying inclusion of *Scutellosaurus* in this group. Evolutionary novelties of the skull and lower jaw, including the sinuous lower cheek tooth row, distinguish stegosaurs and ankylosaurs from the most primitive thyreophorans. Of course, it is possible that *Scutellosaurus* evolved its body armor independently of the evolution of body armor in thyreophorans. In this case, the similarity in body armor between *Scutellosaurus* and thyreophorans would reflect evolutionary convergence and not close phylogenetic relationship. At present, though, the body armor of *Scutellosaurus* is best viewed as genuinely thyreophoran, especially because it shows detailed and unique similarity—dorsal keels and ventral excavations—to the body armor of certain other thyreophorans.

Scelidosaurus (see figure 9.2) is another primitive thyreophoran, but was very different from *Scutellosaurus*. Much larger, at least 4 meters long, *Scelidosaurus* had a small skull with simple, leaf-shaped teeth that ran to the tip of the snout. Its limbs were massive, and apparently (the complete forelimb is unknown) the fore- and hind limbs were of nearly equal length. The skull of *Scelidosaurus* lacked armor plating, but its back was covered by numerous bony plates embedded in the skin. These plates were remarkably similar to those of the ankylosaurs. The extremely broad sacrum of *Scelidosaurus* is another feature that unites it with thyreophorans. Because no complete, articulated skeleton of *Scelidosaurus* has been discovered, the arrangement of the armor plates on its back remains somewhat uncertain. The most complete known skeleton (see figure 9.2), described by Richard Owen in 1863, suggests that the plates formed a broad covering across the back and sides of the dinosaur as in later ankylosaurs.

As in *Scutellosaurus*, much of the anatomy of *Scelidosaurus* is primitively ornithischian. But this quadruped (facultative biped?), with its extensive body armor and broad sacrum, can be more readily allied with the thyreophorans. Indeed, some paleontologists have gone so far as to assign *Scelidosaurus* to the stegosaurs or the ankylosaurs. But because the specific evolutionary novelties that distinguish stegosaurs and ankylosaurs are not present in *Scelidosaurus*, it is best regarded as neither stegosaur nor ankylosaur, but as a primitive thyreophoran.

Scutellosaurus fossils are known from the Lower Jurassic of Arizona, whereas those of *Scelidosaurus* come from the Lower Jurassic of Great Britain. Another poorly known primitive thyreophoran is *Tatisaurus*, known from a single jaw collected in the Lower Jurassic of China. Known primitive thyreophorans were so different from each other and so widely separated geographically that we can be sure much more remains to be discovered about the origin and early evolution of the shield-bearing dinosaurs.

STEGOSAURIA

The **Stegosauria,** meaning "plated lizards" because of the armor plates on their backs, were medium-sized to large (up to 9 meters long), quadrupedal, herbivorous ornithischians. They had small heads, short and massive forelimbs, long, columnar hind limbs and short, stout feet that bore hooves on the ends of the toes. The key evolutionary novelty of stegosaurs was the vertical bony plates and spines arranged in single or double rows along the neck, back, and tail. The most primitive-known stegosaur is *Huayangosaurus* from the Middle Jurassic of China. Other, more advanced, stegosaurs are placed in the family Stegosauridae.

THE GENUS *HUAYANGOSAURUS*

The most primitive stegosaur, **Huayangosaurus** (figure 9.4) from the Middle Jurassic of Sichuan Province, China is placed in its own family, Huayangosauridae. This 4.3-meter-long stegosaur had spike-shaped armor along the midline of its body and additional rows of small armor plates along each side of the row of spikes. Unlike stegosaurids, *Huayangosaurus* had a rather deep (tall) skull with a short snout. The eye sockets were located relatively far forward, above the posterior cheek teeth. *Huayangosaurus* was smaller and less massive than stegosaurids and their fore- and hind limbs were more neatly equal in length. Other differences between *Huayangosaurus* and stegosaurids may be found in details of the structure of the shoulder and hip girdles.

Huayangosaurus is known from several complete skeletons and is thus one of the best-known stegosaurs. Claims of older, Early Jurassic stegosaurs are based on very incomplete fossil evidence and are difficult to substantiate. But to examine the

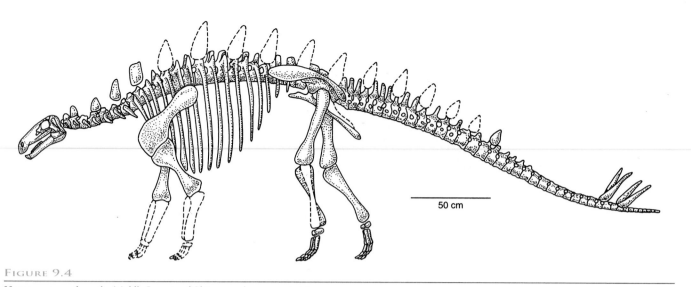

FIGURE 9.4

Huayangosaurus from the Middle Jurassic of China was the most primitive stegosaur.

origin of stegosaurs, we must still bridge the considerable and unfathomed anatomical gap between primitive Early Jurassic thyreophorans such as *Scelidosaurus* and the most primitive stegosaur, *Huayangosaurus*.

STEGOSAURIDAE

All stegosaurs other than *Huayangosaurus* are placed in the family **Stegosauridae.** Stegosaurids are easily distinguished from *Huayangosaurus* by their relatively low skulls, characterized by long snouts and posteriorly located eye sockets (behind the cheek-tooth row), larger size and more massive skeletons, and the relatively long hind limbs. Best known and typical of the stegosaurids is ***Stegosaurus*** (figure 9.5) from the Upper Jurassic of the western United States. Other well-known stegosaurids are *Kentrosaurus* from the Upper Jurassic of Tanzania and *Tuojiangosaurus* (figure 9.6) from the Upper Jurassic of China. The remaining stegosaurids are known from much less complete fossils.

THE GENUS *STEGOSAURUS*

Like all stegosaurids, *Stegosaurus* had only a midline row of armor plates. The exact arrangement of these plates has been debated (box 9.1), but the alternating, offset row of plates seen in most skeletal reconstructions is favored here (see figure 9.5).

Stegosaurus had a low, slender, and, for an animal that weighed 1 to 2 tons, a very small head. The tip of the snout formed a narrow, toothless beak. The cheek teeth were leaf-shaped with small denticles on their edges, as in many groups of plant-eating dinosaurs. These teeth did not, however, form the dental batteries seen in the ornithopods (see Chapter 8). The brain in the skull of *Stegosaurus* was truly tiny and is estimated to have weighed about 70 to 80 grams (2.5 to 2.9 oz.). Indeed, the small skull and tiny brain of *Stegosaurus* have led to the popular notion that it was one of the "dumbest" dinosaurs (but see box 9.2).

The long neck and tail of *Stegosaurus* are typical features of stegosaurids. The powerfully built forelimbs of this dinosaur featured a shoulder blade and humerus with thick bony crests for the attachment of massive shoulder and upper arm

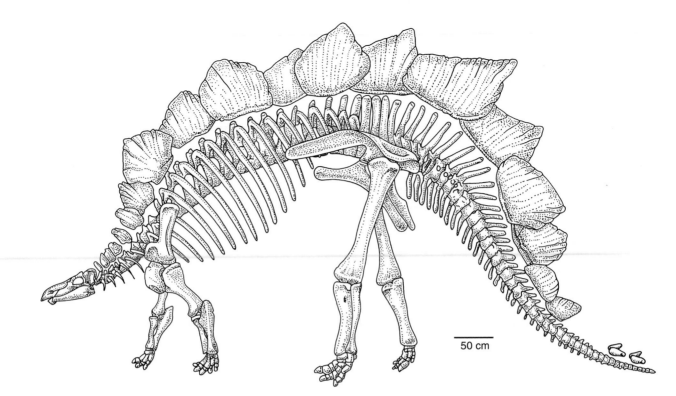

FIGURE 9.5

Late Jurassic *Stegosaurus* was characteristic of the more advanced stegosaurs, the stegosaurids.

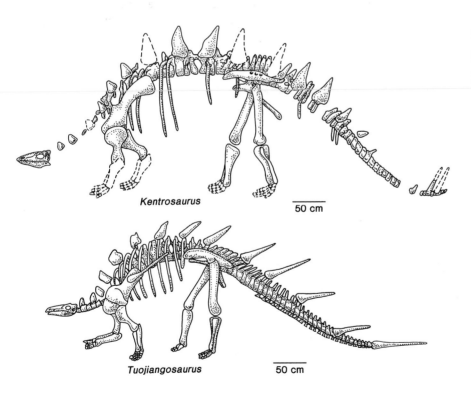

Kentrosaurus

50 cm

Tuojiangosaurus

50 cm

FIGURE 9.6

Tuojiangosaurus from the Upper Jurassic of China, and *Kentrosaurus* from the Upper Jurassic of Tanzania are other well-known stegosaurids.

BOX 9.1

STEGOSAUR PLATES: TWO ROWS OR ONE?

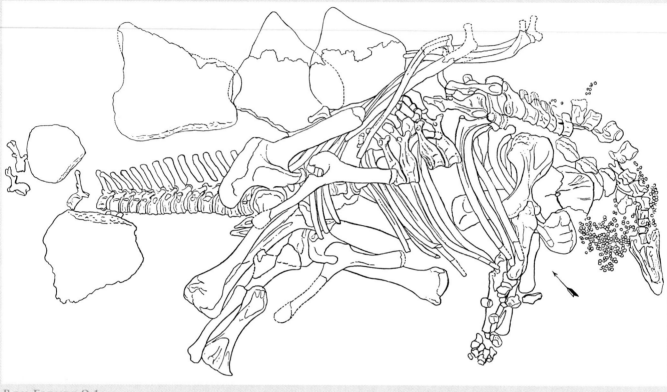

BOX FIGURE 9.1A

This skeleton of *Stegosaurus* from Colorado, shown here as it was found in the rock, provides some of the best direct evidence of the arrangement of the plates of *Stegosaurus*.

Source: C. W. Gilmore, U.S. National Museum Bulletin, 89, 1914.

As in other thyreophorans, the armor plates of *Stegosaurus* were anchored in the skin and not attached to other bones, so they usually fell out of place before fossilization. One of the oldest clues to their arrangement remains the best clue, even today, and is seen in the remarkably well-preserved fossil skeleton of a *Stegosaurus* from Colorado described in 1901 (box figure 9.1A). This skeleton was found lying on its side, and shows some overlap in the anterior and posterior ends of successive plates. But rather than clearly demonstrating the arrangement of plates on the back of *Stegosaurus*, it has fostered two opposing views.

Prior to the discovery of the Colorado specimen, Yale University paleontologist O. C. Marsh reconstructed the skeleton of *Stegosaurus* with its plates arranged in a single row (box figure 9.1B). The overlapping plates of the Colorado specimen, however, suggested to Smithsonian paleontologist Frederick

muscles. They suggest a semi-sprawling posture for the forelimb when walking. The forefoot had five short, broad toes with hoof-like tips. In contrast, the hind limbs of *Stegosaurus* were extremely long and pillar-like. The long, columnar femur that lacked broad flanges of bone suggests an upright hind limb walking posture. Unlike the forefeet, the hind feet of *Stegosaurus* bore three short, stout toes with hooves.

The armor of *Stegosaurus* included numerous, small, knob-like plates that were distributed in the skin over most of the body. Most prominent, though, were the plates along the backbone. The plates immediately behind the head were small and flat, and had irregularly-shaped edges. Large, diamond-shaped plates followed and extended down the back onto the tail. The plates were largest over the hips. Two pairs of long spikes were located at the end of the tail. The plates were not solid

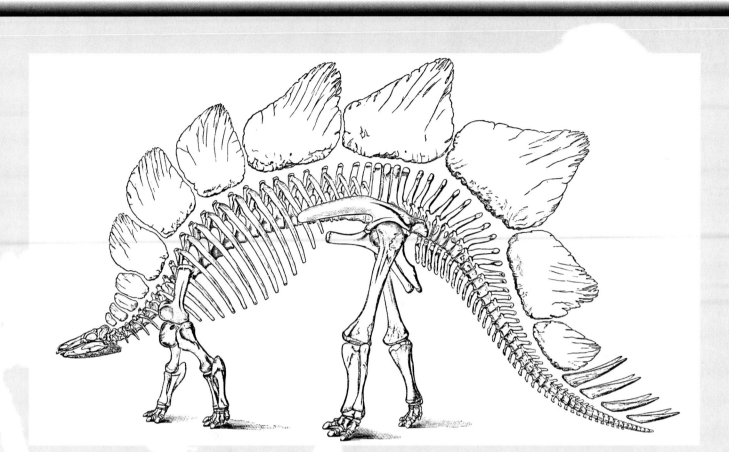

BOX FIGURE 9.1B

The first reconstruction of *Stegosaurus* by O. C. Marsh, in 1891 showed a row of plates that do not overlap.

From Edwin H. Colbert, *The Great Dinosaur Hunters and Their Discoveries*. Copyright © 1984 Edwin H. Colbert. Reprinted by permission of Dover Publications, Inc., Mineola, NY.

Lucas that the plates were arranged in an alternating pattern in two rows (see figure 9.5). But those who defended Marsh's original reconstruction suggested that the overlap of the plates of the Colorado specimen was a result of distortion of the skeleton after the dinosaur died.

Paleontologist and artist Stephen Czerkas recently reviewed ideas about the arrangement of *Stegosaurus* plates and argued they were arranged in a single row, as Marsh originally believed. Czerkas pointed out that on the Colorado skeleton, only the anterior and posterior tips of the plates overlap. If there were two rows of plates, he reasoned, we would see more overlap. Czerkas also noted, as had some earlier paleontologists, that the neck, back, and tail of *Stegosaurus* were long enough to allow the plates to be arranged in a single row with just a slight overlap of plates in the neck, shoulder, and back regions. Yet, despite the force of Czerkas's arguments, most paleontologists still find impressive the argument that the plates of *Stegosaurus* functioned best as radiators when arranged in two alternating rows, as shown in figure 9.5. Indeed, recently discovered skeletons of *Stegosaurus* from Colorado and Utah confirm the overlap of plates.

sheets of bone; instead, their surfaces were covered with grooves and channels (figure 9.7) and their interiors contained large canals. Clearly, blood could flow into and around the plates of *Stegosaurus*.

FUNCTION OF THE PLATES OF *STEGOSAURUS*

For nearly a century, paleontologists believed that *Stegosaurus* used its plates as defensive armor. Various illustrations from earlier times showed *Stegosaurus* protecting itself from attacking predators with its plates. Some drawings even showed the plates lying nearly flat against the sides of the dinosaur's body, even though, in this situation, relatively little of the back and flanks of the dinosaur were shielded (figure 9.8).

BOX 9.2

THE BRAIN OF *STEGOSAURUS*

The small brain size of *Stegosaurus* is legendary. Variously described as "the size of a walnut" or "smaller than a kitten's brain," the brain of *Stegosaurus* has led to the popular notion that it was one of the "dumbest" dinosaurs (box figure 9.2A).

Our knowledge of the brain of *Stegosaurus*, or for that matter the brain of any dinosaur, rests on **endocasts** (short for "endocranial casts"). An endocast is a cast (replica) of the inside of the dinosaur's braincase. It is prepared by carefully cleaning the rock out of the interior of a dinosaur skull and then filling the cleaned braincase with soft rubber (usually latex) that can be pulled out of the opening for the spinal cord after the rubber cures. The flexible rubber must be compressed to pull it out through the spinal cord opening, but then it regains its shape. The resulting endocast is an accurate replica of the overall shape and size of the brain cavity, and it also records the positions of the major nerves and blood vessels that entered and exited the brain.

The endocast of the brain of *Stegosaurus* reveals a typically reptilian brain that had much more in common with the brain of a lizard than with the brain of a mammal (box figure 9.2B). The brain of *Stegosaurus* was long and low and

THE FAR SIDE   **By GARY LARSON**

Dinosaur cranial capacity

BOX FIGURE 9.2A

Stegosaurus are seen as incredibly stupid by most of the public.

There are two reasons to question the idea that the plates of *Stegosaurus* were defensive armor. The first, as already stated, is that these plates, however they were arranged, covered only a small portion of the back and flanks of the dinosaur, leaving the belly and legs entirely unprotected. The second is the vascularization of the plates, which suggests that they were regularly and extensively filled with blood. It simply does not make sense to expose a blood-filled structure to an attacker.

A much more reasonable interpretation of the function of the plates of *Stegosaurus* stems from a rigorous analysis undertaken by James Farlow and colleagues at Yale University during the late 1970s. These scientists argued, by analogy with living reptiles, that the plates of *Stegosaurus* functioned as radiators and solar panels that helped to regulate the dinosaur's body temperature. Pumping blood through the plates would have increased the surface area over which the blood was exposed so it could rapidly be cooled (in the shade) or heated (in the sun). A similar process cools the water in an automobile engine when the water is pumped into the radiator where numerous flat chambers increase the surface area. Living lizards also achieve rapid heating of their blood by flattening their bodies on warm rocks in the sun to increase the surface area over which their blood is exposed.

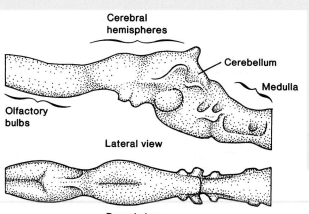

Cerebral
hemispheres

Cerebellum

Medulla

Olfactory
bulbs

Lateral view

Dorsal view

BOX FIGURE 9.2B

The endocast of *Stegosaurus* resembles that of a living lizard.

it lacked much of a curve in the region of the cerebrum. The front of the brain, which included the olfactory bulbs associated with the sense of smell, was extraordinarily large, but the cerebrum and cerebellum were small, while the medulla was long and large (box figure 9.2B). The endocast of *Stegosaurus* displaces only about 56 milliliters of water. A living lizard enlarged to the size of *Stegosaurus*, however, would have an endocast volume of about 110 milliliters. The endocast of a living, fully grown house cat displaces about 30 milliliters of water. The average walnut from a grocery store displaces only 15 to 20 milliliters of water. And when we look at the endocasts of a variety of dinosaurs, *Stegosaurus* does have one of the smallest brain volumes relative to its body size (see Chapter 15).

Stegosaurus thus does not stand out as particularly "brainy" by any standard. Nevertheless, its brain was bigger than a walnut or a kitten's brain, so the intelligence of *Stegosaurus* has been somewhat maligned. Furthermore, stegosaurs were very successful land animals for at least 100 million years, more than 30 times the duration of the human species. Perhaps the best conclusion we can reach about stegosaur intelligence is that these dinosaurs were as intelligent as they had to be!

Some who have wondered how a 1- to 2-ton *Stegosaurus* functioned with a 2- to 3-ounce brain have pointed to the enlarged spinal cavity in its hip region as the possible location of a "second brain." However, no living reptile has a "second brain" located in the hip region. This enlargement, which is a cavity at least 20 times the size of a stegosaur brain, may have been an area where extra nerves met from the tail and hind limbs. But a more likely explanation is that this cavity of *Stegosaurus* was for the storage of fat and sugar, as is seen today in some birds, such as ostriches.

Farlow and colleagues tested the idea of *Stegosaurus* plates functioning as radiators and solar panels by modeling a *Stegosaurus* as a metal cylinder with slots on top into which they could place small metal plates. When this cylinder was heated, it was found to cool most quickly when the plates were diamond-shaped and arranged in two alternating rows. This strongly suggests that the plates of *Stegosaurus* functioned most effectively as radiators and solar panels when arranged in two alternating rows as shown in most reconstructions of *Stegosaurus* (see figure 9.5).

This analysis of the function of the plates of *Stegosaurus* seems convincing, but does it apply to the other stegosaurs? *Huayangosaurus* had spikes, not plates, and the arrangement and shape of the plates of other stegosaurids, such as *Kentrosaurus* and *Tuojiangosaurus*, are not as functionally optimal as *Stegosaurus*. Furthermore, the paired tail spikes of *Stegosaurus* do not fit into the model of thermoregulation and probably did function as defensive structures. Perhaps the best explanation is that stegosaur midline armor originally evolved as defensive spikes such as those of *Huayangosaurus*. In some later stegosaurs, such as *Stegosaurus*, the shape and arrangement of the midline armor became modified for optimum efficiency as radiators and solar panels. The earlier stegosaurids may have had less efficient radiators and solar

FIGURE 9.7

The plates of *Stegosaurus* were not solid sheets of bone, but were instead covered with grooves and canals for blood vessels.

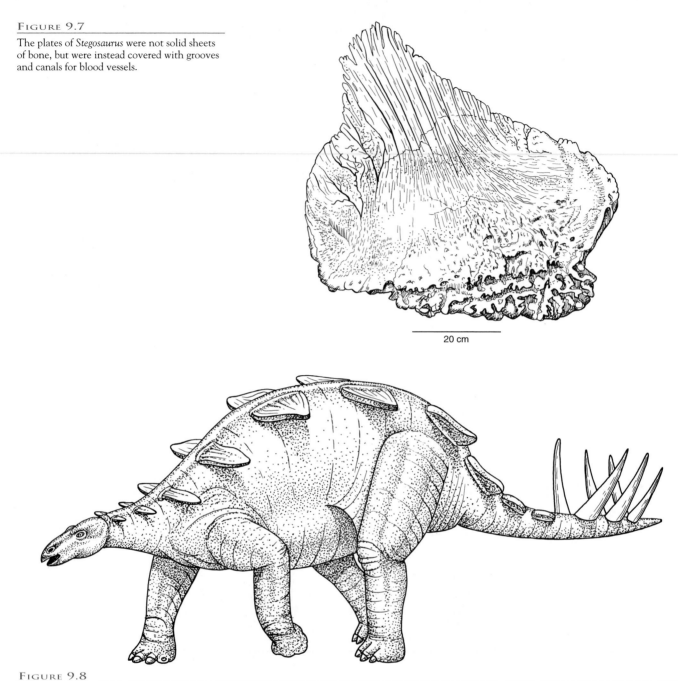

20 cm

FIGURE 9.8

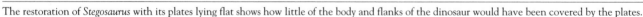

The restoration of *Stegosaurus* with its plates lying flat shows how little of the body and flanks of the dinosaur would have been covered by the plates.

panels and may still have employed the plates, to some extent, in defense. Whatever else stegosaurs did with their midline armor, it might also have functioned in display for recognizing members of the same species.

STEGOSAUR LIFESTYLES AND EVOLUTION

Stegosaur skulls and teeth indicate they were plant eaters that cropped vegetation with their horny beaks, then sliced it with their teeth before swallowing it. Their limb structures suggest they were habitual quadrupeds that weighed as much as 2 tons. Stegosaurs probably could have reared up on their pillar-like hind limbs, but they grazed primarily on vegetation at a height of 1 meter or less above the ground.

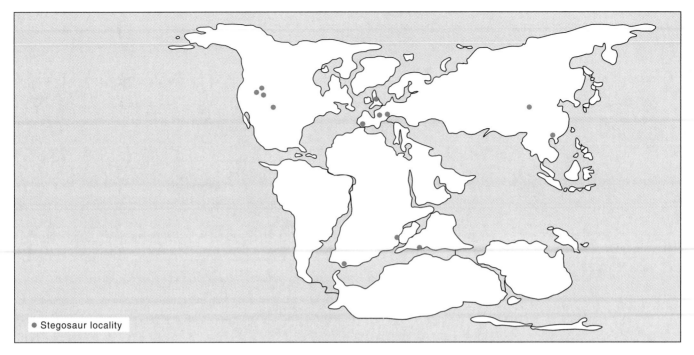

● Stegosaur locality

FIGURE 9.9

This map of stegosaur distribution shows that they lived nearly worldwide during the Late Jurassic.

Stegosaurs first appeared in China during the Middle Jurassic, but by the Late Jurassic they had achieved a nearly worldwide distribution (figure 9.9) and reached the zenith of their diversity, with at least 8 genera. Stegosaurs were among the dominant, large plant eaters of the Late Jurassic, and their fossils are common in Upper Jurassic nonmarine rocks, especially in southern China, the western United States, and eastern Africa.

The Cretaceous record of stegosaurs is much more sparse, and by then they were clearly past their peak. The Cretaceous decline of stegosaurs is usually linked to the appearance of new types of plants (the flowering plants), new types of plant-eating dinosaurs (especially the large ornithopods), or both. The discovery of apparent Late Cretaceous stegosaurs in India during the 1970s, however, suggests they survived in at least one place nearly to the end of the reign of the dinosaurs.

ANKYLOSAURIA

The ankylosaurs ("fused lizards," because of the rod of fused vertebrae in their backs) were medium-sized to large (up to 9 meters long), quadrupedal, plant-eating ornithischians. They had small heads with leaf-shaped, non-interlocking teeth, similar to the teeth of stegosaurs. The broadly arched ribs of ankylosaurs formed a very wide body, which was covered with small round or square armor plates that produced a fairly continuous shield over its dorsal surface (figure 9.10). Some ankylosaurs had spikes or spines as part of their body armor, and others had a club at the end of the tail. Their limbs were robust, the forelimbs were about two-thirds to three-fourths the length of the hind limbs, and their short, stout feet bore hooves.

The low skulls of ankylosaurs (width between the eyes exceeds height of the skull), the closure of the fenestrae in front of the eye and on top of the skull, the added dermal bones on the skull, and the extensive body armor and modifications of the rib cage and hip girdle to form a base for this armor are among the many distinctive evolutionary novelties of the **Ankylosauria.** These primarily Cretaceous dinosaurs comprise two families, the **Nodosauridae** and **Ankylosauridae.**

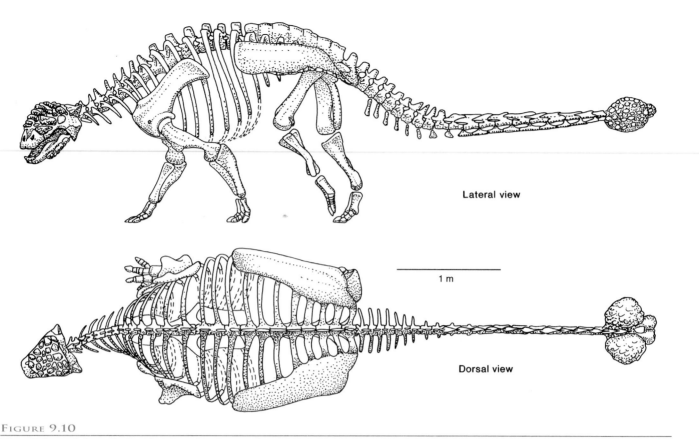

Lateral view

1 m

Dorsal view

FIGURE 9.10

This ankylosaur skeleton displays the key evolutionary novelties of ankylosaurs.

NODOSAURIDAE

Nodosaurid ankylosaurs are distinguished from ankylosaurids by their narrow skulls that lacked armor and horns at the posterior corners, the presence of spines in their armor, and the lack of ossified tail tendons or a tail club. **Nodosaurus** (figure 9.11) from the Upper Cretaceous of Wyoming and Kansas is typical of the family. Other well-known nodosaurids are *Sauropelta* from the Lower Cretaceous of Wyoming and Utah, *Panoplosaurus* from the Upper Cretaceous of Alberta, Canada and *Edmontonia* from the Upper Cretaceous of Canada and the United States.

Because the skull of *Nodosaurus* has not been discovered, we rely on the skull of **Panoplosaurus** as an example of a typical nodosaurid skull. This skull (see figure 9.11) was small and narrow, had a pointed snout, and lacked the horns at the posterior corners and extra armor that were characteristic of ankylosaurids. The lateral temporal fenestra was open, the cheek teeth were leaf-shaped, and the beak was toothless. As in stegosaurs and other ankylosaurs, the teeth of *Panoplosaurus* were not arranged into a dental battery.

The skeleton of *Nodosaurus* represents a 5.5-meter-long nodosaurid. The neck was short, and the long tail had no club at its tip. The entire body was covered with regular bands of bony plates that formed a thick and heavy covering. At present, it is not known whether bony spikes were part of the body armor of *Nodosaurus*, as in most other nodosaurids (figure 9.12). The hind limbs of *Nodosaurus* were longer than the forelimbs, and its feet were short and stout and bore hooves.

ANKYLOSAURIDAE

Ankylosaurids present a striking contrast to nodosaurids because of their wide, armored heads (as wide as long), which had long, triangular horns at their posterior corners and lateral temporal fenestrae completely covered with bony armor. Few

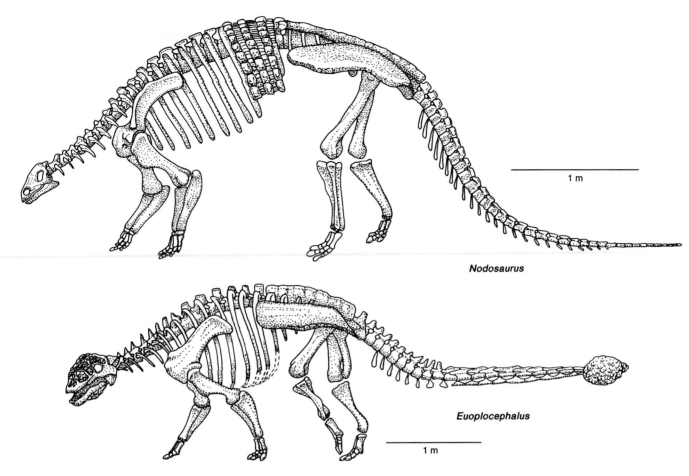

Nodosaurus

Euoplocephalus

1 m

FIGURE 9.11

The skeleton of *Nodosaurus*, to which the skull of *Panoplosaurus* has been added, is typical of nodosaurids and contrasts well with the skeleton of *Euoplocephalus*, a typical ankylosaurid.

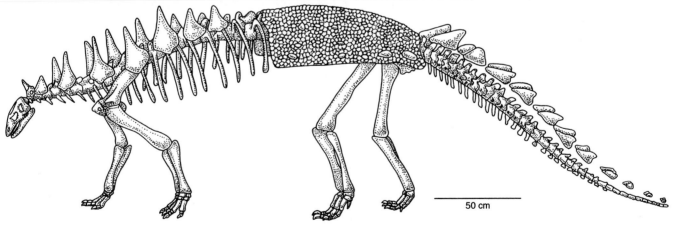

50 cm

FIGURE 9.12

It is not known whether *Nodosaurus* had spike-shaped body armor, but other nodosaurids did, such as *Polacanthus* shown here.

or no spines were present in the body armor of ankylosaurids, and their last few tail vertebrae were braced by ossified tendons. The tip of the ankylosaurid tail bore a club made up of two large and two small plates of bone (figure 9.13).

Euoplocephalus (see figure 9.11) from the Upper Cretaceous of Canada and the United States is a characteristic ankylosaurid that displays all the

BOX 9.3

ANKYLOSAURID NASAL PASSAGES

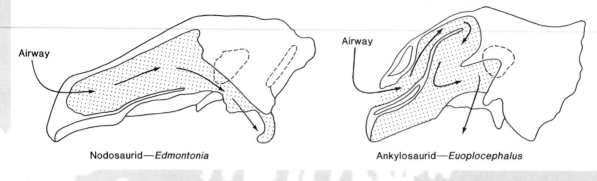

Airway

Airway

Nodosaurid—*Edmontonia*

Ankylosaurid—*Euoplocephalus*

BOX FIGURE 9.3

Unlike nodosaurids, ankylosaurids had folded, S-shaped nasal passages, as shown in these cross sections of the skull of the nodosaurid *Edmontonia* and the ankylosaurid *Euoplocephalus*.

Ankylosaurids are easily distinguished from nodosaurids by a variety of anatomical features, in particular the uniquely shaped nasal passages of ankylosaurids. As in most dinosaurs, the nasal passages of nodosaurids were paired tubes that ran from the nostrils directly back to the throat (box figure 9.3). By contrast, ankylosaurid nasal passages followed a folded, S-shaped path (see box figure 9.3), and, on either side of the nasal passages, ankylosaur skulls were honeycombed with complex sinuses (see box figure 9.3). Furthermore, in the Mongolian Cretaceous ankylosaurids *Pinacosaurus* and *Saichania*, thin, blade-like bones have been found in the nasal passages. These bones resemble the bones called "turbinals" present in the nasal passages of many mammals, including humans.

What was the function of the folded nasal passages, sinuses, and "turbinals" of ankylosaurids? As we have so often seen, they probably had multiple functions, not just a single one. The ankylosaurid nasal passages and sinuses are reminiscent of those in the skulls of hadrosaurian dinosaurs, so ankylosaurids may have used them to make characteristic noises, as has been suggested for hadrosaurs (see box 8.3). Other possible functions include strengthening of the skull, providing space for glands, improving the sense of smell, and moistening the air before it entered the lungs. Perhaps the folded nasal passages and sinuses performed all of these functions simultaneously and also helped to produce characteristic nasal sounds.

features typical of the family. This medium-sized to large ankylosaurid (6 to 7 meters long) had a limb skeleton similar to that of *Nodosaurus*, but more massive. Large slabs of bone covered the skull of *Euoplocephalus* to armor it completely.

The body armor of *Euoplocephalus* consisted of bands of bony plates that ran across the body and tail as well as smaller, bony studs planted throughout the skin. Probably weighing as much as 2 tons, *Euoplocephalus* is one of the best-known ankylosaurids. Other well-known ankylosaurids include *Ankylosaurus* from the Upper Cretaceous of the United States and Canada and *Pinacosaurus* and *Saichania* from the Upper Cretaceous of China and Mongolia.

ANKYLOSAURS: MESOZOIC TANKS

Modern military tank design is based on balancing three factors: speed, armor, and firepower. An increase in tank speed results from a decrease in armor and firepow-

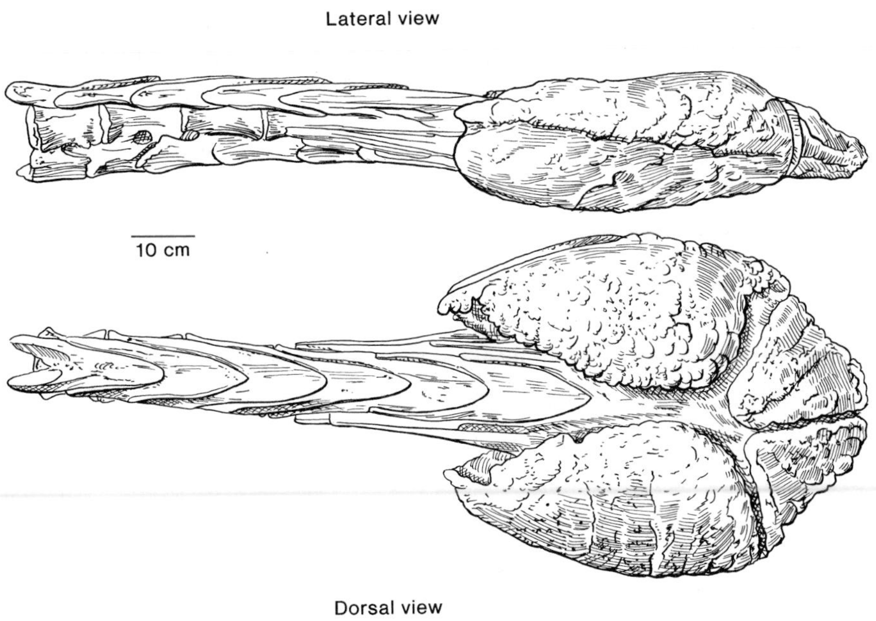

Lateral view

10 cm

Dorsal view

FIGURE 9.13

The tail club of ankylosaurids was made of two large and two small dermal plates.

er (weight) and vice versa. The ankylosaur design of a dinosaurian tank clearly sacrificed speed for the sake of heavy armor. Increased firepower, in the form of powerful jaws and large teeth, was also obviously avoided by ankylosaurs.

The robust and heavy limbs of ankylosaurs were not designed for speed, but for slow and powerful walking. The chassis upon which ankylosaur armor was hung consisted of a wide rib cage with broad ribs and a remarkably broad sacrum (see figure 9.10). Huge ilia hung down from the sacrum, draped over the upper thighs to provide additional protection. A heavy armor coating of round or rectangular plates was laid over this chassis. Plates arranged in rows and not sutured to each other helped the ankylosaur maintain some flexibility in the body covering.

Nodosaurids stopped with this design, so they probably maintained a modicum of speed. But ankylosaurids went a step further in sacrificing speed for increased armor. Thus, the head acquired bony plating, and a tail club evolved to add some firepower to the slower ankylosaurid tank.

There seems little doubt that, when attacked, an ankylosaur did not try to flee or counterattack. Instead, it squatted down, presenting a nearly impervious back to its attacker. Because of the ankylosaur's low slung body and great weight, its attacker would have found it difficult to flip the "tank" over to get at its belly. When attacked, ankylosaurids would also have protected their blind backsides by swinging their massive tail clubs back and forth.

ANKYLOSAUR EVOLUTION

The oldest-known ankylosaur is *Sarcolestes* from the Middle Jurassic of Europe. Although known only from part of a lower jaw, the teeth and an armor plate attached to the jaw identify *Sarcolestes* as an ankylosaur. Other Jurassic ankylosaurs are also from Europe and are based on fragmentary fossils.

Two types of Mesozoic "tanks" evolved among the ankylosaurs: the somewhat lighter nodosaurids and the very heavy ankylosaurids. But the hallmark of ankylosaur evolution was conservatism. Once the basic, heavily-armored, tank-like body plan of these dinosaurs appeared, it was modified very little throughout their evolution.

It is clear that by the Cretaceous the evolutionary split between nodosaurids and ankylosaurids had taken place. At least 11 genera of Cretaceous nodosaurids are known from Europe, North America, and Australia. Fragmentary ankylosaur fossils from South America and Antarctica may also be of nodosaurids. Nodosaurids reached their greatest diversity during the Early to Middle Cretaceous, but did survive into the Late Cretaceous in the form of *Panoplosaurus* and *Edmontonia* in North America.

Ankylosaurids are known only from the Cretaceous of North America, Europe, and Asia. They encompass at least 9 genera, one of which, *Ankylosaurus*, at 8 to 9 meters long, was the largest ankylosaur. Ankylosaurids reached their greatest diversity during the Late Cretaceous, but were not particularly abundant in the fossil record.

S U M M A R Y

1. Thyreophoran dinosaurs include two closely related groups, Stegosauria and Ankylosauria, as well as the primitive thyreophorans *Scutellosaurus* and *Scelidosaurus*.

2. The presence above or alongside the vertebral column of one or more rows of dermal armor plates distinguishes thyreophorans from other dinosaurs.

3. The key evolutionary novelty of stegosaurs is the vertical bony plates and spines arranged in single or double rows along the neck, back, and tail.

4. *Huayangosaurus* from the Middle Jurassic of China is the oldest and most primitive known stegosaur.

5. All other stegosaurs are stegosaurids, best represented by *Stegosaurus* from the Upper Jurassic of the United States.

6. The plates of *Stegosaurus* were highly vascularized and probably had a temperature-regulation function.

7. Stegosaurs reached the zenith of their diversity, at least 8 genera, and achieved a nearly worldwide distribution during the Late Jurassic. The Cretaceous decline of the stegosaurs may have been due to the appearance of new vegetation (flowering plants) and/or the evolution of new types of plant-eating dinosaurs.

8. One of the key evolutionary novelties of ankylosaurs is the possession of extensive body armor.

9. Two types of ankylosaurs, nodosaurids and ankylosaurids, had evolved by the Early Cretaceous and were distinguished from each other by differences in skull structure and body armor.

10. Ankylosaurs were the tanks of the Mesozoic and adopted a defensive strategy based on impervious armor.

11. Although the oldest ankylosaur is of Middle Jurassic age, the conservative evolution of this group of dinosaurs took place primarily during the Cretaceous.

K E Y   T E R M S

Ankylosauria
Ankylosauridae
armor plates
endocast
Euoplocephalus

Huayangosaurus
Nodosauridae
Nodosaurus
Panoplosaurus
Scelidosaurus

Scutellosaurus
Stegosauria
Stegosauridae
Stegosaurus
Thyreophora

REVIEW QUESTIONS

1. What features identify a dinosaur as a thyreophoran?

2. Why is *Scutellosaurus* identified as a thyreophoran, and why is it easier to assign *Scelidosaurus* to the thyreophorans?

3. What are the evolutionary novelties of stegosaurs and how does *Huayangosaurus* exemplify them?

4. How are stegosaurids distinguished from *Huayangosaurus*?

5. What do paleontologists believe were the arrangement and function of the plates of *Stegosaurus*? Why?

6. How does the evolution of stegosaurs differ from that of ankylosaurs in terms of timing, distribution, and amount of morphological change?

7. How are ankylosaurs distinguished from other dinosaurs? How are nodosaurid ankylosaurs distinguished from ankylosaurids?

8. What defensive strategy did ankylosaurs employ?

FURTHER READING

Colbert, E. H. 1981. Primitive ornithischian dinosaur from the Kayenta Formation of Arizona. *Museum of Northern Arizona Bulletin* 52, 61 pp. (Complete description of the primitive thyreophoran *Scutellosaurus*.)

Coombs, W. P., Jr. and Maryanska, T. 1990. Ankylosauria; in Weishampel, D. B., Dodson, P., and Osmólska, H., eds., *The Dinosauria*. Berkeley: University of California Press, pp. 456–83. (A detailed technical review of the ankylosaurs.)

Coombs, W. P., Jr., Weishampel, D. B., and Witmer, L. M. 1990. Basal Thyreophora; in Weishampel, D. B., Dodson, P., and Osmólska, H., eds., *The Dinosauria*. Berkeley: University of California Press, pp. 427–34. (A detailed technical review of the primitive thyreophorans.)

Czerkas, S. A. 1987. A reevaluation of the plate arrangement of *Stegosaurus stenops*; in Czerkas, S. J. and Olson, E. C., eds., *Dinosaurs Past and Present Volume II*. Los Angeles: Natural History Museum of Los Angeles County and University of Washington Press, pp. 83–99. (Reviews the ideas about the arrangement of the plates of *Stegosaurus* and argues for a single row of plates.)

Farlow, J. O., Thompson, C. V., and Rosner, D. E. 1976. Plates of the dinosaur *Stegosaurus*: forced convection heat loss fins? *Science*, v. 192, pp. 1123–25. (Proposed the idea that the plates of *Stegosaurus* functioned as the cooling fins of radiators.)

Galton, P. M. 1990. Stegosauria; in Weishampel, D. B., Dodson, P., and Osmólska, H., eds., *The Dinosauria*. Berkeley: University of California Press, pp. 435–55. (A detailed technical review of the stegosaurs.)

CERATOPSIANS AND PACHYCEPHALOSAURS

T he horned dinosaurs, Ceratopsia, are among the dinosaurs most familiar to us. *Triceratops*, usually in combat with a *Tyrannosaurus rex*, has been a staple of dinosaur movies for decades. Less familiar are the dome-headed dinosaurs, Pachycephalosauria, close relatives of the ceratopsians. Here we examine the anatomy, classification, evolution, and probable habits of these two groups of dinosaurs.

The ceratopsians and pachycephalosaurs share a common evolutionary ancestry that justifies linking them into a single group called **Marginocephalia** (figure 10.1). This is despite the fact that, on first appearance, horned and dome-headed dinosaurs appear to be strikingly different. But a few key evolutionary novelties—especially the development of at least a small **frill** (a shelf of bone projecting from the back of the skull)—suggest a close relationship between the two groups. Marginocephalian dinosaurs were primarily of Late Cretaceous age. They were plant-eating ornithischians closely related to ornithopods.

CERATOPSIA

Ceratopsian dinosaurs were one of the most diverse groups of plant-eating dinosaurs of the Late Cretaceous. They comprise two groups: Psittacosauridae, for the sole genus **Psittacosaurus** from the Early Cretaceous of Asia, and Neoceratopsia, from the Cretaceous of Asia and North America. Evolutionary novelties that unite

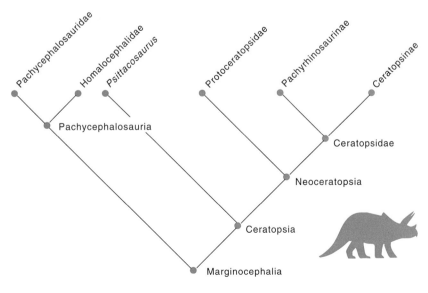

FIGURE 10.1

Ceratopsians and pachycephalosaurs share a common ancestry and thus represent one group of dinosaurs, the Marginocephalia.

133

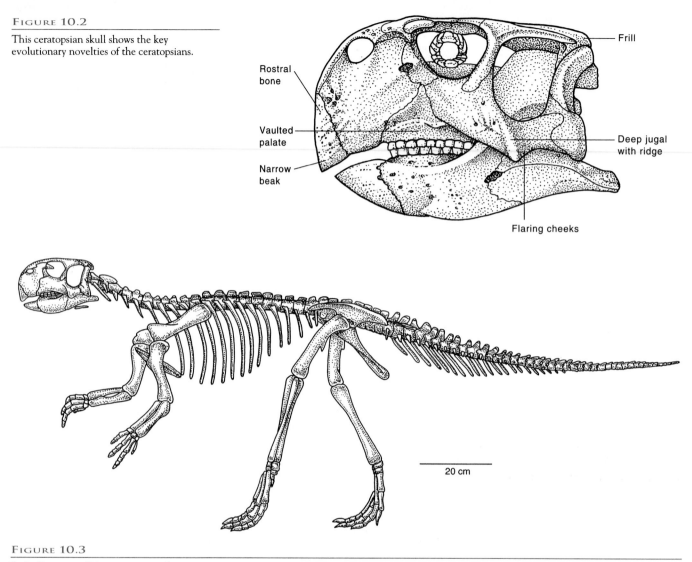

FIGURE 10.2

This ceratopsian skull shows the key
evolutionary novelties of the ceratopsians.

Rostral
bone

Vaulted
palate

Narrow
beak

Frill

Deep jugal
with ridge

Flaring cheeks

FIGURE 10.3

Early Cretaceous *Psittacosaurus* was the most primitive ceratopsian.

ceratopsians are possession of a rostral bone in the skull, a skull with a narrow beak
and flaring jugals (cheeks), a deep jugal with a distinct ridge, a frill, and a highly
vaulted palate in the front of the mouth (figure 10.2). The morphology and distribution of ceratopsian fossils suggests they originated in Asia and spread to North
America, where they were highly successful until their extinction at the end of the
Cretaceous. They were among the last dinosaurs.

THE GENUS *PSITTACOSAURUS*

The "parrot dinosaur" *Psittacosaurus* (figure 10.3) well represents the primitive,
ancestral structure of the Ceratopsia. As many as seven species of *Psittacosaurus* are
known from the Lower Cretaceous of eastern Asia, whose remains include many
complete skulls and skeletons. For many years, psittacosaurs had been allied with
the ornithopods, but recent analysis of their excellent fossil record supports the
identification of *Psittacosaurus* as the earliest ceratopsian.

Psittacosaurus possessed all the key evolutionary novelties of the Ceratopsia
even though it had only the most rudimentary of frills. Indeed, the posterior end of
the skull roof just barely overhung the back end of the skull. The short snout, the
high position of the nostrils, the tall rostrum that superficially resembled a parrot's
beak, and the reduction of the functional toes of the hand to three are diagnostic
features of *Psittacosaurus* among ceratopsians.

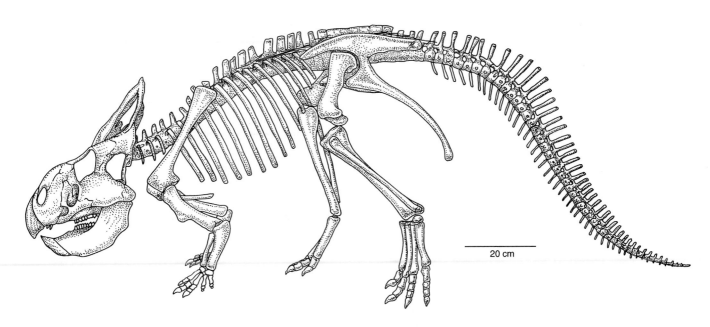

Late Cretaceous *Protoceratops* was characteristic of primitive neoceratopsians, the protoceratopsids.

The cheek teeth of *Psittacosaurus* had broad, flat wear surfaces with self-sharpening edges but did not occlude precisely. Their placement in the jaws was inset from the sides of the skull, suggesting the presence of cheek pouches. *Psittacosaurus* did not exceed 2 meters in length, and its skeletal structure was much more like that of a primitive ornithischian rather than other ceratopsians. In particular, the hind limb was longer than the forelimb, and the forefoot had only three functional toes, whereas the hind foot had four slender toes. The neck was short, and the tail was moderately long. Ossified tendons were present in some species of *Psittacosaurus* along the spine in the back and hip region.

The teeth of psittacosaurs were characteristic of plant eaters. They were usually well worn, and polished stones (gastroliths) associated with some psittacosaur skeletons suggest that significant amounts of vegetation were milled in the stomach. The forelimbs of *Psittacosaurus* were about 58 percent of hind limb length, indicating this dinosaur was a facultative biped. Psittacosaurs were probably able to grasp with their hands; their first finger diverged from the other two (see figure 10.3). If this was the case, psittacosaurs were primarily bipeds, using the hands to grasp vegetation while eating.

The psittacosaurs were widespread and reasonably common dinosaurs in Asia during the Early Cretaceous. They represent well the ancestry of a subsequent, much more diverse and impressive group of dinosaurs, the Neoceratopsia.

NEOCERATOPSIA

If you visited a Late Cretaceous landscape in western North America, you would surely have seen a **neoceratopsian.** These dinosaurs were among the most diverse and abundant dinosaurs at that time and place. Neoceratopsians are divided into two families: the primarily Asian protoceratopsids and the western North American ceratopsids. Evolutionary novelties that distinguish the neoceratopsians from the psittacosaurs include an extremely large head, broad and prominent frill, pointed and sharply keeled rostrum, and limb structures associated with obligate quadrupedalism (figure 10.4).

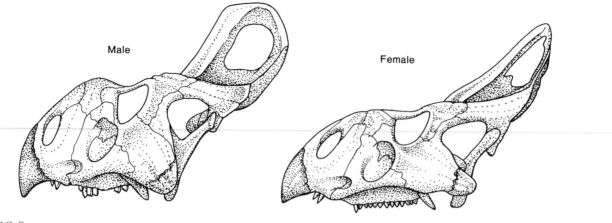

Male Female

FIGURE 10.5

Differences in skull size and shape distinguish male and female *Protoceratops*.

The fossil record of neoceratopsians is one of the best of any group of dinosaurs. Many complete skeletons and well-preserved skulls have been discovered.

PROTOCERATOPSIDAE

Protoceratopsids were small (1 to 2.5 meters long), primitive neoceratopsians that include the well-known genera **Protoceratops** (see figure 10.4) and *Bagaceratops* from Mongolia, and *Montanoceratops* and *Leptoceratops* from North America. All proto-ceratopsids were of Late Cretaceous age, but they truly represent a stage of cer-atopsian evolution intermediate between the psittacosaurs and the ceratopsids. Thus, *Protoceratops* (see figure 10.4), here considered a typical protoceratopsid, had a relatively larger skull and a much longer frill than *Psittacosaurus*. The fore- and hind limbs of *Protoceratops* were of more nearly equal lengths than in *Psittacosaurus*, and the limbs were more massive with broader feet. Thus, *Protoceratops* was much more like a ceratopsid than is *Psittacosaurus*.

Yet, unlike ceratopsids, the frill of *Protoceratops* was still rather short, *Protoceratops* had no horns, and its nostrils were small. These features identify *Protoceratops* (and all protoceratopsids) as neoceratopsians more primitive than cer-atopsids. Indeed, the ancestors of the ceratopsids must have looked very much like *Protoceratops*.

LIFESTYLE OF PROTOCERATOPS

Fossils of *Protoceratops* come from areas that were deserts during the Late Cretaceous. In those deserts, extensive dune fields were dotted by intermittent lakes and streams. The dozens of skeletons, skulls, and nests of eggs of *Protoceratops* indicate that these dinosaurs nested communally and were gregarious. The eggs were laid in ring-shaped clutches in shallow depressions scooped out of the dune sand.

Measurements of *Protoceratops* indicate that as adults these dinosaurs had skulls of two different shapes (figure 10.5). One type of skull had a larger and more erect frill than the other and a prominent bump on the snout. It seems likely, by analogy with living animals, that these two skull types represent males and females of a single species of *Protoceratops*.

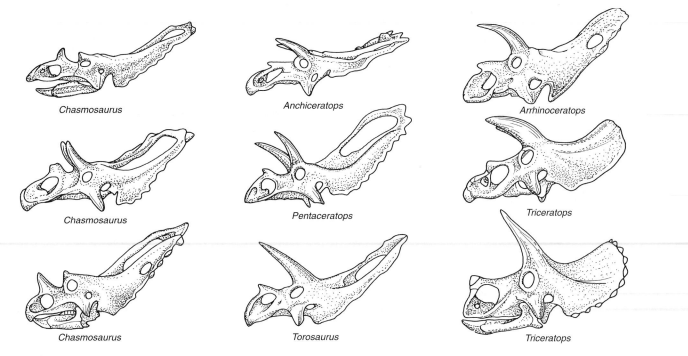

FIGURE 10.6

The skulls of ceratopsids displayed a variety of horn types and frill shapes.

We can thus envision groups of *Protoceratops* living in the deserts of central Asia during the Late Cretaceous, foraging for the vegetation that grew in wetter places in the desert, and nesting communally.

CERATOPSIDAE

The **ceratopsids** were large (4 to 8 meters long), habitual quadrupeds. Their distinctive evolutionary novelties include very large skulls (1 to 2.4 meters long) that had large nostrils, prominent frills, and a variety of horns (figure 10.6). Ceratopsids are known only from the Late Cretaceous of North America. Claims of ceratopsids from Asia and South America have been based on fossils that are too fragmentary to be identified or that have been misidentified.

Paleontologists recognize two different types of ceratopsids: **pachyrhinosaurines** and **ceratopsines** (figure 10.7). The pachyrhinosaurines are considered the more primitive of the two because they had a relatively short and high face and a short frill. They also had horns near the nostrils (nasal horns) that were much larger than the paired horns behind the eyes (postorbital horns). In contrast, the more advanced ceratopsines had long, low faces, long frills, and postorbital horns that were usually larger than the nasal horns. Ceratopsines include the largest of all ceratopsids, *Torosaurus, Triceratops,* and *Pentaceratops,* which had skulls as much as 2.8 meters long and bodies as long as 8 meters.

Pachyrhinosaurine fossils are known primarily from Montana, Alberta, Canada, and Alaska. Ceratopsines, however, were more widespread. Their fossils extend from Alberta to Texas, and fragmentary ceratopsid fossils from Alaska and Mexico may also be of ceratopsines. *Triceratops* is the most famous ceratopsine, and we examine it here as a typical ceratopsid.

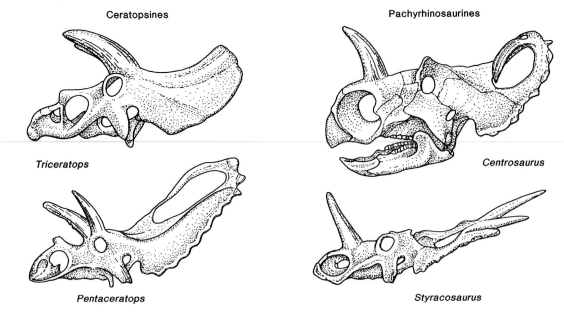

Ceratopsines

Pachyrhinosaurines

Triceratops

Centrosaurus

Pentaceratops

Styracosaurus

FIGURE 10.7

Paleontologists distinguish two types of ceratopsids, pachyrhinosaurines and ceratopsines, based on skull features.

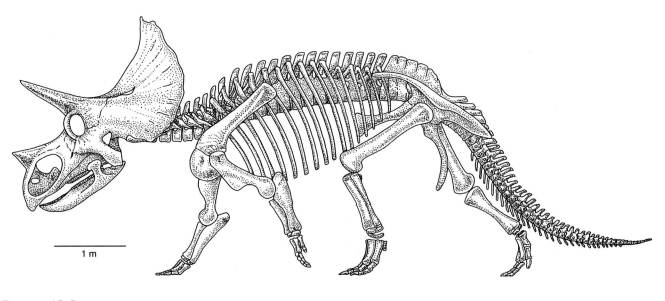

1 m

FIGURE 10.8

Late Cretaceous *Triceratops* was the best-known ceratopsid.

THE GENUS *TRICERATOPS*

In many ways, *Triceratops* (figure 10.8) is a typical ceratopsine. It had a long, low snout and large postorbital horns. But unlike other ceratopsines (see figure 10.6), *Triceratops* had a short frill that lacked openings (fenestrae). The edge of the frill of *Triceratops* was lined with small, conical bones called epoccipitals, a feature seen in some other ceratopsids, including *Centrosaurus* and *Pentaceratops*.

As in all ceratopsids, the teeth of *Triceratops* formed a complex dental battery, in which adjacent teeth were locked together in longitudinal rows and vertical columns (figure 10.9). As the teeth along the cutting edge wore out, they were lost and replaced from below by new teeth. Ceratopsid teeth and dental batteries were thus very similar (convergent) to those of some hadrosaurids (see Chapter 8).

To move the jaws and operate its dental battery, *Triceratops* had large, jaw-moving muscles anchored in the frill. Three forward-pointing horns projected from the skull: two large ones above each orbit and a much smaller one above the nostril. The bone of these horns and over the frill and much of the skull bore numerous grooves and channels for blood vessels. It seems likely that the horns of *Triceratops* had keratinous sheaths, as do the horns of living cows.

As in other ceratopsids, the forelimbs and hind limbs of *Triceratops* were of nearly equal length, thus identifying them as obligate quadrupeds. This interpretation is supported by the short, slender tail of *Triceratops*, which clearly was not used as a counterbalance to walk. Ossified tendons were present only in the hip region of *Triceratops*, and the pelvis was fused to the backbone along 10 sacral vertebrae, 4 or 5 more than was usual among dinosaurs.

The solid fusion of the backbone and hip of *Triceratops* suggests great stability and power in walking. The massive hind limbs with four toes that were broad and hooved are consistent with this idea. The deep rib cage of *Triceratops* supported a massive shoulder girdle and forelimbs. The forelimbs may have been held in a sprawling posture, whereas the hind limbs were upright, though this has been debated (see box 10.1). The first four vertebrae of the neck were fused together (co-ossified) to provide extra support for the extremely heavy head.

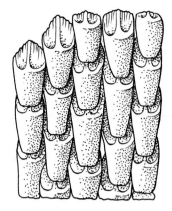

FIGURE 10.9

Ceratopsid teeth formed a complex dental battery.

FUNCTION OF THE HORNS AND FRILL

We usually see artistic depictions of *Triceratops* in a defensive posture, fending off the attack of a large meat-eating dinosaur with its horns and frill. But a careful examination of ceratopsian horns and frills suggests that they were not primarily defensive structures. Indeed, the horns and frills probably performed several functions.

The large muscles that opened and closed the jaws of ceratopsians were attached mainly to the frill (figure 10.10). Different sizes and shapes of frills probably reflected differences in the jaw muscles of various ceratopsians. The extremely large frills of neoceratopsians provided attachment sites for enormous jaw muscles that exerted great chewing forces.

Beyond its relationship to chewing, the ceratopsian frill (and horns) must have functioned as display. Different frill sizes and shapes were probably species-specific identifiers and, within some species, may also have expressed sexual dimorphism. Recent analyses of variation in frill size and shape in *Protoceratops* and *Chasmosaurus* suggest that males and females of the same species differed in features of the frill, horns, and other parts of the skull (see figure 10.5). Similar kinds of differences between males and females of the same species are seen among some living mammals. Deer, in which male and female horns (antlers) differ, are a good example.

Another possible function of the ceratopsian frill was thermoregulation. Ceratopsian frills were highly vascularized; the bone contained numerous canals and grooves for blood vessels (figure 10.11). Like the plates of *Stegosaurus* (see Chapter 9), the ceratopsian frill could have been used to spread the dinosaur's blood over a wide surface area, thus allowing its rapid heating and cooling. The frill of ceratopsians consisted of highly vascularized bone that in life was covered with huge, jaw-closing muscles. It is difficult to envision the frill as a helmet or shield used in combat. The horns might have had some defensive function, but their use primarily in display seems more likely.

CERATOPSIAN EVOLUTION

Ceratopsians first appeared in Asia during the Early Cretaceous, about 100 million years ago. Although the horned dinosaurs shared a common ancestry with the ornithopods, that common ancestor has not been discovered.

FIGURE 10.10

The frills of ceratopsians provided sites for the attachment of jaw muscles.

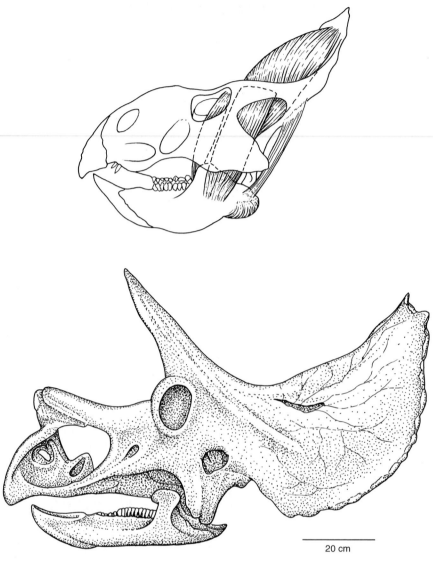

20 cm

FIGURE 10.11

The frill of *Triceratops* was highly vascularized. It was covered with channels and grooves for blood vessels.

The modest diversification of Asian ceratopsians culminated in *Protoceratops*. By 75 million years ago, ceratopsians had emigrated from Asia to western North America where they became remarkably successful (figure 10.12). They were among the most common and most diverse of the Late Cretaceous plant-eating dinosaurs. Indeed, *Triceratops* was one of the last known dinosaurs (box 10.2).

PACHYCEPHALOSAURIA

The dome-headed dinosaurs, **pachycephalosaurs,** were bipedal ornithischians with greatly thickened bones of the skull roof. Two families—Homalocephalidae and Pachycephalosauridae—encompass the 15 known genera of pachycephalosaurs from the Cretaceous of Europe, Madagascar, North America, and Asia.

BOX 10.1

UPRIGHT OR SPRAWLING CERATOPSIANS?

All paleontologists agree that the hind limbs of ceratopsians were held in an upright stance with the limb essentially vertical and almost directly under the pelvis. But sharp differences of opinion exist about how the forelimb was held by ceratopsians. Some paleontologists favor a semi-sprawling or sprawling forelimb in which the ceratopsian humerus was held obliquely or even parallel to the ground. Others favor a fully upright forelimb posture in which the humerus was held vertical to the ground (box figure 10.1A). Indeed, ceratopsian trackways from Colorado apparently indicate these dinosaurs walked with nearly upright (semi-sprawling) forelimbs (see figure 13.6).

The most rigorous analyses of ceratopsian forelimb posture based on bones favor the sprawling or semi-sprawling stance. These studies argue that the shape of the ceratopsian humerus, the size and shape of the shoulder and elbow joints, and the inferred alignment of forelimb muscles based on these shapes, make a habitually upright forelimb in ceratopsians impossible.

We can easily gain some insight into these analyses by comparing the humerus of a living lizard (a sprawler), a living rhinoceros (an upright walker), and a *Triceratops* (box figure 10.1B). The *Triceratops* humerus most closely resembles that of the lizard in having broad flanges of bone designed for the attachment of large shoulder (deltoid) and chest (pectoral) muscles. In the lizard, these relatively large muscles are needed to hold and move the humerus horizontally during walking. In contrast, the rhinoceros does not have such relatively large shoulder and chest muscles (and bony attachments for them on its humerus), because it walks with its legs in a vertical position. Given the shape of the humerus of *Triceratops* and other ceratopsians, it may seem reasonable to conclude that they walked with the humerus in a semi-sprawling or sprawling posture.

Nevertheless, the only known ceratopsian footprints seem to indicate an upright forelimb posture. The bone and footprint evidence thus present an apparent contradiction not easy to resolve. Perhaps the answer lies in suggesting that *Triceratops* twisted the backbone and front part of the body, so that the forefeet were planted much closer together when walking than normally occurs when walking on a sprawling limb. Clearly, more research is needed here!

BOX FIGURE 10.1A

Some paleontologists have argued that ceratopsians held the forelimb vertically.

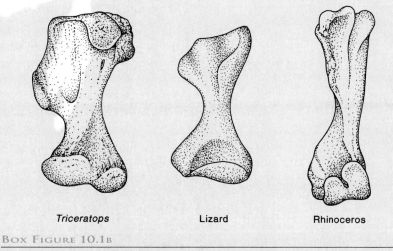

Triceratops   Lizard   Rhinoceros

BOX FIGURE 10.1B

When the humeri of a living Komodo dragon, a living rhinoceros, and a *Triceratops* are compared, it is easy to see that the ceratopsian resembles more closely the lizard.

BOX 10.2

HOW MANY SPECIES OF *TRICERATOPS?*

Nobody else ever collected ceratopsians like John Bell Hatcher. From 1889 to 1892, Hatcher collected 32 ceratopsian skulls in eastern Wyoming and shipped them to Yale University. Most of those skulls belong to *Triceratops*, and they formed much of the basis for some of the 16 species of *Triceratops* named during the nineteenth and twentieth centuries. This great diversity of *Triceratops* species has long played a major role in the ideas about dinosaur extinction. This is because these ceratopsians were among the last dinosaurs, and their high diversity supports the notion of dinosaur prosperity just prior to their extinction.

Recently, paleontologists John Ostrom of Yale University and Peter Wellnhofer of the Bavarian State Museum in Munich, Germany challenged the idea of the existence of many species of *Triceratops* at the end of the Cretaceous.

These paleontologists were motivated by a desire to answer a nagging question. Did so many different species of *Triceratops* inhabit the area from Colorado to Wyoming to Montana during a mere 2 million years? Indeed, today, and at many times during the past, large terrestrial vertebrates, such as elephants, are not very diverse—one species generally has a very wide geographic range. A good example is provided by North American bison during and since the last "Ice Age," when no more than three species were indigenous to North America.

So, how many species of *Triceratops* were there? According to Ostrom and Wellnhofer, only one! They concluded so because variation in horn and skull shape among *Triceratops* (box figure 10.2) is comparable to the variation in horn and skull shape we see today in a single species of bovid. Ostrom and Wellnhofer pointed out that, formerly, paleontologists believed

every *Triceratops* skull of a different shape represented a different species. Instead it is likely that a single "herd" of *Triceratops* from Late Cretaceous Wyoming would have encompassed all the variety in skull and horn structure seen in the 16 previously named species of *Triceratops*.

Ostrom and Wellnhofer's reduction of the species of *Triceratops* from 16 to 1 is not above criticism. It would certainly be best to have a sample of *Triceratops* skulls from a single location. Such a sample would closely approximate an extinct population of these dinosaurs, and thus allow an accurate assessment of skull and horn variation in a single *Triceratops* species. But even if Ostrom and Wellnhofer are wrong, and there were as many as 5 different species of *Triceratops*, it is still far fewer than the 16 named by earlier paleontologists. So, our view of the prosperity of these ceratopsians just prior to dinosaur extinction needs to be revised.

HOMALOCEPHALIDAE

The more primitive pachycephalosaurs were the **homalocephalids** from the Upper Cretaceous of Asia. They were characterized by a flat, table-like skull roof, which was of even thickness from side to side and pitted dorsally (figure 10.13). In addition, the skulls of homalocephalids had open supratemporal fenestrae, and short canine-like teeth were present in both the upper and the lower jaws. The remaining teeth, however, were small and had sharp, serrated edges for slicing vegetation.

Best known and characteristic of the homalocephalids is *Homalocephale* from the Cretaceous of Mongolia (see figure 10.13). The highly ornamented (pitted and knobby) skull roof is a distinctive feature of *Homalocephale*. The postcranial skeletons of homalocephalids have not yet been discovered.

PACHYCEPHALOSAURIDAE

Pachycephalosaurids were advanced pachycephalosaurs characterized by a prominent, dome-like thickening of the skull roof and no supratemporal openings (see figure 10.13). The dome was produced by fusing and thickening the frontal and parietal bones. It is important to stress that these bones were thickened, yet the volume of the brain of pachycephalosaurids was not increased (figure 10.14). Unlike the flat skull roofs of homalocephalids, the domed skull roofs of pachycephalosaurids were smooth, not pitted.

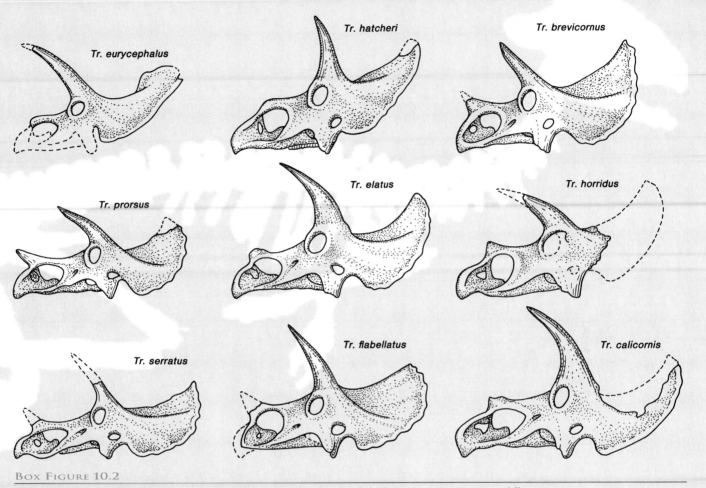

Tr. eurycephalus

Tr. hatcheri

Tr. brevicornus

Tr. prorsus

Tr. elatus

Tr. horridus

Tr. serratus

Tr. flabellatus

Tr. calicornis

Box Figure 10.2

Skulls of *Triceratops* from the Late Cretaceous of Wyoming show variation that led paleontologists to name many different species.

There are at least 11 species of pachycephalosaurids known from the Cretaceous of Europe, Madagascar, North America, and Asia. The North American genus **Stegoceras** (figure 10.15) is the best known and is typical of the family.

The skull of *Stegoceras* had the high, smooth dome characteristic of pachycephalosaurids. In addition, a bony shelf was present around the dome. No supratemporal openings remained, whereas the teeth of *Stegoceras* were similar to those of homalocephalids and indicate it was a plant eater.

No complete pachycephalosaurid skeleton is known, but the best-known skeleton, that of *Stegoceras* (see figure 10.15), indicates that pachycephalosaurids had many of the features we associate with ornithopods. Thus, *Stegoceras* has much longer hind limbs than forelimbs, and a long tail with vertebrae tightly joined by ossified tendons. It is features such as these that long justified inclusion of the pachycephalosaurids in the Ornithopoda. Unique features of the pachycephalosaurid postcranial skeleton, however, are numerous. They include the long and low ilium bone of the pelvis, which contacted six to eight sacral vertebrae. Also, the joint surfaces between pachycephalosaurid vertebrae were ridged and thus "locked" together to stabilize the back. Finally, the head of a pachycephalosaurid was set at an angle to its vertebral column; in a normal posture, the head hung down so that the nose pointed at the ground and the "dome" pointed forward.

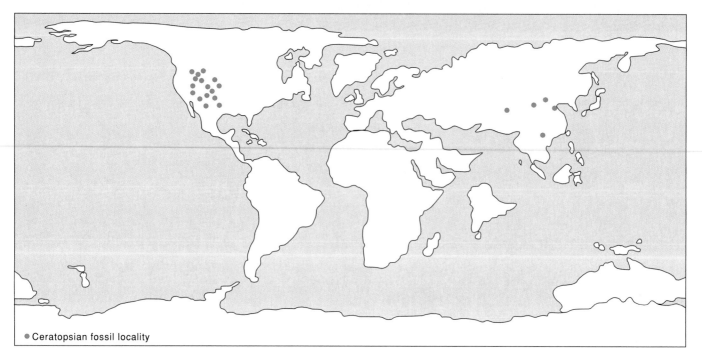

FIGURE 10.12

Ceratopsian fossils are known only from Asia and North America.

FIGURE 10.13

The skull of *Homalocephale* was characteristic of the homalocephalids, whereas that of *Stegoceras* typified the pachycephalosaurids.

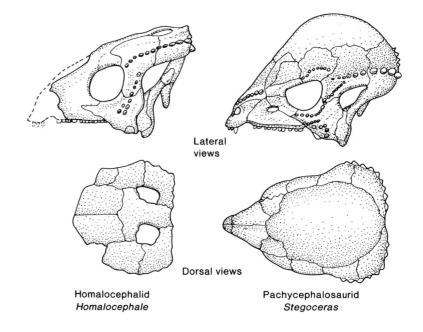

Lateral
views

Dorsal views

Homalocephalid
Homalocephale

Pachycephalosaurid
Stegoceras

HEAD BUTTING

The function of the peculiar, thickened skulls of pachycephalosaurids has long fascinated paleontologists. Most now agree that pachycephalosaurids used their skulls to **butt heads** against other dinosaurs, including each other (figure 10.16), much as do many living bovids. Features of the pachycephalosaurid skull and skeleton designed to resist impacts are

1. The greatly thickened dome of the skull, which protected the brain

2. The shortened base of the skull

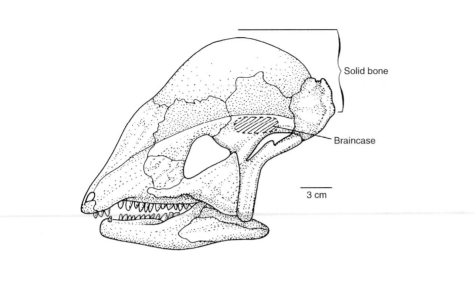

FIGURE 10.14
Pachycephalosaurids had greatly thickened bones of their skull roof, but did not have an increased brain volume.

Solid bone

Braincase

3 cm

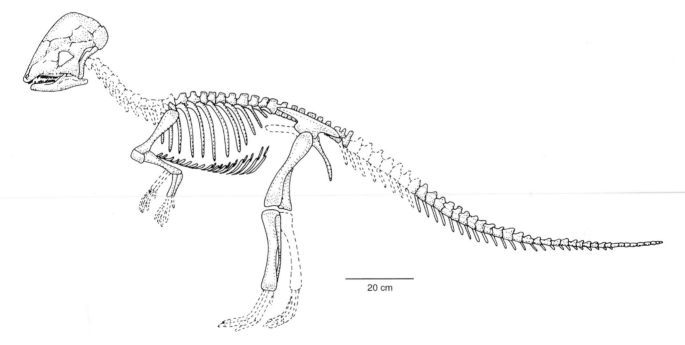

FIGURE 10.15

This skeletal reconstruction of *Stegoceras* is the most complete that can be made for any pachycephalosaur.

3. The inclination of the skull relative to the vertebral column

4. The widely expanded back of the skull

5. The strengthening of the vertebral column described above

6. The reinforced upper lip of the hip socket

All of these features strongly support the idea that pachycephalosaurids either directly butted heads or used their heads to butt the flanks of other pachycephalosaurs (or other dinosaurs).

FIGURE 10.16

Paleontologists believe pachycephalosaurids butted heads to defend territory and maintain their social structure.
© Mark Hallett

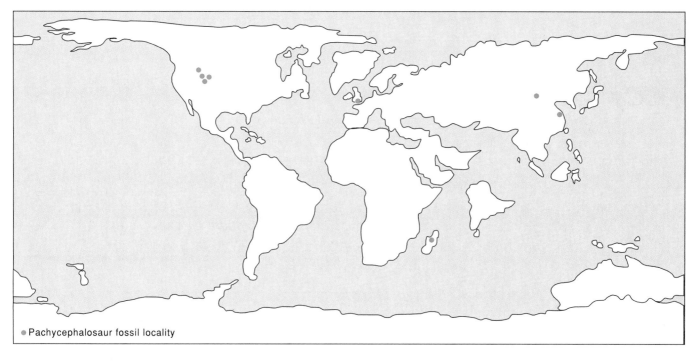

• Pachycephalosaur fossil locality

FIGURE 10.17

Pachycephalosaur fossils have been collected mostly in Asia and North America, but also are known from Europe and Madagascar.

Today, head and flank butting occurs in mammals such as bighorn sheep. The butting is usually for competition among males for territory and/or access to females. It is reasonable to conclude that pachycephalosaurids butted heads and flanks for the same social reasons as these living mammals.

EVOLUTION OF PACHYCEPHALOSAURS

The oldest-known pachycephalosaur is *Yaverlandia* from the Lower Cretaceous of Great Britain. It, however, was not the most primitive pachycephalosaur, which suggests that much more about early pachycephalosaurs remains to be discovered. It also means that the homalocephalids and pachycephalosaurids, origin unknown, had already diverged from each other by the Early Cretaceous.

The subsequent evolutionary history of the pachycephalosaurs is similar to the history of the Ceratopsia. Primitive pachycephalosaurs (homalocephalids) underwent a limited diversification in Asia, where some lived in the same environments as *Protoceratops* (figure 10.17). A more diverse group of advanced pachycephalosaurs (pachycephalosaurids) lived in North America from Alberta to Wyoming. The pachycephalosaurid *Majungatholus*, however, from the Upper Cretaceous of Madagascar is anomalous. It is totally isolated from other pachycephalosaur fossils and thus suggests that an undiscovered fossil record of pachycephalosaurs exists in southern Asia and, probably, Africa.

The distribution of pachycephalosaur fossils indicates they preferred inland rather than coastal environments. In rocks deposited on coastal plains, pachycephalosaur fossils consist mostly of their isolated and highly durable skull caps, which may have been transported many kilometers by rivers. The most complete, well-preserved, and numerous of pachycephalosaur fossils are found in rocks deposited on inland flood plains and in deserts.

The structures for head butting present in the skulls and skeletons of pachycephalosaurids suggest social behavior like that of some living sheep and goats. It is tempting to speculate that pachycephalosaurids lived in herds and defended territory, maintaining their social structure by butting heads.

In North America, pachycephalosaurs existed through nearly the end of the Cretaceous. They were among the last dinosaurs.

S U M M A R Y

1. Ceratopsians and pachycephalosaurs are closely related and belong to a single group of dinosaurs, the Marginocephalia.

2. Ceratopsians consist of two groups, psittacosaurids and neoceratopsians, distinguished from other dinosaurs by features of the skull that include presence of a frill.

3. *Psittacosaurus* from the Lower Cretaceous of Asia well represents the primitive, ancestral structure of the Ceratopsia. Neoceratopsians differ from *Psittacosaurus* in their extremely large heads, prominent frills, and pointed, sharply keeled beaks.

4. Protoceratopsids were primitive neoceratopsians from the Cretaceous of Asia and North America, having short frills and no horns.

5. Ceratopsids were advanced neoceratopsians from the Cretaceous of North America, having long frills and horns.

6. Pachyrhinosaurines, with relatively short faces and frills, were primitive ceratopsids.

7. Ceratopsines, with relatively long faces and frills, were advanced ceratopsids.

8. The horns and frills of neoceratopsians functioned in display and thermoregulation, and the frills provided attachment sites of jaw muscles. They were not primarily used in defense.

9. Ceratopsians lived during the Cretaceous in Asia and North America. They were most successful during the Late Cretaceous in western North America, where ceratopsids were among the last dinosaurs.

10. Pachycephalosaurs were bipedal ornithischians with greatly thickened bones of the skull roof.

11. Primitive pachycephalosaurs, the Homalocephalidae, had flat skull roofs ornamented with pits.

12. Advanced pachycephalosaurs, the Pachycephalosauridae, had smooth, domed skull roofs.

13. Pachycephalosaurid skulls and skeletons contained a variety of features that suggest these dinosaurs butted heads like some modern sheep and goats.

14. Pachycephalosaurs lived during the Cretaceous in Europe, Madagascar, North America, and Asia.

KEY TERMS

butt heads
Ceratopsia
Ceratopsidae
Ceratopsinae
frill

Homalocephale
Homalocephalidae
Marginocephalia
Neoceratopsia
Pachycephalosauria
Pachycephalosauridae

Pachyrhinosaurinae
Protoceratops
Protoceratopsidae
Psittacosaurus
Stegoceras
Triceratops

REVIEW QUESTIONS

1. What features distinguished the ceratopsians and pachycephalosaurs as marginocephalians?

2. What features distinguish *Psittacosaurus* from neoceratopsians?

3. Describe the lifestyle of *Protoceratops*.

4. What features of *Triceratops* identify it as a typical ceratopsine? How is it different from a pachyrhinosaurine?

5. Discuss and evaluate the possible functions of the horns and frills of ceratopsians.

6. What are the two types of pachycephalosaurs, and how are they distinguished from each other?

7. Why do most paleontologists think pachycephalosaurs butted heads? Why would pachycephalosaurs do this?

8. What are the similarities and differences in the evolution of ceratopsians and of pachycephalosaurs?

FURTHER READING

Dodson, P. and Currie, P. J. 1990. Neoceratopsia; in Weishampel, D. B., Dodson, P., and Osmólska, H., eds., *The Dinosauria*. Berkeley: University of California Press, pp. 593–618. (A detailed technical review of the neoceratopsians.)

Galton, P. 1970. Pachycephalosaurids—dinosaurian battering rams. *Discovery* (Yale Peabody Museum of Natural History), v. 6, pp. 23–32. (Discusses the head-butting habits of pachycephalosaurs.)

Lehman, T. M. 1989. *Chasmosaurus mariscalensis*, sp. nov., a new ceratopsian dinosaur from Texas. *Journal of Vertebrate Paleontology*, v. 9, pp. 137–62. (This technical article describes the variation in a sample of *Chasmosaurus* from a bone bed in Texas.)

Maryanska, T. 1990. Pachycephalosauria; in Weishampel, D. B., Dodson, P., and Osmólska, H., eds., *The Dinosauria*. Berkeley: University of California Press, pp. 564–77. (A detailed technical review of the pachycephalosaurs.)

Ostrom, J. H. and Wellnhofer, P. 1986. The Munich specimen of *Triceratops* with a revision of the genus. *Zitteliana*, v. 14, pp. 111–58. (Taxonomy of the species of *Triceratops*.)

Sereno, P. C. 1990. Psittacosauridae; in Weishampel, D. B., Dodson, P., and Osmólska, H., eds., *The Dinosauria*. Berkeley: University of California Press, pp. 579–92. (A detailed technical review of the psittacosaurs.)

THE DINOSAURIAN WORLD

Dinosaurs existed for about 160 million years, from the Late Triassic, 225 million years ago, to the end of the Cretaceous, 65 million years ago. This interval of time can be called the "age of dinosaurs," whereas the entire Mesozoic Era is usually termed the "age of reptiles."

Dinosaurs did not live and evolve in isolation during the age of dinosaurs. They coexisted with plants and other animals in climates and on landscapes very different from those of today. Furthermore, dinosaurs changed dramatically—by evolution and by extinction—during the age of dinosaurs. This chapter examines these changes and briefly reviews the geography, climate, vegetation, and animal life that made up the dinosaurian world.

LATE TRIASSIC: THE BEGINNING OF THE AGE OF DINOSAURS

Dinosaurs first appeared during the Late Triassic, and this interval of time, 225 to 208 million years ago, is known as the beginning, or dawn, of the age of dinosaurs. During the Late Triassic, most dinosaurs were small and rare, and other reptiles dominated the landscape.

GEOGRAPHY AND CLIMATE

During the Late Triassic, all the continents were amalgamated into a single supercontinent that geologists call **Pangaea** (figure 11.1). Much earlier, during the Late Permian more than 250 million years ago, Pangaea coalesced from two supercontinents: **Gondwana** (now broken up into South America, Africa, Antarctica, Australia, India, and Madagascar) and **Laurasia** (now broken up into Europe, part of Asia, and North America). Later, during the Jurassic, it separated again. After Pangaea assembled, the world had only one ocean, a sort of expanded Pacific Ocean called **Panthalassa** (see figure 11.1). A sea along the southern shore of Asia that indented Pangaea between Africa and Europe is called the **Tethys Sea** (see figure 11.1). During the post-Triassic separation of Gondwana from Laurasia the Tethys expanded progressively westward, successively creating the Mediterranean, central Atlantic, and Caribbean ocean basins.

By the Late Triassic, Pangaea had started to break up in the Caribbean and Mediterranean areas. Yet the topography of Pangaea during the Late Triassic seems to have been relatively subdued. There were relatively few large mountain ranges and few volcanoes.

There were no polar ice caps during the Late Triassic, and there is no evidence of glaciers or of cold, snowy winters. Indeed, climates were generally much warmer and more **equable** (less varied with latitude) than they are today, a situation that continued for the entire age of dinosaurs. Recent computer modeling,

FIGURE 11.1

During the Late Triassic the continents were united in one supercontinent, Pangaea, surrounded by one ocean, Panthalassa.

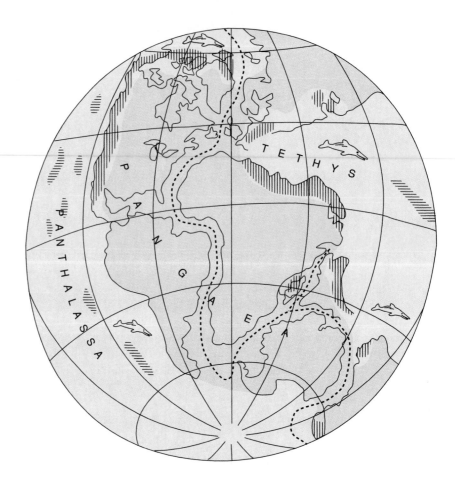

FIGURE 11.2

Ammonoids were successful in the Late Triassic seas.

however, coupled with rock and fossil evidence, indicates that Late Triassic Pangaean climates were strongly **monsoonal.** An arid season alternated with a very wet season on the warm Pangaean supercontinent during the Late Triassic.

LIFE IN THE SEA

The Late Triassic seas were warm and shallow, except for the far offshore portions of Panthalassa, from which few rocks and fossils have been preserved. Clams and snails were particularly common in the Late Triassic seas, as were the **ammonoid** cephalopods (figure 11.2). Corals built low mound-like reefs in many parts of the Late Triassic sea floor.

Sharks and heavily scaled bony fishes also were successful during the Late Triassic. Long-necked marine reptiles, called **plesiosaurs,** first appeared during the Late Triassic, and **ichthyosaurs,** a remarkable case of evolutionary convergence of reptiles with fish-like bodies, were abundant and diverse during the Late Triassic. Indeed, the largest animal known to have lived in the Late Triassic seas was *Shonisaurus,* a 10-meter-long ichthyosaur (figure 11.3).

VEGETATION

Late Triassic vegetation was very different from present-day vegetation. Ferns and the now-extinct seed ferns dominated the understory. Trees that stood above them were cycads and cycadedoids, conifers, and gingkoes. These types of plants, all of which survive today—although cycads and ginkgoes are rare—belong to a group of plants having exposed seeds called **gymnosperms.**

Most paleontologists believe flowering plants, called **angiosperms,** in which the seed is covered, did not evolve until the Early Cretaceous. But there is one Late Triassic plant, **Sanmiguelia** (figure 11.4), that looks remarkably like a palm, which

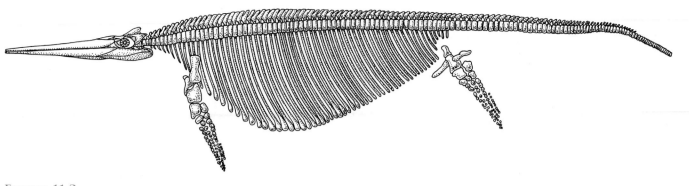

FIGURE 11.3

The 10-meter-long ichthyosaur *Shonisaurus* was the largest animal in the Late Triassic seas.

is a primitive type of angiosperm. This has led some paleontologists to argue that flowering plants first evolved during the Late Triassic. However, even if this were true, the Late Triassic landscape was dominated by ferns, conifers, and other types of plants now extinct or nearly extinct.

VERTEBRATES

Dinosaurs appeared in a world dominated by large (up to 2 meters long) amphibians (the **labyrinthodonts**) and thecodonts, especially the meat-eating **rauisuchians** and phytosaurs, and the plant-eating aetosaurs (figure 11.5). One of the largest meat eaters of the Late Triassic was a rauisuchian thecodont, 5-meter-long *Postosuchus*. Other plant eaters common when dinosaurs first appeared were rhynchosaurs and dicynodonts, two groups well adapted to eating tough, fibrous vegetation, that became extinct soon after the appearance of dinosaurs. Indeed, these types of reptiles, and amphibians, as well as all of the thecodonts, became extinct at or just before the end of the Triassic. This was one of the major extinctions of the Mesozoic.

Other land animals of the Late Triassic include the first turtles, pterosaurs, and mammals, groups that appeared nearly simultaneously with the dinosaurs. The Late Triassic was an important turning point in the history of life on land, with many new types of animals appearing and several other types suffering extinction.

DINOSAURS

Dinosaurs had a nearly worldwide distribution during the Late Triassic. But they were neither conspicuous nor abundant during the Late Triassic, except perhaps at the very end of the Triassic, when they were extremely common in some fossil deposits.

Most Late Triassic dinosaurs were relatively small (up to 3 meters long) and included *Staurikosaurus*-like predators and *Lesothosaurus*-like plant eaters, although the large prosauropods, like *Plateosaurus*, were plant eaters as long as 8 meters. Unlike their contemporaries, the Late Triassic dinosaurs had an upright limb posture designed to make them fast bipedal and quadrupedal walkers and runners. Some paleontologists argue that this gave the dinosaurs an advantage over other reptiles, and explains why they survived and prospered after the Triassic, when many other types of reptiles became extinct. Others suggest that a change in vegetation and an increasingly arid climate favored the dinosaurs during the Late Triassic and Jurassic, while bringing about the extinction of the other reptiles. Whichever explanation is accepted, dinosaurs did not really dominate the land until after the end of the Triassic.

FIGURE 11.4

The palm-like Late Triassic plant *Sanmiguelia* is thought by some paleontologists to have been an angiosperm.

Phytosaurs (left), shared most Late Triassic landscapes with early dinosaurs.

© Doug Henderson

EARLY AND MIDDLE JURASSIC: THE DINOSAURS DOMINATE

During the Early and Middle Jurassic, 208 to 157 million years ago, dinosaurs became the largest and most successful group of land vertebrates. But the fossil record of the establishment of dinosaur dominance is not as complete as their record in the Late Triassic and the Late Jurassic. This is partly because vast deserts covered parts of Pangaea during the Early and Middle Jurassic, especially in western North America and southern Africa, and few dinosaur fossils other than footprints are found in the resulting eolian rocks (figure 11.6). Another reason we know less about Early and Middle Jurassic dinosaurs than about earlier or later dinosaurs is simply a lack of exploration. This has begun to change recently, so that new discoveries of Early and Middle Jurassic dinosaurs have been among the important discoveries of the last couple of decades.

GEOGRAPHY AND CLIMATE

By the end of the Middle Jurassic, Pangaea had broken apart to the point where Laurasia and Gondwana were connected only in the western Mediterranean (figure 11.7). Nevertheless, the Pangaean monsoonal circulation of the Late Triassic still

FIGURE 11.6

Eolian sandstones, crossbedded by wind, are the most common Lower and Middle Jurassic rocks in western North America.

FIGURE 11.7

By the Middle Jurassic, Gondwana and Laurasia were almost completely separated.

influenced climate across the vast supercontinent. Highly arid climates developed in parts of Pangaea during the Early and Middle Jurassic. This was especially true in western North America, which was covered by a vast sand sea during much of this time (figure 11.8).

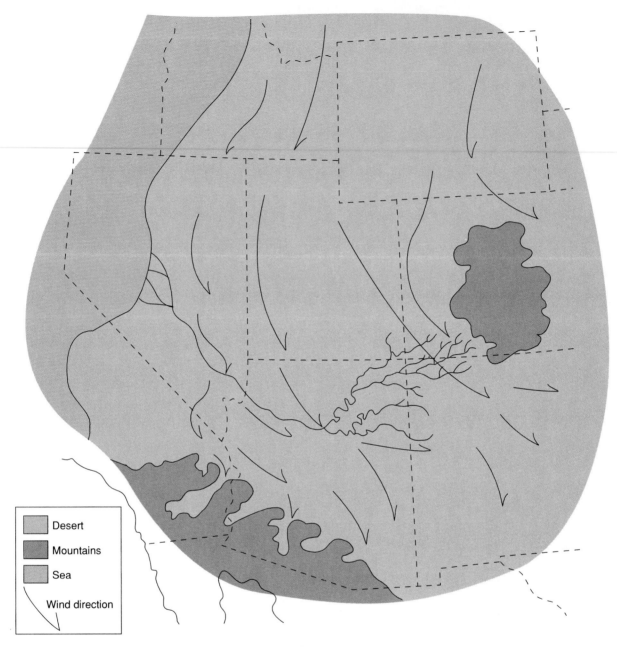

FIGURE 11.8

A vast desert covered much of western North America during the Early and Middle Jurassic.

Map of desert taken from *An Odyssey in Time: The Dinosaurs of North America* by Dr. Dale Russell. Reproduced with permission of Canadian Museum of Nature, Ottawa, Canada.

LIFE IN THE SEA

Early and Middle Jurassic seas were populated by animals similar to those that inhabited the Late Triassic seas, except that most Jurassic animals were larger than their Triassic predecessors. There was also a greater diversity of marine animals during the Early and Middle Jurassic. Thus, for example, huge plesiosaurs were the largest marine predators of the Early and Middle Jurassic (figure 11.9).

FIGURE 11.9

Three-meter-long plesiosaurs were the largest animals in the Early and Middle Jurassic seas.

VEGETATION

Cycads, cycadeoids, conifers, and ginkgoes were the trees of the Early and Middle Jurassic, as they had been during the Late Triassic. Cycads (figure 11.10), however, were the dominant trees throughout the Jurassic, and paleontologists who study fossil plants call this period in earth's history "the age of cycads." Seed ferns became extinct at the end of the Triassic, and ferns were not as common during the Early and Middle Jurassic as they had been during the Late Triassic, partly because climates worldwide may have been drier.

DINOSAURS AND OTHER VERTEBRATES

Dinosaurs dominated life on land during the Early and Middle Jurassic. Thecodonts were extinct, and most of the large amphibians had also disappeared (see box 11.1). All of the large meat eaters and plant eaters were dinosaurs. Examples include *Dilophosaurus*, a 6-meter-long theropod and *Datousaurus*, a 12- to 14-meter-long sauropod. All other terrestrial vertebrates of the Early and Middle Jurassic were relatively small animals, such as mammals, pterosaurs, turtles, crocodiles, and so forth. Clearly, dinosaurs had come to rule the landscape.

LATE JURASSIC: THE GOLDEN AGE OF DINOSAURS

Unlike the earlier part of the Jurassic, paleontologists have an extensive fossil record of dinosaurs and other organisms that lived during the Late Jurassic. The record indicates that the largest dinosaurs that ever lived, including the largest land animals

FIGURE 11.10

Cycads were the dominant trees of the Jurassic.
© Doug Henderson

of all time, evolved during the Late Jurassic. This aspect of the Late Jurassic dinosaurs, as well as their wide geographic range, variety, and abundance is the reason the Late Jurassic is called the "golden age" of dinosaurs.

GEOGRAPHY AND CLIMATE

By the Late Jurassic, Laurasia and Gondwana were totally separated by the Tethys Sea (figure 11.11). World sea level was high, and much of Laurasia and significant parts of Gondwana were inundated by seawater. This created what are called **epicontinental seas,** which were seas atop continental crust unlike today's oceans and seas, which are mainly atop the denser oceanic crust.

Climates during the Late Jurassic were still influenced by the monsoonal circulation pattern of earlier times, but less so as Pangaea broke up and a circumequatorial seaway (Tethys) began to influence air circulation patterns. Overall, Late Jurassic climates seem to have resembled those of the Early and Middle Jurassic, but were probably a bit warmer.

LIFE IN THE SEA; VEGETATION

Life in the seas and vegetation on land during the Late Jurassic were generally similar to those of the Early and Middle Jurassic. An exception is the extensive reefs built on Late Jurassic sea floors, probably the result of higher sea levels that flooded the continental shelves.

DINOSAURS AND OTHER VERTEBRATES

Late Jurassic dinosaurs are well known, especially from the western United States, southern China, and eastern Africa. Huge sauropods, large stegosaurids, and small-to medium-size ornithopods (hypsilophodontids and iguanodontids) were the dominant plant eaters. Allosaurid theropods were the big meat eaters. Almost all other

BOX 11.1

THE DINOSAUR NATIONAL MONUMENT OF CHINA

The most important Middle Jurassic dinosaur locality known lies just outside of the city of Zigong in Sichuan Province of southern China. Chinese geologists discovered this locality in 1972, and since then the bones of many dinosaurs and a variety of other vertebrates have been excavated from an area of 1,800 square meters. Many complete dinosaur skeletons were removed from the Zigong locality, but many more were left in the ground, excavated in relief, for viewing by visitors to the Zigong Dinosaur Museum (box figure 11.1), which was built over the dinosaur locality and opened in 1987. The idea of building an exhibition facility over an ongoing dinosaur excavation was borrowed by the Chinese from Dinosaur National Monument in Utah, and the Zigong Dinosaur Museum may truly be called China's dinosaur national monument.

The Middle Jurassic dinosaurs from Zigong include the oldest and most primitive stegosaur, *Huayangosaurus*, and hypsilophodontid, *Agilisaurus*. Also present, and dominating the dinosaur bones in the excavation, are two sauropods, *Datousaurus* and *Shunosaurus*. These sauropods were much smaller than the Late Jurassic sauropods, but the

BOX FIGURE 11.1

The Zigong Dinosaur Museum is the "Dinosaur National Monument" of China.

composition of the Zigong dinosaur quarry—mostly sauropods and stegosaurs—is very similar to that of the great dinosaur quarries of Late Jurassic age in the western United States. This suggests that the composition of dinosaur communities, particularly the dominance of plant-eating sauropods and stegosaurs,

was a feature of both the Middle and Late Jurassic world. The Zigong dinosaurs also indicate that stegosaurs and hypsilophodontids had already evolved by the Middle Jurassic. This Chinese dinosaur locality thus provides a unique glimpse of the dinosaurs of the Middle Jurassic.

land vertebrates were relatively small (some crocodiles were an exception), truly dwarfed by the gigantic dinosaurs. Dinosaur domination of the earth was complete, and the zenith of dinosaurian evolution, in terms of body size, had been reached (figure 11.12).

EARLY CRETACEOUS: A TRANSITION

The Early Cretaceous, 145 to 100 million years ago, was a time of profound changes in the history of life on land, for it was during the Early Cretaceous that flowering plants appeared and began their rise to dominance among land plants. This change in vegetation may lie at the core of a major transition in dinosaur evolution that took place during the Early Cretaceous.

GEOGRAPHY AND CLIMATE

Worldwide sea level continued to rise from the Late Jurassic into the Early Cretaceous, inundating more of the continents. Gondwana fragmented, and the Atlantic Ocean basin began to form (figure 11.13).

FIGURE 11.11

Laurasia and Gondwana were totally separated by the Late Jurassic.

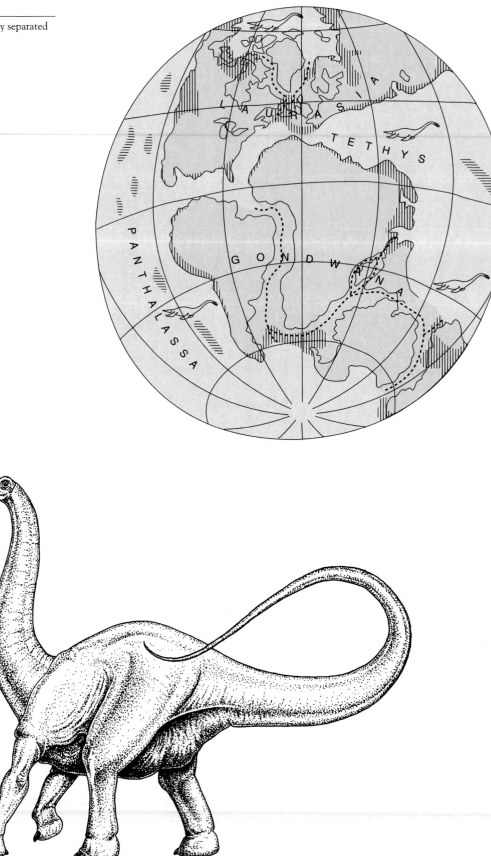

FIGURE 11.12

The largest dinosaurs of all time, gigantic sauropods such as *Diplodocus*, lived during the Late Jurassic.

FIGURE 11.13

During the Early Cretaceous, Gondwana fragmented, and the Atlantic Ocean basin began to form.

World climates became even warmer and much wetter, producing a worldwide **greenhouse** climate that persisted throughout most of the Cretaceous. The world was warm, equable, and ice-free, and the pole-to-equator temperature gradient during the Cretaceous, by one estimate, was only about 20° centigrade. Today, it is 41° centigrade.

LIFE IN THE SEA

The Early Cretaceous saw the diversification of new types of plankton, especially those types that are now common in the world's oceans. Modern types of bony fishes, as well as predatory snails and crabs, also began to diversify. Whereas corals had been the dominant reef builders of the Triassic and Jurassic, during the Early Cretaceous the **rudists,** a group of clams, took center stage in building reefs (figure 11.14).

VEGETATION

Although the gymnosperm floras of the Triassic and Jurassic continued to dominate the land well into the Cretaceous, flowering plants (angiosperms) were to take over rapidly (figure 11.15).

During the Early Cretaceous, conifers stole dominance from the cycads, thus ending the Jurassic "age of cycads." But about 100 million years ago, near the end of the Early Cretaceous, angiosperms first appeared, and by the Late Cretaceous they were more diverse than the conifers. Today there are about 100,000 species of angiosperms and only about 550 species of conifers.

FIGURE 11.14

During the Cretaceous, reefs like this cliff-forming one were built by rudist clams.

FIGURE 11.15

Flowering plants first appeared near the end of the Early Cretaceous, and by the end of the Cretaceous, as shown here, they dominated the landscape.

© Doug Henderson

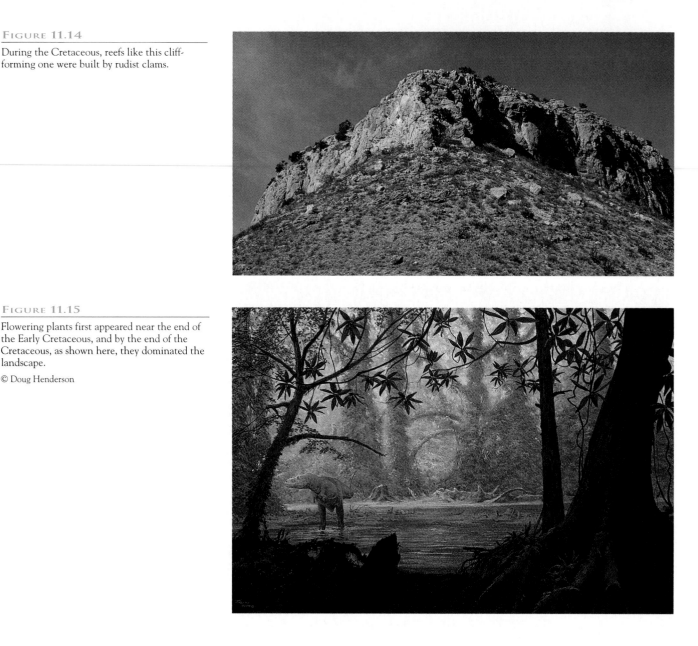

DINOSAURS AND OTHER VERTEBRATES

Dinosaurs of the Early Cretaceous differed somewhat from those of the Late Jurassic. Ornithopods (for example, *Iguanodon*) were generally larger, and sauropods were smaller. Nodosaurid ankylosaurs first became common, whereas stegosaurs virtually disappeared. Indeed, by the end of the Early Cretaceous, iguanodontid and hypsilophodontid ornithopods and sauropods (except in South America) had joined the stegosaurs in practically becoming extinct. Most other land vertebrates of the Early Cretaceous were rather similar to those of the Late Jurassic, but significant changes took place among mammals. Specifically, placental and marsupial mammals first appeared near the end of the Early Cretaceous.

A major change in global climate and vegetation took place during the Early Cretaceous, so it is not difficult to understand the profound transition in dinosaurs that we see between the end of the Jurassic and the beginning of the

FIGURE 11.16

By the Late Cretaceous, Laurasia and Gondwana were almost completely fragmented and sea level was elevated worldwide.

Middle Cretaceous. Dominant Late Jurassic dinosaurs, the sauropods, stegosaurs, hypsilophodontids, and iguanodontids, gave way to a totally different **dinosaur fauna,** a transition that occurred in the Early Cretaceous.

MIDDLE AND LATE CRETACEOUS: THE LAST DINOSAURS

Dinosaurs of the Middle and Late Cretaceous, 100 to 65 million years ago, were very different from the dinosaurs of the earlier portions of Mesozoic time. New types of dinosaurs appeared during the Middle and Late Cretaceous, many of them plant eaters probably better adapted to feeding on angiosperms than were the plant-eating dinosaurs of the Late Jurassic. These new types of dinosaurs dominated the landscape until all dinosaurs became extinct at the end of the Cretaceous.

GEOGRAPHY AND CLIMATE

By Late Cretaceous time, Gondwana had separated into its constituent continents, and Laurasia was split significantly by the enlarging of the northern Atlantic Ocean basin (figure 11.16). Sea level was at an all-time high, and most of the continents were drowned by epicontinental seas.

Climates worldwide were hot and wet like a greenhouse. Tropical and subtropical zones are estimated to have extended as far poleward as 45° N and 70° S. Indeed, one paleontologist has aptly described the Late Cretaceous world as "wall-to-wall Jamaica." Near the end of the Cretaceous, however, this began to change as the sea level fell again.

FIGURE 11.17

Mosasaurs were giant marine lizards of the Middle and Late Cretaceous.

LIFE IN THE SEA

The Middle and Late Cretaceous seas saw the continuing diversification of modern types of marine life—certain plankton, bony fishes, crabs, and snails—that had begun to diversify during the Early Cretaceous. It also saw the end of some very successful groups, including the ammonoids and the rudist and inoceramid (platelike) clams. A group of marine animals unique to the Middle and Late Cretaceous was the mosasaurs (figure 11.17), large marine lizards that were also at the top of food chains in the Middle and Late Cretaceous seas.

VEGETATION

Flowering plants diversified rapidly during the Middle and Late Cretaceous. By the end of the Cretaceous, they had virtually replaced the gymnosperms as the dominant land plants.

DINOSAURS AND OTHER VERTEBRATES

Dinosaurs of the Middle and Late Cretaceous were mostly hadrosaurid ornithopods, ceratopsians, ankylosaurs, and tyrannosaurid and coelurosaurian theropods. Sauropods were common only in South America. These dinosaurs coexisted with turtles, crocodiles, lizards, mammals, and other, generally smaller vertebrates. These dinosaurs were generally not as large as some of those of the Late Jurassic, but they appear to have been more diverse and were very widespread (figure 11.18, box 11.2).

BOX 11.2

CRETACEOUS DINOSAURS FROM ANTARCTICA

Dinosaur fossils have long been known from all the continents except Antarctica. But this changed in 1986, when scientists from Argentina discovered fragmentary remains of an ankylosaur in Upper Cretaceous rocks on James Ross Island off of the Antarctic Peninsula. Three years later, British scientists discovered fossils of a hypsilophodontid from nearby Vega Island. In 1994, American paleontologists reported the discovery of *Cryolophosaurus*, a crested theropod, from Jurassic strata in the Transantarctic Mountains, about 650 km from the South Pole.

The meager record of Antarctic dinosaurs probably will grow with further exploration. But it already is of importance because it documents nearly polar dinosaurs in the southern hemisphere during the Late Cretaceous.

Due to the drifting of the continents, reconstructions of the position of Antarctica during the Late Cretaceous suggest that the Antarctic dinosaur localities were then just north of 60° S, which is only a few degrees north of their present location. There is no evidence that there was a polar ice cap in Antarctica during the Late Cretaceous. But because of the tilt of the Earth's axis, Antarctica would have experienced months of virtual darkness during the Late Cretaceous winters, just as it does today. This polar winter would have been a cold one, even during the Late Cretaceous when there was no Antarctic ice cap.

How did dinosaurs, which we usually think of as warm-weather animals, survive in Antarctica during the Late Cretaceous? Two possibilities exist. One is that contrary to popular belief, dinosaurs were not just warm-weather animals, but were warm-blooded, like living mammals and birds, and thus could endure very cold temperatures. The evidence for warm-blooded dinosaurs, however, is very debatable (see Chapter 15). A more likely solution to the problem of Antarctic dinosaurs may be that dinosaurs did not live there all year-round, but undertook seasonal migrations, as birds do today.

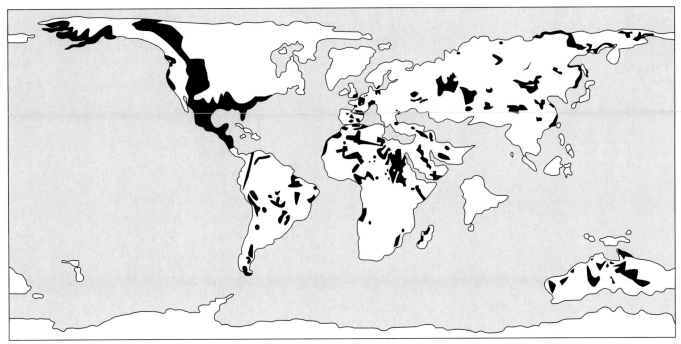

❭ Cretaceous rocks

FIGURE 11.18

Rocks containing the fossils of Late Cretaceous dinosaurs have a worldwide distribution.

TABLE 11.1   THE FIVE DINOSAUR FAUNAS

		Fauna	Theropoda	Sauropodomorpha	Ornithopoda	Thyreophora	Marginocephalia
Cretaceous	Late	5	Carnosauria: (Tyrannosauridae) Coelurosauria: (Ornithomimosauridae) (Dromaeosauridae) (Oviraptorosauridae)		Hadrosauridae	Ankylosauria: Ankylosauridae	Neoceratopsians: Protoceratopsidae Ceratopsidae Pachycephalosauria
Cretaceous	Early	4		Sauropoda: Small Sauropods (Titanosaurids)	Large Ornithopods: Iguanodontidae	Ankylosauria: Nodosauridae Stegosauria: A few Stegosaurids	Psittacosaurs
Jurassic	Late	3	Carnosauria: (Allosauridae)	Sauropoda: Large Sauropods	Medium Ornithopods: Hypsolophodontidae Iguanodontidae	Stegosauria: Large Stegosaurids	
Jurassic	Middle / Early	2		Sauropoda: Small Sauropods (Cetiosaurids)	Small Ornithopods: Hypsilophodontidae	Stegosauria: Small Stegosaurids Primitive Thyreophorans	
Triassic	Late	1	Ceratosauria Also Primitive Saurischians	Prosauropods	Primitive Ornithischians		

FIVE DINOSAUR FAUNAS

If we think of each successive and distinct association of dinosaurs during the Mesozoic as a dinosaur fauna, we can recognize five such faunas (table 11.1):

1. The Late Triassic dinosaur fauna, dominated by relatively small meat eaters and plant eaters with some large prosauropods

2. The Early and Middle Jurassic dinosaur fauna consisting mostly of sauropods, stegosaurs, and small ornithopods

3. The Late Jurassic dinosaur fauna, generally similar to that of the Early and Middle Jurassic, but including the largest dinosaurs and allosaurids

4. The transitional, Early Cretaceous dinosaur fauna, in which ankylosaurs and large ornithopods dominated, whereas the numbers of sauropods and stegosaurs dwindled

5. The Middle and Late Cretaceous dinosaur fauna dominated by hadrosaurs, ceratopsians, ankylosaurs, coelurosaurs, and tyrannosaurids

These five dinosaur faunas reflect changing environments and organisms throughout the 160 million years of the age of dinosaurs. They thus indicate that much evolution and extinction of dinosaurs took place during the Mesozoic.

SUMMARY

1. Dinosaurs appeared during the Late Triassic when all the continents were united in a single supercontinent, Pangaea.

2. Climates on Late Triassic Pangaea were warm and monsoonal, and the vegetation was dominated by ferns and gymnosperms.

3. Dinosaurs were not the dominant land vertebrates of the Late Triassic; thecodonts were.

4. Thecodonts and many other land vertebrates became extinct at or just before the end of the Triassic.

5. Dinosaurs established themselves as the dominant land vertebrates by the end of the Middle Jurassic.

6. Early and Middle Jurassic dinosaurs were mostly prosauropods, sauropods, and stegosaurs.

7. The Late Jurassic was the golden age of dinosaurs; the largest dinosaurs lived then, and sauropods, stegosaurs, hypsilophodontids, and allosaurids were the dominant dinosaurs.

8. During the Early Cretaceous, dinosaurs were in transition as vegetation changed and world climate became wetter and warmer.

9. The Middle and Late Cretaceous dinosaurs were mostly hadrosaurs, ceratopsians, ankylosaurs, coelurosaurs, and tyrannosaurids.

KEY TERMS

ammonoid
angiosperm
dinosaur fauna
epicontinental sea
equable
Gondwana

greenhouse
gymnosperm
ichthyosaur
labyrinthodont
Laurasia
monsoonal
Pangaea

Panthalassa
plesiosaur
rauisuchian
rudist
Sanmiguelia
Tethys Sea

REVIEW QUESTIONS

1. Describe world geography during the Late Triassic and how it changed during the age of dinosaurs.

2. How did world climate change during the age of dinosaurs?

3. What major changes in vegetation took place during the age of dinosaurs? How might these changes have influenced dinosaur evolution?

4. What were the five dinosaur faunas of the age of dinosaurs, and how did they differ from each other?

FURTHER READING

Behrensmeyer, A. K., Damuth, J. D., DiMichele, W. A., Potts, R., Sues, H.-D., and Wing, S. L. 1992. *Terrestrial Ecosystems through Time.* Chicago: The University of Chicago Press. 568 pp. (Provides a detailed review of Mesozoic terrestrial vegetation, animal life and climate on pp. 327–72.)

Benton, M. J. 1986. The Late Triassic tetrapod extinction events; in Padian, K., editor, *The Beginning of the Age of Dinosaurs.* Cambridge, England: Cambridge University Press. pp. 303–20. (A technical review of the Late Triassic extinctions.)

Colbert, E. H. 1965. *The Age of Reptiles.* New York: W.W. Norton & Co., 228 pp. (Somewhat outdated, but otherwise an excellent review of Mesozoic life.)

Dodson, P. 1990. Counting dinosaurs: how many kinds were there?: *Proceedings of the National Academy of Science,* vol. 87, pp. 7608–12. (A technical examination of changing dinosaur diversity during the Mesozoic.)

Fastovsky, D. E. 1989. Dinosaurs in space and time: the geological setting; in Culver, S. J., editor, *The Age of Dinosaurs.* Knoxville, Tennessee: The Paleontological Society [Short Courses in Paleontology Number 2]. pp. 22–33. (Reviews the geological setting of dinosaurs with emphasis on North America.)

Hallam, A. 1965. *Jurassic Environments.* London: Cambridge University Press. 269 pp. (Provides an overview of the Jurassic world.)

Russell, D. A. 1989. *An Odyssey in Time: The Dinosaurs of North America.* Toronto: University of Toronto Press. 240 pp. (A colorful review of the geological and environmental context of North American dinosaurs.)

Sereno, P. C. 1995. Dinosaurs and drifting continents: *Natural History,* vol. 104, no. 1, pp. 40–47. (Discusses recently discovered Cretaceous dinosaurs from Africa and their significance to continental drift).

Stanley, S. M. 1989. *Earth and Life Through Time* (second edition). New York: W.H. Freeman & Co. 689 pp. (Chapters 15 and 16 review the Mesozoic world and its life.)

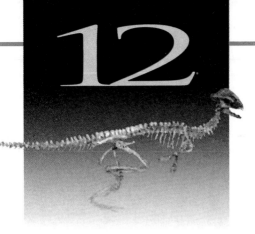

DINOSAUR HUNTERS

The history of the discovery of dinosaurs is full of adventure. Fantastic discoveries, exotic places, physical hardships, danger, and dynamic personalities are just some of the elements of this history. Sometimes it is easy to lose sight of the fact that what we know about dinosaurs is the result of nearly two centuries of collecting dinosaur fossils by amateurs and professionals worldwide. It is their discoveries, beginning in the 1820s, that have shaped scientific views about dinosaurs. Indeed, if we examine both the history of dinosaur discoveries and the history of scientific ideas about dinosaurs, there is a notable correlation. New discoveries have led to new ideas, so that ideas about dinosaurs have changed dramatically since the 1820s.

This chapter does not present a comprehensive history of the discovery and collection of dinosaurs. That history merits a book all its own, and is well told in the books listed as "Further Reading" at the end of this chapter. Instead, the focus here is on how dinosaur discoveries have shaped scientific ideas about the "terrible lizards."

EARLIEST DISCOVERIES

The scientific study of dinosaurs began in England during the 1820s, although it is clear that many cultures, such as the ancient Chinese, had encountered dinosaur bones long before then. The first dinosaur to be described scientifically was the theropod **Megalosaurus** (see Chapter 6), named by British geologist and naturalist **William Buckland** (1784–1856) in 1824. However, two years earlier, Mary Ann Mantell, the wife of British country doctor **Gideon Mantell** (1790–1852), discovered dinosaur teeth and bones in Sussex. In 1825, Mantell named those fossils (figure 12.1) **Iguanodon,** because they resemble the teeth of a living iguana (*odont* is Greek for tooth).

Neither Buckland nor Mantell knew the fossils they described as dinosaurs, but they did recognize them as the remains of large, extinct reptiles. Similar, fragmentary fossils of reptiles continued to be found in Britain through the 1830s. These included a partial skeleton of an armored reptile named **Hylaeosaurus** by Mantell in 1833, as well as other fragments that formed the basis for the names *Cetiosaurus, Poekilopleuron,* and *Thecodontosaurus.*

At that time, the foremost authority on fossil reptiles in Britain was **Richard Owen** (1804–1892), a comparative anatomist who worked for most of his career at the Royal College of Surgeons and, later, the British Museum of Natural History, both in London (figure 12.2). In 1842, Owen published a comprehensive review of British fossil reptiles in the *Report of the British Association for the Advancement of Science*. There, Owen coined the term **Dinosauria,** from the Greek roots *deinos*, "terrible," (Owen actually meant "fearfully great") and *sauros*, "lizard" or "reptile." Owen included *Megalosaurus, Iguanodon,* and *Hylaeosaurus* in the Dinosauria, but

FIGURE 12.1

These lithographs of teeth of *Iguanodon* are from Mantell's original 1825 article.

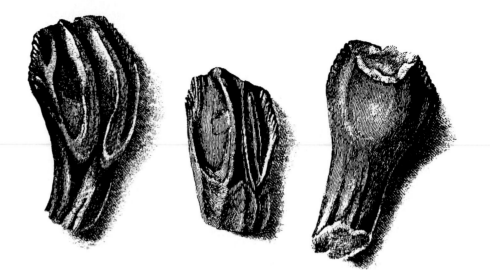

FIGURE 12.2

Richard Owen coined the word Dinosauria in 1842.

Courtesy The Natural History Museum (Neg. #T02985/N)

other British fossil reptiles known to him and subsequently shown to be dinosaurs, were excluded. For example, Owen identified the theropod *Poekilopleuron* as a crocodile, the prosauropod *Thecodontosaurus* as a lizard, and the sauropod *Cetiosaurus* as a gigantic marine crocodile. Owen characterized dinosaurs as having teeth set in bony sockets, large sacra composed of five fused vertebrae, ribs with two heads, a complex shoulder girdle, long hollow limb bones, and mammal-like feet. In fact, Owen saw several of the features of dinosaurs as more mammal-like than reptile-like, and he even speculated that dinosaurs had hearts and respiratory systems very similar to those of living mammals.

Yet, despite Owen's comparisons of dinosaurs to mammals, his work and that of his contemporaries produced a very reptilian image of the dinosaurs. This image, the first comprehensive scientific view of the dinosaurs, emerged in the 1850s through Owen's collaboration with artist and sculptor **Benjamin Waterhouse Hawkins.** Between 1852 and 1854, this collaboration produced various paintings by Hawkins (figure 12.3) and, most notably, several life-size sculptures of dinosaurs for the grounds of the Crystal Palace exhibition center at Sydenham, now a London suburb, where they still stand (see figure 18.4). As a publicity stunt just before the sculptures were unveiled, Hawkins organized a dinner for 20 scientists held inside the hollow body of the life-size *Iguanodon*.

The Owen-Hawkins collaboration produced images of dinosaurs as bulky, lizard- and toad-like brutes. These images differ greatly from current concepts of dinosaurs and are demonstrably wrong. But to be fair to Owen, Hawkins, and their contemporaries, we need to remember the context that produced these incorrect restorations of dinosaurs. First, let us remember that not a single complete skeleton of a dinosaur had yet been discovered in 1854. Thus, many aspects of dinosaur size, shape, and appearance were necessarily highly speculative. In fact, the most complete dinosaur skeleton available to Owen was a very incomplete *Iguanodon* that had been found in a quarry at Maidstone in Kent. Mantell had studied this skeleton and used it to reconstruct a complete skeleton of *Iguanodon* (figure 12.4). A spike of bone that was part of this skeleton was placed by Mantell on the nose of the dinosaur and also appears there on Hawkins's sculpture. But the discovery of complete *Iguanodon* skeletons at Bernissart, Belgium in 1878 (see box 8.2), revealed this to be a thumb, not a nose spike.

Because Owen and his contemporaries lacked complete dinosaur skeletons, they filled in the gaps from their knowledge of living reptiles, especially lizards and crocodiles. This knowledge was also heavily colored by an image of reptiles as stupid and sluggish brutes, prejudices that are still with us (see box 15.1).

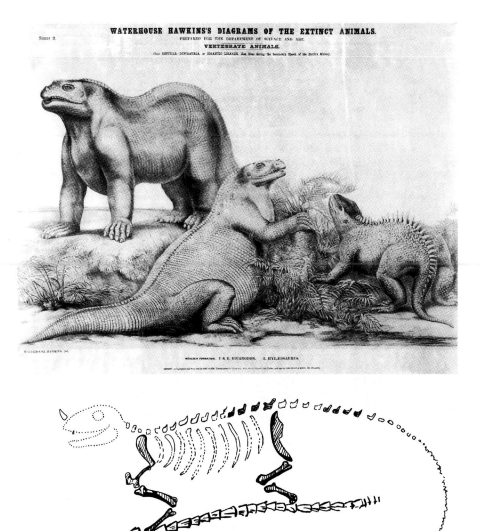

WATERHOUSE HAWKINS'S DIAGRAMS OF THE EXTINCT ANIMALS.
PREPARED FOR THE DEPARTMENT OF SCIENCE AND ART.
VERTEBRATE ANIMALS.

Iguanodon

FIGURE 12.3

Benjamin Waterhouse Hawkins created these images of dinosaurs.

Courtesy The Natural History Museum (Neg. #T045151N)

FIGURE 12.4

Mantell reconstructed the skeleton of *Iguanodon* with the thumb spike on the dinosaur's nose.

The incomplete knowledge of dinosaurs and prejudices about living reptiles inspired the Owen-Hawkins restorations of dinosaurs during the 1850s. What emerged was the concept of ponderous, dim-witted, and terrible lizards, or "dinosaurs as reptiles."

COMPLETE SKELETONS

The first dinosaur fossils brought to scientific attention in North America were teeth found in 1855 in what is now Montana. They were studied by **Joseph Leidy** (1823–1891), a Philadelphia anatomist who is considered the founder of vertebrate paleontology in the United States. Leidy (figure 12.5) was familiar with British publications on dinosaurs, and he recognized the similarities between the teeth from Montana and those of *Megalosaurus* and *Iguanodon*. The names Leidy coined for the Montana teeth included **Deinodon,** "terrible tooth," and **Trachodon,** "rough tooth," and these were the first North American dinosaurs to be described scientifically.

FIGURE 12.5

Joseph Leidy is shown here with the femur of *Hadrosaurus*.

But a far more significant discovery was in store for Leidy much closer to home. In 1868, he examined a partial skeleton of a dinosaur found by a farmer digging in a marl pit near Haddonfield, New Jersey. This was the most complete skeleton of a dinosaur yet discovered, and Leidy christened it **Hadrosaurus,** "heavy lizard."

The Haddonfield skeleton had nearly complete forelimbs and hind limbs, and Leidy realized that the dinosaur must have been an upright biped, not a sprawling quadruped like the Owen-Hawkins *Iguanodon*. This change in dinosaur posture was soon reflected in a life-size model of *Hadrosaurus* in New York's Central Park constructed in 1868 by Benjamin Waterhouse Hawkins.

The skeleton of *Hadrosaurus* may have forced some rethinking of the posture and appearance of dinosaurs by 1870. But a true revolution in scientific understanding was to take place between 1870 and 1900 because of the discovery of many more nearly complete dinosaur skeletons.

These skeletons came from western North America during what has been called the **"great dinosaur rush."** The many dinosaur skeletons were primarily collected for and studied by two paleontologists, **Edward Drinker Cope** (1850–1897) and **Othniel Charles Marsh** (1831–1899). Cope (figure 12.6) was born into a wealthy Quaker family, was a protégé of Leidy, though largely self-taught, and worked and lived mainly in Philadelphia, where he used his family fortune to support his paleontological research. Marsh (see figure 12.6) was trained primarily in Europe and was the first professor of paleontology at Yale University, where he started the Peabody Museum of Natural History. It was named after his wealthy uncle, George Peabody, who underwrote many of Marsh's paleontological endeavors.

Neither Cope nor Marsh personally collected many dinosaurs themselves. Instead, they employed collectors who scoured much of the American West, from the Dakotas to New Mexico, discovering and collecting dinosaurs and many other

FIGURE 12.6

Edward Drinker Cope (left) and Othniel Charles Marsh (right), scientific rivals, studied most of the dinosaur fossils discovered during the "great dinosaur rush" of the nineteenth century.

(*left*) Courtesy Ewell Sale Stewart Library, Academy of Natural Sciences of Philadelphia
(*right*) Courtesy John Ostrom, Yale Peabody Museum

fossils, then shipping them back to Cope in Philadelphia, and Marsh in New Haven for preparation, study, and description. For a variety of reasons, a tremendous personal rivalry arose between Cope and Marsh, as each tried to outdo the other in paleontological discoveries. This rivalry, which began in the early 1870s, lasted until Cope's death in 1897. It benefited paleontology by fueling the discovery of many new fossils, but it also led Cope and Marsh to sometimes publish their research too hastily and make many unnecessary mistakes.

Tremendous new dinosaur discoveries, particularly by Marsh's collectors, brought to science many new types of dinosaurs and complete skeletons. Thus, Marsh first described some of the best-known dinosaurs, Jurassic giants such as *Stegosaurus*, *Brontosaurus*, and *Allosaurus*, from the dinosaur quarries worked by his collectors at **Como Bluff** in Wyoming. Indeed, beginning in 1891, Marsh published remarkably accurate reconstructions of the nearly complete skeletons of many of the dinosaurs his collectors had discovered (figure 12.7). Furthermore, Marsh proposed a comprehensive classification of the dinosaurs in 1882 (see box 6.1). His terminology, reconstructions, and ideas vitally shaped scientific conceptions about dinosaurs. His collectors, some of whom went on to become paleontologists themselves (box 12.1), also discovered many new types of dinosaurs.

Cope devoted less attention to dinosaurs than did Marsh, but his collectors' discoveries were also very significant. And Cope was more willing to speculate on the appearance and habits of the dinosaurs than was Marsh. So, we find Cope introducing the idea that sauropods were aquatic in 1897 (see figure 7.19) and directing artist **Charles R. Knight** to draw two active and agile fighting theropods (see figure 18.7). Indeed, the scientific legacy of Cope and Marsh's ideas about dinosaurs is well summed up in the artwork of Charles R. Knight.

Knight painted and sculpted dinosaurs largely in collaboration with paleontologist **Henry Fairfield Osborn** (1857–1935), a protégé of Cope who founded the Department of Vertebrate Paleontology at the American Museum of Natural History. After Cope and Marsh died, the "great dinosaur rush" continued, partly financed by the American Museum of Natural History. **Barnum Brown** (1873–1963) collected dinosaurs for the American Museum all over the American West. And one of Cope's collectors, **Charles Hazelius Sternberg** (1850–1943), collected dinosaurs freelance for many museums, especially in Alberta, Canada, and New Mexico. Indeed, it would be fair to say that Brown and Sternberg (figure 12.8) collected more dinosaurs than anyone else in history.

FIGURE 12.7

Marsh published many very accurate reconstructions of dinosaur skeletons, some of which are shown here.

From Edwin H. Colbert, *The Great Dinosaur Hunters and Their Discoveries*. Copyright © 1984 Edwin H. Colbert. Reprinted by permission of Dover Publications, Inc., Mineola, NY.

BOX 12.1

JOHN BELL HATCHER

John Bell Hatcher (box figure 12.1) began his paleontological career as one of O. C. Marsh's hired collectors and went on to become an outstanding paleontologist in his own right. Born in 1861 in Virginia, Hatcher was raised on a farm and as a young man worked in a coal mine to save money for a college education.

In 1884, Hatcher received a bachelor's degree in geology from Yale College and was immediately hired by Marsh to collect fossils. Although Hatcher collected fossils for Marsh until 1893, the relationship between the two men was rough. They squabbled often over Hatcher's salary and over the nature and schedule of Hatcher's duties. Yet, despite the bickering, Hatcher made truly amazing discoveries for Marsh, many of fossil mammals in what are now the states of

Wyoming and South Dakota. His great dinosaur discoveries were made during the field seasons of 1889 to 1892, when he collected the skulls and skeletons of 50 (!) ceratopsians in eastern Wyoming (see box 10.2). Most of these were of *Triceratops*, and even now represent much of what we know about that dinosaur.

After Hatcher left Marsh's employ, his dinosaur-collecting days ended. He participated in mammal fossil-collecting expeditions to Argentina from 1896 to 1899 and shortly thereafter took a position at the Carnegie Museum of Natural History. Hatcher had been a sickly child, and as an adult he suffered from rheumatoid arthritis and various other maladies. His death, from typhoid fever in 1904, at the age of 42, cut short the career of one of America's most promising paleontologists.

BOX FIGURE 12.1

John Bell Hatcher.

FIGURE 12.8

Barnum Brown (left) and Charles Hazelius Sternberg (right) were the greatest dinosaur collectors of all time.

Photos Courtesy Department of Library Services, American Museum of Natural History

Primarily through the artistry of Charles R. Knight, the dinosaurs available to Osborn and his colleagues at the beginning of this century produced an image of dinosaurs fundamentally different than the Owen-Hawkins collaboration. Multiple skeletons allowed for accurate, upright postures and body shapes in dinosaurs. Huge, bipedal theropods and strange, armored ankylosaurs, stegosaurs, and ceratopsians were not extrapolations from a handful of bones, but real animals based on many articulated skeletons. Yet, despite the huge increase in knowledge of dinosaurs since 1854, their image as ponderous, dim-witted brutes (figure 12.9) remained. True, there

FIGURE 12.10

Louis Dollo's reconstruction of the skeleton of
Iguanodon was based on more than two dozen
complete skeletons from Bernissart.

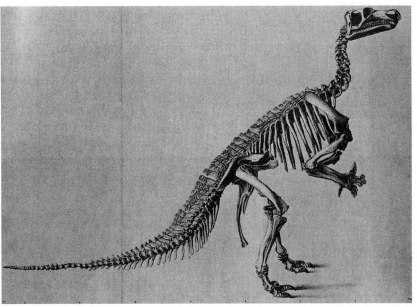

were exceptions, such as the Cope-Knight fighting theropods (see figure 18.7), but
dinosaurs as reptiles, with all the supposed negative reptilian attributes, remained
the predominant scientific view.

It would be incorrect to think that all the great discoveries and new ideas
about dinosaurs between the 1850s and the early 1900s took place only in North
America. Dinosaurs continued to be collected in Europe, and in 1878 complete
skeletons of *Iguanodon* were discovered in **Bernissart, Belgium** (see box 8.2). Belgian
paleontologist **Louis Dollo** (1857–1931) studied these fossils, and provided a reconstruction of *Iguanodon* (figure 12.10) fundamentally different from the early attempts
of Mantell, Owen, and Hawkins.

Ideas about other aspects of dinosaur science were not confined to North
America, either. For example, in 1887 British paleontologist **Harry G. Seeley**
(1839–1909) proposed a classification of dinosaurs that divided them into two
groups: Saurischia and Ornithischia. This classification (see Chapter 2) differed from
those of Cope and Marsh (figure 12.11), but is the one still used today.

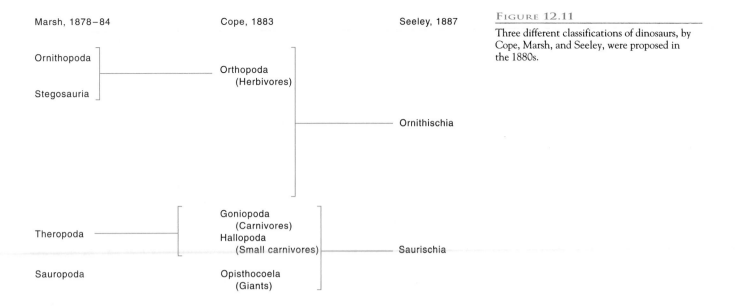

Marsh, 1878–84	Cope, 1883	Seeley, 1887

Ornithopoda

Stegosauria

Orthopoda
(Herbivores)

Ornithischia

Theropoda

Goniopoda
(Carnivores)
Hallopoda
(Small carnivores)

Sauropoda

Opisthocoela
(Giants)

Saurischia

FIGURE 12.11

Three different classifications of dinosaurs, by Cope, Marsh, and Seeley, were proposed in the 1880s.

FIGURE 12.12

Werner Janensch, with local field workers, is shown here collecting dinosaurs in East Africa.

Courtesy Museum Für Naturkunde, Berlin

In many ways, the science of dinosaur paleontology came into its own during the second half of the nineteenth century. The discovery of a variety of dinosaurs, and especially of articulated, essentially complete dinosaur skeletons, made this possible. But the emphasis remained on the reptilian nature of the dinosaurs, even though a more thorough knowledge of their anatomy was available.

TWO GREAT EXPEDITIONS

It is fair to say that scientific opinions about dinosaurs did not change significantly between the turn of the century and World War II. Much time was still spent analyzing the products of the great dinosaur discoveries of the previous half century, and new discoveries continued to be made, such as Barnum Brown's discovery of *Tyrannosaurus rex* in Montana in 1902. Whatever new ideas arose in dinosaur science between 1900 and 1945 were largely the result of two great expeditions.

The first of these took place between 1907 and 1912 at **Tendaguru Hill** in what was then German East Africa and is now Tanzania. These expeditions were led by German paleontologists **Werner Janensch** and Edward Hennig, who brought

BOX 12.2

THE STORY BEHIND THE CENTRAL ASIATIC EXPEDITIONS

The principal purpose of the Central Asiatic Expeditions, which collected fossils in the Gobi Desert in 1922, 1923, 1925, 1928, and 1930, was not to collect dinosaurs. Instead, the expeditions were initiated because Henry Fairfield Osborn believed that the origin of humankind was to be found in Asia.

Roy Chapman Andrews (box figure 12.2), who was the leader of the Central Asiatic Expeditions, first went to China in 1916 to collect living mammals for the American Museum of Natural History. The idea of collecting fossils in Asia came to Andrews only in 1919, when he met a Swedish geologist, Johan Gunnar Andersson (1874–1960). Andersson was employed by the Chinese government as a mining geologist and adviser. As an adjunct to his official duties, which began in 1914, Andersson amassed an extensive collection of archaeological materials and mammal fossils in eastern China. This collection must have impressed Andrews, who later discussed it with Osborn. Osborn was also aware of a fossil human tooth bought from a Chinese druggist and described by German paleontologist Max Schlosser in 1903. Schlosser boldly suggested, largely on the basis of this fossil, that the origin of humankind was to be found in Asia, a suggestion heartily endorsed by Osborn. Thus, Schlosser's and Andersson's fossils and theories about human origins and the bold, adventurous spirit of Andrews provided the basis for the Central Asiatic Expeditions. Ironically, no human fossils were found, but a large number of other fossil mammals, as well as dinosaurs and dinosaur eggs were discovered.

BOX FIGURE 12.2

Roy Chapman Andrews.

Courtesy Department of Library Services, American Museum of Natural History (Neg. #410927)

thousands of bones of Jurassic dinosaurs, including several nearly complete skeletons, back to Berlin (figure 12.12). The Tendaguru dinosaurs included articulated skeletons of a new dinosaur, then the largest land animal of all time, the gigantic sauropod *Brachiosaurus*. Tendaguru dinosaurs also included several types, such as *Brachiosaurus* itself, also known from the western United States. This provided a dinosaur based stratigraphic correlation (see box 3.2) and demonstrated a broader geographic distribution for some dinosaurs than had previously been suspected. Most importantly, the extensive dinosaur collections from Tendaguru demonstrated that significant dinosaur collections could be made in parts of the world outside of Europe and western North America.

The second great dinosaur expedition (actually a series of expeditions) of the first half of this century further emphasized that great dinosaur finds were waiting outside of Europe and North America. This series of expeditions, the **Central Asiatic Expeditions** of the American Museum of Natural History, led by **Roy Chapman Andrews,** collected fossils in the **Gobi Desert** of China and Mongolia during the 1920s and 1930s. Although the primary purpose of the expedition was not to collect dinosaurs (box 12.2), workers unearthed a rich lode of them in the Cretaceous beds of the Gobi, including the primitive ceratopsian *Protoceratops*, and the small theropods *Oviraptor* and *Velociraptor*, among others. Most famous of the discoveries of the Central Asiatic Expeditions, however, were the nests of dinosaur eggs discovered at Bayn-Dzak, Mongolia (figure 12.13).

These expeditions, like the German efforts at Tendaguru, brought to light new types of dinosaurs and new information about dinosaur biology and distribution, all of which significantly added to our scientific understanding of dinosaurs. New analyses of dinosaurs, such as Swedish paleontologist Carl Wiman's 1923 interpretation of the hollow tube on the head of the hadrosaurid *Parasaurolophus* as a

FIGURE 12.13

Dinosaur eggs were discovered by the Central Asiatic Expeditions at the "flaming cliffs" of Bayn-Dzak, Mongolia.

Courtesy Department of Library Services, American Museum of Natural History (Neg. #410767)

resonating chamber, also appeared in the first half of the twentieth century. But the overall image of dinosaurs did not change from that at the turn of the century. Dinosaurs as reptiles, as viewed by Cope, Marsh, and Osborn and as painted by Charles R. Knight, remained substantially intact.

THE CALM BEFORE THE STORM?

Curiously, dinosaur paleontology was relatively quiet between the 1940s and the early 1970s. Dinosaurs continued to be collected during this time, and some outstanding discoveries were made, such as the skeletons of hundreds of *Rioarribasaurus* found in Upper Triassic strata in northern New Mexico by the American Museum in the late 1940s. Other Triassic dinosaurs were discovered in Brazil and Argentina, and dinosaur collecting became a worldwide activity, with important discoveries made in such far-flung locales as southern Africa, India, and China. Between 1947 and 1949, Soviet paleontologists led expeditions back to Mongolia and uncovered many new Cretaceous dinosaurs. These and other discoveries helped to fill in scientific understanding of the dinosaurs and the world they inhabited, but they did not fundamentally alter the prevailing, turn-of-the-century view of dinosaurs as reptiles.

Proof of this is best seen in the work of two men, Czechoslovakian artist **Zdenek Burian** and American paleontologist **Edwin H. Colbert.** Burian's paintings of dinosaurs, many painted during the 1950s (figure 12.14), show the heavy influence of Charles R. Knight, and well reflect turn-of-the-century ideas about dinosaur biology and behavior. Colbert, an outstanding researcher on dinosaurs and other reptiles, wrote many popular books on dinosaurs from the 1940s through the 1960s. Several of his books featured Knight's paintings and popularized the scientific image of dinosaurs as reptiles.

FIGURE 12.14

This dramatic and often copied painting of *Brachiosaurus* by Zdenek Burian reflects turn-of-the-century ideas about the appearance and behavior of the giant sauropods.

Courtesy Jiri Hochman

THE DINOSAUR RENAISSANCE

Although major new ideas about dinosaurs did not emerge during the 1940s, 1950s, and 1960s, dinosaur science was not dead. Instead, those years were a period when new ideas about dinosaurs were incubating, ready to hatch during the early 1970s.

During the 1960s, the joint **Polish-Mongolian Paleontological Expeditions** revisited the Gobi Desert. Again, new dinosaurs were to be had, especially small and very bird-like theropods. Also during the 1960s, field crews from Yale University, led by paleontologist **John Ostrom,** explored the Lower Cretaceous dinosaur-bearing strata along the Montana-Wyoming border. Their most significant discovery was also a small theropod, *Deinonychus.*

The skeletons of the small theropods from Mongolia and of *Deinonychus* suggested very active and agile animals, quite different from the ponderous, dim-witted brutes of the dinosaurs-as-reptiles image. Furthermore, in the 1970s Ostrom argued persuasively in several scientific publications that dinosaurs were the ancestors of birds (see Chapter 16).

The ideas about highly active and agile theropods and dinosaurs as bird ancestors were clearly not just based on the discoveries and the research of the 1960s. They could also be found in speculations published by some paleontologists as far back as the 1870s. However, in the 1970s, one bold paleontologist, **Robert Bakker,** challenged paleontological orthodoxy by arguing the case for warm-blooded and active dinosaurs that were much more bird-like in their biology and behavior than paleontologists had previously envisioned. Bakker thereby started a dinosaur renaissance that has totally revolutionized the scientific study of dinosaurs. After Bakker's initial proposals, in the last 20 years, paleontologists have used a wealth of new information on the biology of living reptiles, mammals, and birds, as well as new techniques, many computer-aided, to analyze dinosaur fossils.

This renaissance in the study and interpretation of dinosaur fossils continues today. Renewed interest in collecting dinosaurs has resulted in discoveries in Antarctica, Alaska, Australia, and just about every other place that dinosaur fossils might be had. New interpretations of dinosaur phylogeny, rooted in cladistic analysis, prevail. Spirited scientific debate about dinosaur metabolism (see Chapter 15) and the causes of dinosaur extinction (see Chapter 17) are ongoing. Discoveries of nests and baby dinosaurs in Montana (see Chapter 14) and a revitalized interest in dinosaur footprints (see Chapter 13) have produced a wealth of informed speculation about dinosaur behavior. This new research has reshaped our entire scientific view of dinosaurs. The "dinosaurs-as-reptiles" view of ponderous, dim-witted brutes has given way to the view of dinosaurs as fast, active, and agile animals, more akin to living birds, their apparent descendants, than to living reptiles. This view of dinosaurs as bird ancestors has also been brought to life by many talented artists, some of them well schooled in dinosaur science.

The **dinosaur renaissance,** however, has not been without its excesses. Galloping sauropods and feathered theropods have little or no supporting evidence. And, no matter how fast, active, agile, and bird-like dinosaurs may have been, it is impossible to view a 50-ton sauropod as anything other than a huge, slow-moving, powerful, and not particularly brainy animal. New discoveries and new analyses continue to support an image of the dinosaurs, not as the ponderous reptiles of the turn-of-the-century paleontologist, but as bird-like—the most distinctive animals to have ever lived.

CHANGING IDEAS IN DINOSAUR SCIENCE

The history of dinosaur discoveries presented here emphasizes the interplay of discoveries and scientific ideas about dinosaurs. It reveals three distinct concepts of the dinosaurs during the 170 or so years that they have been studied scientifically (figure 12.15).

The first concept, of the 1850s, was based on a very incomplete knowledge of dinosaur anatomy and on a view of living reptiles as slow-moving and stupid. Dinosaurs were seen as huge, ponderous, and dim-witted reptiles.

The second concept emerged by the turn of the century, and was founded on a far more extensive knowledge of dinosaur anatomy. Nevertheless, the idea of dinosaurs as reptiles, however unique dinosaurs as reptiles might have been, remained.

The third, and current concept of dinosaurs emerged during the 1960s. Dinosaurs were seen as fast, active, agile, bird-like animals. This concept is based on new discoveries of bird-like theropods, on a new understanding of the biology of living animals, and on the recognition of dinosaurs as the ancestors of birds.

Which concept is the correct one? Certainly, it is as easy to dismiss the 1850s view of dinosaurs now as it was in 1900. And the turn-of-the-century second concept of dinosaurs is clearly wrong for theropods and in several other ways. Today's concept of dinosaurs stems from the analysis of much more information than did the earlier concepts, so it seems closer to the truth than the older concepts. But what will our concept of dinosaurs be in the next century?

1850s

1920s

1990s

FIGURE 12.15

These three views of *Iguanodon* reflect changing scientific ideas about dinosaurs over more than 150 years.

SUMMARY

1. Dinosaurs first came to scientific attention in Britain during the 1820s.

2. Richard Owen coined the word *Dinosauria*, meaning "terrible lizards," in 1842.

3. The first restorations of dinosaurs, in the 1850s, reflected terribly incomplete knowledge of dinosaur anatomy and prejudices about living reptiles. Dinosaurs were portrayed as ponderous, sluggish, and dim-witted brutes.

4. The "great dinosaur rush" of the 1870s and 1880s in western North America brought to science many more dinosaurs, including nearly complete skeletons, described principally by two American paleontologists, E. D. Cope and O. C. Marsh.

5. By the beginning of the twentieth century, many dinosaurs could be reconstructed with fair accuracy, but scientific views of dinosaurs still stressed their slow-moving and slow-witted reptilian nature.

6. Two great dinosaur-collecting expeditions of the first half of this century—to East Africa in 1907–1912 and to the Gobi Desert during the 1920s and 1930s—brought more dinosaurs to scientific attention, but they did not alter the prevailing view of dinosaurs as reptiles.

7. Between 1940 and 1970, still more dinosaur discoveries were made, but they too failed to alter turn-of-the-century views of dinosaurs as reptiles.

8. A new concept of dinosaurs as fast, active, agile, and bird-like emerged in the 1970s following new discoveries of small theropods, a new understanding of the biology of living animals, and the recognition of dinosaurs as the ancestors of birds.

KEY TERMS

Roy Chapman Andrews
Robert Bakker
Bernissart, Belgium
Barnum Brown
William Buckland
Zdenek Burian
Central Asiatic Expeditions
Edwin H. Colbert
Como Bluff
Edward Drinker Cope
Deinodon
Deinonychus
dinosaur renaissance

Dinosauria
Louis Dollo
Gobi Desert
"great dinosaur rush"
Hadrosaurus
John Bell Hatcher
Benjamin Waterhouse Hawkins
Hylaeosaurus
Iguanodon
Werner Janensch
Charles R. Knight
Joseph Leidy

Gideon Mantell
Othniel Charles Marsh
Megalosaurus
Henry Fairfield Osborn
John Ostrom
Richard Owen
Polish-Mongolian Paleontological
    Expeditions
Harry G. Seeley
Charles Hazelius Sternberg
Tendaguru Hill
Trachodon

REVIEW QUESTIONS

1. What were the first dinosaurs described in Europe? In North America? Who described them?

2. Who introduced the term *Dinosauria* and what does it mean?

3. What was the scientific evidence behind the Owen-Waterhouse dinosaur sculptures?

4. How did the "great dinosaur rush" influence scientific understanding of dinosaurs?

5. What was the turn-of-the-century scientific image of the dinosaurs, and why did that image remain unchanged until the 1970s?

6. How did the two great dinosaur-collecting expeditions of the first half of this century contribute to our knowledge of dinosaurs?

7. What is the current concept of dinosaurs and on what is it based?

FURTHER READING

Colbert, E. H. 1984. *The Great Dinosaur Hunters and Their Discoveries*. Mineola, New York: Dover Publications Inc., 283 pp. [republication of the 1968 book *Men and Dinosaurs*]. (The most extensive history of dinosaur collecting through the 1960s.)

Desmond, A. J. 1979. *The Hot-Blooded Dinosaurs*. New York: The Dial Press, 238 pp. (An excellent history of changing ideas about dinosaurs.)

Horner, J. R. and Gorman, J. 1988. *Digging Dinosaurs*. New York: Workman Publishing, 210 pp. (The story of the discovery of dinosaur nests and babies in Montana.)

Kielan-Jaworowska, Z. 1969. *Hunting for Dinosaurs*. Cambridge: MIT Press, 177 pp. (The story of the Polish-Mongolian paleontological expeditions.)

Ostrom, J. H. and McIntosh, J. S. 1966. *Marsh's Dinosaurs*. New Haven: Yale University Press, 388 pp. (The history of collecting at Como Bluff and many previously unpublished lithographs of Jurassic dinosaurs prepared for O. C. Marsh.)

Owen, R. 1842. Report on British fossil reptiles: *Report of the British Association for the Advancement of Science*, vol. 11, pp. 60–204. (The word *Dinosauria* is coined on p. 103.)

Sternberg, C. H. 1985. *Hunting Dinosaurs in the Bad Lands of the Red Deer River, Alberta, Canada*. Edmonton: NeWest Press, 235 pp. [republication of the 1932 second edition of the original book]. (The story of Sternberg's work in Canada and many other locales.)

DINOSAUR TRACE FOSSILS

When we think of dinosaur fossils, what comes to mind are the complete skeletons that are the mainstays of the world's great natural history museums. To collect dinosaurs does mean unearthing such skeletons, or at least finding a skull or some bones. But there is also an important record of dinosaurs preserved in their trace fossils—skin impressions, footprints, eggs, gizzard stones (gastroliths), and feces (coprolites) (figure 13.1). Such "trace fossils" (though, technically speaking, only the tracks and skin impressions are trace fossils) provide important evidence of dinosaur behavior and distribution that significantly augments the information gleaned from studying their bones (body fossils). The last two decades have witnessed a resurgence in the study of dinosaur trace fossils, particularly footprints. In this chapter we evaluate the behavioral and distributional significance of dinosaur footprints, eggs, gastroliths, and coprolites. Dinosaur skin impressions are discussed in Chapter 14.

Skin impressions

Stomach stones (gastroliths)

Eggs

Nests

Tracks

Fossilized feces (coprolites)

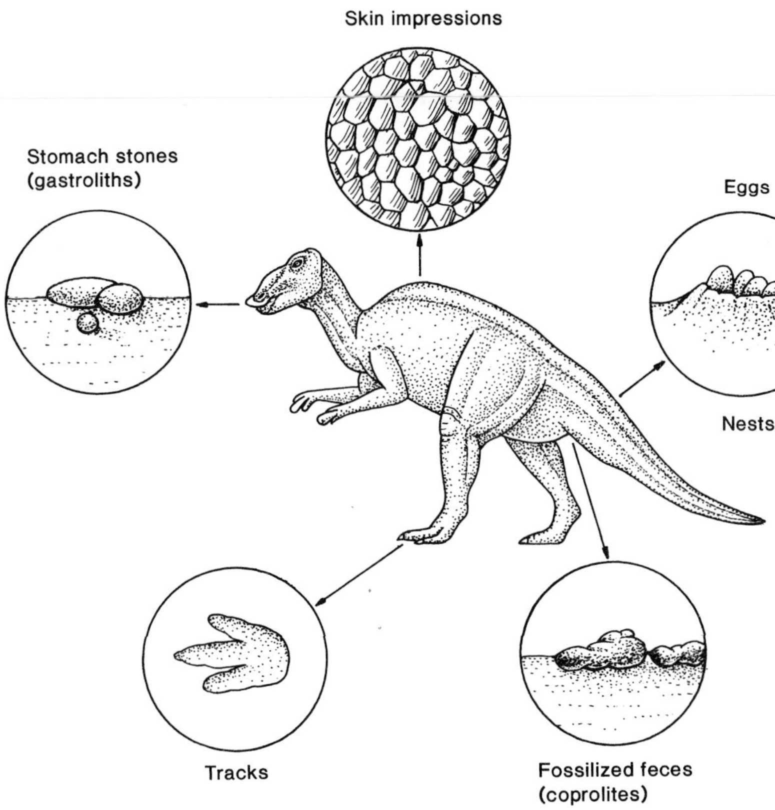

FIGURE 13.1

Dinosaur fossils include skin impressions, footprints, eggs, gastroliths, and coprolites. Technically speaking, only the tracks and skin impressions are trace fossils.

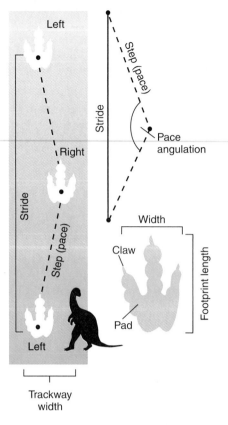

FIGURE 13.2

A sequence of footprints is a trackway. Pace, stride, and pace angle can usually be measured from a dinosaur trackway.

DINOSAUR FOOTPRINTS

Dinosaur footprints have been discovered in Upper Triassic through Upper Cretaceous rocks and on all the continents except Antarctica. Indeed, in many regions dinosaur footprints are often the only dinosaur fossils known. They also provide important information about the posture, gait, foot structure, speed, and social behavior (see Chapters 7 and 14) of dinosaurs that cannot be learned from a study of their skeletons alone. In order to interpret dinosaur footprints, we must first understand how they are identified and learn some associated terminology.

UNDERSTANDING DINOSAUR FOOTPRINTS

A dinosaur **footprint** results from the interaction between the structure of a living dinosaur's foot and the land surface (substratum) upon which it walked. A series of consecutive footprints of an individual dinosaur is a trackway, and this is an obvious example of "fossilized behavior." To understand this behavior, we must first measure the **trackway** and each footprint, thus calculating the foot length, stride, and **pace lengths,** and pace (or step) angles (figure 13.2). These measurements and the shapes of the footprints themselves provide the basis for identifying the dinosaur that made them.

Identifying dinosaur footprints begins by matching them with the known foot structures of dinosaur skeletons (figure 13.3). For example, the three-toed footprints of some theropod and ornithopod dinosaurs seem rather similar, but theropod footprints can be easily distinguished by their long, slender toes, claws and lack of "heel" impressions, features absent in ornithopod footprints (figure 13.4).

The problem with matching dinosaur footprints to skeletons is that many footprints are known for which no matching skeletons exist. There is also the problem of the distinctiveness of dinosaur feet and footprints. For example, many types of hadrosaurid dinosaurs are distinguished by little more than their different skull shapes. As far as paleontologists can determine, the feet of these different hadrosaurids were of essentially one uniform structure. This means that hadrosaurid footprints are of no use in distinguishing different types of hadrosaurids that are told apart by skull shapes. Despite this, distinctive dinosaur footprint types may be recognized in certain deposits, even though the identity of the footprint-maker remains unknown.

FIGURE 13.3

Dinosaur foot skeletons can sometimes be matched to footprint shapes.

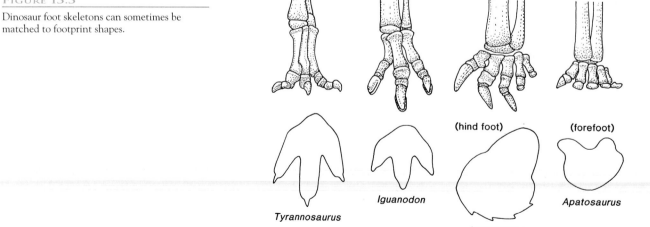

Tyrannosaurus

Iguanodon

(hind foot)

Apatosaurus

(forefoot)

Apatosaurus

BOX 13.1

A THEROPOD FOOTPRINT BY ANY OTHER NAME

Latinized scientific names are given not just to body fossils, but to trace fossils as well. This is especially true of dinosaur footprints, for which hundreds of different names have been proposed. Unfortunately, many paleontologists who proposed names for types of dinosaur footprints failed to consider variation in footprint size and shape during an individual dinosaur's life span. They also failed to consider variation in the substratum upon which the dinosaur walked, as well as variation in a dinosaur's speed and gait. These sources of variation can produce rather different looking footprints, even though only one type of dinosaur, or even a single dinosaur individual, made the footprints (box figure 13.1A).

The result of this failure to consider variation has been a plethora of names for dinosaur footprints, many of them synonyms. Perhaps no footprints have suffered more from such naming than those of theropods. Such footprints belong to bipedal dinosaurs with three toes bearing long claws that touched the substratum. They range in age from Late Triassic to Late Cretaceous and have been described from all the continents except Antarctica. A variety of names is still applied to them, even when the sources of variation discussed above are considered (box figure 13.1B). Such names are useful in discussing theropod footprint distribution, but paleontologists should be cautious and take into account the many possible sources of variation before naming theropod and other dinosaur footprints.

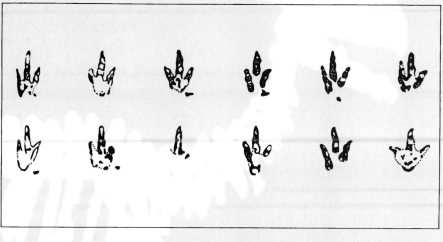

BOX FIGURE 13.1A

These theropod footprints from a single trackway show remarkable variation in shape.

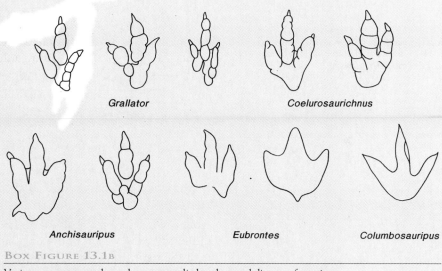

Grallator   *Coelurosaurichnus*

Anchisauripus   *Eubrontes*   *Columbosauripus*

BOX FIGURE 13.1B

Various names, some shown here, are applied to theropod-dinosaur footprints.

Because of the need to discuss different types of dinosaur footprints in a concise way, distinctive types of dinosaur footprints are given Latinized scientific names similar to, but not the same as, the names assigned to dinosaur body fossils. These names, however, were sometimes created without considering various factors that affected the shapes of the footprints (box 13.1).

The most important of these factors is that a footprint represents the interaction of a foot with the substratum. In other words, the type of substratum, and where in the substratum the footprint is preserved, can very much affect the footprint's shape (figure 13.5). It is particularly important to recognize that a dinosaur footprint may be the original footprint on the surface of the substratum or one of a

FIGURE 13.4

Theropod and ornithopod footprints are somewhat similar but can be distinguished by the features shown here.

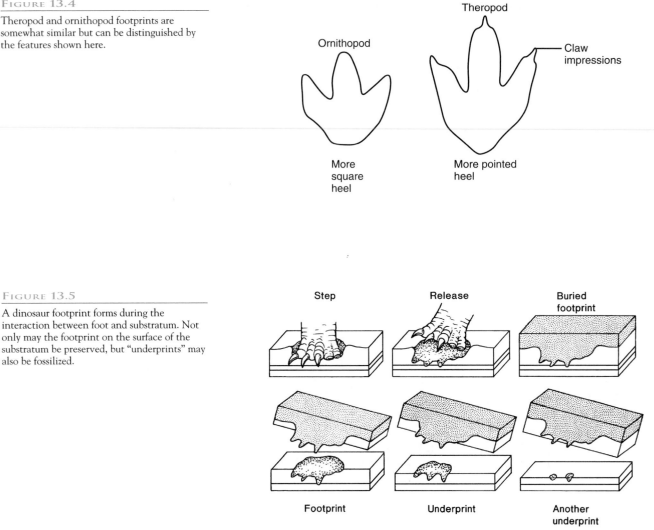

FIGURE 13.5

A dinosaur footprint forms during the interaction between foot and substratum. Not only may the footprint on the surface of the substratum be preserved, but "underprints" may also be fossilized.

series of "underprints" in all the sediment layers underneath the surface that were disturbed by the weight of the dinosaur. The underprints can look quite different from the surface footprint, so we need to be careful to distinguish footprints from underprints when naming dinosaur footprints.

INTERPRETING DINOSAUR FOOTPRINTS

Dinosaur footprints document the former presence of dinosaurs in places, time intervals, and environments where dinosaur-body fossils are often absent. Footprints also provide important evidence about the posture and gait of dinosaurs. For example, the footprints of theropods confirm the erect posture and bipedality of these dinosaurs inferred by studying their skeletons, but the footprints of ankylosaurs and ceratopsians (figure 13.6) may suggest more upright forelimb postures and gaits than have been inferred by studying their limb structures. This has been a source of debate over the posture and gaits of these dinosaurs (see box 10.1). Perhaps the most important piece of information paleontologists derive from studying dinosaur footprints is an estimate of dinosaur speed (box 13.2). Footprints are the only reliable information from which to obtain such estimates.

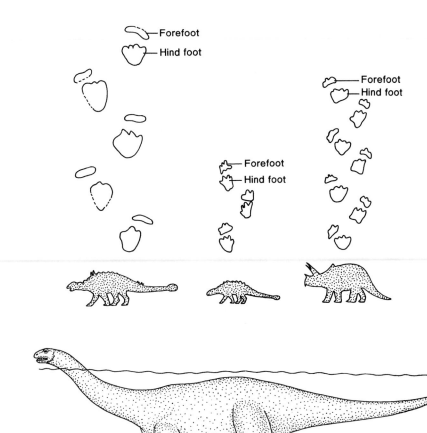

FIGURE 13.6

These trackways of ankylosaurs and of a ceratopsian suggest more erect forelimb postures than do studies of their bones.

FIGURE 13.7

The original interpretation of a swimming sauropod (above) has been reexamined to show that most of the footprints are underprints (below).

FOOTPRINT MYTHS

Although much important information comes from studying dinosaur footprints, many myths and misconceptions about dinosaurs are also based on footprints. Foremost among these are supposed human footprints associated with dinosaur footprints (box 13.3) and the idea that sauropods were aquatic.

The idea of swimming sauropods is based on footprints of Early Cretaceous age along the Paluxy River near Glen Rose, Texas, studied by paleontologist Roland T. Bird during the 1930s and 1940s. In a 1941 article, Bird analyzed the trackway of a single sauropod that consists almost entirely of shallow forefoot impressions. Bird explained the lack of hind-foot impressions as a result of the sauropod's hindquarters being buoyed up in fairly deep water so that only its front feet touched the bottom (figure 13.7).

BOX 13.2

SPEED ESTIMATES FROM DINOSAUR FOOTPRINTS

Dinosaur speed can be estimated from footprints using a method developed by British researcher R. MacNeill Alexander. Here's how it's done. A **stride** is the distance from one point on a footprint to the same point on the next print of the same foot (see figure 13.2). When dinosaurs walked, they took short strides; when dinosaurs ran, they took longer strides. Long-legged dinosaurs, of course, took longer strides than smaller ones, whether walking or running. So we can't simply use stride length to estimate dinosaur speeds, because a longer-legged dinosaur, such as *Tyrannosaurus*, would take longer strides than a shorter-legged dinosaur, such as *Ornithomimus*, when both dinosaurs were walking (or running). Instead, we eliminate the effect of leg length on speed in order to use stride length to estimate a dinosaur's speed. This is most easily done by dividing the length of the dinosaur's stride by its leg length to arrive at the relative stride of the dinosaur:

$$\text{Relative stride} = \frac{\text{length of stride (in meters)}}{\text{leg length (in meters)}}$$

In this calculation, leg length is the distance from the hip joint to the ground when the dinosaur is in a normal standing posture. Note that relative stride is dimensionless (not a length in meters) because dividing stride length in meters by leg length in meters eliminates the dimension.

But how do we determine the leg lengths of dinosaurs that left only fossil footprints? Measuring the leg lengths of complete dinosaur skeletons and then trying to match them to footprints might seem to be the most direct approach. This, however, is seldom possible because deciding which skeletons correspond to which footprints is never obvious. Furthermore, many footprints cannot be matched to the feet of known dinosaur skeletons. Nevertheless, measurements of skeletons of a wide variety of dinosaurs indicate that their feet are about one-fifth as long as their legs. In other words, a *Tyrannosaurus* with a foot (or footprint) length of 0.64 meters had a leg length of 5 × 0.64

meters = 3.2 meters. If the footprints of this *Tyrannosaurus* showed a stride of 4.16 meters, then its relative stride would be the stride length divided by leg length: 4.16/3.2 = 1.3.

Now that we can calculate the relative stride of any dinosaur, we need a way to convert relative stride into an estimate of movement speed. To do so, we need to examine the relationship between relative stride length and speed in living animals, such as mammals. This is done by measuring the relative strides of mammals clocked at different speeds during walking and running. When measuring speed, however, we face the problem that larger animals move faster than smaller ones, even if they have the same relative strides. This is similar to the stride and leg-length problems faced earlier.

To resolve this problem, we need to divide the actual speed of the mammal by some dimension of body size, in this case the square root of leg length × gravitational acceleration. (The use of this dimension of body size is dictated by the laws of physics.) This gives us a value called **dimensionless speed.**

$$\text{Dimensionless speed} = \frac{\text{actual speed (in meters per second)}}{\sqrt{\begin{array}{l}\text{leg length (in meters)} \times \text{gravitational}\\ \text{acceleration (in meters per second}^2)\end{array}}}$$

(Use the square root key on your pocket calculator to calculate the denominator.) Dimensionless speed thus allows us to estimate equivalent speeds despite the size (dimensions) of an animal.

The relationship between relative stride and dimensionless speed for living mammals (box figure 13.2) produces a trend that accords with intuition. The longer the relative stride, the faster the dimensionless speed. It also allows us to estimate dinosaur speeds simply by finding the dimensionless speed for a living mammal that corresponds to the relative stride length of the dinosaur (see box figure 13.2). For the relative stride length of the *Tyrannosaurus* mentioned earlier, 1.3, the dimensionless speed is 0.4. To estimate the actual speed of the dinosaur, we can plug this value into the equation for dimensionless speed, and solve that equation for actual speed.

Recent careful reexamination of this sauropod trackway, however, reveals that most of the sauropod footprints are underprints. A hindfoot impression is also present. This discounts the evidence of swimming sauropods based on the Texas footprints.

DINOSAUR EGGS

Dinosaur **eggs** were first discovered in France in 1869, but the most famous dinosaur eggs were those discovered in Mongolia in 1923 (figure 13.8). Today, dinosaur eggs are best known from the Upper Cretaceous of Asia and the western United States, though they have also been described from France, Spain, India, and Argentina, the oldest being of Late Triassic age.

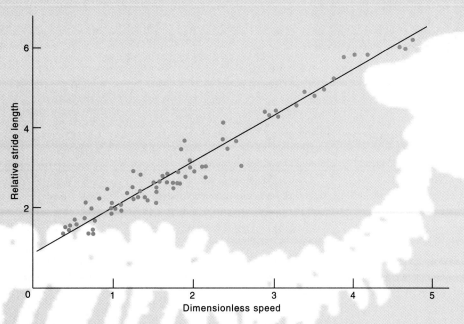

BOX FIGURE 13.2

This plot of relative stride length against dimensionless speed is based on data from living mammals and ostriches. Note that both axes of the plot are dimensionless.

Source: Data from R. McNeil Alexander, *Dynamics of Dinosaurs and Other Extinct Giants*, Columbia University Press, 1989.

Dimensionless speed = $\dfrac{\text{actual speed}}{\sqrt{\text{leg length} \times \text{gravitational acceleration}}}$

Actual speed = $\dfrac{\text{dimensionless speed} \times}{\sqrt{(\text{leg length} \times \text{gravitational acceleration})}}$

Note that gravitational acceleration = 10 meters per second^2.

So

Actual speed = $0.4 \times \sqrt{2.56 \text{ meters} \times 10 \text{ meters/second}^2}$

Actual speed = 2 meters/second (about 4.5 miles per hour)

This is a brisk walk for a human. Applying this method to a variety of dinosaur trackways produces estimated speeds that range from walks to fast runs of as much as 43 kilometers/hour (a 4-minute mile is 25 kilometers/hour) by some theropods (see table 13.1). Some trackways thus document very fast dinosaurs, which helps to dispel the old idea that dinosaurs were slow, lumbering behemoths. Most trackways, however, record normal walking speeds—presumably because this was the typical mode of progression among dinosaurs.

Other ways of estimating dinosaur speeds have been devised. These methods are not strictly based on footprints because they rely on body-weight estimates, angulation of the limbs, and other factors requiring skeletal information. The method presented here simply relies on footprints and measurements (length of foot and of leg) easily derived from them.

Dinosaur eggshells were composed of organic matter and an inorganic mineral, crystalline calcium carbonate, as in the eggshells of living reptiles and birds. The well-organized, interlocking crystals of calcium carbonate made the dinosaur eggshell rigid, and thus gave it a good chance of being fossilized. The fact that few dinosaur eggs are known that are older than Late Cretaceous has led some paleontologists to speculate that many primitive dinosaurs may have laid soft-shelled eggs lacking an extensive mineral matrix.

The shapes of dinosaur eggs vary considerably, ranging from spherical to almost cylindrical (figure 13.9). Some kinds of dinosaurs had eggs with characteristic mineral textures, and some eggs contain well-preserved embryos or are closely associated with the skeletons of hatchling and/or adult dinosaurs. These circumstances allow most dinosaur eggs to be identified as those of a particular type of dinosaur.

BOX 13.3

DID HUMANS WALK WITH DINOSAURS?

Most of us have heard claims of human footprints found with dinosaur footprints. Such claims contradict what we know from the body fossil record, namely that dinosaurs became extinct 65 million years ago, more than 60 million years before humans evolved. Most of these claims come from one of the great dinosaur footprint localities, the limestone bed of the Paluxy River, just west of the town of Glen Rose in Somervell County, Texas.

There, thousands of footprints of Early Cretaceous theropod and sauropod dinosaurs have been studied by paleontologists since the first investigations by Roland T. Bird of the American Museum of Natural History in the 1930s. However, the first supposed human footprints associated with these dinosaur footprints were found in 1910. Since that time, many "human footprints" have been discovered and studied, especially by so-called "creation scientists" intent on overturning the standard paleontological interpretation of Earth history. Indeed, the "human footprints" from near Glen Rose have figured prominently in books and films by creationists who assert that humans and dinosaurs lived side by side.

During the 1980s, qualified paleontologists carefully reexamined the "human footprints" from near Glen Rose. They found that most of them were not footprints at all, but erosional features only remotely similar to human footprints. Others were actually eroded bipedal dinosaur footprints. And some of the "human footprints" were manmade—chiselled in rock—and are not even accurate replicas of a human foot (box figure 13.3). Indeed, we now know that several residents of Glen Rose have, over the years, supplemented their incomes by carving human-like footprints for sale to unsuspecting passersby.

Careful scientific scrutiny reveals that no authentic human footprints are associated with dinosaur footprints near Glen Rose or anywhere else. There

BOX FIGURE 13.3
A human footprint carved in Glen Rose, Texas during the 1930s.

Courtesy Glen J. Kuban

remains absolutely no evidence that humans walked with the dinosaurs.

FIGURE 13.8
This nest of dinosaur eggs was discovered in Mongolia in 1923. Originally identified as *Protoceratops* eggs, they are now known to belong to a small theropod.

Courtesy Department of Library Services, American Museum of Natural History (Neg. #410765)

TABLE 13.1 DINOSAUR SPEEDS

Dinosaurs	Number of trackways	Height at hip (m)	Velocity (km/hr)
Sauropods	2	1.5–3.0	4
Ornithomimid	1	1.2	6
Ornithopods	10	<1.0	16
Ornithopod	1	1.2	7
Ornithopods	5	1.0–1.2	6–10
Ornithopods	2	0.2–0.6	2–3
Ornithopod	1	0.9	7
Ornithopods	3	1.0–2.6	4–6
Ornithopod	1	1.8	4
Theropods	2	0.4–0.6	5–8
Theropods	10	<1.0	13
Theropods	15	1.2–1.9	6–43
Theropods	2	1.5–2.1	5–10
Theropod	1	0.6	10
?Theropods	2	1.0–1.2	8
Theropod	1	1.4	10
?Theropods	4	1.0–1.2	6–9
?Theropods	7	0.8–1.3	4–8
Theropods	17	0.8–1.5	5–16
Theropods	8	1.5–2.3	3–9
Theropod	1	1.6	8
Theropod	1	1.1	8
Theropods	3	0.6	7–8
Theropods	3	0.3–1.2	2–11
Theropod	1	1.1	7

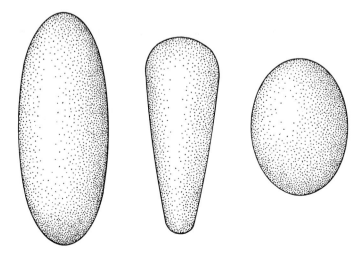

FIGURE 13.9

Shape and size of dinosaur eggs vary considerably.

FIGURE 13.10

These polished (left) and unpolished (right) cross sections of a hypsilophodontid egg show some of the bones of the embryonic dinosaur.

Courtesy Museum of the Rockies

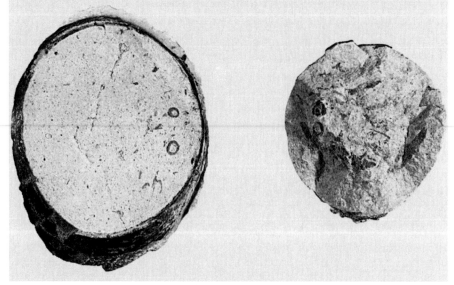

The largest dinosaur eggs, those of sauropods, were more than 30 cm long. Eggs are known from most dinosaur groups, including theropods, prosauropods, sauropods, ceratopsians, and ornithopods. However, only ornithopod eggs have been described as containing well-preserved embryos. It is reasonably certain that all dinosaurs reproduced by laying eggs.

The eggs of some dinosaurs were laid in hollow mounds or in shallow pits. The sizes of the clutch varied, but as many as 20 eggs in one clutch have been documented for the hadrosaurid *Maiasaura*. Some clutches appear to have been laid in **nests** that also contain hatchlings. A few dinosaur eggs still contain fossilized embryonic dinosaurs inside of them (figure 13.10).

Dinosaur eggs present paleontologists with various types of information. Perhaps most significant is that most, if not all, dinosaurs reproduced by laying eggs. Nests with eggs have also been a source for interpreting the parenting behavior of some dinosaurs (see Chapter 14). Also, dinosaur eggs provide information on dinosaur distribution where dinosaur bones or other trace fossils are not available. Finally, analysis of dinosaur eggs of Late Cretaceous age has figured in speculation about the cause of dinosaur extinction (box 13.4).

DINOSAUR GASTROLITHS

Many living birds and some reptiles swallow stones and hold them in a crop region (gizzard) to grind food to aid digestion. Such gizzard stones, when found with fossils, are called **gastroliths** (from the Greek *gastro*, stomach and *lithos*, rock). Most reports of dinosaur gastroliths are of isolated polished stones from Upper Jurassic and Lower Cretaceous rocks in the western United States that may or may not have been gastroliths. Many different kinds of dinosaur skeletons have been discovered with polished stones in their abdominal cavities, and these stones are undoubtedly gastroliths (figure 13.11).

Highly polished stones found in association with dinosaur skeletons are confidently identified as gastroliths. The stones presumably were polished by grinding against each other and against food while in the dinosaur's crop region. However, similar stones not found associated with dinosaur bones are sometimes also identified as gastroliths. This is particularly true in the Upper Jurassic Morrison Formation of the western United States, where numerous polished stones are often found in

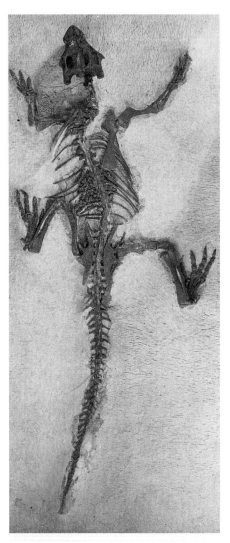

FIGURE 13.11

The polished stones inside the rib cage of this *Psittacosaurus* skeleton are considered gastroliths.

Courtesy Department of Library Services, American Museum of Natural History (Neg. #311488)

BOX 13.4

BRITTLE EGGSHELLS: CAUSE OF DINOSAUR EXTINCTION?

One of the greatest accumulations of dinosaur eggs is in the Upper Cretaceous strata of the Nanxiong basin of southeastern China. Chinese paleontologists there have collected about 20,000 eggshell fragments and about 300 complete eggs, including some found in 24 complete or nearly complete nests. These eggs have been assigned Latin names (box figure 13.4) and are found with very few dinosaur bones. The eggs are from the uppermost Cretaceous sediments in the Nanxiong basin, however, and they must have been laid by dinosaurs during the last few million years before dinosaur extinction. Indeed, in the strata immediately above the dinosaur eggs are found fossils of some of the earliest Tertiary mammals.

Chinese paleontologists and geochemists recently conducted an extensive analysis of the dinosaur egg record from the Nanxiong basin. They found that many of the youngest eggs, those laid just before the extinction of the dinosaurs, had shells that were thin, brittle, and enriched with trace elements such as manganese and strontium. In addition, these fossil eggshells have an unusual ratio of the two common isotopes of the oxygen atom, O^{16} and O^{18}.

The Chinese scientists considered these abnormalities to be the result of dry climates and an excess supply of trace elements in southeastern China at the end of the Cretaceous. They maintained that plant-eating dinosaurs ingested an abnormally high amount of these trace elements, and the dinosaurs that preyed upon them thus also ate the trace elements in high concentrations. The trace elements adversely affected the formation of eggshells by female dinosaurs, making the shells so brittle that they fractured easily and failed to protect the dinosaur embryos inside. In addition, some of the embryos may have died well before hatching because of the excessive amounts of trace elements. The deaths of so many embryonic dinosaurs resulted in greatly reduced dinosaur populations, producing a major extinction, according to the Chinese scientists.

This explanation of dinosaur extinction relies on too long a chain of reasoning. Perhaps the weakest link in the chain is the assumption that the high levels of trace elements in the dinosaur eggshells were concentrated when the eggshells were formed in the bodies of female dinosaurs. It is more likely that the trace elements were introduced and concentrated during the fossilization of the dinosaur eggs. This might also explain the oxygen-isotope ratios in the eggshells. And even though the youngest Cretaceous eggshells are thinner than the older ones, it is not clear that they were too thin to protect the developing dinosaur embryos. It thus is easy to question the conclusion that the dinosaur eggs of the Nanxiong basin provide evidence of a specific cause of dinosaur extinction. Nevertheless, the dinosaur eggs from the Upper Cretaceous of southeastern China do represent an exceptional record, one deserving of much further analysis.

BOX FIGURE 13.4

Fossil dinosaur eggs are abundant in the Upper Cretaceous of the Nanxiong basin in southeastern China as shown by the range bars of the different kinds of eggs in the left portion of the diagram.

Source: Data from "Extinction of the Dinosaurs Across the Cretaceous-Tertiary Boundary in Nanxiong Basin, Guangdong Province" in *Vertebrata PalAsiatica*, 29(1), 1991.

FIGURE 13.12

Were any of these three types of coprolite from
the Upper Triassic of New Mexico produced by
a dinosaur?

clumps in clay or sandstone where no dinosaur bones are present. Regurgitation
of gastroliths by dinosaurs has been suggested to explain why no fossil bones are associated with the stones. On the other hand, perhaps the bones did not mineralize and
become fossilized at those locations, so that only the gastroliths remain as evidence
that a dinosaur once was there. A more likely explanation is simply that these
stones were polished by the action of wind or water. The best association is polished
stones inside the abdominal cavity of an articulated fossil skeleton. If polished
stones are not found associated with dinosaur bones we cannot confidently term
them gastroliths. Indeed, one paleontologist has cleverly labelled such stones
"gastromyths."

Today, living animals swallow stones to relieve hunger pangs, to serve as
ballast while swimming, or to aid in grinding and crushing food. All three possibilities have been invoked to explain why some dinosaurs evidently swallowed stones.
Relief of hunger pangs is difficult to document in a dinosaur, and because dinosaurs
were generally not aquatic animals, it seems unlikely they swallowed the stones for
ballast. If anything, it is most probable that dinosaur gastroliths aided digestion
much as the gizzard stones do in many of today's birds. The fact that many sauropod skeletons contain gastroliths may explain how these tiny-headed behemoths
ground up the vast quantities of vegetation they must have consumed.

DINOSAUR COPROLITES

The term **coprolite,** from the Greek roots *copros* (feces) and *lithos* (rock), is applied
to fossilized feces. Coprolites are known from a wide variety of animals of different
ages ranging from crustaceans to extinct humans. They provide paleontologists
with direct evidence of an extinct animal's diet. But their use is greatly limited
because we are unable, except in rare cases, to link confidently a given coprolite
to the animal that produced it. This limitation especially affects dinosaurs. Few
bona fide dinosaur coprolites have been identified, and there has been little
analysis of them.

Coprolites from a Late Triassic fossil locality in New Mexico provide a good
example of the problems encountered in trying to interpret them. This locality produces bones and teeth of dinosaurs and a variety of other reptiles, large amphibians,
and fishes. Three types of coprolites are present (figure 13.12).

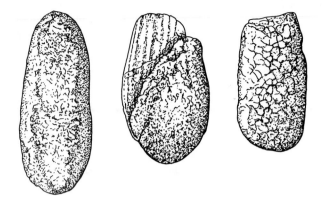

FIGURE 13.13

These dinosaur coprolites are from the Cretaceous of India. The coprolite on the far left is 16.5 cm long; the other two are about 7 cm long.

The most common coprolites are small (up to 2 centimeters long) and cigar-shaped and do not contain noticeable bone fragments or fish scales. The next most common type also lack bone and scale fragments, but have spiral grooves on their surfaces. The third, least common, type of coprolite is much larger than the other two types, and contains bone and scale fragments. What kind of animal produced each type of coprolite and are any of them dinosaur coprolites?

The spiral grooves of the second type of coprolite are typical of fishes. The third type obviously belongs to a fish-eater, but that could be any of several different kinds of reptiles or large amphibians known from the locality. What animal produced the first type of coprolite is unknown, and there is no way to be certain any of the coprolites was produced by a dinosaur.

What we need is a fossil locality where only dinosaur bones are associated with coprolites, or coprolites so large that only dinosaurs could have produced them. Such localities are known, and contain coprolites as large as 29 centimeters long. Known dinosaur coprolites are mostly of predatory dinosaurs. (figure 13.13). This is probably because the feces of these dinosaurs were rich in phosphatic minerals from the undigested bones of their prey and thus fossilized more readily than did the feces of plant-eating dinosaurs, which lacked such minerals.

At present, few dinosaur coprolites have been identified, and little analysis of them has been undertaken. This means that collecting and studying dinosaur coprolites remains a largely untapped field of research that may teach us more about the behavior and diets of dinosaurs.

Summary

1. Dinosaur trace fossils are skin impressions, footprints, eggs, gastroliths, and coprolites.

2. Dinosaur footprints provide important information about dinosaur posture, gait, speed, behavior, and distribution.

3. Estimates of dinosaur speeds from trackways range mostly from walks to fast runs of as much as 43 kilometers/hour for theropods.

4. There are many myths surrounding dinosaur footprints, including the idea that humans walked side by side with dinosaurs, and that sauropods swam in the sea.

5. Dinosaur footprints receive scientific names, but attention is not often paid to several sources of variation when naming dinosaur footprints.

6. Dinosaur eggs are known from most kinds of dinosaurs and indicate that dinosaurs laid hard-shelled eggs like those of living birds.

7. Dinosaur gastroliths can only be identified with certainty when polished stones are found associated with dinosaur skeletons. Dinosaurs probably used gastroliths primarily to crush and grind food.

8. Dinosaur coprolites have been little analyzed, largely because it is difficult to identify the kind of dinosaur that produced a specific coprolite.

Key Terms

coprolite
dimensionless speed
egg
footprint (track)

gastrolith
"gastromyth"
nest
pace (or step) angle

pace length
stride
trackway

Review Questions

1. What are the principal types of dinosaur trace fossils?

2. What types of information can paleontologists obtain from dinosaur footprints?

3. How is the speed of a dinosaur estimated from a trackway?

4. Estimate the speed of a dinosaur with a stride length of 1 meter and a leg length of 1.2 meters.

5. Which dinosaurs laid eggs?

6. What types of information can paleontologists obtain from dinosaur eggs?

7. How are dinosaur gastroliths identified?

8. Why might some dinosaurs have swallowed stones?

9. Why is it difficult to interpret dinosaur coprolites?

FURTHER READING

Alexander, R. McNeill. 1989. *Dynamics of Dinosaurs and Other Extinct Giants*. New York: Columbia University Press, 167 pp. (Chapter 3 explains how to estimate dinosaur speeds from dinosaur footprints.)

Bird, R. T. 1941. Did *Brontosaurus* ever walk on land? *Natural History*, vol. 53, pp. 60–67. (This is the original article on swimming sauropods.)

Carpenter, K., Hirsch, K. F., and Horner, J. R., editors. 1994. *Dinosaur Eggs and Babies*. Cambridge: Cambridge University Press, 372 pp. (Up-to-date technical coverage of dinosaur eggs.)

Gillette, D. D. and Lockley, M. G., editors. 1989. *Dinosaur Tracks and Traces*. Cambridge: Cambridge University Press, 454 pp. (A collection of 50 technical articles on dinosaur footprints and eggs.)

Lockley, M. G. 1991. *Tracking Dinosaurs: A New Look at an Ancient World*. Cambridge: Cambridge University Press, 238 pp. (A very readable introduction to the study and interpretation of dinosaur footprints.)

Lockley, M. G. and Hunt, A. P. 1995. *Dinosaur Tracks and Other Fossil Footprints of the Western United States*. New York: Columbia University Press, 338 pp. (Thoroughly reviews all dinosaur tracks from the western U.S.)

Lockley, M. G. and Rice, A. 1990. Did "*Brontosaurus*" ever swim out to sea?: Evidence from brontosaur and other dinosaur footprints: *Ichnos*, vol. 1, pp. 81–90. (Challenges the idea of swimming sauropods introduced in Bird's 1941 article.)

Manley, K. 1993. Surface polish measurements from bona fide and suspected sauropod dinosaur gastroliths, wave and stream transported clasts: *Ichnos*, vol. 2, pp. 167–169. (Describes a laser technique to distinguish gastroliths from river and beach pebbles.)

Milne, D. H. and Schafersman, S. D. 1983. Dinosaur tracks, erosion marks and midnight chisel work (but no human footprints) in the Cretaceous limestone of the Paluxy River bed, Texas: *Journal of Geological Education*, vol. 31, pp. 111–23. (Thoroughly debunks the "human footprints" associated with Cretaceous dinosaur footprints.)

Mossman, D. J. and Sarjeant, W. A. S. 1983. The footprints of extinct animals: *Scientific American*, vol. 248, pp. 74–85. (A popular introduction to the study of fossil footprints.)

Thulborn, R. A. 1991. Morphology, preservation and palaeobiological significance of dinosaur coprolites. *Palaeogeography, Palaeoclimatology, Palaeoecology*, vol. 83, pp. 341–66. (A technical review of dinosaur coprolites.)

Thulborn, T. [R. A.] 1990. *Dinosaur Tracks*. London: Chapman and Hall, 410 pp. (A comprehensive technical review of dinosaur footprints.)

14

DINOSAUR BIOLOGY AND BEHAVIOR

C hapters 6 through 10 presented a survey of the dinosaurs and many conclusions about their biology and behavior. This chapter summarizes some of that information and explores other aspects of dinosaur biology and behavior. The study of dinosaur soft-tissue (non-skeletal) anatomy and behavior is full of speculation, much of it sensational and unwarranted. Here, we shall take a cautious approach to these subjects, presenting reasonable speculation and avoiding science fiction.

DINOSAUR BIOLOGY

Many aspects of dinosaur biology, especially skeletal anatomy, have already been reviewed in this book, and Chapter 15 discusses the complex subject of dinosaur metabolism. The focus of this chapter is on four topics not discussed elsewhere in this book: dinosaur external appearance, weight, growth, and longevity.

EXTERNAL APPEARANCE

Fossilized **skin impressions** are known for ornithopod, theropod, and ceratopsian dinosaurs. They indicate that the skin of these dinosaurs was covered with scales similar to the scales of some living reptiles (figure 14.1). There is no conclusive evidence that any dinosaur was covered with hair or feathers, although some paleontologists believe that small theropods closely related to birds may have had feathers or a feather-like body covering (see Chapter 16).

The color of dinosaurs is totally a matter of conjecture, because the pigment in their skin and scales did not fossilize. Most paleontologists and artists who create paintings or sculptures of dinosaurs use the color patterns of living reptiles, especially lizards, as a guide to the probable colors of dinosaurs. Some artists, however, paint dinosaurs with very flamboyant, bright color patterns unlike those of most living reptiles. These flashy dinosaurs are eye-catching, but no serious student of dinosaurs views the coloration attributed to any dinosaur as anything but speculation.

The posture and overall body shape of a dinosaur is determined by analyzing its skeleton. Skeletal anatomy is a guide to the size, shape, and configuration of the muscles and provides an understanding of how the dinosaur moved (figure 14.2). Of course, this is old news to the readers of this book. What is not old news, and what is not so certain, is how fat or thin a given dinosaur was, whether or not it had flaps of skin on its neck or head as do some modern lizards and birds, and other features of dinosaur external anatomy that are difficult to predict from skeletal anatomy. It is certain that paleontologists' and artists' view of the external appearance of

FIGURE 14.1

This fossilized skin impression of a hadrosaurid shows reptilian scales. Probably all dinosaurs were covered by such scales.

Courtesy Department of Library Services, American Museum of Natural History (Neg. #35608)

FIGURE 14.2

The dinosaur skeleton provides the basis for reconstruction of the shape, size, and arrangement of muscles.

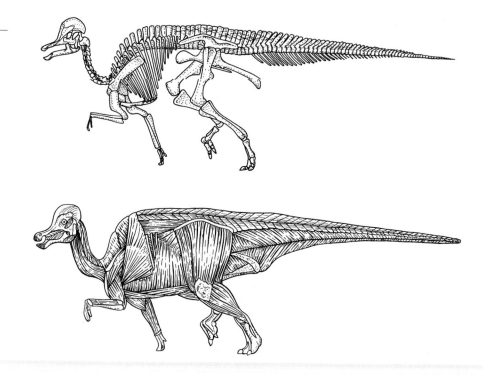

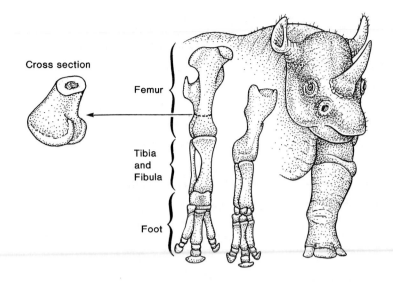

FIGURE 14.3

The cross-sectional area of a limb bone is related to the weight that bone must bear.

Cross section

Femur

Tibia
and
Fibula

Foot

dinosaurs has evolved as new ideas about dinosaur biology and behavior (see Chapter 12) have emerged. Older ideas of sluggish, cold-blooded dinosaurs produced restorations of flabby and lethargic dinosaurs. New ideas of fast, warm-blooded dinosaurs produce renderings of sleek and agile dinosaurs. We can see that ideas about dinosaur external appearance not only involve careful inferences from dinosaur skeletal anatomy, they also require speculation about **coloration** and **soft-tissue anatomy** that cannot be directly inferred from skeletal anatomy. Furthermore, paleontological conceptions about dinosaur biology and behavior have always shaped perceptions of dinosaur external appearance.

WEIGHT

Many popular dinosaur books list weights of dinosaurs. These **weight estimates** are one way to state the size of a dinosaur. Indeed, most dinosaur weight estimates emphasize the very large size of the dinosaurs. How are dinosaur weights estimated?

Two methods are used. One way is measuring the **cross-sectional area** of a weight-bearing limb bone (figure 14.3). The more weight a limb bone bears, the larger its cross-sectional area, and an equation that predicts weight borne from cross-sectional area of a limb bone (usually the femur) can be calculated for living vertebrates. The cross-sectional area of the dinosaur limb bone can be plugged into such an equation.

What is determined, of course, is not the weight of the dinosaur but only the weight supported by the limb bone. A further adjustment upward of this value must be made in order to estimate the dinosaur's body weight. This adjustment depends on the dinosaur's posture and shape, leading to some uncertainty in the weight estimate. Also uncertain is just how applicable the cross-section-to-weight-borne equation is to extinct animals much larger, and presumably heavier, than the living animals from which the equation was originally determined.

Because of these uncertainties, the cross-sectional area method is not the ideal method of estimating a dinosaur's weight. Instead, **scale models** of dinosaurs are the most common way to estimate weights.

Estimating dinosaur weights from scale models is relatively straightforward once a model of known scale (say one-fiftieth the length of the dinosaur) is available. The volume of the model is calculated by displacement of water. That volume is multiplied by the cube of the linear scale of the model so that it becomes the volume of a full-size dinosaur identical in shape to the model. This volume of the

FIGURE 14.4

Different scale models yield different weight estimates of the same type of dinosaur.

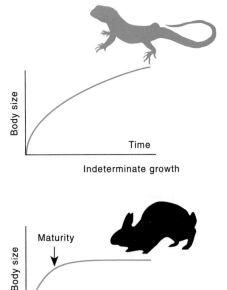

Indeterminate growth

Maturity

Determinate growth

FIGURE 14.5

Living reptiles have indeterminate growth, whereas mammals and birds have determinate growth.

TABLE 14.1	Weight estimates (in approximate metric tons) of some dinosaurs published by two paleontologists, Edwin Colbert and Robert Bakker.	
	Colbert	**Bakker**
Allosaurus	2	1
Tyrannosaurus	7	5
Apatosaurus	31	25
Diplodocus	11	17
Brachiosaurus	78	40
Corythosaurus	4	3
Stegosaurus	2	3.3
Triceratops	8	5

"real" dinosaur is then multiplied by 0.9 kg/liter, which is the mass of a liter of living crocodile, to arrive at a mass (weight) in kilograms (box 14.1).

This method is simple, and it forms the basis of most published dinosaur weight estimates (table 14.1). However, these estimates are only as accurate as the models (figure 14.4). Because we are uncertain exactly how "fleshy" or "lean" dinosaurs were, dinosaur model-making is an imprecise art. Dinosaur weight estimates are full of uncertainty, which is why this book uses skeletal lengths, not weight estimates, to convey the size of a given dinosaur.

GROWTH AND LONGEVITY

Living reptiles grow throughout their lives, although the rate at which they grow decreases as they age (figure 14.5). This type of growth, called **indeterminate growth**, contrasts with the **determinate growth** of mammals and birds. Determinate growth means that after the animal grows to adulthood it stops growing (figure 14.5). In general, rates of determinate growth are faster than those of indeterminate growth (figure 14.6). Another factor affecting growth rate is metabolism; on average, warm-blooded vertebrates grow at least 10 times faster than cold-blooded vertebrates.

BOX 14.1

YOUR OWN ESTIMATES OF DINOSAUR WEIGHTS

Most paleontologists estimate the weights of dinosaurs by using scale models. The more accurate the scale model, the more accurate the weight estimate. You can test this method by using available scale models, such as the plastic dinosaurs you can purchase in a toy store. Here's how to do it.

First, you need the following: solid, waterproof plastic scale models of dinosaurs, a water supply, a calculator, a ruler, and a measuring cup from the kitchen or graduated cylinder from a chemistry lab. The more precisely calibrated the measuring cup or graduated cylinder, the more accurate will be your estimate.

Start by measuring the length of the dinosaur scale model. If your ruler is not metric, convert this measurement into centimeters (1 inch = 2.54 centimeters). Then, determine the actual length of the full-sized dinosaur. Now, divide the length of the actual dinosaur by the length of the model. For a 6.7-meter-long *Stegosaurus* and a 10.2-centimeter-long model, this value is approximately 66, so the model is 1/66th the size of the dinosaur.

Now submerge the model in water to measure its volume (box figure 14.1). Fill the measuring cup or graduated cylinder to a set level, say 5 ounces, or 100 milliliters if the cylinder is metric. Drop in the dinosaur toy. If it doesn't sink, gently push it with your finger or a pen point until it is submerged. Read the new level of the

BOX FIGURE 14.1

The volume of a dinosaur scale model can be determined by measuring the amount of water it displaces. This volume can then be used to estimate the weight of a full-size dinosaur.

water; the difference between it and the original water level is the volume of the scale model. If you must push the model to submerge it, make sure you did not put your finger or the pen point into the water any more than necessary, because that will artificially increase the estimate of the model's volume.

If your estimate of the volume of the model is in fluid ounces, you need to convert it to milliliters (1 fluid ounce = 29.6 milliliters). The 10.2-centimeter-long toy *Stegosaurus* displaces 0.9 ounces or about 27 milliliters.

Now, cube the scale of the model to obtain its cubic scale. The *Stegosaurus* model is 1/66 of the length of the actual dinosaur, so it is $1/66 \times 66 \times 66$ (or 66^3) = 1/287,496 the volume of the actual dinosaur. If we multiply the inverse of this value times the volume of the model we get the volume (in milliliters) of a life-size replica of the toy dinosaur.

So

$$287,496 \times 27 = 7,762,392 \text{ milliliters}$$

Dividing this value by 1,000 converts the volume to liters

$$7,762,392/1,000 = 7,762 \text{ liters}$$

A liter of water weighs 1 kilogram, and the average living crocodile weighs 0.9 kilograms per liter. If we apply this to our *Stegosaurus*, the weight of a dinosaur with a volume of 7.762 liters should be:

$$7,762 \text{ liter} \times 0.9 \text{ kilograms/liter} = 6,986 \text{ kilograms}$$

A metric ton is 1,000 kilograms, so this is about 7 metric tons. One kilogram = 2.2 pounds, so this is 15,369 pounds, or about 7.7 tons.

What type of growth did dinosaurs have, and how long did an individual dinosaur live? These questions are difficult to answer directly from dinosaur fossils because they provide little direct evidence of the age, in years, of an individual dinosaur. (Recent identification of growth rings in some dinosaur bones may change this, but it is difficult to be certain how long a time interval is represented by each ring.) But if we examine dinosaurs for which eggs or hatchlings and full-size adult individuals are known, we can use the growth rates of living vertebrates as a guide.

The ceratopsian *Protoceratops* is a good example. The adult weight of a full-size *Protoceratops* has been estimated, from scale models, to have been 177 kilograms. The estimated weight of the hatchling is 0.43 kilograms, if hatchling weight represents 90 percent of the weight of the egg, which is calculated from egg volume (= 0.5 liter in *Protoceratops*). If the maximum growth rate for living reptiles applies to this dinosaur, it would have taken 26 to 38 years to reach adult size. A similar

FIGURE 14.6

Warm-blooded vertebrates grow faster than cold-blooded vertebrates.

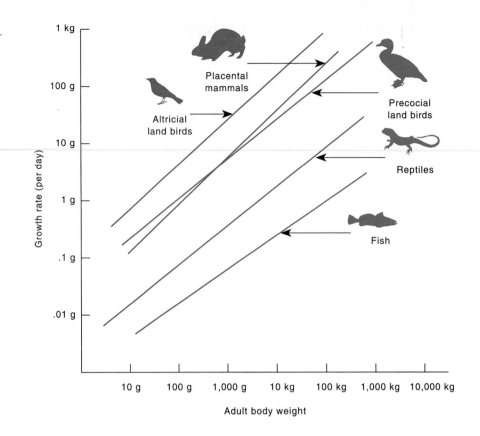

calculation for the European sauropod **Hypselosaurus** (adult weight = 5,300 kilograms, hatchling weight = 2.4 kilograms) indicates 82 to 118 years of growth to reach adulthood. Because much larger sauropods, such as *Brachiosaurus*, weighed four or five times as much as *Hypselosaurus*, the estimated time they would have taken to reach adult size would have been much more than one century, perhaps centuries!

These estimates, of course, assume cold-blooded dinosaurs with reptilian growth rates. But if many dinosaurs were warm-blooded (see Chapter 15), they would have had growth rates comparable to those of living birds and mammals. The time taken by warm-blooded dinosaurs to reach adult size would have been about one-tenth of the estimates given above. *Protoceratops* would have reached adult size in about 3 years, and *Hyselosaurus* would have taken about 10 years. In comparison, living African elephants reach adult size in about 10 years.

Where does this leave us with the question of dinosaur growth rates and longevity? The answer depends on how we view dinosaur metabolism. Because much evidence suggests that many dinosaurs were warm-blooded, dinosaur growth rates and longevity estimates based on living warm-blooded vertebrates are probably correct. This means that it is reasonable speculation that many dinosaurs grew as fast as living warm-blooded vertebrates, and probably lived at least as long as large mammals and birds.

DINOSAUR BEHAVIOR

Although Chapters 6 through 10 discussed many aspects of dinosaur behavior, it is useful to summarize them here and to discuss some subjects mentioned briefly at greater length. Important aspects of dinosaur behavior were feeding and locomotion, reproduction and parenting, attack and defense, and social (group) behavior.

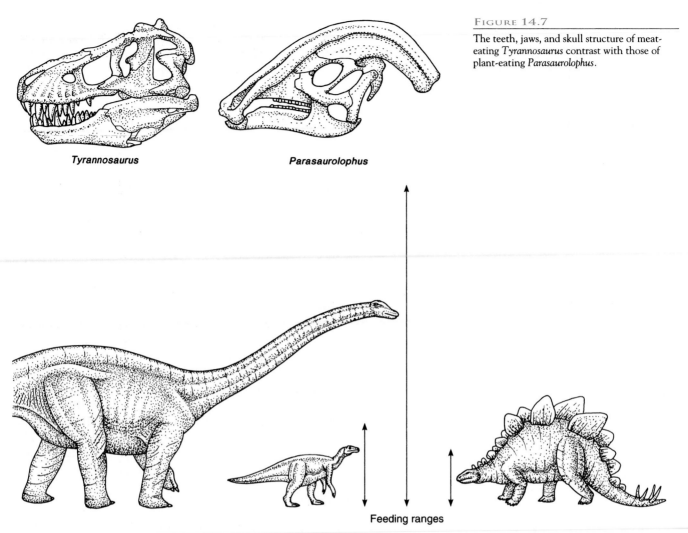

FIGURE 14.7

The teeth, jaws, and skull structure of meat-eating *Tyrannosaurus* contrast with those of plant-eating *Parasaurolophus*.

Tyrannosaurus

Parasaurolophus

Feeding ranges

FIGURE 14.8

Feeding range may provide some clues to the types of plants eaten by some dinosaurs.

FEEDING AND LOCOMOTION

Tooth and jaw structure allow paleontologists to easily distinguish plant-eating from meat-eating dinosaurs (figure 14.7). As we repeatedly saw in Chapters 6 through 10, meat-eating dinosaurs had numerous sharp, serrated, blade-like teeth set in powerful jaws. This was a feeding mechanism designed to stab, tear, and slice flesh. Plant-eating dinosaurs, in contrast, had flatter, leaf-shaped teeth, sometimes arranged in dental batteries, set in massive jaws and skulls. This was a feeding mechanism designed to tear, slice, pulp, and/or grind vegetation. Nevertheless, the feeding of some toothless theropods, such as oviraptorosaurs, and some sauropods, such as diplodocids, is less certain.

It is extremely difficult to determine exactly what kinds of plants or animals a given kind of dinosaur ate. Stomach contents—conifer twigs and needles in hadrosaur mummies, a lizard in *Compsognathus*, and so forth—provide some direct evidence. Gut contents even indicate some meat-eating dinosaurs resorted to cannibalism (box 14.2). Inferences of the **feeding range** of plant-eating dinosaurs—how far above the ground the dinosaur could crop vegetation—suggest some specific types of plant food that may have been favored by different kinds of dinosaurs (figure 14.8). But preserved gut contents are not known for most dinosaurs, and inferences about feeding narrow little the range of possible plant foods. So it remains difficult to identify the specific food items most dinosaurs ate.

BOX 14.2

Dinosaur Cannibals

Cannibalism (animals that devour their own kind) is common among some living predators such as sharks and crocodiles. Evidence of cannibalism exists for some predatory dinosaurs. Most impressive are skeletons of the small ceratosaur **Coelophysis** found at the Upper Triassic Ghost Ranch dinosaur quarry in northern New Mexico. Two of these skeletons have stomachs full of the bones of juvenile *Coelophysis* (box figure 14.2).

We might conclude that these are the bones of young, unborn *Coelophysis* in their mothers' wombs. But, because all evidence indicates dinosaurs reproduced by laying eggs, this conclusion seems unlikely. Instead, cannibalism—the larger *Coelophysis* ate the smaller ones—seems the most reasonable conclusion.

Today, cannibalism occurs in many predatory reptiles and mammals. Most often, a reptile or mammal will eat younger individuals of its species when hungry, simply because they are easy to capture. This may seem cruel, but it may actually make sense in situations where the population density of young

BOX FIGURE 14.2

This juvenile skeleton (stippled bones) of a *Coelophysis* is inside the rib cage of an adult individual.

reptiles/mammals is very high and/or other food is difficult to catch.

The two relatively large adult individuals of *Coelophysis* from Ghost Ranch with small juvenile *Coelophysis* in

their stomachs fits the modern pattern of reptilian cannibalism. Clearly, cannibalism has a long antiquity, at least 210 million years, and may have been common among theropod dinosaurs.

One of the principal reasons most animals, including dinosaurs, move (locomote) is to obtain food. Dinosaur **locomotion** has been discussed at various points in this book, and we can draw some general conclusions.

Dinosaur skeletons indicate, almost without exception, that they were ground-dwelling walkers and runners. There is no strong evidence that any dinosaur was arboreal (lived in trees), although some paleontologists speculate that some small theropods may have been tree climbers. Other than some hadrosaurids, no compelling argument can be presented that any dinosaur was aquatic (living in the water). Indeed, as we saw in Chapter 7, earlier ideas that sauropods were aquatic do not stand up to a critical analysis of sauropod anatomy. Therefore, dinosaurs stand out as a remarkable group of ground-dwelling animals.

Reproduction and Parenting

Chapter 13 discussed the evidence suggesting that dinosaurs reproduced by laying eggs. **Clutches** of eggs are particularly well known for coelurosaurs in Mongolia, the hadrosaurid **Maiasaura** in Montana, and the French sauropod *Hypselosaurus*.

Most significant for interpretations of dinosaur reproductive and parenting behavior have been the Montana egg sites. There, at a place called "egg mountain" (figure 14.9), a number of clutches of eggs attributed to two dinosaurs—the hadrosaurid *Maiasaura* and the hypsilophodontid *Orodromeus*—have been

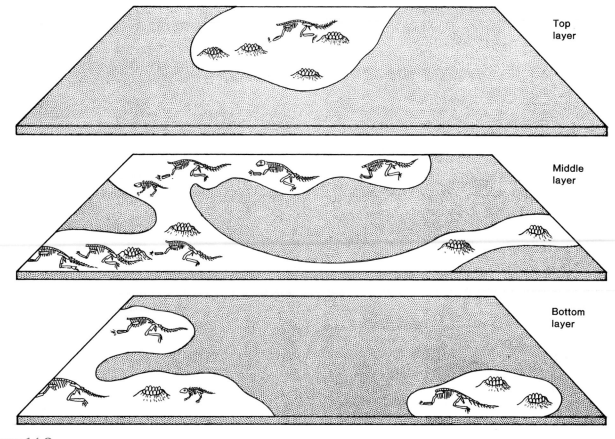

FIGURE 14.9

Nests and dinosaur bones have been discovered at egg mountain in Montana.

discovered (figure 14.10). These clutches are in oval to subcircular crater-like depressions with raised rims. It is almost certain the eggs were not exposed to the air after being laid, but were covered with a thin layer of soil or vegetation (figure 14.11).

Numerous skeletons of hatchling dinosaurs are found around these nests, as are some bones and footprints of adult dinosaurs of the same species as the hatchlings. This provides circumstantial (though not incontrovertible) evidence of parental care.

There is very suggestive evidence of parental care of young dinosaurs in the hadrosaurid *Maiasaura* (figure 14.12), but what of other dinosaurs? Certainly the **nests** and hatchlings of coelurosaurs and *Hypselosaurus* could have been cared for as were those of *Maiasaura*. But no evidence of such care is preserved. Other dinosaurs, such as the cannibalistic *Coelophysis* (box 14.2) probably did not care for their young beyond the amount of care characteristic of living crocodilians. There may have been a spectrum of parental care among dinosaurs, ranging from no care to the feeding and protection of hatchlings among some types of hadrosaurids.

ATTACK AND DEFENSE

How predatory dinosaurs hunted and how they and other dinosaurs defended themselves are subjects for which there is some good hard evidence and much unfounded speculation.

Chapter 6 discussed ideas about how carnosaurs hunted. In general, most paleontologists view the very large carnosaurs, the tyrannosaurids, as solitary hunters, and smaller carnosaurs as pack hunters when taking big game, such as sauropods.

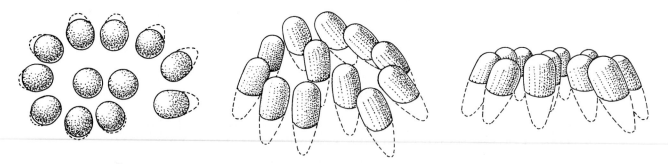

FIGURE 14.10

These three views: (top, oblique, and side) are of an *Orodromeus* clutch from egg mountain.

FIGURE 14.11

This artist's restoration of a *Maiasaura* nest includes a layer of vegetation that may have covered the eggs.

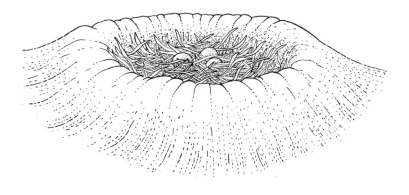

FIGURE 14.12

This skeleton of a very young *Maiasaura* is about 1 meter long and provides a remarkable record of the early growth of a hadrosaurid.

Courtesy Museum of the Rockies

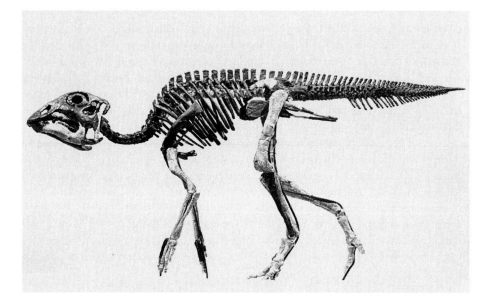

FIGURE 14.13

At least three defensive strategies evolved in plant-eating dinosaurs. Ceratopsians and ankylosaurs had body armor. Sauropods (not shown) were gigantic. The defensive strategy of hadrosaurs is not easily determined.

Pack-hunting in dromaeosaurids is also reasonable speculation, but most other coelurosaurs probably were solitary hunters of small animals such as insects and lizards.

Defensive behavior varied greatly in dinosaurs. Among the predatory dinosaurs, perhaps the most that can be said is that they followed the maxim "the best defense is a good offense." Their speed and agility, and their slashing teeth and claws, must have been used to defend against enemies, as do many predators today.

Among the plant-eating dinosaurs, three different defensive strategies appear to have evolved (figure 14.13). In the sauropods, huge body size and powerful whip-like tails provided defense against enemies. Some sauropods, such as titanosaurids, evolved body **armor.** But defensive armor was the hallmark of most ornithischians. This armor ranged from the impervious plating of ankylosaurs to the spiked tails of stegosaurs, and from the horns of ceratopsids to the thickened skulls of pachycephalosaurids.

Ornithopods were the exception. They lacked body armor and must have defended themselves from attackers in other ways—by speed, by camouflage, or by fleeing to the water or by some sort of group defensive behavior. But it is not clear which one (or more) of these strategies ornithopods employed. Indeed, defensive behavior probably varied greatly among the ornithopods, from the small and speedy hypsilophodontids to the large, spike-thumbed iguanodontids.

GROUP BEHAVIOR

The evidence for **group behavior** (gregariousness or sociality) among dinosaurs can be listed as follows:

1. Display structures—ceratosaur crests, tubes and crests on hadrosaur skulls, and so forth—suggest sociality among some groups of dinosaurs. These display structures presumably would have enabled the recognition of potential mates or opponents in a social group.

2. Sexual dimorphism (differences between males and females of the same species) of these display features and other structures (for example, tusks) in some dinosaurs also supports sociality. Often (though not always), sexual dimorphism among living social animals allows them to distinguish males from females and provides males with display/defensive structures that aid in the defense of territory and the acquisition of mates.

3. The change in shape during growth of some dinosaur display structures could indicate the need to distinguish juveniles from adults in a social group.

4. Multiple dinosaur fossils (**mass-death assemblages**) might also indicate group behavior. Dinosaurs that lived in groups would, occasionally, die in groups. However, many dinosaur mass-death assemblages, such as the Late Jurassic fossils at Dinosaur National Monument in Utah, represent river-transported accumulations of carcasses (figure 14.14). Few dinosaur mass-death assemblages may actually represent groups of animals that lived and died together.

5. The evidence for parental care and nesting behavior discussed earlier also suggests some sort of group behavior among hadrosaurids.

6. Finally, and regarded by many paleontologists as the strongest evidence, multiple trackways of dinosaurs that walked in the same direction suggest social behavior. Indeed, many dinosaur track sites preserve more than one trackway of the same type of dinosaur, all heading the same way (figure 14.15). Because so many tracksites document this pattern, an alternative interpretation—that at each site individual dinosaurs walked, at different times, to a common goal—seems unlikely.

The six points of evidence above suggest some form of group behavior among dinosaurs, especially theropods, ornithopods, and sauropods. But they don't allow us to infer the exact types of **social structures** of these dinosaurs. Some books talk of dinosaurs living in "herds." But a **herd** is a complicated and specific kind of social group in which a dominant animal (usually a male) leads other animals. No unequivocal evidence for herd behavior exists among dinosaurs, although much evidence for social groupings exists for many different types of dinosaurs.

FIGURE 14.14

The dinosaur skeletons and bones at Dinosaur National Monument, Utah were accumulated primarily by river transport, not by the sudden death of a group of dinosaurs.

Courtesy Dinosaur National Monument, Herm Hoops

FIGURE 14.15

Most of these Early Jurassic dinosaur trackways in Massachusetts are heading in the same direction and suggest the possibility of group behavior.

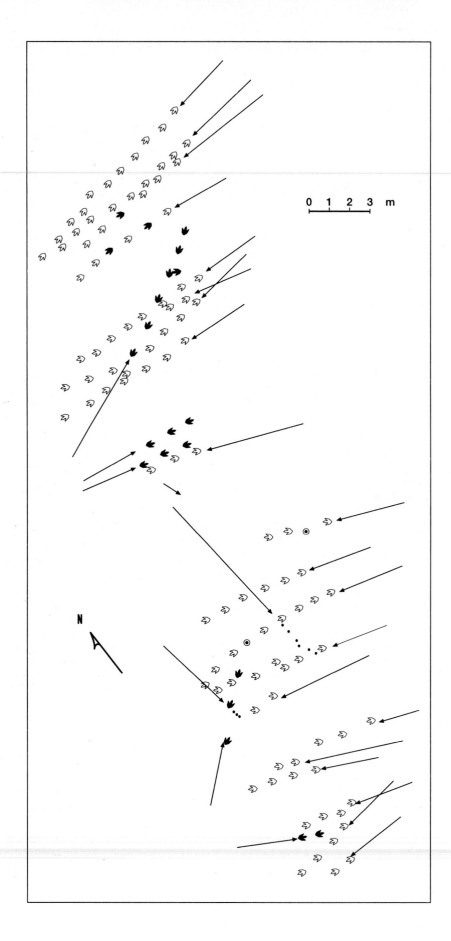

S U M M A R Y

1. Fossilized skin impressions suggest all dinosaurs had reptilian scales covering their bodies. There is no conclusive evidence of hairy or feathered dinosaurs.

2. Dinosaur coloration does not fossilize and is usually arrived at in renderings by analogy to the coloration of living reptiles.

3. Restorations of the external appearance of dinosaurs have evolved with changing ideas about the biology and behavior of dinosaurs.

4. Dinosaur-weight estimates are based mostly on scale models and are only as accurate as the models.

5. Living reptiles have indeterminate growth, whereas mammals and birds have determinate growth.

6. Dinosaur growth rates and longevity based on living reptilian growth rates are those of very slow-to-mature and long-lived dinosaurs. However, dinosaur rates based on living warm-blooded-animal rates are much faster and suggest times of dinosaur maturation and longevity comparable to those of living mammals and birds.

7. Although jaw and tooth structures allow paleontologists to distinguish meat-eating from plant-eating dinosaurs, it is seldom possible to determine exactly what food a dinosaur ate.

8. The skeletons of all dinosaurs identify them as ground-dwelling walkers and runners. Few, if any, dinosaurs lived in the trees or in water.

9. All dinosaurs probably laid eggs, some in nests that may have been protected and, after hatching, tended by adult dinosaurs.

10. Dinosaurs defended themselves in a variety of ways, from speedy escape to impervious body armor.

11. Several lines of evidence suggest group behavior, especially in some theropods, ornithopods, and sauropods. But the exact kinds of social structures of these dinosaurs cannot be determined, and there is no evidence of herd behavior among dinosaurs.

K E Y   T E R M S

armor
cannibalism
clutch
Coelophysis
coloration
cross-sectional area
determinate growth

feeding range
group (social) behavior
herd
Hypselosaurus
indeterminate growth
locomotion
Maiasaura

mass-death assemblage
nest
scale models
skin impressions
social structure
soft-tissue anatomy
weight estimates

R E V I E W   Q U E S T I O N S

1. When you examine a restoration of a dinosaur, what features are inferred from sound skeletal evidence and what features are based on speculation?

2. Critique the dinosaur restoration in figure 16.9.

3. How have changing ideas about dinosaurs influenced dinosaur restorations?

4. How are dinosaur weights estimated?

5. Which estimate of the growth rate of a dinosaur is preferable, one based on growth rates of living reptiles or one based on living mammals and birds? Why?

6. How long did an individual *Brachiosaurus* live? What variables affect your estimate?

7. How do paleontologists determine what dinosaurs ate, and what are the limitations of these determinations?

8. What does the locomotion of dinosaurs tell us about where they lived?

9. What sort of parental care did hadrosaurids confer on their young? What evidence supports your answer?

10. List the defensive strategies employed by different types of dinosaurs. What is the evidence to indicate which dinosaurs employed a particular strategy?

11. What is the evidence for group behavior among dinosaurs?

FURTHER READING

Case, T. J. 1978. Speculations on the growth rate and reproduction of some dinosaurs: *Paleobiology*, vol. 4, pp. 320–28. (A technical analysis of dinosaur growth rates based on the growth rates of living reptiles.)

Colbert, E. H. 1962. The weights of dinosaurs: *American Museum Novitates*, no. 2076:1–16. (Weight estimates of dinosaurs using scale models.)

Coombs, W. P., Jr. 1989. Modern analogs for dinosaur nesting and parental behavior: *Geological Society of America, Special Paper*, no. 238, pp. 21–53. (Draws analogies between the nesting and parental behavior of living birds and of dinosaurs.)

Horner, J. R. 1984. The nesting behavior of dinosaurs: *Scientific American*, vol. 250, pp. 130–37. (A popular review of the dinosaur nests from Montana.)

Ostrom, J. H. 1972. Were some dinosaurs gregarious? *Palaeogeography, Palaeoclimatology, Palaeoecology*, vol. 11, pp. 287–301. (A technical review of the trackway evidence for social behavior in dinosaurs.)

Ostrom, J. H. 1986. Social and unsocial behavior in dinosaurs. *In: Animal Behavior and Evolution*. Oxford: Oxford University Press, pp. 41–61. (A very readable review of the behavior of dinosaurs.)

HOT-BLOODED DINOSAURS?

P aleontologists long considered dinosaurs to have had the reptilian metabolism popularly referred to as cold-blooded. But in 1970, paleontologist John Ostrom of Yale University suggested that dinosaur metabolisms may have been more mammal- or bird-like than reptilian. There soon followed an article in *Scientific American* by paleontologist Robert Bakker titled "Dinosaur Renaissance" in which was presented evidence and analysis to support warm-bloodedness in all dinosaurs. Bakker thereby initiated debate, still ongoing, about the nature of dinosaur metabolism. In this chapter, we review the evidence supporting mammal- or bird-like dinosaur metabolism and evaluate the debate over this complex and fascinating subject.

SOME TERMS AND CONCEPTS

Before studying dinosaur metabolism, we need to become conversant with some basic terminology and concepts. **Metabolism** is best defined as the chemical processes that provide energy to and repair the cells of an organism. In popular terms, vertebrate metabolisms either are **cold-blooded** (fishes, amphibians, and reptiles) or **warm-blooded** (mammals and birds). The nearly equivalent technical terms are **ectothermic** (for cold-blooded) and **endothermic** (for warm-blooded or its exaggerated synonym, **hot-blooded**), based on the Greek roots *ecto* (outside), *endo* (inside), and *thermos* (temperature).

Ectotherms (figure 15.1) receive most, or all, of their body heat from an external source, usually directly from the sun. In contrast, endotherms generate most, or all, of their body heat internally. Endotherms characteristically have high rates of heat production, so their metabolism has been called **tachymetabolic** (*tachys* is Greek for rapid). Ectotherms, however, typically have a slower metabolism, which is called **bradymetabolic** (*bradys* is Greek for slow). Vertebrates that maintain a nearly constant body temperature (usually ± 2° centigrade) are called **homeotherms,** whereas those in which body temperature varies daily, seasonally, or throughout their life cycles are **heterotherms** (from Greek *homeos*, similar, and *heteros*, different).

Today, different metabolisms are found in different kinds of vertebrates. The very diverse and dominant land vertebrates, mammals and birds, are endotherms, whereas the less diverse reptiles and amphibians are ectotherms. The current success of endotherms relative to ectotherms has incorrectly fueled the notion that ectothermy is an inferior type of metabolism (box 15.1). Also, the great difference in metabolism between living endotherms and ectotherms suggests a marked dichotomy in vertebrate metabolism, endotherm on one side, ectotherm on the other. But endothermy and ectothermy describe only the broad ends of a spectrum of vertebrate metabolisms (see figure 15.1). Some ectotherms, such as tuna, maintain high body temperatures, whereas some endotherms, such as tenrec shrews, are hard

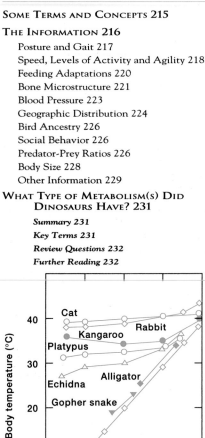

FIGURE 15.1

Endotherms (the cat, rabbit, kangaroo, platypus, and echidna) maintain a relatively constant body temperature, whereas the body temperature of ectotherms (the alligator, gopher snake, and salamander) varies with the ambient (outside) temperature.

From John H. Ostrom, "The Evidence for Endothermy in Dinosaurs" in *A Cold Look at the Warm-Blooded Dinosaurs*, Roger D. K. Thomas and Everett C. Olson (eds.), AAA Selected Symposium. Copyright © 1980 by the AAAS.

BOX 15.1

MISCONCEPTIONS ABOUT METABOLISM

The fact that today vertebrate endotherms are more successful than ectotherms has helped create the misconception that ectothermy is an inferior metabolism. Furthermore, because we are mammals most of us see mammals as superior to cold-blooded amphibians and reptiles. Indeed, many people find reptiles repulsive, for the reasons so well stated by Carolus Linnaeus in 1797: "Reptiles are abhorrent because of their cold body, pale color, cartilaginous skeleton, filthy skin, fierce aspect, calculating eye, offensive smell, harsh voice, squalid habitation, and terrible venom." Small wonder that most of our pets are mammals and birds, not reptiles.

But it is simply a mistake to view ectotherms as inferior to endotherms. Instead, we should realize that both represent equally viable types of vertebrate metabolisms, each with advantages and disadvantages. So consider some of the advantages of the relative slow ectothermic metabolism of an animal receiving most of its body heat from the sun. Such an animal needs to eat much less than a comparable-sized endotherm, thus reducing the problems associated with obtaining food. Most ectotherms can endure much greater

BOX FIGURE 15.1

Ectothermic reptiles are typically seen as inferior to endothermic mammals.

temperature extremes than endotherms can, because their body temperature can vary widely, and does not need to be held within a narrow range. These advantages explain, for example, why in some of the hottest deserts on earth, in western Australia, ectothermic lizards abound, whereas there are few mammals. The endothermic mammals simply cannot find enough food nor endure the extreme temperatures of these deserts.

Although ectothermy may not be inferior to endothermy, the question of superior metabolism has often been behind efforts to demonstrate that dinosaurs were endotherms. Some paleontologists cannot believe that dinosaurs could have been as successful as they were if they had been ectotherms. No doubt, few living lizards would agree!

pressed to maintain a high constant body temperature. There is great variety in existing vertebrate metabolism, and there is no reason why such variety should not have been present during the past, even in the age of dinosaurs.

THE INFORMATION

Metabolism is determined by chemical reactions in the enzymes, blood, and internal organs. None of these structures in dinosaurs are known to have fossilized, so it might seem there is very little direct information about dinosaur metabolism. Indeed, wouldn't we need a time machine and a thermometer in order to determine the body temperatures and metabolisms of dinosaurs? (figure 15.2)

Fortunately, fossils preserve quite a variety of information on dinosaur metabolism, although much of it is indirect. This information can be organized into 11 categories and most of it, as we shall see, has been interpreted in different ways.

THE FAR SIDE By GARY LARSON

An instant later, both Professor Waxman
and his time machine are obliterated,
leaving the cold-blooded/warm-blooded
dinosaur debate still unresolved.

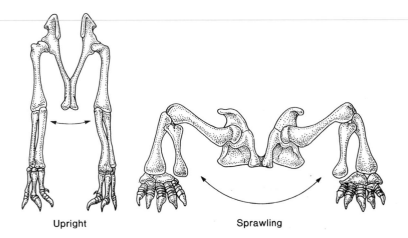

Upright   Sprawling

FIGURE 15.3

Upright posture characterizes living
endotherms, whereas living ectotherms have a
sprawling posture.

POSTURE AND GAIT

Living ectotherms have sprawling postures and gaits, whereas living endotherms,
with a few exceptions, have upright postures and gaits (figure 15.3). The exceptions
are mostly aquatic mammals, such as seals and walruses, that have sprawling limbs
admirably adapted to propelling them through the water. Living vertebrates show
a nearly perfect correlation between posture and metabolism. This correlation may
indicate that extinct animals with an upright posture, the dinosaurs, were
endotherms.

FIGURE 15.4

The theropod *Deinonychus* well displays many skeletal features suggestive of speed, sustained high activity, and agility.

Two criticisms can be leveled at this conclusion. First, no cause-and-effect relationship has been established between posture and metabolism. Maybe ectotherms can have an upright posture, some (the dinosaurs?) did in the past, and it is only a coincidence that all living ectotherms happen to be sprawlers.

A second criticism is that not all dinosaurs may have had an upright posture. Stegosaurs, ankylosaurs, and ceratopsians have been reconstructed with upright hind limbs and sprawling or semi-sprawling forelimb postures. What does this indicate about their metabolisms? Does it mean (facetiously) their posterior halves were endothermic and anterior halves ectothermic? It probably indicates that factors other than metabolism, such as the heavy skulls and armor of stegosaurs, ankylosaurs, and ceratopsians, which forced a slow and powerful sprawling forelimb posture, also determined a dinosaur's posture.

Despite these criticisms, the correlation between posture and metabolism in living vertebrates is striking. A subset of this correlation, that all living bipeds are endotherms, also suggests that bipedal dinosaurs were endotherms. But to believe that these correlations indicate endothermic dinosaurs, we must agree that posture is controlled by metabolism, a conclusion still open to some debate.

SPEED, LEVELS OF ACTIVITY AND AGILITY

High levels of activity characterize living endotherms, whereas today's ectotherms generally are slower, more sluggish, and less agile. The qualifier "generally" needs to be used here because some living ectotherms, for example sea turtles, are

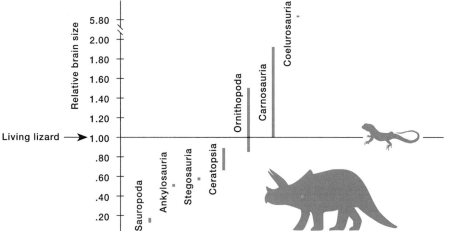

FIGURE 15.5

Dinosaurs have a range of relative brain sizes when compared to a living lizard.

capable of great speed and agility, if only for short periods of time. Nevertheless, evidence for speed, sustained activity, and agility in dinosaurs would be more consistent with them having had an endothermic rather than an ectothermic metabolism.

Speed, sustained activity, and agility in dinosaurs is evident in their skeletal structures, brain size, and brain complexity, and in the speeds estimated from dinosaur trackways. As we saw in Chapters 5 through 10, the skeletons of some dinosaurs, especially small theropods and ornithopods, in many ways resemble those of fast-running birds and mammals. Key features of this resemblance include elongate, slender limbs and limb joints indicating an ability to flex acutely at the elbow, wrist, knee, and ankle joints. Hollow bones, large claws, limb proportions indicative of habitual bipedality, and long, rigid tails for precision balance during running contribute to the impression of speed and agility in some dinosaurs (figure 15.4). Some theropod and ornithopod dinosaurs thus seem to have been every bit as quick and agile as living birds and mammals, suggesting that these dinosaurs may have been endotherms.

Some paleontologists assert that the larger dinosaurs, such as ceratopsians, galloped like living endothermic rhinoceroses. But this argument is inconsistent with the limb structures and trackways of the large, quadrupedal plant-eating dinosaurs, which indicate they were slow, powerful walkers. The skeletal evidence for speed, high levels of activity, and agility in dinosaurs, and the inference of endothermy from this evidence, is confined to theropods and ornithopods.

Relative brain size and complexity provides a second line of evidence of speed, high activity levels, and agility in some dinosaurs. These characteristics of living endotherms require great motor and sensory control by larger and more complex brains than in living ectotherms. If we compare the relative brain sizes of dinosaurs to that of a living ectothermic lizard (figure 15.5), theropods and most ornithopods appear to have been relatively "brainy." But sauropod, ankylosaur, stegosaur, and ceratopsian brain sizes fall well below the line set by the lizard.

Brain complexity in dinosaurs can only be inferred from endocasts of empty fossil skulls (see box 9.2). These empty skulls act as molds that reproduce the brain's overall configuration, and the location and number of the associated blood vessels and nerves. Dinosaur brain casts, however, reveal typically reptilian levels of brain complexity (figure 15.6). These casts do not preserve special structures, such as extremely large cerebral hemispheres, that might be linked to speed, high activity levels, and agility.

FIGURE 15.6

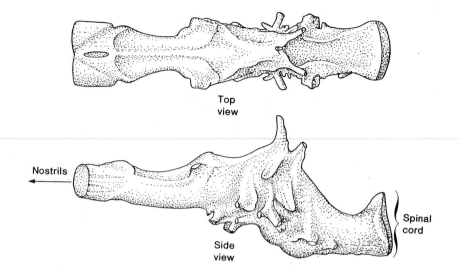

A third line of evidence for dinosaur speed, activity, and agility comes from their trackways. In Chapter 13 we saw that dinosaur speeds can be estimated from trackways. Most dinosaur trackways indicate slow walking, which is the normal speed of all living vertebrates, ectotherms, and endotherms alike. But, a few trackways document small theropods running as fast as a living antelope.

So the evidence for speed, high activity levels, and agility among dinosaurs seems to support endothermy only in small theropods and ornithopods. But some paleontologists point out, as we did at the beginning of this discussion, that some living ectotherms can be very fast, active, and agile. It might be that speedy, active, and agile theropods and ornithopods were ectotherms.

FEEDING ADAPTATIONS

Living endotherms maintain a constant high body temperature and a fast metabolism by consuming and processing large amounts of food (energy). This means they eat more per body weight and process that food more quickly than ectotherms. Key to rapid processing are the teeth, jaws, and skulls of many endotherms, which allow the food to be broken down rapidly into small pieces, thereby increasing the food's surface area and releasing important nutrients so that the endothermic digestive system can rapidly assimilate them. If dinosaurs had tooth, jaw, and skull structures that indicate extensive processing of the food in the mouth, that might be evidence they had an endothermic metabolism.

When we look at the teeth, jaws, and skulls of dinosaurs, however, only among ornithopods do we find structures similar to the **"food processors"** of living endotherms. The powerful jaws and extensive dental batteries of ornithopods such as hadrosaurids are similar to the jaws and teeth of living endothermic horses or elephants that extensively grind the vegetation they consume (figure 15.7).

This might be taken to indicate that only the ornithopods possessed "food processors" suggestive of endothermy. But the teeth, jaws, and gastric mills of sauropods and some of the armored ornithischians don't indicate food processing inferior to that of living plant-eating birds. Theropod food processing doesn't look much different from the slicing of meat undertaken by living meat-eating mammals such as wild dogs and cats. We also need to remember that the large size of most dinosaurs would have forced them to process and consume large amounts of food, whether they were ectotherms or endotherms. Furthermore, the ornithopod grinding mechanism may simply reflect their dietary preference for tough, hard-to-process plant foods.

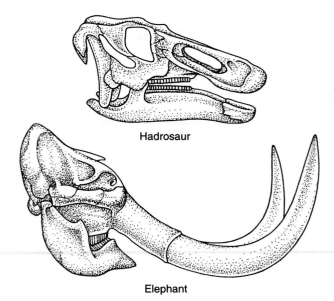

Hadrosaur

Elephant

FIGURE 15.7

The dental batteries and powerful jaws of hadrosaurs resemble those of some living plant-eating mammals, such as the elephant.

We simply cannot be certain what the food processors of dinosaurs indicate about their metabolism. The need to consume large amounts of food to support huge body masses, specialization on tough food items, or the need to feed a rapid, endothermic metabolism could explain the tooth, jaw, and skull structures of some dinosaurs, especially the ornithopods.

BONE MICROSTRUCTURE

The external layer of bone of many living ectotherms contains few channels for blood vessels. In contrast, the **compact bone** of many living endotherms is full of large numbers of blood vessels (figure 15.8). This is thought to reflect the quick metabolism of endotherms, which requires rapid exchange of elements stored in bone such as calcium and phosphorus. It stands to reason that if dinosaur compact bone had many channels for blood vessels, then this would indicate endothermy.

Well-preserved dinosaur bone can be cut into thin wafers, and the microscopic structure of the bone can be determined. This has been done for all major groups of dinosaurs and reveals compact bone with numerous channels similar to that of many living endotherms (figure 15.9).

This might seem conclusive evidence for endothermy in all dinosaurs, but the correlation between metabolism and compact bone microstructure is not a perfect one in living vertebrates. Some large ectotherms (turtles and crocodiles) have compact bone with many channels, whereas some small living endotherms (certain mammals and birds) lack numerous blood channels in their compact bone. This suggests that bone microstructure may be more related to size than to metabolism, making the **bone microstructure** of dinosaurs inconclusive evidence of endothermy.

Another aspect of dinosaur bone microstructure is the recent identification of growth rings in the bone. These growth rings have been found in the bone of many kinds of dinosaurs, including some ornithopods, theropods, and ceratopsians. The rings are characteristic of the bone of living ectothermic reptiles. Periodic pauses in bone growth due to seasonal (or annual) temperature fluctuations cause the rings to form. Their presence in the bone of some dinosaurs may be compelling evidence of ectothermy. However, the bone of other dinosaurs, such as the ornithopod *Dryosaurus*, lacks growth rings and more resembles endothermic bone.

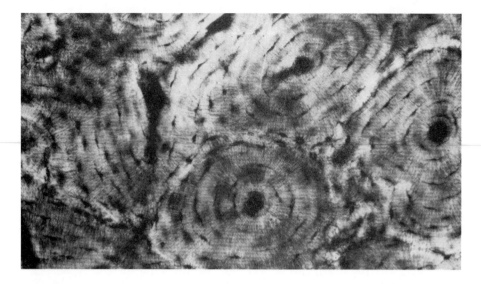

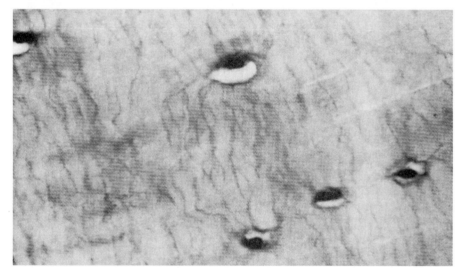

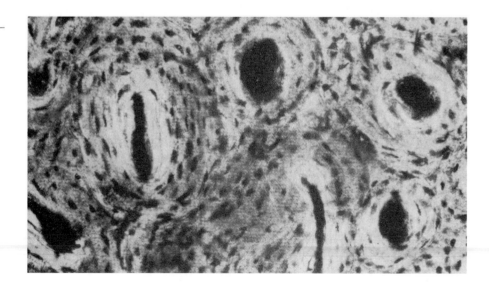

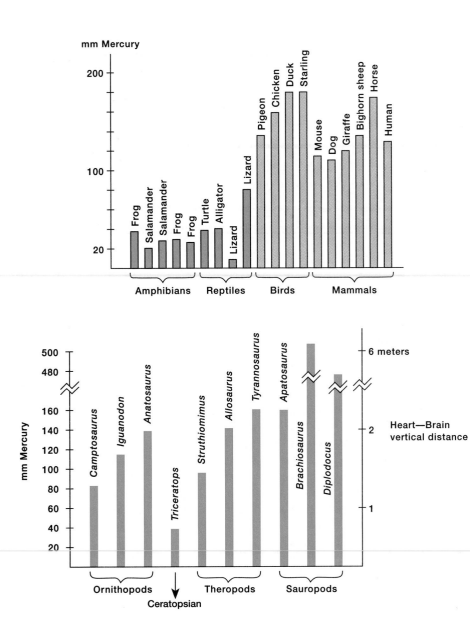

FIGURE 15.10

Living endotherms have higher blood pressures than do ectotherms.

From John H. Ostrom, "The Evidence for Endothermy in Dinosaurs" in *A Cold Look at the Warm-Blooded Dinosaurs*, Roger D. K. Thomas and Everett C. Olson (eds.), AAA Selected Symposium. Copyright © 1980 by the AAAS.

FIGURE 15.11

Dinosaur blood pressures can be estimated from their heart-brain vertical distances.

From John H. Ostrom, "The Evidence for Endothermy in Dinosaurs" in *A Cold Look at the Warm-Blooded Dinosaurs*, Roger D. K. Thomas and Everett C. Olson (eds.), AAA Selected Symposium. Copyright © 1980 by the AAAS.

BLOOD PRESSURE

An endothermic metabolism requires high blood pressure and rapid blood circulation to move energy quickly through the body. Thus, living endotherms have consistently higher **blood pressures** than do ectotherms (figure 15.10). If we could estimate dinosaur blood pressures, this might indicate whether or not they were endotherms.

But how can we do this? It turns out quite easily if we recognize that a primary function of the vertebrate heart is to pump blood to the brain, which is usually elevated above the level of the heart. In other words, the vertical distance between the heart and the brain should be related, in some way, to the blood pressure, because sufficient pressure must be maintained to move blood to the brain, or the animal dies.

It is possible to estimate blood pressure based on the vertical distance between the heart and brain of a dinosaur (figure 15.11). Such an estimate is based on the heart-brain distance/blood pressure relationship of living vertebrates and also requires certainty of the posture of the dinosaur. Blood pressure estimates suggest high, endothermic levels for most dinosaurs (*Triceratops* is a notable exception) and

FIGURE 15.12

Living endotherms have a four-chambered
heart, crocodiles have an imperfectly divided
four-chambered heart, and other ectotherms
have a two-chambered heart.

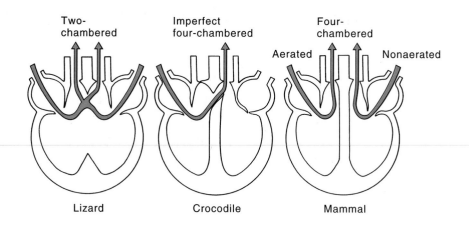

an incredibly high blood pressure (more than 400 millimeters of mercury!) for sauropods. It is questionable whether blood pressure as high as that estimated for sauropods could be maintained by any vertebrate circulatory system without an explosion. So, it seems likely that sauropods may have used arterial valves or muscular contractions in the neck, as do living giraffes, to help bring blood to the brain, and thus would have had a much lower blood pressure than estimated. Estimates of blood pressure, however, are consistent with endothermy in most dinosaurs, although critics point out that large heart-brain vertical distances in dinosaurs could be the determining factor here, not metabolism.

A second, speculative aspect of dinosaur blood pressure concerns the structure of the dinosaurian heart. Living endotherms have a fully divided **four-chambered heart** that separates aerated from nonaerated blood and thus acts as a double pump, producing high pressure for the aerated blood and lower pressure for nonaerated blood. This mechanism is especially significant because by lowering the pressure of the nonaerated blood, it prevents the rupture of tiny blood vessels characteristic of the lungs of endotherms. In contrast, ectothermic hearts have only two chambers that do not efficiently separate the aerated from the nonaerated blood. An exception is living crocodiles that have an imperfectly divided four-chambered heart (figure 15.12).

The closest living relatives of dinosaurs—birds and crocodiles—have four-chambered hearts. So some paleontologists believe that dinosaurs had four-chambered hearts as well. Dinosaur hearts have not fossilized, so this remains speculation. But if dinosaurs did have four-chambered hearts, and if their high estimated blood pressure simply doesn't reflect large heart-brain vertical distances, these lines of evidence suggest endothermy among most dinosaurs.

GEOGRAPHIC DISTRIBUTION

Today, ectotherms cannot live in the extremely cold climates near the poles simply because there is not enough solar energy there with which to warm their bodies (figure 15.13). However, endothermic mammals and birds, such as polar bears and penguins, are capable of living in those colder regions of the globe not inhabited by ectotherms. So if the geographic distribution of dinosaur fossils indicates that they lived in cold climates, this might suggest endothermy in dinosaurs.

The current geographic distribution of dinosaur fossils encompasses Cretaceous localities as far north as Alaska, the Northwest Territories of Canada, and Svalbard (Spitzbergen) and as far south as Antarctica (figure 15.14). These are places where ectotherms do not live today. But the Cretaceous world was not as cold toward the poles as is today's world, and because of continental drift, these Cretaceous dinosaur localities were not as poleward as they are today. Despite this, these locations would still have been far enough poleward during the Cretaceous to have

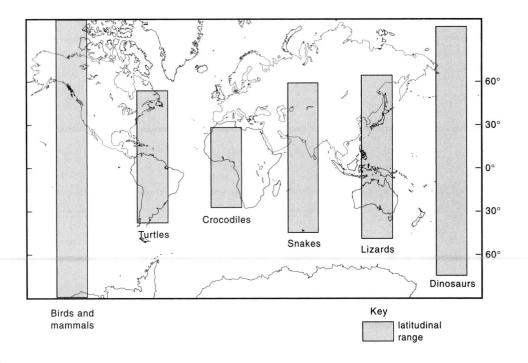

Birds and
mammals

Key

latitudinal range

FIGURE 15.13

Today, ectotherms do not live in cold poleward regions.

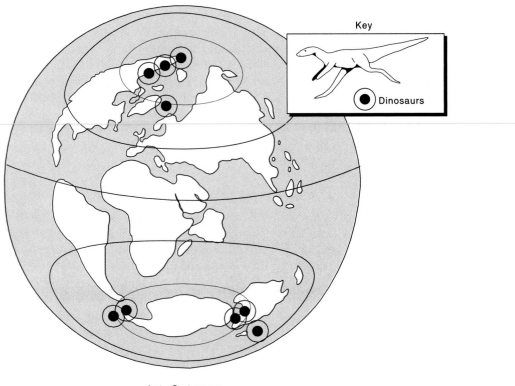

Late Cretaceous

FIGURE 15.14

Cretaceous dinosaur fossils have been collected much farther north and south than ectotherms live today.

experienced the **polar "night"**—winter months of virtually continuous darkness. This darkness would have prevented ectotherms from living in poleward regions, even if there were no polar ice caps and temperatures were warmer during the Cretaceous.

It also has been suggested that the poleward Cretaceous dinosaur fossils do not represent dinosaurs that lived in these regions year-round. Instead, they may represent dinosaurs that migrated over large areas and were only living poleward during the warmer, brighter portion of the year. So a hadrosaurid might have migrated the 3,000 kilometers from Alaska to Alberta in a given year, a trek of 60 days at a speed of 50 kilometers per day. Given the possibility of migration, it is difficult to argue that dinosaur geographical distribution supports endothermy.

BIRD ANCESTRY

Dinosaurs are the ancestors of birds (see Chapter 16). Living birds are endotherms (figure 15.15), and there is no reason to doubt that all extinct birds, including Late Jurassic *Archaeopteryx*, the first bird, were endotherms. Indeed, the small size, skeletal structure, insulating feathers, and powered flight of *Archaeopteryx* strongly suggest an endothermic metabolism. The question thus arises, did endothermy in birds first evolve in *Archaeopteryx*, or did the theropod ancestors and close relatives of birds have an endothermic metabolism?

This question can't be answered definitively. As already discussed, many features of the small theropods are consistent with endothermy. That they gave rise to the birds, and are very bird-like in many ways, are also consistent with endothermy. Although the endothermy of birds may indicate endothermy in at least some theropods, it provides no clues to the metabolism of the other dinosaurs.

SOCIAL BEHAVIOR

Today, complex social behaviors are characteristic of many endotherms (figure 15.16) and uncommon among ectotherms. The evidence reviewed in Chapter 14 suggests that some dinosaurs may have lived in groups and had some form of sociality based on visual display and parental care of young dinosaurs. On face value, this is consistent with endothermic dinosaurs. But some living reptiles form social groups to hunt and administer minimal care to their young, and not all living endotherms form social groups; some live solitary lives. Indeed, social behavior is not normally viewed as being caused by metabolism, but instead is related to other factors, such as the distribution of food resources in an animal's habitat. So the inferred social behavior of some dinosaurs at best is consistent with, but not strong evidence for, their endothermy.

PREDATOR-PREY RATIOS

Living endotherms need to consume more energy than do comparable-sized ectotherms. This means that a 150 kilogram lion eats more food, and more frequently, than a 150 kilogram crocodile. Therefore, in the wild, a lion must have more food items (prey) than a crocodile (figure 15.17). The **predator-prey ratio,** the body mass of predators to their potential prey, thus should differ for endothermic and ectothermic predators. Endothermic predator-prey ratios should be lower (less predator mass per prey) than the ratio for ectotherms. Extrapolating this to dinosaurs predicts that predatory dinosaurs should be rare relative to their potential prey dinosaurs if the predatory dinosaurs were endotherms, and more common if they were ectotherms.

A survey of dinosaur fossil collections reveals that predatory dinosaurs are relatively rare. For example, the greatest dinosaurian predator of all time, *Tyrannosaurus rex*, is known from a handful of skeletons and a few other isolated bones. One of the most extensive dinosaur collections ever made, from the Upper Cretaceous badlands in Dinosaur Provincial Park, Alberta, Canada, contains only 3 to 5 percent predatory dinosaurs (figure 15.18). On face value, the scarcity of predatory dinosaurs suggests that they (and only they, because this tells us nothing about the metabolism of their prey) were endotherms.

FIGURE 15.15

Living birds are endotherms.

FIGURE 15.16

Today, complex social behavior is characteristic of endotherms.

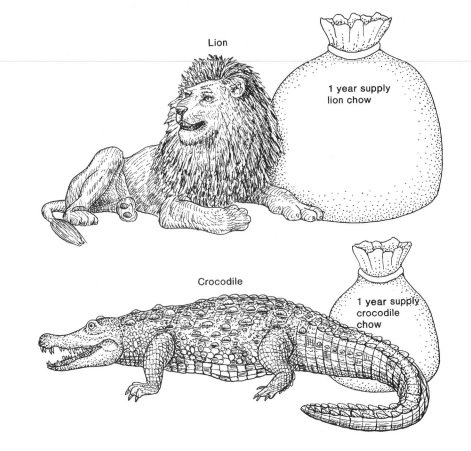

FIGURE 15.17

A 150-kilogram lion (endotherm) eats more food than a 150-kilogram crocodile (ectotherm) in a given period of time.

Lion

1 year supply lion chow

Crocodile

1 year supply crocodile chow

FIGURE 15.18

Predatory dinosaurs are extremely rare in the dinosaur collections from the Upper Cretaceous of Dinosaur Provincial Park, Canada.

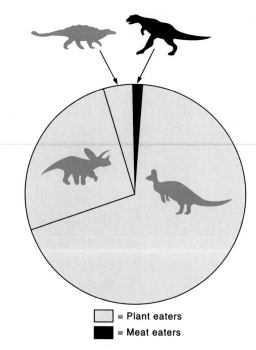

☐ = Plant eaters
■ = Meat eaters

Larger volume: less surface area relative to volume

Smaller volume: more surface area relative to volume

FIGURE 15.19

Because of the surface area-to-volume relationship, smaller spheres (and animals) have more surface area relative to volume than larger spheres (or animals).

There are, however, two insurmountable problems with using predator-prey ratios to infer dinosaur metabolism. First, it is not clear that the ratio of predators to prey today is simply determined by the food requirements of the predators. Other factors, such as food availability for the prey, are important as well. The second problem, and a very big one, is that we cannot be certain that collections of dinosaur fossils reflect the actual predator-prey ratios of dinosaurs. Taphonomic processes (see box 3.1) destroy many potential fossils, and may have biased the dinosaur-fossil record against predators or toward prey. If dinosaur predators and prey did not always inhabit the same environments, then fossil collections would not necessarily reflect their actual abundances. In light of these problems, studying predator-prey ratios of dinosaurs seems an unsatisfactory way to infer dinosaur-predator metabolism.

BODY SIZE

Body size has already been mentioned as a factor in the evaluation of several of the lines of evidence for dinosaur metabolism. It is a very important factor in any consideration of vertebrate metabolism, because body size influences metabolism, and the metabolism of a vertebrate must be consistent with its body size.

To understand why this is so, we need to understand the relationship between the body size of an animal and its surface area. This relationship is best portrayed by two spheres, one large and one small (figure 15.19). The volume of a sphere is $^4/_3 \pi r^3$, where r is the radius of the sphere. The surface area of a sphere is $^2/_3 \pi r^2$, where r also is the radius. As a sphere becomes larger, its volume increases as the cube of its radius, whereas its surface area only increases as a square of its radius. The guaranteed result is that a larger sphere has a smaller surface area relative to its large volume, and a smaller sphere has much more surface area relative to volume.

Although this may not strike you as intuitively correct, a quick calculation should convince you. Consider two spheres, one with a radius of 5 centimeters and the other with a 10 centimeter radius. Calculate the surface areas and volumes of both spheres, and then divide the surface area of each sphere by its volume. The result is that the surface area of the smaller sphere is 59 percent of its volume, whereas that of the larger sphere is only 30 percent of its volume. Smaller spheres have relatively larger surface areas than do larger spheres.

If we transfer this basic geometry to animals, we realize that small animals have much more surface area relative to their volume than do large animals. Much of metabolism is generating body heat, and the surface area of an animal determines how readily it can acquire heat from an external source, or how rapidly it loses its body heat. Small animals, such as mice and hamsters, have such large surface areas relative to their volume (or mass) that they lose heat very fast. As endotherms, they have an insulating coat of fur to help retard heat loss and use their very tachymetabolic metabolism to generate more heat to replace that being lost rapidly. They also shiver frequently to generate more body heat and hide in burrows or under vegetation to slow heat loss.

In contrast, an elephant has a much lower surface area-to-volume ratio than a mouse. Its problem, as an endotherm, lies in overheating because an elephant loses heat very slowly. For this reason, elephants have little in the way of insulating body hair and use their large ears as heat radiators by pumping blood into large vessels in the ears, thereby cooling it by increasing the blood's surface area. Elephants also employ behavioral mechanisms to avoid overheating, such as bathing in rivers several times a day.

Ectotherms that receive most of their body heat from the sun also are affected by the surface area-to-volume relationship. Because of their relatively large surface areas, small lizards can heat and cool themselves rapidly. But because of its large size, a crocodile is slower to warm up and cool down.

Dinosaurs also must have been affected by the **surface area-to-volume relationship,** and this has to constrain our interpretation of dinosaur metabolism. Large dinosaurs, those that weighed about 1,000 kilograms or more, had very low surface areas relative to their volumes. This has inspired calculations that suggest very large dinosaurs, especially full grown sauropods, would have overheated if they had had an endothermic metabolism. Indeed, these dinosaurs would have been inertial homeotherms ("gigantotherms," box 15.2), huge animals with a nearly constant body temperature due to their large size (which, via the surface area-to-volume relationship produces thermal inertia) even though they might have had relatively slow, ectothermic metabolisms. Small dinosaurs, including baby and juvenile sauropods, based on their surface area-to-volume relationship, could have been either ectotherms or endotherms.

Dinosaur body size considered in light of the surface area-to-volume relationship makes endothermy in adult sauropods and some of the other larger dinosaurs (body weight well above 1,000 kilograms) seem improbable. It suggests that the largest dinosaurs were gigantotherms, but leaves open the question of the metabolism of small dinosaurs. Indeed, small juvenile dinosaurs may have had a metabolism different from their metabolism later in life at large adult sizes, so many dinosaurs could have been heterotherms.

OTHER INFORMATION

Very recently, two new kinds of information have been analyzed to determine dinosaur metabolism. This information focuses on bone chemistry and on bones characteristic of the nasal passages of endotherms.

The most common form (what chemists call an isotope) of the oxygen atom in nature has an atomic weight of 18 (abbreviated ^{18}O), whereas the next most common form has an atomic weight of 16 (^{16}O). The bone of any vertebrate incorporates both forms of oxygen into its mineral matrix. The relative amount (ratio) of ^{18}O to ^{16}O in the bone depends on temperature. Some scientists have argued that in an endotherm the ratio of ^{18}O and ^{16}O should vary little between the limb bones and the bones in the core of the body (such as vertebrae) because the body temperature is nearly the same at both locations. They also argue that the temperatures of the extremities and body core are very different in an ectotherm, so the oxygen ratios should be very different at each location.

A consistency of oxygen ratios has been demonstrated in the extremities and core of the skeleton of *Tyrannosaurus rex,* suggestive of endothermy. However, there may be a problem with the basic argument underlying this conclusion. Various

BOX 15.2

GIGANTOTHERMY

BOX FIGURE 15.2
Very large dinosaurs, such as sauropods, probably were gigantotherms.
© Mark Hallett

In Chapter 7 we discussed the metabolism of sauropod dinosaurs, identifying them as animals that maintained a nearly constant body temperature by virtue of their great bulk, or inertial homeotherms. Recently, the term inertial homeotherm has been replaced by the more colorful word **"gigantotherm,"** referring to an animal that maintains a constant high body temperature by virtue of its large size.

How large must an animal be to qualify as a gigantotherm? Recent studies suggest that ectotherms at least as large as 1,000 kilograms are gigantotherms. The most studied example of a living ectothermic gigantotherm is the leatherback turtle. This large reptile lives in the sea, migrating from the tropics to the Arctic oceans on a regular basis. The 1,000 kilogram adult leatherbacks have metabolic rates well below those of comparable-sized mammals. Yet gigantothermy enables leatherbacks to

stay warm in frigid waters. If anything, the leatherbacks have trouble dumping heat and staying cool in tropical waters and on the warm beaches where they lay their eggs.

The example of the leatherback shows that large size can be conducive to maintaining a constant body temperature. All large vertebrates, especially the large dinosaurs (box figure 15.2), must experience some degree of gigantothermy.

studies of living mammals and birds show that temperature varies considerably between their cores and extremities, at least as much as in living alligators. The reasoning behind using the oxygen ratios to determine metabolism thus may be flawed.

Living mammals and birds have small bones in their nasal passages called **respiratory turbinates.** These bones increase the surface area over which blood and moist tissues are exposed to that air. Respiratory turbinates thus play a vital role in the rapid breathing and high rate of oxygen consumption characteristic of the endotherms. It is difficult to imagine an animal being endothermic without respiratory turbinates.

Preliminary studies have failed to locate respiratory turbinates in the skulls of some theropod dinosaurs, which suggests that they were not endotherms. However, respiratory turbinates are very small, delicate bones that might not readily fossilize. More research in this area is needed and anticipated.

WHAT TYPE OF METABOLISM(S) DID DINOSAURS HAVE?

Having reviewed the many lines of information bearing on hypotheses of dinosaur metabolism, you should see how difficult it is to present a simple answer to the question about what type of metabolism(s) dinosaurs had. The following answers, however, are offered by different paleontologists.

1. All dinosaurs were ectotherms.

2. All dinosaurs were endotherms.

3. Dinosaurs were a diverse group of animals metabolically, some (at least some theropods and ornithopods) were endotherms and others were ectotherms.

4. Large dinosaurs, the sauropods and big ornithischians, were gigantotherms as adults. Juveniles of these large dinosaurs, and the smaller dinosaurs, may have been either endotherms or ectotherms.

The evidence presented in this chapter suggests neither of the first two extreme views of dinosaur metabolism is correct. The third and fourth views, some combination of them or some variant, appear to best explain the evidence. There is, indeed, no simple answer to the question of what type of metabolism the dinosaurs had.

SUMMARY

1. Warm-blooded vertebrate metabolisms are endothermic and tachymetabolic.

2. Cold-blooded vertebrate metabolisms are ectothermic and bradymetabolic.

3. Numerous lines of evidence have been brought to bear on the nature of dinosaur metabolism including; posture and gaits, speed, activity levels and agility, feeding adaptations, bone microstructure, blood pressure, geographic distribution, bird ancestry, social behavior, predator-prey ratios, and body size.

4. Many of these lines of evidence are consistent with endothermy in at least some theropods and ornithopods, but most evidence does not support endothermy in the other dinosaurs.

5. Very large dinosaurs, such as the sauropods, were gigantotherms.

6. The evidence does not support extreme views of dinosaur metabolism, in other words, that all were ectothermic, or all were endothermic.

7. The evidence suggests a probable variety of metabolisms in dinosaurs, including endotherms and ectotherms, some of which were also heterotherms and gigantotherms.

KEY TERMS

blood pressure
bone microstructure
bradymetabolic
brain complexity
cold-blooded
compact bone
ectotherm
endotherm

"food processors"
four-chambered heart
gigantotherm
heterotherm
homeotherm
hot-blooded
metabolism

polar "night"
predator-prey ratio
relative brain size
respiratory turbinates
surface area-to-volume relationship
tachymetabolic
warm-blooded

REVIEW QUESTIONS

1. Define the following seven terms: endotherm, ectotherm, tachymetabolic, bradymetabolic, homeotherm, heterotherm, and gigantotherm. Use each word in a paragraph describing dinosaur metabolism.

2. What are some common misconceptions about ectotherms and why are they wrong?

3. Which of the 11 lines of information presents the most convincing evidence for endothermic dinosaurs? Which presents the weakest?

4. Explain the surface area-to-volume relationship and its bearing on dinosaur metabolism.

5. What type(s) of metabolism(s) did dinosaurs have? Defend your answer.

FURTHER READING

Bakker, R. T. 1975. Dinosaur renaissance: *Scientific American*, v. 232, pp. 48–78. (The original article that argues all dinosaurs were endotherms.)

Bakker, R. T. 1986. *The Dinosaur Heresies*. New York: William Morrow and Co., Inc., 481 pp. (Much of this book argues the case for endothermic dinosaurs.)

Farlow, J. O. 1990. Dinosaur energetics and thermal biology; in Weishampel, D. P., Dodson, P., and Osmólska, H., editors, *The Dinosauria*. Berkeley: University of California Press, pp. 43–55. (Presents the idea of dinosaur heterometabolism.)

Ruben, J. 1995. The evolution of endothermy in mammals and birds: from physiology to fossils: *Annual Review of Physiology*, vol. 57, pp. 69–95. (Critiques some key assumptions and evidence marshalled to support dinosaur endothermy.)

Spotila, J. R., O'Connor, M. P., Dodson, P., and Paladino, F. V. 1991. Hot and cold running dinosaurs: body size, metabolism and migration: *Modern Geology*, vol. 16, pp. 203–27. (Presents the evidence for dinosaur gigantothermy.)

Thomas, R. D. K. and Olson, E. C., editors. 1980. *A Cold Look at the Warm-Blooded Dinosaurs*. Boulder: American Association for the Advancement of Science, 514 pp. (A collection of 12 technical articles that present various evidence and points of view on dinosaur metabolism.)

Vickers-Rich, P. and Rich, T. H. 1993. Australia's polar dinosaurs: *Scientific American*, vol. 269, No. 1, pp. 50–55. (Reviews Australian dinosaurs and their implications for ideas about dinosaur migration and endothermy.)

16

THE ORIGIN OF BIRDS

Several times in this book dinosaurs are identified as the ancestors of birds. This should have a major effect on our view of the dinosaurs. Instead of thinking of them as huge lizard- or elephant-like animals, we should see dinosaurs as bird-like behaviorally (see Chapter 14). Dinosaurs are no longer just a long extinct group of animals because their descendants, the birds, live today as one of the world's most successful animal groups. In this chapter, we develop the evidence for a dinosaur ancestry of birds and discuss some aspects of the evolution of the "feathered dinosaurs."

WHAT IS A BIRD?

There are about 9,000 species of living **birds,** making them the most diverse group of vertebrates except for the bony fishes. All birds belong to a single class of vertebrates, the **Aves** (from the Latin word for bird). It is difficult to imagine a person who has not seen a bird and cannot readily distinguish it from other animals. This distinction, of course, is based primarily on the powered flight and feathers that are the hallmarks of birds. The **feathers** of birds are intricate structures (figure 16.1) that not only form flight surfaces (flight feathers) but also insulate the bird (downy feathers).

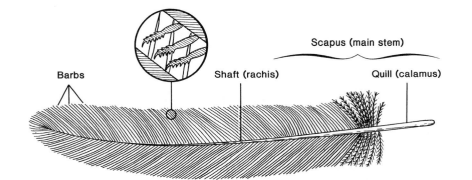

Barbs — Shaft (rachis) — Scapus (main stem) — Quill (calamus)

FIGURE 16.1

Bird feathers, the most distinctive avian feature, are intricate structures.

FIGURE 16.2

Avian long bones are hollow, have thin walls, and are braced by struts.

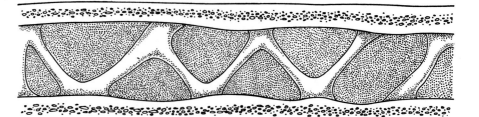

FIGURE 16.3

The respiratory system of a bird is more than just its lungs. It includes air sacs connected to hollow bones.

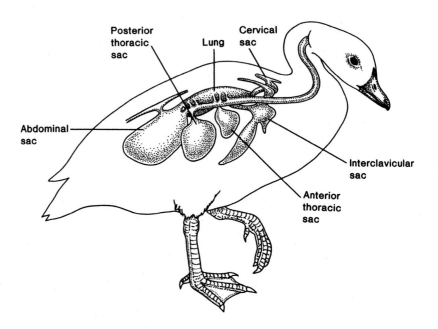

Like their flight feathers, skeletal features unique to birds are associated with flight. The limb bones are hollow and are much more lightly constructed (they have thinner walls) than were those of theropod dinosaurs. Braces and struts within bird long bones (figure 16.2) provide structural support for their thin walls, and the long bones are **pneumatic.** This means that air passes through small openings or ducts in the bones when the bird respires. These **pneumatic ducts** are connected to **air sacs** and the bird's lungs (figure 16.3). Avian air sacs not only lighten a bird, but they also supplement its lungs by acting both as a supercharger that increases the efficiency of respiration, and as a cooling system for the fast avian metabolism. Because birds lack sweat glands, they are strictly air-cooled by their lungs and air sacs.

A second unique aspect of the avian skeleton is the fusion of many bones to form more rigid structures, which is particularly evident in the hind limb, pelvis, sacrum, and skull (figure 16.4). For example, the collarbones are fused to form a single bone, the furcula (the "wishbone"). Such fused structures contain far fewer separate bones than the same structures in most other vertebrates, including theropod dinosaurs.

Other distinctive features of all but the most primitive birds include modifications of the forelimb skeleton to form wings (figure 16.5). The sternum (breastbone) is very large and keeled. The coracoid bone is very long and forms a brace with the sternum, and a large groove for the passage of a large tendon is present in the shoulder girdle. These structures are designed to anchor the huge and powerful chest muscles needed to flap the wings for flying. The limb itself is modified to

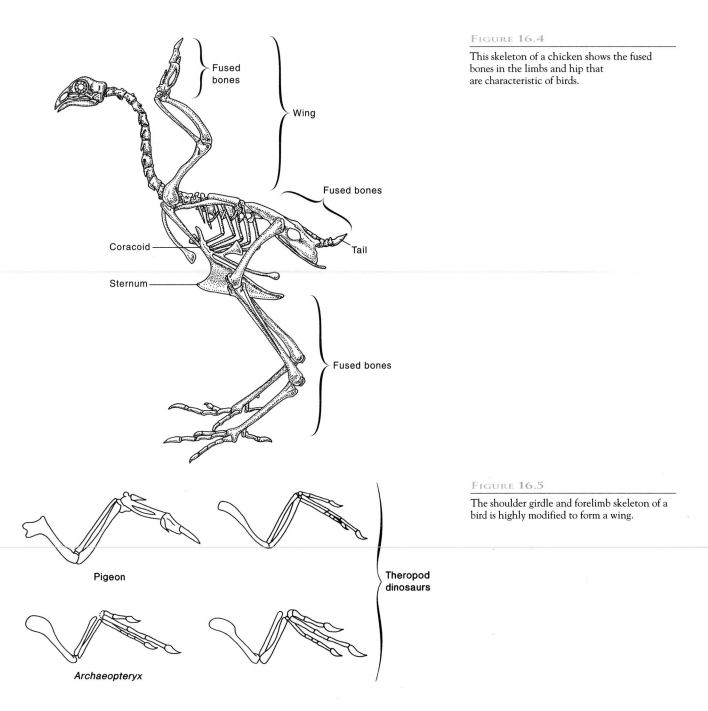

FIGURE 16.4

This skeleton of a chicken shows the fused bones in the limbs and hip that are characteristic of birds.

Fused bones

Wing

Fused bones

Tail

Coracoid

Sternum

Fused bones

FIGURE 16.5

The shoulder girdle and forelimb skeleton of a bird is highly modified to form a wing.

Pigeon

Theropod dinosaurs

Archaeopteryx

form a wing. The carpals are fused so that the wrist is a simple hinge joint. The digits and metacarpals also are fused, and the joints at the wrist and elbow are modified to allow folding of the wing. Pores in the ulna anchor flight feathers.

THE FIRST BIRD: ARCHAEOPTERYX

Most paleontologists consider Late Jurassic **Archaeopteryx** (figure 16.6) to be the first bird. It provides a unique glimpse of an animal in many ways part dinosaur, part bird. *Archaeopteryx* thus represents what paleontologists would call a "transitional form" between two major groups of animals, the reptiles (dinosaurs) and birds. In popular terms, *Archaeopteryx* is a **"missing link."**

FIGURE 16.6

Late Jurassic *Archaeopteryx* was the first bird.

Fossils of *Archaeopteryx* come from only one place, the Upper Jurassic **Solnhofen Limestone** in Bavaria, Germany. There, during the Late Jurassic, a quiet lagoon was present behind coral reefs. Tiny fragments of calcium carbonate and the carbonate shells of microscopic marine organisms were deposited on the bottom of the lagoon. The result was the preservation of delicate structures of the larger organisms that died there, making the Solnhofen Limestone an incredible graveyard of fossilized soft tissues. Indeed, the hallmark of the fossils of *Archaeopteryx*, their preserved feathers, is but one example of the high quality of fossilization in the Solnhofen Limestone.

The first known fossil of *Archaeopteryx* is a single feather discovered in 1860. Since then, five skeletons have been discovered. The most exquisite, found in 1877, is in the Humboldt Museum in Berlin, Germany (figure 16.7). The *Archaeopteryx* specimens have been intensively studied for more than one century, and more has been written about them than about any other collection of six fossils pertaining to one genus.

The skeleton of *Archaeopteryx* shares many features with small theropod dinosaurs. Indeed, some specimens of *Archaeopteryx* were originally identified as theropod (or pterosaur) before their feather impressions were recognized.

Archaeopteryx was about the size of a crow or pigeon. Its skull had teeth, and very few of its bones were fused to each other—dinosaurian, not avian features. The hollow limb bones of *Archaeopteryx* had thick walls that lacked pneumatic openings, unlike the thin-walled, pneumatic limb bones of later birds.

FIGURE 16.7

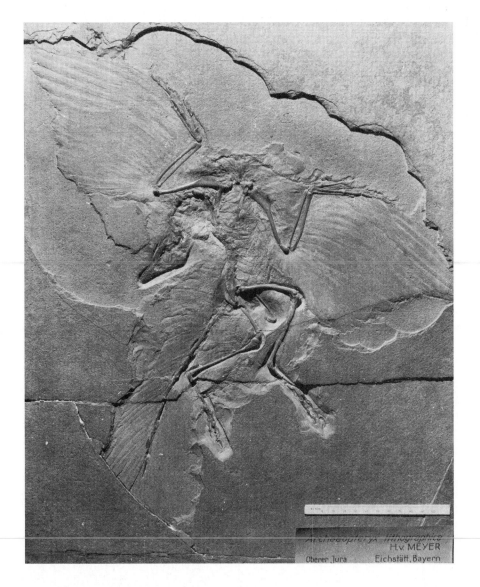

The Berlin specimen of *Archaeopteryx* is the
most exquisitely preserved fossil of the first bird.

Courtesy John Ostrom, Yale Peabody Museum

No sternum (breastbone) is known for *Archaeopteryx*, so it apparently
lacked the main anchor for flight muscles seen in other birds. Nevertheless, the forelimbs of *Archaeopteryx* indicate it was capable of powered flight. Although
Archaeopteryx had a **furcula** (a wishbone; distally fused clavicles) like other birds,
this feature was present in some tetanuran theropods (see Chapter 6). The shape
of the pelvis of *Archaeopteryx*—the pubis apparently pointed posteriorly (although
this is still debated)—was very avian and also resembled that of some theropods.
The long, bony tail of *Archaeopteryx* also sets it apart from other birds.

The forelimb of *Archaeopteryx* was theropod-like. It had three fully
developed digits and a flexible and unmodified wrist, radius, and ulna. But the
hind limb of *Archaeopteryx* was very bird-like. The head of the femur was turned
medially, and the knee and ankle joints were hinges. The fibula was reduced, the
proximal tarsals were fused to the tibia, and the distal tarsals were fused to the
metatarsals. The long metatarsals were partly fused to each other, and there were

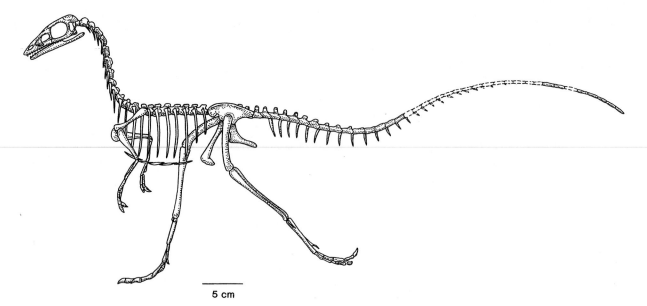

5 cm

FIGURE 16.8

Compsognathus is a small theropod dinosaur about the same size and the same geologic age as *Archaeopteryx*.

FIGURE 16.9

Reconstructions of feathered theropods, such as this one of Cretaceous *Velociraptor*, are highly speculative.

Courtesy Gregory Paul

three slender, forward-facing digits and a fourth digit that faced backward. Most of these avian features of the hind limb of *Archaeopteryx* were also present in small theropods. Compare them, for example, in *Archaeopteryx* and *Compsognathus*, a theropod of similar size contemporaneous with *Archaeopteryx* (figure 16.8).

There was actually only one feature of *Archaeopteryx* that no theropod dinosaur possessed. This was feathers, which in structure and arrangement clearly ally *Archaeopteryx* with birds. To call *Archaeopteryx* a "feathered dinosaur," in other words, to recognize it as an animal with an essentially theropod skeleton and avian feathers, is a reasonable conclusion.

Nevertheless, it is not certain that *Archaeopteryx* will maintain its position as the "missing link" between dinosaurs and birds. Some features of *Archaeopteryx* identify it as too specialized to have been the ancestor of later birds. Indeed, *Archaeopteryx*

BOX 16.1

ARCHAEOPTERYX: AN EVOLUTIONARY DEAD END?

Recent discoveries of Early Cretaceous birds in Mongolia, Spain, and China challenge the central role occupied by *Archaeopteryx* in the initial evolution of birds. Many paleontologists not only regard *Archaeopteryx* as the link between dinosaurs and birds, but they see it as the ancestor of later birds. The newly discovered Early Cretaceous birds (box figure 16.1) lived only a few million years after *Archaeopteryx*. Yet these Early Cretaceous birds were remarkably diverse and much more similar to later birds than to *Archaeopteryx*. For example, their specialized skeletons indicate that they were capable of sustained powered flight. A huge evolutionary gap thus exists between *Archaeopteryx* and these Early Cretaceous birds.

Some paleontologists believe that this gap could not have been bridged during the relatively short interval of geologic time between Late Jurassic *Archaeopteryx* and the Early Cretaceous birds. In other words, to identify *Archaeopteryx* as the ancestor of these birds would require impossibly fast rates of evolution. Instead, they argue, *Archaeopteryx* represents a side branch, or dead end, in the early evolution of birds. Another bird (or birds) still undiscovered must be the ancestor of the Early Cretaceous advanced birds.

BOX FIGURE 16.1

Cathayornis, from the Lower Cretaceous of China, was a surprisingly advanced bird that lived only a few million years after *Archaeopteryx*.

This argument, however, may be based on an unwarranted assumption about rates of evolution. Perhaps when birds first appeared they did evolve at unusually fast rates. This would have happened if birds diversified quickly to take advantage of the new adaptive opportunities that must have been available to flying vertebrates that could sustain powered flight. If so, the rapid evolution of the advanced Early Cretaceous birds from Late Jurassic *Archaeopteryx* during a few million years seems plausible. Also, let us not forget that "a few million years" really *is* a lot of time.

It is difficult to decide whether or not rates of early bird evolution were fast enough for *Archaeopteryx* to have been the ancestor of the advanced Early Cretaceous birds. But it is easy to see that the recent discoveries of advanced Early Cretaceous birds shed new light on the early evolution of birds. Clearly, a diverse and widespread group of birds capable of sustained powered flight evolved shortly after birds first appeared.

seems to be more closely related to theropod dinosaurs than to later birds (box 16.1). Some paleontologists, therefore, classify it as a theropod, not a bird. They argue that the feathers of *Archaeopteryx* are not uniquely avian features, and if we discovered equally well preserved theropod fossils, many of them would also have feather impressions (figure 16.9). Of course, this is speculation, because no feathered theropods are known. So for the time being we may continue to identify *Archaeopteryx* as a bird because of its feathers. But new discoveries of theropods may change this.

OTHER POSSIBLE ANCESTORS OF BIRDS

Although most paleontologists agree that dinosaurs were the ancestors of birds, a vocal group of dissenters exists. Some of these paleontologists argue that birds evolved directly from archosaurs more primitive than dinosaurs—the thecodonts. This old idea is difficult to disprove because many thecodonts certainly were sufficiently primitive to have been the ancestors of birds. But to argue for a thecodont

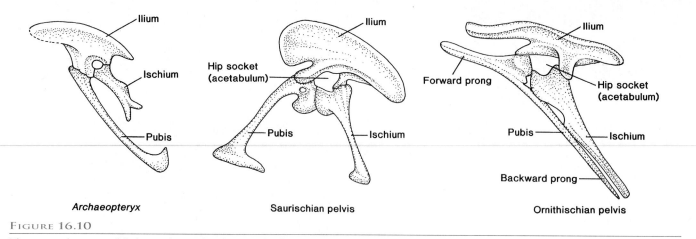

FIGURE 16.10

The avian pelvis is a modified saurischian pelvis that superficially resembles the ornithischian pelvis.

ancestry of birds is to ignore the many evolutionary novelties shared by dinosaurs and birds that indicate they are more closely related to each other than either is to a thecodont.

Another perspective on bird origins is held by those paleontologists who point to some features shared by birds and primitive crocodiles. These features of the jaw and middle ear, however, probably reflect evolutionary convergence between crocodiles and birds because these animals are otherwise very dissimilar.

Two ideas to avoid about the origin of birds are that the ornithischian dinosaurs and the pterosaurs were avian ancestors. Certainly, the pelvis of birds does somewhat resemble that of the ornithischian (bird-hipped) dinosaurs. But a closer look (figure 16.10) reveals that the avian pelvis is actually a highly modified saurischian pelvis.

Pterosaurs were flying archosaurs that first appeared during the Late Triassic and became extinct at the end of the Cretaceous. Pterosaurs lacked feathers and the evolutionary novelties shared by dinosaurs and birds. As noted in Chapter 5, pterosaurs were archosaurs closely related to dinosaurs, but that's as close as their relationship was to birds. Flight must have evolved twice, quite separately, among the archosaurs. Once in pterosaurs and once in birds.

ORIGIN AND EVOLUTION OF AVIAN FLIGHT

Because the hallmark of birds, including *Archaeopteryx*, is their feathers and other skeletal modifications for flight, it is natural to ask how avian flight originated. Two major hypotheses have been advanced and remain the subject of controversy.

An old idea is that the immediate ancestors of *Archaeopteryx* lived in the trees, or were arboreal. These arboreal theropods evolved feathers to glide from branch to branch and to the ground. Flight powered by flapping the wings evolved later. Indeed *Archaeopteryx* itself has claws that indicate it was capable of climbing trees.

An alternative hypothesis is that the immediate ancestors of *Archaeopteryx* were ground-living, fast runners (cursorial). According to this hypothesis (figure 16.11), feathers evolved to insulate the dinosaur and, on the arms, provided additional surface area to aid in catching insects. Enlargement of these feathers followed to provide support and thrust when the newly evolved wings were flapped. This hypothesis of the origin of avian flight can be termed the **cursorial hypothesis,** and the older hypothesis can be called the **arboreal hypothesis.**

FIGURE 16.11

Two hypothetical stages in the cursorial origin of avian flight show a proto-bird catching insects with feathered hands (above) and a later, winged proto-bird like *Archaeopteryx* (below).

Two strong criticisms of the arboreal hypothesis have been presented. First, the wings of gliders, such as "flying" squirrels, are very different from those of birds. For example, in gliders the wing membrane is attached to the body and extends between the fore- and hind limbs, very different than the wing membrane of birds. This suggests that *Archaeopteryx* was not an arboreal glider, so no evidence is available for this gliding stage of evolution, which is required by the arboreal hypothesis.

Second, as we know from Chapter 6, the hind-limb skeletons of theropod dinosaurs, and of *Archaeopteryx*, were those of fast ground runners. Indeed, there is no evidence that any theropod dinosaur was arboreal. Therefore, for the arboreal theory to stand we must believe that fossils of arboreal theropods and of arboreal gliding "protobirds" will be found.

The principal criticism of the cursorial hypothesis is that the mechanism of catching insects with feathered hands does not seem practical. Also, some paleontologists have difficulty imagining what adaptive advantage the early stages of flapping the arms would have conferred on theropods. If anything, this might have slowed a theropod trying to catch insects or running away from a predator. Also, *Archaeopteryx* apparently was arboreal, but no known theropod was, so there is a missing arboreal predecessor of *Archaeopteryx*. Yet despite these criticisms, many paleontologists favor the cursorial hypothesis, mostly because the arboreal hypothesis seems much less plausible.

FIGURE 16.12

Wingless diving birds of the Early Cretaceous, such as *Baptornis* shown here, still had teeth.

EVOLUTION OF BIRDS

A book on dinosaurs would be remiss if it did not include a brief overview of the evolution of the descendants of dinosaurs, the birds.

Despite claims of older birds (box 16.2), Late Jurassic *Archaeopteryx* still remains the oldest-known bird. Cretaceous birds were much more advanced than *Archaeopteryx*, although some still had teeth (figure 16.12). During the Early

BOX 16.2

A TRIASSIC BIRD?

In 1986, newspapers reported the discovery of a fossil bird in Upper Triassic strata in West Texas (box figure 16.2). These reports provoked great interest among paleontologists as well as the general public because, until that time, Late Jurassic *Archaeopteryx* was considered to be the oldest fossil bird. Not only was the "fossil bird" from West Texas about 70 million years older than *Archaeopteryx*, it was also a contemporary of some of the earliest dinosaurs. This must mean that the divergence of birds from dinosaurs took place virtually at the onset of dinosaur evolution.

Five years later, in 1991, the "bird fossil" from West Texas was formally described in a scientific publication. This pheasant-sized animal was named **Protoavis** (first bird), but the fossil may not be of a bird at all! Indeed, paleontologists who are experts on the origin of birds are not convinced it is avian.

The fossils of *Protoavis* come from a bone bed where they were disarticulated and jumbled in a layer of clay. It is not clear that they represent a single kind of animal or even a single individual animal. Most *Protoavis* bones, especially limb bones, cannot be distinguished from those of early dinosaurs. A supposed fragment of the **furcula (wishbone)** exists but does not particularly resemble a wishbone. Most of the pieces of the "skull" of *Protoavis* are just that—pieces, many badly damaged and distorted, that do not clearly fit together. So, to interpret them as showing avian features—and it is in the skull that the avian features of *Protoavis* are sought—

BOX FIGURE 16.2

This reconstruction of the supposed Triassic bird, *Protoavis*, began to appear in newspapers in 1986.

requires much interpretation, so much so that many paleontologists feel reasonable interpretation has given way to unreasonable speculation. No convincing evidence exists that *Protoavis* is a bird.

If *Protoavis* is not a bird, what is it? Most, if not all, of it appears to be, as mentioned above, the bones of a Late Triassic dinosaur. *Protoavis* also provides a good example of the caution both paleontologists and the general

public need to exercise when reading media reports of new fossil discoveries. Only when these discoveries are adequately documented in scientific publications and reviewed by professional paleontologists can their authenticity be evaluated. Five years after the first newspaper reports, the avian status of *Protoavis* did not stand up to critical scrutiny. *Archaeopteryx* remains the oldest-known fossil bird.

Cretaceous, highly specialized, flightless diving birds as well as very proficient flyers evolved. This early diversity among birds may indicate an ancestry older than *Archaeopteryx* or that other Late Jurassic birds remain to be discovered.

Mononykus (figure 16.13) from the Upper Cretaceous of Mongolia has very peculiar, spike-like forelimbs. Although originally identified as a very early, flightless bird, some paleontologists argue that *Mononykus* is a bizarre coelurosaurian dinosaur. Truly modern toothless birds appeared by the beginning of the Cenozoic. During the last 65 million years, birds have been one of the most successful groups of vertebrates (figure 16.14).

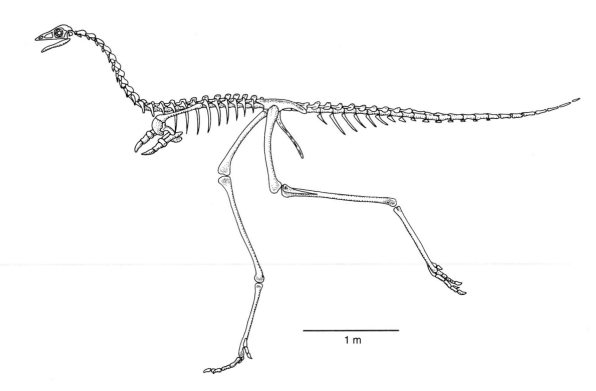

FIGURE 16.13

Mononykus, recently discovered in the Upper Cretaceous of Mongolia, has been deemed either a flightless bird or a bizarre theropod.

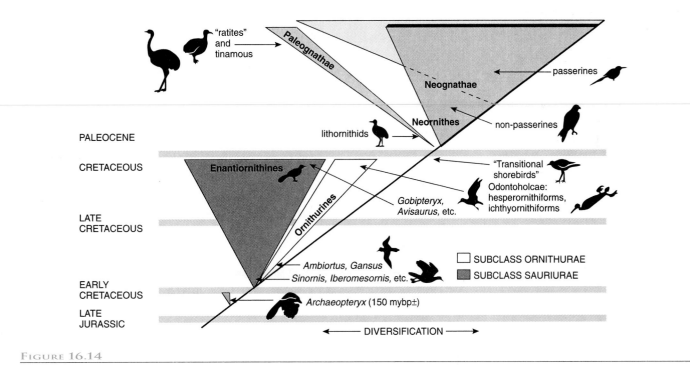

FIGURE 16.14

Birds have been very diverse and successful during the last 65 million years.

Reprinted with permission from Alan Feduccia "Explosive Evolution in Tertiary Birds and Mammals" in *Science*, vol. 267. Copyright 1995 American Association for the Advancement of Science.

Birds have delicate, hollow bones, most are small animals, and many live in dry or forested environments. For these reasons, the fossil record of birds is less extensive than that of reptiles and mammals. Yet, despite this, we have fossils of water birds, land birds, and giant, flightless birds (**ratites**) at least as far back as the

FIGURE 16.15

Giant flightless birds, such as *Diatryma* shown here, appeared as early as 58 million years ago.

Paleocene. The giant, flightless ratites are particularly interesting (figure 16.15) because they evolved from flying ancestors and so represent a return to the flightless habits of the theropod ancestors of birds.

SIGNIFICANCE OF DINOSAURS AS BIRD ANCESTORS

As stated at the beginning of this chapter, identifying dinosaurs as the ancestors of birds should have a major impact on how we view the dinosaurs. We should no longer think of them as reptile-like in many aspects of their biology. Instead, much about dinosaur biology and behavior was very avian, as explained elsewhere in this book.

If dinosaurs were so bird-like, should we classify them with reptiles? Perhaps not, although various answers to this question have been proposed (box 16.3). Regardless of the classification used, the close relationship of birds to dinosaurs is well established.

SUMMARY

1. Birds are feathered vertebrates with skeletons highly modified to be lightweight and rigid to enable sustained powered flight.

2. *Archaeopteryx*, from the Upper Jurassic of Germany, is the oldest known bird.

3. Skeletal features of *Archaeopteryx* are essentially those of small theropod dinosaurs.

4. Evolutionary novelties of the skeleton shared by theropod dinosaurs and birds provide strong evidence that birds descended from dinosaurs.

5. There is little or no evidence that birds are descended from thecodonts, crocodiles, ornithischian dinosaurs, or pterosaurs.

6. There are two hypotheses of the origin of avian flight, the arboreal and the cursorial hypotheses.

7. Many paleontologists favor the cursorial hypothesis, which states that flight originated in a ground-running animal that evolved feathers and flapped its wings to gain stability and additional thrust when catching insects.

8. Modern birds evolved by the beginning of the Cenozoic.

9. Recognition of dinosaurs as the ancestors of birds forces us to rethink much of dinosaur anatomy and behavior and stress their bird-like aspects.

BOX 16.3

BIRDS AS DINOSAURS

The cladogram of theropod dinosaurs presented earlier in this book (see figure 6.1) can be modified slightly to show where most paleontologists believe birds belong, which is as close relatives of the coelurosaurs (box figure 16.3). If this cladogram is turned directly into a classification, that classification would simply identify birds as a particular type of tetanuran theropod, of the same rank in the Linnaean hierarchy as "coelurosaurs." In this classification, birds are just another type of coelurosaur.

Some paleontologists have taken such a classification to heart. They cast doubt on the significance of "dinosaur extinction," because, after all, the avian dinosaurs (= feathered dinosaurs, = birds) are still with us, some 9,000 species strong (see Chapter 17). These paleontologists speak flippantly of "carving the dinosaur" at a Thanksgiving dinner. In a more serious vein, they argue that putting the birds in a class distinct from that which contains the dinosaur obscures their close relationship.

This may be the case, but putting birds into the class of dinosaurs also obscures the key evolutionary novelties of birds—their feathers, skeletal features, and physiological mechanisms for sustained,

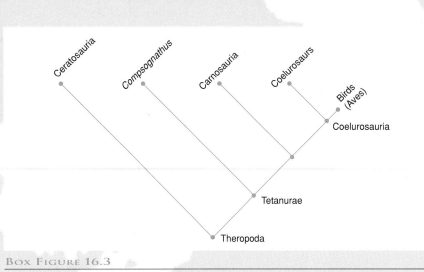

BOX FIGURE 16.3

This cladogram indicates that birds are closely related to coelurosaurs.

powered flight. Despite the many similarities of theropod dinosaurs to birds, and their shared evolutionary novelties, birds are unique vertebrates. It is this uniqueness, and the great diversity of birds, that long ago led to their recognition as a separate class of vertebrates called Aves. For these reasons some paleontologists prefer to distinguish this class from dinosaurs. But, others place dinosaurs (or at least theropod dinosaurs) in the Aves, and, as mentioned above, still

others abandon Aves as a separate class and include birds in the Theropoda.

These differing classifications of birds reflect different philosophies of how a phylogeny should be turned into a classification. They do not reflect different ideas on the phylogenetic relationships of birds. All but a few paleontologists agree that the birds, or the non-dinosaurian Aves, or the avian theropods, or whatever you choose to call them, were descended from theropod dinosaurs.

K E Y   T E R M S

air sacs
arboreal hypothesis
Archaeopteryx
Aves
bird

cursorial hypothesis
feathers
furcula (wishbone)
"missing link"
pneumatic

pneumatic ducts
Protoavis
ratites
Solnhofen Limestone

REVIEW QUESTIONS

1. How is a bird's skeleton designed to make powered flight possible?

2. What evolutionary novelties were shared by theropod dinosaurs and birds?

3. Why do most paleontologists consider *Archaeopteryx* to be a bird? What similarities does it show to theropod dinosaurs?

4. What other possible ancestors of birds have been identified, and why are arguments for a dinosaur ancestry of birds more convincing?

5. Compare and contrast the arboreal and cursorial hypotheses of the origin of avian flight. Which do you favor, and why?

6. What do Cretaceous birds suggest about the origin and early diversification of the Aves?

7. What impact does their recognition as the ancestors of birds have on our ideas about dinosaurs?

FURTHER READING

Chatterjee, S. 1991. Cranial anatomy and relationships of a new Triassic bird from Texas: *Philosophical Transactions of the Royal Society of London Series B,* v. 332, pp. 277–342. (Technical description of *Protoavis*.)

Feduccia, J. A. 1980. *The Age of Birds.* Cambridge: Harvard University Press, 196 pp. (A very readable and thorough book on the evolution of birds.)

Feduccia, J. A. 1993. Evidence from claw geometry indicating arboreal habits of *Archaeopteryx: Science,* v. 259, pp. 790–93. (Presents evidence that *Archaeopteryx* perched in trees.)

Hecht, M. K., Ostrom, J. H., Viohl, G., and Wellnhofer, P., editors. 1985. *The Beginnings of Birds.* Eichstatt: Freunde des Jura-Museums Eichstatt, 382 pp. (A collection of 38 technical articles on bird origins based on a conference held in Germany in 1984.)

Kurochkin, E. N. 1985. Lower Cretaceous birds from Mongolia and their evolutionary significance: *Acta XVIII Congressus Internationalis Ornithologici,* vol. 1, pp. 191–99. (Challenges the idea that *Archaeopteryx* was the ancestor of later birds.)

Ostrom, J. H. 1976. *Archaeopteryx* and the origin of birds: *Biological Journal of the Linnaean Society,* v. 8, pp. 91–182. (A comprehensive technical article on the origin of birds.)

Ostrom, J. H. 1979. Bird flight: How did it begin?: *American Scientist,* v. 67, pp. 46–56. (A semitechnical review of the origin of flight in birds.)

Padian K., editor. 1986. The origin of birds and the evolution of flight: *Memoirs of the California Academy of Sciences,* v. 8, 152 pp. (A collection of technical articles on the origin of birds and related subjects.)

DINOSAUR EXTINCTION

The most frequently asked question about dinosaurs is, why (or how) did they become extinct? To attempt to answer that question, we need to examine one of the most highly charged scientific debates about dinosaurs. This debate is ongoing, and it has produced two radically different explanations of dinosaur extinction. One explanation links the extinction of dinosaurs to the impact of a comet or meteorite that exploded upon striking the earth 65 million years ago. The other explanation sees dinosaur extinction as the outgrowth of changes in topography, climate, vegetation, and/or animal life at the end of the Cretaceous that resulted in the **"ecological collapse"** of the dinosaurs. Other explanations of dinosaur extinction, some quite well known, are based on much less (or no) evidence than these two possibilities (box 17.1). Therefore, this chapter focuses on the two current hypotheses about the cause of dinosaur extinction.

THE TERMINAL CRETACEOUS EXTINCTION

Dinosaur extinction was part of a more pervasive extinction that occurred at the end of the Cretaceous, usually called the **terminal Cretaceous extinction,** or the extinction at the Cretaceous-Tertiary boundary (or K-T boundary for short, K for Cretaceous and T for Tertiary). The terminal Cretaceous extinction was only one of several major extinctions in the history of life (figure 17.1). But it was not the largest; that "honor" is held by the extinction that occurred at the end of the Permian, 250 million years ago.

The terminal Cretaceous extinction was not just the extinction of the dinosaurs. It included the extinction of several types of organisms, both in the sea and on land. Paleontologists estimate that at least 15 percent of the families (or approximately 100 families) of shelled marine invertebrates became extinct in the sea during the terminal Cretaceous extinction. Particularly hard-hit groups were the **ammonoid** cephalopods, relatives of living octopuses and squids, which suffered total extinction; clams and snails, which suffered significant losses including the total extinction of the **rudists,** reef-building clams, and the **inoceramids,** thin-shelled, plate-like clams; and the marine reptiles, the **mosasaurs** (marine lizards) and the long-necked **plesiosaurs** (figure 17.2). Major changes also occurred in the marine plankton, and the microscopic shelled protozoans known as **Foraminifera** also suffered heavy losses (figure 17.3). On land, the pterosaurs and dinosaurs became extinct, several types of **marsupial mammals** disappeared, and a few types of plants died out (figure 17.4). However, most mammals, reptiles (lizards, snakes, turtles, and crocodiles), and birds were apparently not affected by the extinction.

BOX 17.1

Many explanations of dinosaur extinction lack supporting evidence, but, ironically, these are some of the most widely-known explanations of dinosaur extinction. Perhaps the best-known explanation is that dinosaurs became extinct because Late Cretaceous mammals ate their eggs. Today, very few mammals eat eggs, humans and mongooses notwithstanding. There is no evidence of egg eating by Late Cretaceous mammals. Furthermore, mammals coexisted with dinosaurs throughout the Mesozoic reign of the dinosaurs. Why, then, would **egg-eating mammals** have had an adverse effect on dinosaurs only at the end of the Cretaceous? Egg eating by mammals thus can be rejected as an explanation of dinosaur extinction.

Some explanations of dinosaur extinction rely on extreme changes in climate at the end of the Cretaceous. One argument is that dinosaurs were so large they could not hibernate, so they were unable to cope with extremely cold climates at the end of the Cretaceous. A contrasting argument is that temperatures at the end of the Cretaceous became so hot that dinosaurs literally "roasted" to death. Both of these explanations of surviving at the end of the Cretaceous point to the small size and/or ability of mammals and small reptiles to hibernate as reasons why they were able to cope with one or the other temperature extreme.

The problem is that there is no evidence for extremely hot or cold climates at the end of the Cretaceous, although the impact of a meteor or comet may have produced a geologically short period of intense dark and cold.

Today, some plants, called converters, absorb and concentrate elements like selenium, which are poisonous in large amounts. Large amounts of selenium are present in some volcanic ashes. Thus arose the argument that increased volcanic activity at the end of the Cretaceous produced increased **selenium** in plants eaten by herbivorous dinosaurs, which was also passed on to the meat-eating dinosaurs when they preyed upon the plant eaters. The selenium poisoned the dinosaurs, bringing about their extinction. Of course, the case for an increase in volcanic activity at the end of the Cretaceous is not convincing, a fossil record of the selenium converting plants does not exist and no explanation can be offered about why non-dinosaurian plant eaters, some mammals, and non-dinosaurian reptiles were not poisoned. Selenium poisoning is an inadequate explanation of dinosaur extinction.

The longest running extraterrestrial cause of dinosaur extinction is a supernova. It has been estimated that a nearby **supernova** could generate a tremendous rise in the radiation in the atmosphere, immediately killing or causing massive chromosomal mutations in the dinosaurs that would have made them sterile or at least incapable of producing viable offspring. At present, however, no remnant of a nearby 65-million-year-old supernova has been detected by astronomers. Also, the supernova explanation is hard pressed to explain why many organisms survived the Cretaceous.

Thinning of and trace elements in dinosaur eggshells at the end of the Cretaceous as a cause of dinosaur extinction was discussed in Chapter 13 (see box 13.3). There, we saw that high levels of trace elements in dinosaur eggshells may have been introduced during fossilization. Also, it has not been demonstrated that the dinosaur eggs with relatively thin shells were not viable eggs. A similar problematic explanation is that disease extinguished the dinosaurs. Not only is there no evidence for this, but a worldwide epidemic or plague among the dinosaurs exceeds the scope of any known disease and seems implausible.

This review of some popular, yet unsupported, explanations of dinosaur extinction still leaves a residuum of fantastic ideas beyond scientific inquiry. The most popular of these is that extraterrestrial beings either hunted the dinosaurs into extinction or trapped them all and carried them off into space (box figure 17.1). Clearly, these ideas are the stuff of science fiction stories, not of the scientific inquiry into dinosaur extinction.

It is important to recognize that more than just dinosaurs became extinct at the end of the Cretaceous. The broad nature of the extinctions calls for an explanation beyond one that would account for just the disappearance of the dinosaurs. Furthermore, the selectivity of the extinctions (many types of organisms survived the Cretaceous) needs to be explained. Hence we are looking for a cause of dinosaur extinction that is consistent with what we know about the breadth and selectivity of the terminal Cretaceous extinction.

Spacemen killing off the dinosaurs is an explanation of dinosaur extinction for which there is no evidence.

NATURE OF THE EVIDENCE

We must not only consider the breadth and selectivity of the terminal Cretaceous extinction in the search for a cause, but the evidence of the extinction—the rocks and fossils and their distribution in geologic time and space—must be considered. Indeed, the evidence holds center stage in the search for the cause of the extinction, because most debate about the cause of the terminal Cretaceous extinction focuses on disagreements over the evidence and how it should be interpreted.

This is best understood if we make a clear, conceptual distinction between the evidence itself, or the pattern of the terminal Cretaceous extinction, and the processes that produced it. This distinction between **pattern** and **process** is a

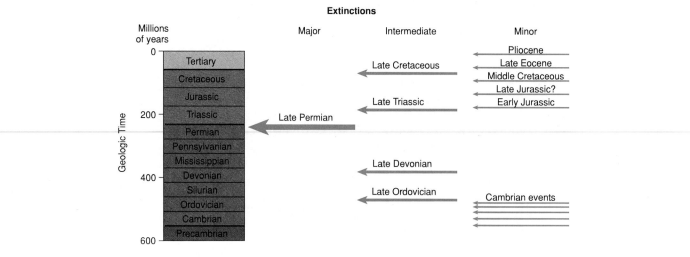

Extinctions

FIGURE 17.1

The terminal Cretaceous extinction was one of several major extinctions in the history of life.

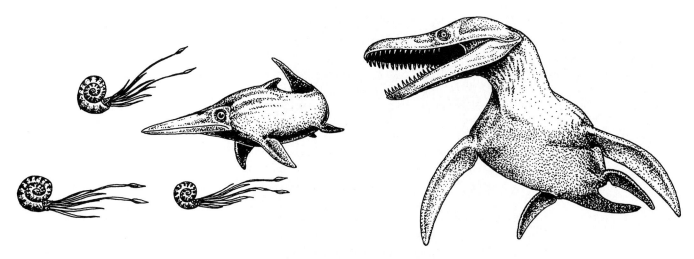

FIGURE 17.2

Several types of marine organisms, including those shown here, became extinct at the end of the Cretaceous.

FIGURE 17.3

Foraminifera are microscopic shelled protozoans; they suffered heavy losses during the terminal Cretaceous extinction.

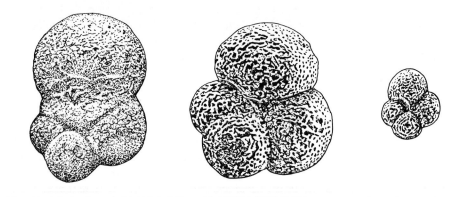

fundamental one in paleontology. It involves distinguishing the fossils themselves and the rocks that contain them as patterns to be described, from the processes (for example, evolution and sedimentation) that produced the patterns. Processes can only be inferred from patterns, not observed, much as a detective might infer the process of a crime from the patterns represented by the evidence of the crime.

The pattern of the terminal Cretaceous extinction, and particularly the extinction of dinosaurs, is a subject of great disagreement among paleontologists. This disagreement lies at the core of debate over the cause of the extinction. Different patterns, especially distributions of dinosaur fossils through geologic time, suggest different causes of extinction. One possible pattern suggests a sudden and simultaneous cause of dinosaur extinction, whereas a different pattern suggests a more gradual and long-term cause of their disappearance (figure 17.5). What pattern best describes the fossil record of the last dinosaurs?

Before answering this question, let us consider another aspect of the nature of the evidence of dinosaur extinction, namely its completeness. The last interval of Cretaceous time is termed the **Maastrichtian,** after the town of Maastricht in Belgium, and it lasted about 6 million years, from 71 to 65 million years ago. Maastrichtian dinosaurs were the last dinosaurs, and are known from a variety of locations worldwide. But most of these Maastrichtian dinosaur localities are millions of years older than the end of the Cretaceous, and thus do not include the last dinosaurs, which are those of latest Cretaceous age. Furthermore, many of these localities yield only a few dinosaur fossils, or eggs, or have not been collected and studied extensively. Only late Maastrichtian dinosaur localities in western North America yield enough dinosaur fossils and have been collected and studied sufficiently to produce a detailed pattern of the distribution in geologic time of the last dinosaurs. These localities extend in an arc from the high plains of southern Alberta to the Big Bend of Texas (figure 17.6). Although some other localities have been analyzed to explain dinosaur extinction, almost all localities that can produce a reliable pattern are restricted to a small portion of the world in western North America. This, of course, should make us cautious about the pattern of dinosaur extinction, because it can only be drawn from a limited area and then *assumed* to represent a global pattern.

Bearing this in mind, two patterns of dinosaur extinction have been constructed from the late Maastrichtian localities in western North America. One pattern is of decreasing dinosaur abundance and diversity during the Maastrichtian, the other of an undiminished or increasing dinosaur presence, followed by a sudden disappearance at the end of the Maastrichtian (see figure 17.5). The first pattern, of course, suggests a gradual disappearance of dinosaurs over a period of a few million years, whereas the second suggests a sudden, catastrophic extinction of the dinosaurs.

Many paleontologists believe that the first pattern accurately reflects what happened to dinosaurs at the end of the Cretaceous. But others believe that strong evidence supports the second pattern. Debate over the two patterns is ongoing, with new evidence being accumulated and described to support one pattern or the other. This makes it difficult to choose one pattern over the other at present. Instead, we can best focus our attention on how the two patterns are arrived at and why they differ.

Documentation of how dinosaur diversity (the number of different kinds of dinosaurs) changed during the Maastrichtian is only as good as the sampling and identifications on which it is based. We need extensive collections of dinosaur fossils from as many Maastrichtian fossil layers as possible and as accurate as possible (ideally to the genus and species) identifications of those fossils. This might sound straightforward, but extensive collecting of dinosaur fossils is expensive and time-consuming. Also, many of the fossils collected are not complete dinosaur skeletons or skulls, and thus are difficult to identify precisely (figure 17.7).

Dinosaurs and pterosaurs became extinct at the end of the Cretaceous.

© Mark Hallett

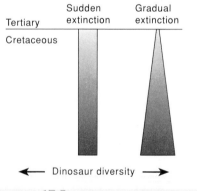

FIGURE 17.5

Two patterns of dinosaur extinction, one gradual and the other sudden, have been described.

Different amounts of collecting, different degrees of geologic time resolution (in other words, many versus few fossil layers), and differing identifications account for the two conflicting patterns seen in the Maastrichtian dinosaurs of western North America. Also, collections from different areas, even from two nearby locations in Montana, suggest different patterns, partly because of different degrees of preservation at different locations.

Two contrasting patterns of dinosaur extinction have thus arisen. Even a third one had been proposed that claims dinosaurs survived the Cretaceous (box 17.2). Choosing among these patterns is critical, because each suggests a very different cause of dinosaur extinction, one gradual, the other sudden. But, as of this writing, the jury is still out on which pattern is the accurate one. Until this is decided, debate about dinosaur extinction will continue.

COMET (METEORITE) IMPACT

Having revealed the impasse over the pattern of dinosaur extinction, it might seem anticlimactic to discuss possible causes. But the two current explanations of dinosaur extinction present possible explanations of the alternative patterns and one or the other, or a combination of both, stands a good chance of being correct.

In 1979, Nobel physics laureate Luis Alvarez, his geologist son, Walter Alvarez, and two nuclear chemists, Frank Asaro and Helen Michel, proposed that a comet (or meteorite) the size of a mountain (10 kilometers in diameter) collided with the earth 65 million years ago and caused the terminal Cretaceous extinction (figure 17.8). They based this proposition on chemical analysis of a thin, 65-million-year-old clay layer at **Gubbio** in northern Italy. This clay layer was deposited at the bottom of the sea at the end of the Cretaceous, and the chemical analysis revealed it contains an unusually high concentration of the platinum-group metal **iridium.** Iridium is very rare on the earth's surface except in some rock deposits mined for gold and platinum. The rocks at Gubbio are clearly not such a deposit. Most of the iridium on earth comes from meteorites and other matter from space, so the Alvarez team decided that the high concentration in the 65-million-year-old clay at Gubbio must have settled in the dust produced by a huge cometary impact.

FIGURE 17.6

Maastrichtian dinosaur localities in western North America provide the only extensive record of dinosaur extinction.

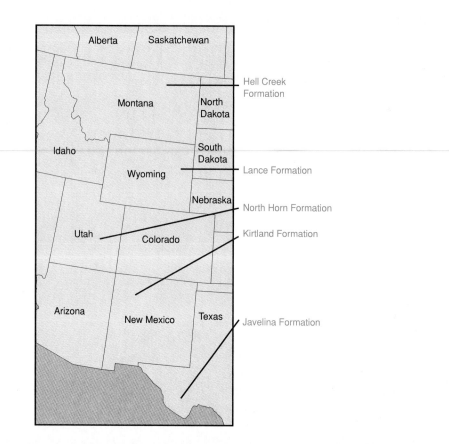

FIGURE 17.7

Fragmentary dinosaur fossils of Maastrichtian age, such as this one, are difficult to identify precisely.

BOX 17.2

PALEOCENE DINOSAURS?

For more than a century, paleontologists have marked the end of the Cretaceous with the disappearance of the dinosaurs. This means that the youngest dinosaur fossils are of Late Cretaceous age, and, conversely, the discovery of a dinosaur fossil is taken to indicate the rocks at the discovery site are no younger than Late Cretaceous. Despite this, some paleontologists claim to have discovered younger dinosaur fossils, of Paleocene age, thus demonstrating that not all of the dinosaurs became extinct at the end of the Cretaceous. These claims have come from such farflung locales as China, India, Peru, Bolivia and, in the United States, New Mexico and Montana. If substantiated, they seriously challenge well-accepted ideas about the timing of dinosaur extinction.

But most of these claims cannot be substantiated simply because the Paleocene age of the dinosaur fossils cannot be verified. This is because few of the supposed Paleocene dinosaur fossils have been found associated with, or directly above in the strata, other types of fossils of unquestioned Paleocene age. A good example of this is provided by supposed Paleocene dinosaur footprints from Bolivia. These footprints are found in an exposure of a rock formation that contains no Paleocene fossils. But many kilometers away, the same formation contains fossils of mammals and fishes of Paleocene age, so it has been suggested that the entire formation, including the dinosaur footprints, is of Paleocene age. However, many kilometers of forest intervene between the two exposures, so it cannot be demonstrated that the dinosaur footprints are the same age or younger

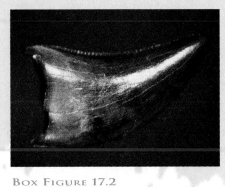

BOX FIGURE 17.2

This isolated dinosaur tooth from Montana was found associated with Paleocene fossils of mammals and pollen.

Courtesy Dr. J. Keith Rigby, Jr.

than the Paleocene fishes and mammals. They might just as well be older!

A lack of direct association with Paleocene fossils eliminates all but one of the current claims of Paleocene dinosaurs. This remaining claim comes from Montana, where dinosaur fossils are found in direct association, mixed in the same rock layer, with fossil mammals and pollen of Paleocene age. These dinosaur fossils are isolated teeth—mostly of hadrosaurids, ceratopsians and small theropods—and fragments of bone (box figure 17.2). This might seem convincing proof of Paleocene dinosaurs were it not for the possibility that these dinosaurs have been reworked from older, Cretaceous strata.

A fossil is said to be reworked if, after initial fossilization in the rock, it was exhumed and redeposited in an overlying, younger layer of rock. Reworking of small fossils may be common, especially in fluvial environments. Imagine, for example, isolated dinosaur teeth and parts

of dinosaur bones buried and fossilized on a Late Cretaceous river floodplain. Subsequently, during the Paleocene, large river channels carve out and scour into the floodplain. In so doing, older Upper Cretaceous floodplain deposits containing the dinosaur fossils are eroded and carried off by the running water. They become mixed with younger sediments and fossils and are subsequently deposited on channel bottoms and margins, producing a mixture of Cretaceous and Paleocene fossils.

Most paleontologists believe this is the explanation of how dinosaur fossils and Paleocene mammal and pollen fossils came to be associated in Montana. They point to the small size of the dinosaur fossils and the fact that the association is in river-channel deposits as evidence the dinosaur fossils are reworked. But proponents of the Paleocene age of these dinosaur fossils point to the lack of damage, abrasion, and weathering of the dinosaur teeth as evidence against them having been reworked. They argue that we should see some mechanical damage of the dinosaur teeth by the process of erosion, exhumation, transport, and reburial that reworking entails.

But is this really the case? Cretaceous shark teeth found reworked in rocks as young as Eocene show no evidence of mechanical damage. Therefore, we might expect reworking of dinosaur teeth to occur without appreciable alteration of the fossils.

There thus seems to be no convincing evidence for Paleocene dinosaurs. The search for them, however, continues, and we can expect claims of Paleocene dinosaurs to continue as long as dinosaur extinction is studied.

FIGURE 17.8

A cometary impact at the end of the Cretaceous may have looked like this.

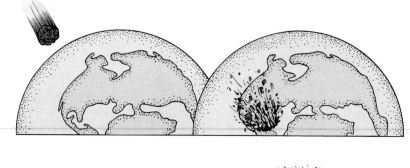

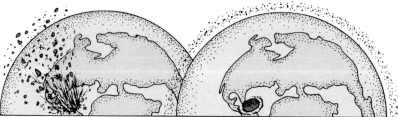

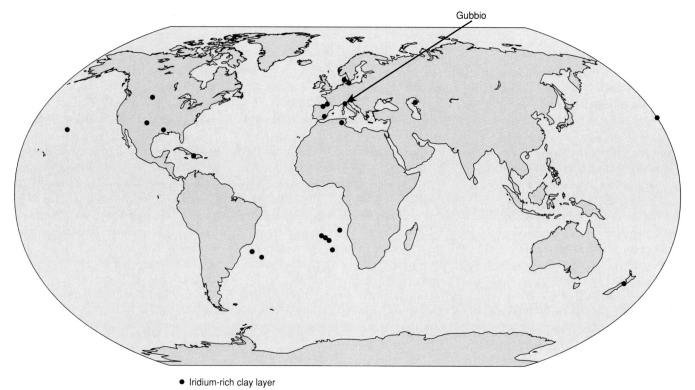

Gubbio

• Iridium-rich clay layer

FIGURE 17.9

An iridium-rich clay layer has been identified at the Cretaceous-Tertiary boundary at many sites worldwide.

This idea elicited both criticism and enthusiasm in the scientific community, and much effort was expended in the 1980s to either refute or support the comet impact and its inferred results. Further chemical analysis of the Gubbio clay layer revealed it contains other elements (such as osmium) not common on earth except as the result of meteoritic infall. The high concentration of iridium was also identified in 65-million-year-old rock layers at dozens of localities worldwide (figure 17.9). Another peculiarity of these layers is that they contain microscopic droplets of **"shocked quartz,"** a type of quartz grain with laminar deformations only known to be generated by high speed shock in laboratories, nuclear test sites, and near impact craters (figure 17.10).

BOX 17.3

THE CHICXULUB IMPACT STRUCTURE

In 1990, a group of American geologists announced the discovery of a huge impact structure of terminal Cretaceous age, and this structure has since been proclaimed the "smoking gun" behind the terminal Cretaceous extinctions. Located on the northwestern coast of Mexico's Yucatán Peninsula (box figure 17.3), the **Chicxulub** (pronounced CHICKS-uh-loob) structure is a circular collapse feature with an estimated diameter of about 300 kilometers. Diverse and impressive evidence makes Chicxulub look like the place where a huge comet (or meteorite) crashed into the earth at the end of the Cretaceous. This evidence includes:

1. The Chicxulub structure itself has many features diagnostic of an impact crater, including the concentrically collapsed crust under it.

2. A layer of melted rock underlies the structure. The numerical age of this melt layer has been calculated at 65 million years, exactly the Cretaceous-Tertiary boundary. And the melted rocks are unusually rich in iridium.

3. Above the melted rocks are well-sorted debris that is most easily understood as rock fragments that fell back into the crater after the impact.

4. Tidal wave deposits of the same age as the structure have been identified in the southern Gulf of Mexico and the western Atlantic.

5. Deposits of rock debris thrown out of the crater (called ejecta) have been found in Haiti and northeastern Mexico. These deposits are full of shocked mineral grains and melted rock droplets.

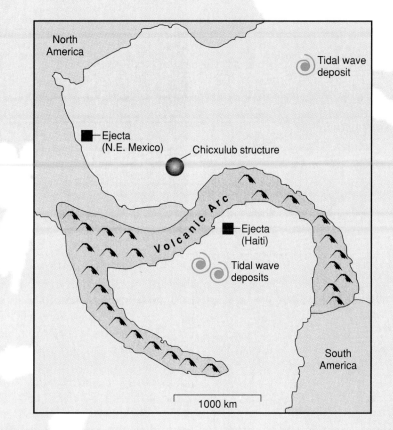

BOX FIGURE 17.3

This paleogeographic map of the Caribbean at the end of the Cretaceous shows the Chicxulub impact structure and some related rock features.

The case for Chicxulub being the site where the comet (meteorite) plowed into the earth at the end of the Cretaceous seems incontrovertible, though some critics still argue the structure is of volcanic origin.

At the end of the Cretaceous, much of the rock present at the site of the Chicxulub structure consisted of anhydrite, a mineral rich in sulfur. Some scientists suggest that the impact released huge amounts of sulfur into the atmosphere. The sulfur combined with water, producing sulfuric acid and a devastating acid rain. Acidic dust then filled the upper atmosphere, blocking out sunlight and causing a decade of freezing or near-freezing temperatures worldwide.

The search for the terminal Cretaceous cometary impact crater also energized research on the detection of ancient impact craters on the earth's surface (box 17.3). This research identified about 16 impact craters that could be the right age to have been the site of the terminal Cretaceous cometary impact. Most of these craters are in and around the Atlantic Ocean basin, and the possibility of multiple comet impacts at the end of the Cretaceous has been suggested.

FIGURE 17.10

Shocked quartz grains provide evidence of a cometary impact at the end of the Cretaceous.

Courtesy Charles Naeser; photograph by Glenn Izett

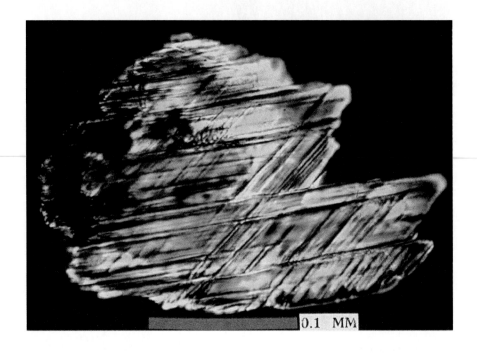

0.1 MM

At the time of this writing, the evidence that one or more comets struck the earth at the end of the Cretaceous seems conclusive to most geologists and paleontologists. But some geologists, notably French volcanologists, have argued that massive volcanic eruptions at the end of the Cretaceous produced the iridium-rich layer. These geologists point to huge Late Cretaceous volcanoes that were present in India, Siberia, and other locations as the source of the iridium-rich layer. This source, however, could not provide the shocked quartz and some other features peculiar to the iridium layer, and for this reason most scientists discount volcanism as the likely source of the layer.

Although it now seems certain that one or more comets collided with Earth 65 million years ago, how and whether or not that would have caused the terminal Cretaceous extinction is much less certain. Initially, the Alvarez team suggested that the impact generated dust that produced global darkness, causing the extinctions. This dust would have stopped plant photosynthesis and cooled global temperatures, resulting in a deep freeze. Other possible effects of the impact include nitric acid rain resulting from heating of the atmosphere by the entering comet or a worldwide greenhouse (after the impact deep freeze) produced by water vapor that would have been lofted into the atmosphere if the comet landed in the ocean.

Currently, there is no clear agreement on the precise effect of the comet impact, but there is general agreement that it produced a **global catastrophe.** Whether this catastrophe caused the terminal Cretaceous extinctions, or whether it was a violent perturbation weathered by most organisms, is still hotly debated.

We might best think of this by concluding that the iridium-rich layer is a pattern indicative of a specific process, a comet impact. Now, the question becomes, does the pattern of dinosaur and other Late Cretaceous fossil distribution support the comet impact and the resulting catastrophe as the cause of the extinction?

One advantage of the comet impact explanation is that it predicts a sudden and simultaneous pattern of terminal Cretaceous extinction. Many fossil patterns, such as those constructed by some paleontologists for Maastrichtian dinosaurs, don't indicate a sudden and simultaneous end. But proponents of the comet impact explanation argue that these patterns are based on an incomplete sampling of fossils or incomplete preservation of latest Maastrichtian fossils. There is some evidence to support their contention. For example, recent dinosaur collecting by paleontologist Peter Sheehan and colleagues at the Milwaukee Public Museum in eastern Montana and western North Dakota reveals no evidence of a gradual decline of

FIGURE 17.11

Badlands of the Hell Creek Formation in eastern Montana provide the most extensive record known of dinosaur extinction.

Courtesy David Fastovsky

dinosaurs at the end of the Cretaceous. In contrast, other intensively sampled locations suggest gradual decline and ecological collapse of dinosaurs during the Maastrichtian. One of these studies represents the most serious challenge to the sudden, catastrophic extinction of dinosaurs posited by the comet impact explanation, and is discussed below.

GRADUAL EXTINCTION

The badlands developed in the upper Maastrichtian and Paleocene strata in eastern **Montana** represent the most extensively sampled record of dinosaur extinction on earth (figure 17.11). The upper Maastrichtian rocks are the **Hell Creek Formation** overlain by lower Paleocene strata of the Tullock Formation. The end of the Cretaceous, and the boundary of the two formations, has generally been placed at a layer of coal called the Z-coal bed. An iridium-rich layer is found just below this coal bed.

Since the 1950s, paleontologists William Clemens of the University of California at Berkeley and Robert Sloan of the University of Minnesota, and numerous colleagues and students, have collected fossils from these rocks. This collecting has produced an unparalleled record of the evolution of terrestrial plants and animals during the transition from Cretaceous to Tertiary.

Much of this record does not suggest a sudden, catastrophic extinction at the end of the Cretaceous (figure 17.12). For example, placental mammals increase in diversity throughout the Maastrichtian. Non-dinosaurian reptiles, including lizards, snakes, turtles, and crocodiles, show very little extinction at the end of the Cretaceous, with only about 30 percent of their genera disappearing. Dinosaurs became extinct at the end of the Cretaceous, but there was a marked decline in diversity in the Hell Creek Formation from 19 genera at its base, to 12 in the upper 16 meters of the formation, to 7 at the very top.

This pattern of dinosaur decline either is real, or it is an artifact of sampling and biases in preservation. If real, it presents the strongest evidence available of a gradual extinction of dinosaurs during the late Maastrichtian. This evidence, and other patterns of fossil distribution, certainly do not support the sudden extinction predicted by the comet impact explanation. Instead, they suggest complicated ecological factors as a likely cause of dinosaur extinction.

FIGURE 17.12

The fossil record of vertebrates from badlands of the Hell Creek Formation shows some groups diversifying before, and most groups surviving, the end of the Cretaceous. Sharks disappeared locally because of loss of marine habitats.

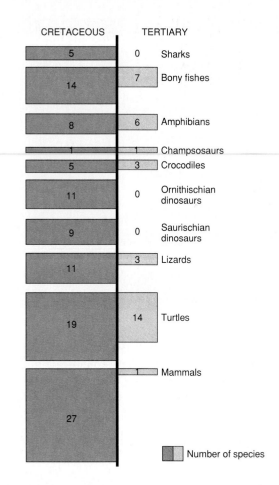

These ecological factors might include cooling and drying of climate because of a worldwide drop in sea level at the end of the Cretaceous, changes in vegetation due to the climate change, and/or competition from diversifying placental mammals that might have posed a real problem for small, juvenile dinosaurs. Certainly such possibilities do not present a cause of dinosaur extinction as simple, and therefore appealing, as a comet impact. But the pattern of dinosaur extinction and other fossil distribution in the Hell Creek Formation suggests to many paleontologists a complex, ecological cause of dinosaur disappearance.

MINIMIZING THE DAMAGE

In recent years a number of paleontologists have questioned the significance of dinosaur extinction. This questioning has taken three tacks.

The first has been to point out that the significance of the entire terminal Cretaceous extinction has been greatly overstated. Today, most of the living species of animals are arthropods and worms that lack fossilizable skeletal parts. There is no reason to believe that these animals did not have a similar diversity during the Late Cretaceous, yet they have left no fossils during that interval of geologic time. This means, of course, that paleontologists have virtually no idea how, if at all, these soft-bodied animals were affected by the terminal Cretaceous extinction. This should lower our confidence in estimates of the magnitude of the terminal Cretaceous extinction. These estimates, which range from a kill of from 40 to 80 percent of the species on earth, apply only to those organisms with fossil records and may greatly overstate the magnitude of the terminal Cretaceous extinction.

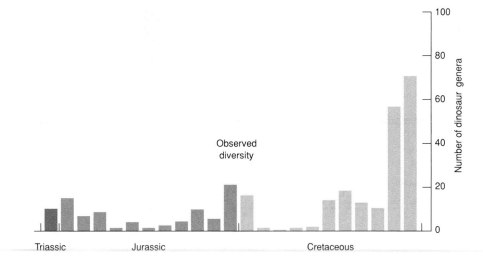

FIGURE 17.13
Dinosaur diversity during the Late Triassic through Late Cretaceous indicates that most dinosaurs disappeared before the end of the Cretaceous.

This is a valuable perspective on the terminal Cretaceous extinction, or for that matter, any extinction being studied in the fossil record. We should always remember that the fossil record is incomplete, and should not interpret it as if it preserves all organisms that lived during the past. Yet, this perspective should not fundamentally alter the significance of dinosaur extinction. The dinosaur fossil record relevant to extinction is, as discussed above, very incomplete, yet it is good enough to demonstrate that dinosaurs did become extinct, and their extinction merits an explanation.

Or did they? The second tack in questioning the significance of dinosaur extinction is to state that dinosaurs are not extinct. They survive as birds, so what is all this fuss about their extinction? This viewpoint, however, merely dodges the issue of dinosaur extinction. The dinosaurs that became extinct at the end of the Cretaceous represented a significant group of animals. The fact that their descendants, the birds, or if you like, one group of feathered dinosaurs, survived the extinction does not diminish the significance of the terminal Cretaceous extinction of dinosaurs. Birds appeared during the Late Jurassic, long before the extinction of the dinosaurs, and it is highly likely their closest relatives among the theropod dinosaurs were extinct long before the Late Cretaceous. It is an interesting question why birds survived the Cretaceous, one that needs to be considered in any attempt to explain the terminal Cretaceous extinctions. But the survival of birds does not diminish the significance of dinosaur extinction.

A third, and final attempt to question the significance of dinosaur extinction stems from a "long view" of the fossil record of dinosaurs. This long view points out that somewhere between 900 and 1,200 genera of dinosaurs are estimated to have lived during the Late Triassic through Late Cretaceous (almost 300 valid genera are known), most of which became extinct before the Late Cretaceous (figure 17.13). The last dinosaurs represent only a small portion of their total Mesozoic diversity, so the extinction of dinosaurs is merely the disappearance of a relatively small fraction of the group.

This argument, like the previous one, dodges the issue of dinosaur extinction. Its faults are best revealed by a terrifying analogy. Suppose the human species became extinct tomorrow. If so, it would be true that most species (and individuals) of humans became extinct before the final disappearance of *Homo sapiens*. Thus, as the dinosaurs, the final extinction of humankind would be the disappearance of only a small fraction of the group. But should this minimize the significance of these final extinctions? Indeed, the final extinction of most groups of organisms involved only a fraction of the species of that group that ever lived. Dinosaur extinction thus remains a significant phenomenon, regardless of the incompleteness of the fossil record, the survival of birds, or the pre-Late Cretaceous diversity of the dinosaurs.

ANSWER THE QUESTION!

After all this discussion, we are still led back to the original question of what caused the extinction of the dinosaurs. The answer to this question, as we now know, depends on which pattern of distribution of the last dinosaurs is correct. One pattern suggests a sudden and simultaneous disappearance of dinosaurs at the end of the Cretaceous and thus supports a major catastrophe, as would be caused by a comet impact. An alternative pattern of gradual decline of the dinosaurs during the late Maastrichtian suggests that complicated ecological changes brought about dinosaur extinction. It just might be that these ecological changes were followed by a comet impact that eliminated the last dinosaurs, thus combining the two most likely causes.

The inability to provide a simple answer to the question of what killed the dinosaurs may disappoint some. But this inability reflects the fact that not all the evidence is in on dinosaur extinction. The disappearance of the dinosaur remains a vigorous field of scientific research and debate.

SUMMARY

1. The two current, and debated, explanations of dinosaur extinction identify as the cause a comet impact or complex ecological changes.

2. Other explanations of dinosaur extinction lack strong evidence and include egg-eating mammals, extreme cold or hot climates, poisoning, a supernova explosion, thinning and trace elements in dinosaur eggshells, disease, and extraterrestrial big-game hunters.

3. The terminal Cretaceous extinction eliminated many types of organisms in the sea and on the land.

4. The broad extent and selectivity of the terminal Cretaceous extinction forces a search for a cause that explains both of these factors.

5. Patterns are the fossils and rocks studied by paleontologists. The processes (evolution and sedimentation) that created these patterns cannot be observed directly.

6. Different distribution patterns of the last dinosaurs reflect different degrees of sampling and precision of identification.

7. Strong evidence, accepted by most geologists, indicates one or more comets collided with the earth 65 million years ago.

8. Supporters of a comet impact causing dinosaur extinction predict a sudden and simultaneous extinction of dinosaurs.

9. According to some paleontologists, the pattern of fossil distribution in the Hell Creek Formation in Montana is not consistent with a comet impact causing the terminal Cretaceous extinction. Instead, it suggests a gradual decline of dinosaurs because of complicated ecological changes.

10. Some paleontologists minimize the significance of dinosaur extinction by noting that the magnitude of the terminal Cretaceous extinction has been overstated, that dinosaurs did not become extinct because birds survived, or that the last dinosaurs represent a small fraction of all dinosaurs that ever lived. These arguments, however, do not diminish the importance of dinosaur extinction.

11. The inability to give a simple answer to the question of what caused dinosaur extinction reflects the fact that all the data are not in on the subject.

KEY TERMS

ammonoid
Chicxulub
"ecological collapse"
egg-eating mammals
Foraminifera
global catastrophe
Gubbio

Hell Creek Formation
inoceramids
iridium
Maastrichtian
marsupial mammals
Montana
mosasaurs
pattern

plesiosaurs
process
rudists
selenium
"shocked quartz"
supernova
terminal Cretaceous extinction

REVIEW QUESTIONS

1. What are some popular ideas about the cause of dinosaur extinction, and why are they not accepted by most paleontologists?

2. Describe the extent of the terminal Cretaceous extinction.

3. How do the extent and selectivity of the terminal Cretaceous extinction affect attempts to determine its cause?

4. Distinguish a pattern from a process and explain how these concepts apply to paleontology.

5. How does the nature of the fossil record of Maastrichtian dinosaurs influence our understanding of dinosaur extinction?

6. Why are two contrasting patterns of dinosaur extinction described by paleontologists?

7. What evidence indicates a comet impact with the earth 65 million years ago? What would be some of the possible effects of such an impact?

8. Did a comet impact cause the extinction of the dinosaurs?

9. What does the fossil record from the Hell Creek Formation in Montana suggest about dinosaur extinction?

10. How have some paleontologists minimized the significance of the extinction of dinosaurs, and what are the strengths and the weaknesses of their arguments?

11. What killed the dinosaurs?

FURTHER READING

Alvarez, W. and Asaro, F. 1990. An extraterrestrial impact: *Scientific American*, vol. 246, pp. 78–84. (An up-to-date review of the comet impact at the end of the Cretaceous and its possible effects.)

Archibald, J. D. 1989. The demise of the dinosaurs and the rise of the mammals; in Culver, S. J., ed., *The Age of Dinosaurs Short Courses in Paleontology Number 2*. Knoxville: The Paleontological Society, pp. 162–74. (A very readable review of the fossil record of the Hell Creek Formation and its bearing on dinosaur extinction.)

Benton, M. J. 1990. Scientific methodologies in collision: The history of the study of the extinction of the dinosaur: *Evolutionary Biology*, vol. 24, pp. 371–400. (Reviews the history of ideas about dinosaur extinction.)

Courtillot, V. E. 1990. A volcanic eruption: *Scientific American*, vol. 246, pp. 85–92. (Argues the case for volcanic eruptions producing the iridium-rich layer at the Cretaceous-Tertiary boundary.)

Raup, D. M. 1986. *The Nemesis Affair*. New York: Norton, 220 pp. (Discusses the asteroid-produced extinction of the dinosaurs within the context of how science works.)

Rigby, J. K., Jr. 1987. The last of the North American dinosaurs; in Czerkas, S. J. and Olson, E. C., eds., *Dinosaurs Past and Present Volume II*. Los Angeles: Natural History Museum of Los Angeles County and University of Washington Press, pp. 119–35. (Presents some of the basis for the claim of Paleocene dinosaurs in Montana.)

Sheehan, P. M., Fastovsky, D. E., Hoffmann, R. G., Berhaus, C. B., and Gabriel, D. L. 1991. Sudden extinction of the dinosaurs: Latest Cretaceous, upper Great Plains, U.S.A.: *Science*, vol. 254, pp. 835–39. (Presents evidence for a pattern of sudden extinction of the dinosaurs.)

18

DINOSAURS IN THE PUBLIC EYE

Dinosaurs are extremely popular, and not a week goes by without some new dinosaur discovery appearing in the newspapers and magazines, or on radio and television. Popular books on dinosaurs, for both children and adults, are legion. Life-size sculptures of dinosaurs adorn museums and parks, and toy dinosaurs are a staple item of toy stores. Paintings and drawings of dinosaurs pervade dinosaur books and museums, and dinosaurs have been the subject of myriad movies, cartoons, and television shows. The word *dinosaur* is part of the English language, and it would be difficult to find an American who hasn't used this word at least once. The word *dinosaur* has been transliterated or translated into almost all the world's languages. For example, in Chinese it is pronounced "kong-long" and literally means "terrible dragon."

The preceding 17 chapters of this book have been concerned with the paleontological understanding of dinosaurs. In this chapter, we take a paleontological perspective on some aspects of the public presentation and perception of dinosaurs.

DINOSAURS: DENOTATION AND CONNOTATION

As stated in Chapter 1, and elaborated in Chapter 5, a dinosaur was a reptile with an upright limb posture. Dinosaurs lived during the Late Triassic through Cretaceous, 225 to 65 million years ago, and were the ancestors of birds. Large size was not a characteristic of all dinosaurs, but they included the largest land animals.

Some of these defining features or **denotation** of the word *dinosaur,* are familiar to most people and appear as the primary definition of dinosaur in dictionaries. But a second definition of dinosaur also appears in them, using *dinosaur* as a word to refer to something unwieldy or out-of-date (figure 18.1). This use of the word *dinosaur* may be thought of as its **connotation,** namely a negative image of something no longer useful and so deservedly extinct.

FIGURE 18.1

Most dictionaries present two definitions of the word dinosaur. Note the incorrect derivation of the word dinosaur at the end of the definitions!

From *The Random House Dictionary of the English Language, Unabridged*, 2d ed. Copyright © 1987 by Random House, Inc. Reprinted by permission of Random House, Inc.

di·no·saur (dī′nə sôr′), *n.* **1.** any chiefly terrestrial, herbivorous or carnivorous reptile of the extinct orders Saurischia and Ornithischia, from the Mesozoic Era, certain species of which are the largest known land animals. **2.** something that is unwieldy in size, anachronistically outmoded, or unable to adapt to change: *The old steel mill was a dinosaur that cost the company millions to operate.* [< NL *Dinosaurus* (1841), orig. a genus name. See DINO-, -SAUR]

No doubt heavy emphasis on the bulkiness of many dinosaurs and their extinction created this connotation of the word *dinosaur*. But, as we have seen in this book, it is hardly deserved. Many dinosaurs were fast and agile animals. Dinosaurs existed for about 150 million years, during most of which they dominated the earth. Their descendants, the birds, are among the most diverse and successful groups of living animals.

So, although dinosaurs are extinct, they should stand as paragons of evolutionary success. Instead, they are often thought of as dim-witted, unwieldy failures, which is an undeserved reputation.

DINOSAURS IN THE NEWS

New discoveries of dinosaurs frequently appear in the news media before they are published in scientific journals and books (figure 18.2). There are two obvious reasons for this. First, paleontologists, like most people, have a natural desire to receive public recognition for their discoveries. Second, publicity about paleontological discoveries is one way to educate the general public about dinosaurs. Funding agencies and scientific institutions, such as museums and universities, seek publicity for dinosaur discoveries made by their paleontologists both to educate the public and to enhance the institution's reputation.

In an ideal world, news reports about dinosaur discoveries should serve the public's desire for up-to-date, factual information on the latest developments in dinosaur research. But there is an unfortunate down side to media coverage of dinosaurs. This, in part, results from journalistic biases and mistakes. Most reporters are not scientists, and some unintentionally introduce factual errors into stories about dinosaurs. Also, because every news story must have an "angle"—an aspect that makes it appealing to the journalists and, they hope, the public—many stories about dinosaurs focus on the sensational and speculative. News stories, whether print, audio, or video, are necessarily short, so they usually cannot present all the evidence that supports their conclusions. Much of the media coverage of dinosaurs is tantalizing but incomplete, and it sometimes contains errors and highly biased and speculative conclusions for which there may be little factual basis.

A second problem with media coverage rests with the paleontologists themselves. The desire for recognition, or the pressures imposed by funding agencies and institutions for results, have sometimes led to sensational news reports about dinosaurs. Subsequent research, however, has revealed that these reports lacked substance, and so misinformed the public. Fortunately, these occurrences are few and far between, and most dinosaur discoveries that appear in the press, if accurately presented by reporters, convey new and significant information.

News reports about dinosaurs will always be with us, so how can you distinguish the good from the bad? Certainly, the more you know about dinosaurs, the

Dinosaur-destroying meteorite might have hit Mexico

London Observer Service

Evidence is mounting that a giant meteorite or comet, believed to have wiped out the dinosaurs 66 million years ago, struck Earth along the coast of Central America.

Scientists have discovered an area in Yucatan, near the Mexican city of Progresso, that has been showered in the past with tiny glass droplets known as tektites and also with "shocked" quartz crystals, the science magazine New Scientist reports this week.

Both would have been flung from the crater caused by the meteorite's impact, says Florentin Maurasse of Florida International University in Miami.

Two other researchers, Alan Hildebrand of the University of Arizona and Glen Penfield of Aero Service in Houston, have reported signs of an ancient, giant crater near the coast of Yucatan.

Geologists have been looking for just such a crater ever since Luis and Walter Alvarez discovered a layer of iridium-rich rock that was created 66 million years ago, just when dinosaur extinctions occurred.

Iridium is rare on Earth but common in meteorites, strongly suggesting that the rock layer, which appears to have covered the world at one time, was created by a giant meteorite crash or explosion that sent a plume of debris round the world. In the ensuing climatic chaos, the world's large dinosaurs were wiped out, it is argued.

But the theory is controversial. Some scientists have pointed out that the dinosaurs did not disappear instantly but took more than a million years to die away. And where is the crater that must have been caused by the impact, they ask.

To answer this last, crucial question, the "big crash" supporters launched a worldwide search for geological signs of the calamity.

In 1988, attention focused on the Caribbean after Joanne Bourgeois of the University of Washington discovered what looked like deposits from giant tidal waves in Texas.

A giant meteorite plunging into the Caribbean would have sprayed massive tidal waves that would have battered the entire southern United States.

Now Hildebrand and Penfield believe they have found where the meteorite must have crashed — in an area near Progresso.

Distributed by Scripps Howard News Service

FIGURE 18.2

News reports about new dinosaur discoveries, such as this one, are common.

Published by permission of *The Observer.* © 1990.

better equipped you will be to make such judgments. But perhaps the best thing to do is be critical of the story, asking yourself, what, if any, biases does it portray? How many facts—actual information on the fossils, their context and the lines of reasoning—does the story contain? Also, if the news story draws conclusions, are alternative possibilities and evidence discussed? Few news stories about dinosaurs may stand up to such critical scrutiny, but by asking yourself these questions you may be able to separate those few stories that mislead and misinform from the wealth of new and useful information.

DINOSAUR BOOKS

A sizeable library is needed to house all the dinosaur books available in bookstores today. These books fall into three categories: children's books (and comics), popular factual books on dinosaurs, and dinosaur fiction. This is not the place to recommend or criticize any specific book, but a few comments on what to look for in dinosaur books, and how they influence the public perception of dinosaurs, are in order.

Many **misconceptions about dinosaurs** are perpetuated in books today. A wide range of children's books on dinosaurs identify the sail-backed reptile *Dimetrodon* as a dinosaur, which it most certainly was not. Comic books often portray humans coexisting with dinosaurs. But perhaps most pervasive in popular books is the image of dinosaurs as animals that did little more than tear each other apart or search for something else, often a human, to eat. Indeed, such dinosaur carnage is so frequent a theme that most people don't realize that the average day of a dinosaur, like that of most living animals, was probably rather peaceful. Dinosaurs slept, reproduced, played, and rested—they were not always locked in mortal combat.

When buying dinosaur books for children the goal should be to avoid such misinformation. However, those of us seeking action and adventure in our reading may not care about accuracy. Indeed, a certain lack of accuracy pervades one of the most influential, though now little read, works of dinosaur fiction. This book (figure 18.3), **Arthur Conan Doyle's *The Lost World*** (1912), is based on the premise that dinosaurs are still living on a high plateau in the Amazon jungle (box 18.1). Although the book contains many misconceptions about dinosaurs, it still makes exciting reading, and its premise has been the basis for many other works of dinosaur fiction and dinosaur movies.

FIGURE 18.3

Arthur Conan Doyle's book *The Lost World* was based on the premise that dinosaurs are living today on a plateau in Amazonia.

THE LOST WORLD

Being an account of the recent amazing adventures of Professor George E. Challenger, Lord John Roxton, Professor Summerlee, and Mr. E. D. Malone of the "Daily Gazette."

BY

ARTHUR CONAN DOYLE

AUTHOR OF

"SIR NIGEL," "THE WHITE COMPANY," "RODNEY STONE," ETC., ETC.

NEW EDITION

WITH ILLUSTRATIONS

LONDON

SMITH, ELDER & CO., 15, WATERLOO PLACE

1914

All rights reserved

Although it is difficult to be too critical of the information about dinosaurs presented in books of fiction, readers should demand accuracy of popular books that purport to present dinosaur science to the public. Again, as in the case of news stories on dinosaurs, your ability to evaluate such books increases as your knowledge of dinosaurs increases. A particularly good measure is the accuracy of the dinosaur restorations and information presented in the book. Do they reflect current scientific thinking about dinosaurs, or are they based on old and outmoded notions? Also, when the book presents topics hotly debated by paleontologists, such as dinosaur metabolism or extinction, does it discuss alternative evidence and ideas? It is the intention of this textbook to meet these criteria and provide you with a standard by which to evaluate other dinosaur books.

This section would not be complete without some mention of the technical scientific literature on dinosaurs. Articles on dinosaurs in scientific journals and scientific books about dinosaurs are available in any university library. These articles and books represent the ultimate written authority on what paleontologists know and think about dinosaurs. But they need to be read critically, because the scientific study of dinosaurs is continually growing and changing through new discoveries and interpretations, as well as spirited scientific debate.

BOX 18.1

CONAN DOYLE'S LOST WORLD

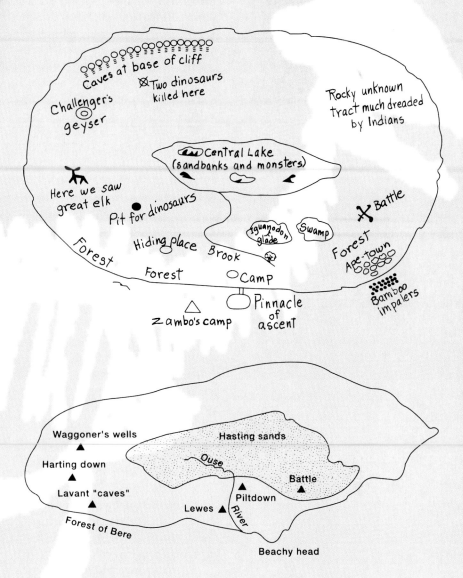

S ir Arthur Conan Doyle is best known as the creator of Sherlock Holmes, the most famous and skilled detective of all time. However, Conan Doyle's 1912 novel, *The Lost World,* has influenced the genre of dinosaur movies since the movie version of the book appeared in 1925.

The Lost World is mainly the story of an expedition, led by British scientist Professor George E. Challenger, to a high plateau in the upper reaches of the Amazon River inhabited by dinosaurs, mastodons, and a belligerent race of ape-men. In the novel, a map of the high plateau shows the expedition's campsites, the village where the ape-men live, locations of dinosaur sightings, and other features (box figure 18.1). It might seem that such a map was a totally imaginative exercise of Conan Doyle's, but it actually had some basis in fact.

Conan Doyle was an avid rock and fossil collector well acquainted with discoveries made in Great Britain. Many of Britain's Early Cretaceous dinosaurs, notably *Iguanodon,* and its most infamous fossil human, the Piltdown man, a scientific hoax discovered in 1912 and debunked in the 1950s, come from a region in southeastern England called the **Weald.** A map of this area shows several points of resemblance to Conan Doyle's map of the lost world (see box figure 18.1).

Thus, the "central lake" corresponds to the Hastings Sands, rocks that contain fossils of *Iguanodon,* and were thought in Conan Doyle's day to represent Early Cretaceous lakes and swamps (now they are considered to be mainly river and beach deposits). Indeed, an *Iguanodon* glade and swamp are present in the lost world. The site of the battle with the ape-men in the lost world nearly matches that of the town of Battle in the Weald. Similarly, Lavant Caves in the Weald is mirrored by the "hiding place" of the lost world, the "brook" mimics the Ouse River and "Challenger's geyser" corresponds to Waggoner's Wells. Finally, Beachy Head in the Weald is a promontory on the British coast that corresponds to the "pinnacle of ascent" of the lost world.

BOX FIGURE 18.1

The map of the lost world in Conan Doyle's *The Lost World* (above) is remarkably similar to a map of the Weald in England (below).

Clearly, Conan Doyle borrowed heavily from fact to create the fictional lost world. But, a tremendous amount of non-fact appears in *The Lost World* as well. Ape-men and mastodons coexist with dinosaurs, and dinosaurs of different geologic time periods live together on the high plateau. Also, long outmoded prejudices about dinosaurs fill the book. Witness, for example, the conclusions of Professor Challenger and his colleague Sumerlee on the intelligence of dinosaurs:

Both were agreed that the monsters were practically brainless, that there was no room for reason in their tiny cranial cavities, and that if they have disappeared from the rest of the world it was assuredly on account of their own stupidity, which made it impossible for them to adapt themselves to changing conditions.

Conan Doyle's book, though in part based in fact, helped to create and perpetuate some common misconceptions about dinosaurs and the dinosaurian world.

DINOSAUR ART

Artists began to create dinosaur art, such as sculptures and paintings, not long after Richard Owen coined the word *dinosaur* in 1842. In 1854, **Benjamin Waterhouse Hawkins** built life-size models of *Iguanodon*, *Megalosaurus* and *Hylaeosaurus* (a nodosaurid ankylosaur) that still stand in London's Crystal Palace Park (figure 18.4). These sculptures, and indeed all dinosaur art, reflect paleontological ideas about the biology and behavior of dinosaurs that were current when the artwork was created. Hawkins' dinosaurs are the massive, toad- and lizard-like giants that Richard Owen and his colleagues conceived from only a fragmentary knowledge of dinosaur anatomy. For example, Hawkins' *Iguanodon* has the spike on its nose, not thumb, as believed by Gideon Mantell in the 1820s.

In Chapters 12 and 14, we saw that new discoveries have radically changed ideas about dinosaur biology and behavior. Dinosaur art has changed as well. By the beginning of the twentieth century, complete skeletons of dinosaurs were known that provided a far better basis for dinosaur sculptures and paintings than was available to Hawkins.

The most famous dinosaur artist then, and perhaps the most influential dinosaur artist of all time, was **Charles R. Knight** (1874–1953) (figure 18.5). Knight painted and sculpted many dinosaurs, mostly with the advice of paleontologist Henry Fairfield Osborn (1857–1935) of the American Museum of Natural History. Although most people don't realize it, the images of dinosaurs created by Charles R. Knight pervaded dinosaur art for more than half a century and shaped the work of many dinosaur artists. His restorations are some of the most familiar, and most copied, images of dinosaurs (figure 18.6).

Knight's dinosaurs reflected accurate anatomical information based on complete skeletons and ideas about dinosaur biology and behavior that were current in the early years of this century. His dinosaurs are very reptilian and often heavy and ponderous, dragging their tails. Sauropods are presented in aquatic settings. Yet some of Knight's artwork was prescient of future ideas about dinosaurs, such as his painting of two agile fighting theropods of the genus *Dryptosaurus* (figure 18.7). During his life, Knight made some 800 drawings, 150 oil paintings, and numerous sculptures of extinct animals, many of dinosaurs. They are an incredible legacy that has influenced the public perception of dinosaurs more than the work of any other artist.

Today, many talented artists sculpt and paint dinosaurs. Their work reflects the latest ideas about dinosaurs, particularly dinosaur's bird-like appearance, speed, and agility. It also embodies much speculation about dinosaurs, such as the feathered theropods depicted in figure 16.9.

Viewing dinosaur art is much like reading books about dinosaurs. The same criteria of accuracy should be applied to your judgment of dinosaur art, tempered, of course, by your own sense of aesthetics.

FIGURE 18.5

Charles R. Knight was the most influential dinosaur artist.

Courtesy Department of Library Services, American Museum of Natural History (Neg. #327667)

FIGURE 18.6

Charles R. Knight's most famous dinosaur painting is this classic confrontation between *Triceratops* and *Tyrannosaurus*.

Courtesy Field Museum of Natural History (Neg. # 59442), Chicago

FIGURE 18.7

One of Knight's early dinosaur paintings, this 1897 view of two theropods, *Dryptosaurus*, fighting, presages later ideas about agile theropods.

Courtesy Department of Library Services, American Museum of Natural History (Neg. #335199)

DINOSAUR TOYS

Dinosaur toys, typically small plastic scale models, are a form of dinosaur sculpture. They should be judged by their anatomical accuracy with respect to complete skeletons of dinosaurs, and unfortunately, most toy dinosaurs fall short of the mark. They are very bulky, garishly-colored, and anatomically inaccurate (note especially the plates on many toy *Stegosaurus*). Many sets of dinosaur toys are full of non-dinosaurs, such as *Dimetrodon*, pterosaurs, mastodons, mammoths, "cave men" and, in some sets, mythical beasts unknown to science.

The most accurate dinosaur toys have been marketed by some of the world's great natural history museums (figure 18.8). These toys, and other toys that lack the flaws mentioned above, provide reasonably accurate scale models of dinosaurs consonant with modern paleontological thought.

DINOSAUR CARTOONS AND MOVIES

The first character to appear in an animated cartoon was a sauropod dinosaur *Gertie the Dinosaur* created by cartoonist **Winson McCay** in 1912 (figure 18.9). Since that time, dinosaurs have been featured in many cartoons, typically coexisting with humans or other animals that did not evolve until long after dinosaur extinction.

FIGURE 18.8

These dinosaur toys, produced by the British Museum, are among the most accurate on the market.

FIGURE 18.9

This scene from the animated cartoon *Gertie the Dinosaur* was drawn and photographed by Winson McCay in 1912.

Dinosaurs got their start in movies in 1925 when Hollywood produced a silent film version of *The Lost World*. The dinosaurs in this movie (figure 18.10) were straight out of the paintings of Charles R. Knight. **Willis Harold O'Brien,** who pioneered the techniques of stop-action photography, joined forces with sculptor **Marcel Delgado** to produce the scale models of the dinosaurs used in the movie. The life-like quality of these models and their movement has seldom been surpassed by later

FIGURE 18.10

An *Allosaurus* kills an *Apatosaurus* in the 1925 silent movie *The Lost World*.

Courtesy Donald Glut

FIGURE 18.11

King Kong kills a *Tyrannosaurus* after a pitched battle in the 1933 movie classic *King Kong*.

Courtesy Donald Glut

dinosaur movies. Few readers of this book have seen the 1925 version of *The Lost World*, but most know the quality of the O'Brien-Delgado dinosaurs from the 1933 classic **King Kong,** on which they also collaborated (figure 18.11).

The Lost World has left an indelible mark on the public perception of dinosaurs for two reasons. First, its premise that dinosaurs are not extinct, but are still living in some remote corner of the globe, has become the basis of many dinosaur movies. And, at the end of the movie (but not in the book), the discoverers of the dinosaurs bring a live sauropod back to London for exhibition. There, the terrified (enraged?) dinosaur escapes, destroying everything in its path until it crashes through a bridge, landing in the Thames for the long swim back to South America. Thus was born the idea, so familiar to dinosaur movie fans, of a prehistoric monster running amok in a modern city.

FIGURE 18.12

A cave man (Victor Mature) fights off an attacking "dinosaur" (actually an enlarged iguana) in *One Million B.C.* (1940).

Courtesy Donald Glut

Almost all dinosaur movies that are not based on the idea of living twentieth-century dinosaurs are time travel movies. We, the viewers, along with the humans in the movie, are transported back in time to the Mesozoic to encounter dinosaurs. A separate subgenre of dinosaur movies is based on the false idea that humans coexisted with dinosaurs, and usually features the misadventures of scantily clad cave women and cave men as they are terrorized by dinosaurs (figure 18.12).

All dinosaur movies are based on fantastic premises, so how are we to judge them from a paleontological perspective? Our only guide must be the scientific accuracy and quality of motion of the dinosaurs themselves. Many movie dinosaurs are nothing more than iguanas or other lizards, sometimes adorned with spikes or plates (see figure 18.12). These movie dinosaurs deserve our scorn as they sprawl across the screen. Other movie dinosaurs, such as **Godzilla,** are utterly fantastic creatures whose resemblance to dinosaurs is at best remote (box 18.3). The remaining movie dinosaurs are scale models, usually based on the art of Charles R. Knight, although some recent dinosaur movies and television shows are based on much more modern restorations. Ironically, the dinosaurs that appeared in the first full-length dinosaur movie, *The Lost World,* were, from a paleontological perspective, for many years about the best dinosaurs to appear in the movies. However, the 1993 movie *Jurassic Park* brought the most modern scientific ideas about dinosaurs to the silver screen (see box 18.2).

DINOSAUR SCIENCE AND PUBLIC DINOSAURS

This review of the public persona of dinosaurs has not been comprehensive. Representations of dinosaurs also appear as jewelry, on postage stamps, as breakfast cereal, and on corporate logos, among other things. The public's view of dinosaurs, however, is generally misinformed. Common misconceptions about dinosaurs include the idea that humans coexisted with dinosaurs, the misidentification

BOX 18.2

Michael Crichton's 1990 novel *Jurassic Park* became the blockbuster movie of the same name released in 1993. The premise of the book (and the movie) is that by extracting dinosaur blood from a Mesozoic mosquito preserved in amber, scientists isolate dinosaur DNA in order to clone living dinosaurs. The long dead, decomposed DNA is incomplete, but the gaps are filled with pieces from the DNA of living frogs.

The living dinosaurs thus cloned are the attraction of a pricey theme park (the "Jurassic Park") located on a remote Caribbean island. The plot unravels as a test of the theme park's accuracy and viability goes terribly awry when a devious computer hacker attempts to steal dinosaur embryos. A dinosaur rampage ensues, and only the luckiest of the good guys (but, alas, not their lawyer!) escape the dinosaur-infested island. The movie thus ends, ripe for a sequel.

Although the theme park is named Jurassic Park, most of its dinosaurs—*Tyrannosaurus*, ceratopsians, hadrosaurs—were Cretaceous denizens. They share the park's limelight with some characteristically Jurassic dinosaurs, such as the brachiosaurs. Cinematic license produces a venom-spitting *Dilophosaurus* that startles its victims by raising a broad flap of skin on its neck—wholly conjectural behaviors and structures for which no fossil evidence exists. And the movie features a terrifying troop of *Velociraptor* (the "raptors") too large and too smart to be the real thing.

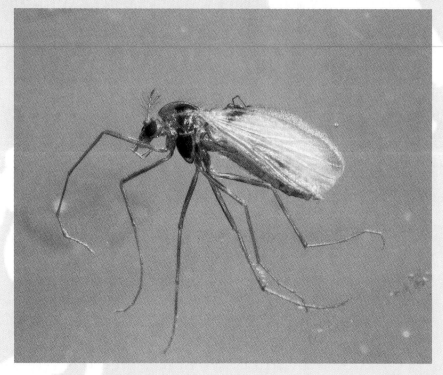

BOX FIGURE 18.2

Most fossil insects preserved in amber are of Cenozoic age, so they postdate the dinosaurs.
Courtesy Museum Für Naturkunde, Stuttgart

Despite these and other flights of fancy, *Jurassic Park* has phenomenal special effects. More than any other movie, it creates dinosaurs more life-like and more closely based on the modern scientific understanding of dinosaurs. Paleontologists and others who watched the movie came as close as they ever will to seeing a dinosaur in the flesh.

But, what about the basic premise of *Jurassic Park*? Can dinosaur DNA be isolated to clone a living, breathing prehistoric monster? Not now, and probably never. The vast majority of insects in amber (box figure 18.2) are of Cenozoic age, so they never had a chance to bite a dinosaur. Dinosaur DNA has been isolated (from bone), but no current technology can begin to replace the missing, decomposed pieces of the phenomenally complex DNA molecule to produce a viable structure. Like many other works of science fiction, *Jurassic Park* is based on an apparently plausible premise, but one well beyond current possibilities.

BOX 18.3

GODZILLA: A LOUSY DINOSAUR

Weight: 50,000 tons
Height: 262'
Chest: 226'
Waist: 254'
Hips: 286'
Tail length: 354'
Foot size: 50'6"

Age: 2,000,000 or more years

Location: Last residence:
The volcanic crater
of Mount Mihara,
Oshima Island,
off the Izu Peninsula

Speed at sea: 45 knots
Speed on land: 40 mph
Maximum speed: Unknown

Nationality: Japanese
Personality: "Profound/Savage"

Godzilla Film Chronology

1.	*Godzilla, King of the Monsters*	November 1954
2.	*Gigantis, the Fire Monster*	April 1955
3.	*King Kong vs. Godzilla*	August 1962
4.	*Godzilla vs. the Thing*	April 1964
5.	*Ghidra, the Three-Headed Monster*	December 1964
6.	*Monster Zero*	December 1965
7.	*Godzilla vs. the Sea Monster*	December 1966
8.	*Son of Godzilla*	December 1967
9.	*Destroy all Monsters*	December 1968
10.	*Godzilla's Revenge*	December 1969
11.	*Godzilla vs. the Smog Monster*	July 1971
12.	*Godzilla vs. Gigan*	March 1972
13.	*Godzilla vs. Megalon*	March 1973
14.	*Godzilla vs. the Bionic Monster*	March 1974
15.	*The Revenge of Mecha-Godzilla*	March 1975
16.	*Godzilla '85*	December 1985
17.	*Godzilla vs. Violante*	December 1989

BOX FIGURE 18.3

Vital statistics and movie credits of Godzilla.

Source: Data from Associated Press release, 1989.

Few movie monsters are as famous as Godzilla. Godzilla is a green, nearly 100-meter-tall, bipedal reptile with fiery, radioactive breath, and dorsal spikes (box figure 18.3). Since it first appeared on the silver screen in the 1954 movie *Godzilla, King of the Monsters*, the Japanese behemoth has been the star of 16 more movies (see box figure 18.3). Memorable images of Godzilla include the creature running amok in Tokyo or other locales in the Japanese islands, destroying buildings, vehicles, and the populace with its huge feet, thick, dragging and swinging tail, and enormous flame-throwing mouth.

Godzilla was created under the direction of Japanese special effects expert Eiji Tsuburaya. An actor inside a suit portrayed the monster as it wreaked havoc on miniature models of Tokyo and other locales. A mechanical model also was used in some scenes.

Generations of Japanese and American moviegoers, especially children, have thrilled to the destructive exploits of and, in some of the movies, sympathetic character portrayed by Godzilla. To many, Godzilla is basically a dinosaur with an overlay of a few novel features of the atomic age, including its appetite for radioactivity.

From a paleontologist's point of view, very little about Godzilla is dinosaurian. True, the overall body shape of Godzilla is basically that of a large theropod. But, everything else is wrong. Godzilla far exceeds the size of any theropod, is much too massively built, has human-like arms and hands, breathes fire, and has spikes on its back like a stegosaur. These are not exaggerations of theropod features, but instead spot Godzilla as a horrific monster not closely related in any way to the theropods despite the filmmaker's premise that Godzilla, hibernating since the Mesozoic, was awakened by American atomic tests at Bikini Atoll during the 1950s.

Nevertheless, don't expect this expose of Godzilla's non-dinosaurian background to curtail its cinematic career and dim its stardom. Like many movie personalities with unsavory private lives and questionable backgrounds, Godzilla's appeal on the screen will transcend its doubtful paternity. We can no doubt expect more Godzilla movies and the continued popularity of this fantastic monster!

of a host of non-dinosaurs as dinosaurs, the image of dinosaurs as beefy, ponderous reptiles, and the vision of a dinosaur as a terrifying, bloodthirsty brute bent only on savagery and carnage.

Clearly there is a gap between scientific knowledge about dinosaurs and public perception. Much of the public's perception of dinosaurs is rooted in outmoded ideas about dinosaurs. Sensationalism and a thirst for action and adventure also pervade the public perception of dinosaurs.

But the gap is narrowing. Paleontologists know that dinosaurs are fascinating and exciting animals that can stir public interest without being embellished by unfounded ideas. Our new and expanded knowledge of dinosaurs, much of it accumulated during the last 20 years, is being communicated in new books, art, toys, and cinema. As public interest in dinosaurs continues to grow, we can look forward to even more paleontological interest and information on these fascinating animals.

S U M M A R Y

1. Dinosaurs are extremely popular and appear in the news media, books, sculptures, paintings, toys, cartoons, television shows, movies, and other items available to the general public.

2. The word *dinosaur* refers to extinct reptiles with an upright limb posture, but also is used to refer to anything that is unwieldy or obsolete. This latter use of the word *dinosaur* is based on their generally large size and extinction, but this connotation of dinosaurs contradicts their success.

3. News reports about new dinosaur discoveries sometimes are inaccurate and misleading. Such reports need to be viewed critically.

4. Dinosaur books frequently perpetuate old, outmoded ideas about dinosaurs and also perpetuate erroneous ideas such as the coexistence of humans and dinosaurs.

5. Dinosaur sculptures and paintings have changed as scientific ideas about dinosaur biology and behavior have changed.

6. Charles R. Knight's paintings and sculptures of dinosaurs have influenced images of dinosaurs more than those of any other artist.

7. Many dinosaur toys are inaccurate scale models of dinosaurs.

8. The first animated cartoon character was a dinosaur (1912).

9. The first full-length movie that featured dinosaurs was the 1925 Hollywood version of Arthur Conan Doyle's *The Lost World*.

10. Most dinosaur movies are based either on the idea of living, twentieth-century dinosaurs, or time travel to the Mesozoic.

11. Many dinosaur movies, like most of the public presentation of dinosaurs, perpetuate outmoded or incorrect ideas about dinosaurs.

12. The gap between dinosaur science and the public perception of dinosaurs is being narrowed by new discoveries and the public's increasing desire to know more about dinosaurs

K E Y   T E R M S

connotation
Marcel Delgado
denotation
dinosaur (two meanings)
dinosaur toys

Arthur Conan Doyle
Godzilla
Benjamin Waterhouse Hawkins
Jurassic Park
King Kong
Charles R. Knight

The Lost World
Winson McCay
misconceptions about dinosaurs
Willis Harold O'Brien
Weald

R E V I E W   Q U E S T I O N S

1. What are the two meanings of the word *dinosaur*? Are they accurate definitions?

2. Why do some news reports present inaccurate information about dinosaurs?

3. What questions should you direct at news reports about dinosaur discoveries to evaluate their accuracy?

4. What misconceptions about dinosaurs are perpetuated by some books, art, and movies?

5. How have paleontological ideas about dinosaurs influenced dinosaur art?

6. What are the subgenres of dinosaur movies?

7. What influence did *The Lost World* have on subsequent dinosaur movies?

FURTHER READING

Conan Doyle, Sir Arthur. 1912. *The Lost World*. Originally serialized in *The Strand* magazine, published as a book in 1914 by Doubleday, New York and reprinted many times. (The story of Professor Challenger's expedition to a high plateau in Amazonia populated by dinosaurs.)

Czerkas, S. M. and Glut, D. F., editors. 1982. *Dinosaurs, Mammoths and Cavemen: The Art of Charles R. Knight*. New York: E. P. Dutton Inc., 120 pp. (Presents a biography of Charles R. Knight and full-color reproductions of many of his paintings of dinosaurs.)

Czerkas, S. M. and Olson, E. D., editors. 1987. *Dinosaurs Past and Present*. Los Angeles: Natural History Museum of Los Angeles County and University of Washington Press, 161 pp. (Volume I) and 149 pp. (Volume II). (Contains pictures of dinosaur artwork featured in an exhibition organized by the Natural History Museum of Los Angeles County and 12 articles about dinosaur art and new ideas about dinosaurs.)

Glut, D. F. 1980. *The Dinosaur Scrapbook*. Secaucas, New Jersey: Citadel Press, 320 pp. (The subtitle of this book is "The Dinosaur in Amusement Parks, Comic Books, Fiction, History, Magazines, Movies, Museums, Television.")

Padian, K. 1988. New discoveries about dinosaurs: Separating the facts from the news: *Journal of Geological Education*, vol. 36, pp. 215–20. (Discusses, using examples, how to distinguish accurate from inaccurate news reports about dinosaur discoveries.)

Robinson, S. 1992. From bones to behemoths a look at dinosaur art and artists: *Rocks and Minerals*, vol. 67, no. 2, p. 110 (Briefly reviews the life and work of numerous dinosaur artists.)

A DINOSAUR DICTIONARY

All of the dinosaur generic names that appear in this book are listed here with a guide to pronunciation, a brief identification of the dinosaur, and the derivation of the genus name. Note that *sauros* is Greek for "lizard" or "reptile."

Abrictosaurus (uh-brick-toe-SORE-us) A heterodontosaurid ornithopod from the Lower Jurassic of South Africa [Greek *abriktos*, "wakeful"]. 100

Acrocanthosaurus (ak-row-KANTH-uh-sore-us) An Early Cretaceous theropod from the United States [Greek *akros*, "high" + *akantha*, "spine"]. 66

Alamosaurus (AL-uh-mo-sore-us) A Late Cretaceous sauropod from the western United States [for Ojo Alamo, a spring in New Mexico]. 90

Albertosaurus (al-BURR-tuh-sore-us) A Late Cretaceous tyrannosaurid from western North America [for Alberta, Canada]. 66

Allosaurus (AL-uh-sore-us) A Late Jurassic allosaurid theropod from North America and East Africa [Greek *allos*, "strange"]. 65

Alxasaurus (AL-kha-sore-us) An early Cretaceous theropod from China [for the Alxa Desert of Inner Mongolia]. 75

Ammosaurus (AM-oh-sore-us) An Early Jurassic prosauropod from North America [Greek *ammos*, "sand"]. 83

Amphicoelias (am-fee-SEE-lee-us) A Late Jurassic sauropod from North America; not considered a valid name, which is *Camarasaurus* [Greek *amphi*, "double" + *koilos*, "hollow"]. 85

Anchisaurus (AN-key-sore-us) An Early Jurassic prosauropod from North America and South Africa [Greek *anchi*, "near or close to"]. 80

Ankylosaurus (ang-KY-low-sore-us) A Late Cretaceous ankylosaur from North America [Greek *ankylos*, "stiff" or "fused"]. 128

Antarctosaurus (ant-ARK-toe-sore-us) A Late Cretaceous sauropod from South America and Asia [Greek *antarktikos*, "southern"]. 90

Apatosaurus (uh-PAT-oh-sore-us) A Late Jurassic sauropod from North America [Greek, *apatel*, "deceit"]. 87

Bagaceratops (bag-uh-SAYR-uh-tops) A Late Cretaceous ceratopsian from Asia [Mongolian *baga*, "small" + Greek *ceratops*, "horned face"]. 136

Barapasaurus (bah-RAP-uh-sore-us) An Early Jurassic sauropod from India [Hindi *bara*, "big" + *pa*, "leg"]. 95

Barosaurus (BAHR-oh-sore-us) A Late Jurassic sauropod from North America and eastern Africa [Greek *barys*, "heavy"]. 87

Brachiosaurus (BRAK-ee-oh-sore-us) A Late Jurassic sauropod from North America and eastern Africa [Greek *brachion*, "arm"]. 88

Brontosaurus (BRON-toe-sore-us) A Late Jurassic sauropod from North America; not a valid name, which is *Apatosaurus* [Greek *bronte*, "thunder"]. 87

Camarasaurus (KAM-uh-ruh-sore-us) A Late Jurassic sauropod from North America [Greek *kamara*, "chamber"]. 87

Camptosaurus (KAMP-toe-sore-us) A Late Jurassic-Early Cretaceous ornithopod from North America and Europe [Greek *kamptos*, "flexible"]. 105

Centrosaurus (SEN-tro-sore-us) A Late Cretaceous ceratopsian from North America [Greek *kentron*, "sharp point"]. 138

Ceratosaurus (sir-AT-oh-sore-us) A Late Jurassic theropod from North America and eastern Africa [Greek *keratos*, "horned"]. 60

Cetiosaurus (SEAT-ee-oh-sore-us) A Middle to Late Jurassic sauropod from England and North Africa [Greek *keteios*, "whale-like"]. 95

Chasmosaurus (KAZ-mo-sore-us) A Late Cretaceous ceratopsian from North America [Greek *chasma*, "opening"]. 139

Chirostenotes (KIY-row-sten-OH-tees) A Late Cretaceous theropod from Canada [Greek *cheir*, "hand" + *stenos*, "narrow"]. 74

Coelophysis (see-low-FY-sis) A Late Triassic theropod from North America [Greek *koilos*, "hollow" and *fysis*, "form"]. 63

Coloradisaurus (col-oh-rah-dih-SORE-us) A Late Triassic prosauropod from Argentina [for the Los Colorados Formation in Argentina]. 82

Compsognathus (comp-sug-NAY-thus) A Late Jurassic theropod from Europe [Greek *kompsos*, "elegant" + *gnathos*, "jaw"]. 65

Cryolophosaurus (cry-uh-LOAF-uh-sore-us) An Early Jurassic theropod from Antarctica [Greek *cryo*, "cold" + *lophos*, "crest"]. 163

Daspletosaurus (das-PLEE-toe-sore-us) A Late Cretaceous theropod from North America [Greek *daspletos*, "frightful"]. 66

Datousaurus (DAH-toe-sore-us) A Middle Jurassic sauropod from China [Chinese *da*, "big" and *tou*, "head"]. 89

Deinodon (DIE-no-don) A name originally given to large theropod teeth from the Upper Cretaceous of North America; not considered valid [Greek *deinos*, "terrible" + *odon*, "tooth"]. 169

Deinonychus (die-NON-ik-us) An Early Cretaceous theropod from North America [Greek *deinos*, "terrible" + *onychos*, "claw"]. 72

Dilophosaurus (die-LOWF-oh-sore-us) An Early Jurassic theropod from North America [Greek *di*, "two" + *lophos*, "crest"]. 60

Diplodocus (di-PLOD-oh-kus) A Late Jurassic sauropod from North America [Greek *diplos*, "double" + *dokos*, "beam"]. 84

Dryosaurus (DRY-oh-sore-us) A Late Jurassic ornithopod from North America and eastern Africa [Greek *dryos*, "tree"]. 104

Dryptosaurus (DRIP-toe-sore-us) A Late Cretaceous theropod from North America [Greek *drypto*, "to tear"]. 272

Edmontosaurus (ed-MON-toe-sore-us) A Late Cretaceous ornithopod from North America [for the Edmonton Formation, Alberta, Canada]. 107

Euhelopus (you-HEE-low-pus) An Early Cretaceous sauropod from China [Greek *eu*, "true" + *helos*, "marsh" + *pous*, "foot"]. 88

Euoplocephalus (you-oh-plo-SEF-uh-lus) A Late Cretaceous ankylosaur from North America [Greek *euoplo*, "well armed" + *kephale*, "head"]. 127

Fabrosaurus (FAB-row-sore-us) An Early Jurassic primitive ornithischian from southern Africa [named for French geologist Jean Fabre]. 53

Hadrosaurus (HAD-row-sore-us) A Late Cretaceous ornithopod from North America [Greek *hadros*, "heavy"]. 170

Haplocanthosaurus (hap-low-KANTH-uh-sore-us) A Late Jurassic sauropod from North America [Greek *haplos*, "single" + *akantha*, "spine"]. 88

Herrerasaurus (her-RARE-uh-sore-us) A primitive saurischian from the Late Triassic of Argentina [named for Argentine rancher Don Victorino Herrera]. 50

Heterodontosaurus (het-ur-oh-DONT-oh-sore-us) An Early Jurassic ornithopod from South Africa [Greek *heteros*, "different" + *odontos*, "tooth"]. 100

Homalocephale (ho-mah-low-SEF-uh-lee) A Late Cretaceous pachycephalosaur from Asia [Greek *homalos*, "level" + *kephale*, "head"]. 142

Huayangosaurus (hwah-YANG-oh-sore-us) A Middle Jurassic stegosaur from China [for Huayang, Shanxi Province, China]. 117

Hylaeosaurus (HI-lee-oh-sore-us) An Early Cretaceous ankylosaur from Europe [Greek *hylaios*, "Wealden"]. 167

Hypselosaurus (HIP-se-low-sore-us) A Late Cretaceous sauropod from Europe [Greek *hypselos*, "high"]. 95

Hypsilophodon (hip-si-LOAF-uh-don) An Early Cretaceous ornithopod from Europe [for the living iguana *Hypsilophus*]. 101

Iguanodon (i-GWA-no-don) An Early Cretaceous ornithopod from Europe and North Africa [iguana, a living lizard, + Greek *odon*, "tooth"]. 105

Kentrosaurus (KEN-tro-sore-us) A Late Jurassic stegosaur from eastern Africa [Greek *kentron*, "spike"]. 119

Leptoceratops (LEP-toe-sayr-uh-tops) A Late Cretaceous ceratopsian from North America [Greek *leptos*, "small" + *ceratops*, "horned face"]. 136

Lesothosaurus (le-SOW-toe-sore-us) An Early Jurassic ornithischian from southern Africa [for Lesotho, Africa]. 53

Lufengosaurus (loo-FUNG-oh-sore-us) An Early Jurassic prosauropod from China (for Lufeng, Yunnan Province, China). 83

Maiasaura (my-uh-SORE-uh) A Late Cretaceous hadrosaur from North America [Greek *maia*, "good mother"]. 207

Majungatholus (mah-JOONG-ah-tho-lus) A Late Cretaceous pachycephalosaur from Madagascar [for Majunga, Madagascar + Latin *tholus*, "dome"]. 147

Mamenchisaurus (ma-MENCH-ee-sore-us) A Late Jurassic sauropod from China [for Mamenchi Ferry, Sichuan Province, China]. 84

Massospondylus (MASS-oh-spon-die-lus) An Early Jurassic prosauropod from North America and southern Africa [Greek *masson*, "longer" + Greek *spondylus*, "vertebra"]. 82

Mononykus (maw-no-NIGH-kus) A late Cretaceous theropod from Mongolia [Greek *mono*, "one" + *onychos*, "claw"]. 242

Montanaceratops (mon-TAN-uh-sayr-uh-tops) A Late Cretaceous ceratopsian from North America [Montana + Greek *ceratops*, "horned face"]. 136

Mussaurus (mus-AW-rus) A hatchling prosauropod from the Late Triassic of Argentina [Latin *mus*, "mouse"]. 82

Nanotyrannus (nan-oh-tie-RAN-us) A Late Cretaceous theropod from North America [Greek *nanos*, "small" + *tyrannos*, "tyrant"]. 66

Nodosaurus (NO-do-sore-us) A Late Cretaceous ankylosaur from North America [Latin *nodus*, "knot" or "swelling"]. 126

Opisthocoelicaudia (oh-PIS-tho-SEE-li-kaw-dee-uh) A Late Cretaceous sauropod from Asia [Greek *opisthe*, "behind" and *koilos*, "hollow" + Latin *cauda*, "tail"]. 88

Orodromeus (or-oh-DROM-ee-us) A Late Cretaceous hypsilophodontid from North America [Greek *oros*, "mountain" + *dromeus*, "runner"]. 104

Ouranosaurus (oh-RAN-oh-sore-us) An Early Cretaceous ornithopod from Africa [from *ouran*, a monitor lizard that lives in the Sahara]. 106

Oviraptor (oh-vi-RAP-tor) A Late Cretaceous theropod from Asia [Latin *ovum*, "egg" + *raptor*, "robber"]. 73

Panoplosaurus (pan-OH-plo-sore-us) A Late Cretaceous ankylosaur from North America [Greek *pan* "everywhere" + *oplo*, "armored"]. 126

Parasaurolophus (par-us-sore-ALL-uh-fus) A Late Cretaceous ornithopod from North America [Greek *para*, "similar" + *Saurolophus*, a related ornithopod]. 108

Parksosaurus (PARKS-oh-sore-us) A Late Cretaceous ornithopod from North America [for Canadian paleontologist W. A. Parks]. 104

Patagosaurus (PAT-uh-go-sore-us) A Middle Jurassic sauropod from South America [for Patagonia, Argentina]. 95

Pentaceratops (PEN-tuh-sayr-uh-tops) A Late Cretaceous ceratopsian from North America [Greek *pente*, "five" + *ceratops*, "horned face"]. 137

Piatnitzkysaurus (pee-yot-NITS-kee-sore-us) A Middle Jurassic theropod from Argentina [for Argentine geologist Alejandro Piatnitzky]. 66

Pinacosaurus (pin-AK-oh-sore-us) A Late Cretaceous ankylosaur from Asia [Greek *pinakos*, "board"]. 128

Pisanosaurus (pee-SAHN-oh-sore-us) A primitive ornithischian from the Late Triassic of Argentina [for Argentine paleontologist Juan Pisano]. 53

Plateosaurus (PLAT-ee-oh-sore-us) A Late Triassic prosauropod from Europe [Greek *plateo*, "broad"]. 80

Poekilopleuron (po-kee-low-PLEW-ron) A Middle Jurassic theropod from Europe [Greek *poikilos*, "mottled" + *pleuron*, "rib"]. 167

Polacanthus (po-luh-KAN-thus) An Early Cretaceous ankylosaur from Europe [Greek *polys*, "many" + *akantha*, "spine"]. 127

Protoceratops (pro-toe-SAYR-uh-tops) A Late Cretaceous ceratopsian from Asia [Greek *protos*, "first" + *ceratops*, "horned face"]. 136

Psittacosaurus (si-TAK-oh-sore-us) An Early Cretaceous ceratopsian from Asia [Greek *psittakos*, "parrot"]. 133

Revueltosaurus (ruh-VWEL-toe-sore-us) A primitive ornithischian from the Late Triassic of North America [for Revuelto Creek, New Mexico, U.S.]. 54

Rhoetosaurus (REET-oh-sore-us) A Middle Jurassic sauropod from Australia [Rhoetus, a mythical giant]. 95

Riojasaurus (ree-OH-ha-sore-us) A Late Triassic prosauropod from Argentina [for La Rioja Province, Argentina]. 80

Saichania (SY-kan-ee-uh) A Late Cretaceous ankylosaur from Asia [Mongolian *saikhan*, "beautiful"]. 128

Sarcolestes (sar-ko-LESS-tees) A Middle Jurassic ankylosaur from Europe [Greek *sarkos*, "flesh" + *lestes*, "robber"]. 129

Saurolophus (sore-uh-LOAF-us) A Late Cretaceous ornithopod from North America and Asia [Greek *sauros*, "lizard" + *lophos*, "crest"]. 109

Sauropelta (sore-oh-PEL-tuh) A Late Cretaceous ankylosaur from North America [Latin *pelta*, "small shield"]. 126

A DINOSAUR DICTIONARY

Saurornithoides (sore-or-nith-OID-eez) A Late Cretaceous theropod from Asia [Greek *ornithoides*, "bird-like"]. 73

Scelidosaurus (skel-id-oh-SORE-us) A primitive thyreophoran from the Lower Jurassic of Europe [Greek *skelidos*, "limb"]. 117

Scutellosaurus (skew-TELL-oh-sore-us) A primitive thyreophoran from the Lower Jurassic of North America [Latin *scutella*, "little shield"]. 115

Seismosaurus (SIGHS-mow-sore-us) A Late Jurassic sauropod from North America [Greek *seismos*, "earthquake"]. 92

Shunosaurus (SHOO-no-sore-us) A Middle Jurassic sauropod from China [*shu* is the ancient Chinese name for Sichuan Province, China]. 89

Staurikosaurus (stor-IK-oh-sore-us) A Late Triassic dinosaur from South America [Greek *staurikos*, "cross," for the constellation the Southern Cross]. 53

Stegoceras (steg-OS-ur-us) A Late Cretaceous pachycephalosaur from North America [Greek *stego*, "covered" + *keras*, "horn"]. 143

Stegosaurus (STEG-oh-sore-us) A Late Jurassic stegosaur from North America [Greek *stego*, "covered"]. 118

Struthiomimus (strooth-ee-oh-MIME-us) A Late Cretaceous theropod from North America [Latin *struthio*, "ostrich" + *mimus*, "mimic"]. 71

Supersaurus (SOO-per-sore-us) A Late Jurassic sauropod from North America [Latin *super*, "above"]. 92

Syntarsus (sin-TAR-sus) An Early Jurassic ceratosaur from North America and southern Africa [Greek *syn*, "together" + *tarsos*, "ankle"]. 63

Szechuanosaurus (sech-WAN-uh-sore-us) A Late Jurassic theropod from China [for Sichuan (Szechuan) Province, China]. 66

Tarbosaurus (TAR-bow-sore-us) A Late Cretaceous theropod from Asia [Greek *tarbos*, "terror"]. 66

Tatisaurus (tah-TEE-sore-us) A primitive thyreophoran from the Lower Jurassic of China [for Tati, Yunnan Province, China]. 117

Tenontosaurus (ten-ON-toe-sore-us) An Early Cretaceous ornithopod from North America [Greek *tenontos*, "sinew"]. 104

Therizinosaurus (THAYR-uh-zeen-uh-sore-us) A Late Cretaceous theropod from Mongolia. 74

Thescelosaurus (THESS-el-oh-sore-us) A Late Cretaceous ornithopod from North America [Greek *theskelos*, "marvelous"]. 104

Titanosaurus (TIE-tan-oh-sore-us) A Late Cretaceous sauropod from Europe, Asia, and South America [for the Titans of Greek mythology]. 90

Torosaurus (TOR-oh-sore-us) A Late Cretaceous ceratopsian from North America [Greek *toreo*, "to perforate"]. 137

Trachodon (TRACK-oh-don) Originally applied to teeth of a Late Cretaceous ornithopod from North America [Greek *trachys*, "rough" + *odon*, "tooth"]. 169

Triceratops (try-SAYR-uh-tops) A Late Cretaceous ceratopsian from North America [Greek *tri*, "three" + *ceratops*, "horned face"]. 137

Tuojiangosaurus (twoa-JEEANG-uh-sore-us) A Late Jurassic stegosaur from China [for the Tuojiang, a river in Sichuan Province, China]. 119

Tyrannosaurus (tie-RAN-oh-sore-us) A Late Cretaceous theropod from North America and Asia [Greek *tyrannos*, "tyrant"]. 66

Ultrasauros (UHL-tra-sore-os) A Late Jurassic sauropod of North America; considered an invalid name, which is *Brachiosaurus* [Latin *ultra*, "excessive"]. 91

Valdosaurus (VAL-doe-sore-us) An Early Cretaceous ornithopod from England [Latin *valdo*, "Wealden"]. 104

Vulcanodon (vul-CAN-oh-don) An Early Jurassic prosauropod from southern Africa [for Vulcanus, Roman god of the forge + Greek *odon*, "tooth"]. 80

Xenotarsosaurus (zeen-oh-TAR-so-sore-us) A Late Cretaceous theropod from South America [Greek *xenos*, "stranger" + *tarsos*, "ankle"]. 64

Yaverlandia (yah-ver-LAND-ee-uh) An Early Cretaceous pachycephalosaur from Europe [for Yaverland Battery, Isle of Wight, England]. 146

Yunnanosaurus (you-NAN-oh-sore-us) An Early Jurassic prosauropod from China [for Yunnan Province, China]. 80

GLOSSARY

Advanced mesotarsal (AM) ankle The ankle of pterosaurs, dinosaurs, and birds, in which the only hinge is between the astragalus-calcaneum and the rest of the foot. The astragalus is much larger than the calcaneum and both bones are rigidly attached to each other and to the tibia. 48

Aetosaur A heavily armored, plant-eating **thecodont** with a **crocodile-normal (CN)** ankle. 48

Ammonoid Any of a group of extinct invertebrates, most of which have coiled shells, that were close relatives of living octopuses, squids, and *Nautilus*. 247

Amniotic egg An egg in which the developing embryo is almost totally surrounded by a liquid-filled cavity enclosed by the amnion, which is a membrane continuous with the skin of the embryo. 43

Amphicoelous Describes a vertebra with sockets (cavities) in the centrum both anteriorly and posteriorly. 85

Anapsid A reptile with a skull that lacks upper and lower **temporal fenestrae.** 45

Angiosperm A vascular plant in which the seed is covered by an ovary, a flowering plant. 150

Archosaurs Diapsid reptiles that include **thecodonts,** crocodilians, **pterosaurs,** and **dinosaurs.** A variety of skeletal evolutionary novelties distinguish the archosaurs from the other diapsids, the **lepidosaurs.** 46

Binomen The two-word name of a species in the **Linnaean hierarchy**; for example, *Tyrannosaurus rex.* 13

Biped An animal that walks on its hind limbs. 33

Bone microstructure The microscopic arrangement of the inorganic matrix and organic component of bone. 221

Bradymetabolic Having a relatively slow **metabolism.** 215

Calcium phosphate The organic mineral matrix of bone. 18

Clade A branch or cluster of branches with a common stem on a **phylogeny**; a **monophyletic group.** 8

Cladistic phylogeny A **phylogeny** based on shared evolutionary novelties. 9

Cladogram A diagram of a **cladistic phylogeny.** 9

Classification The grouping of organisms into categories (taxa). 13

Clutch A nest of eggs. 206

Cold-blooded A popular term referring to an animal that receives most, or all, of its body heat from external sources, usually the sun. **Ectothermic** is a virtual synonym. 215

Compact bone The dense, tightly woven exterior layer of most vertebrate bones. 221

Connotation The meaning suggested by a word other than what it explicitly names or describes. See also **denotation.** 265

Convergence The evolution of similar features in two distinct **clades.** 8

Coprolite Fossilized feces. 17

Cretaceous Period The last period of the **Mesozoic Era,** approximately 145 to 65 million years ago. 28

Cross-sectional area The area of the surface at right angles to the axis [of a bone]. 201

Deltaic Having to do with a delta, a triangular body of sediment formed where a river enters a large, quiet body of water, either the sea or a lake. 25

Denotation The direct, specific meaning of a word, in contrast to its **connotation.** 265

Dental battery A large number of teeth cemented to each other to form an extensive shearing and grinding surface. 36

Determinate growth The pattern of growth of **endothermic** animals that stop growing at maturity. 202

Diapsid A reptile with two **temporal fenestrae** on each side of its skull. 45

Dimensionless speed The actual speed of an animal divided by some dimension of its body size. 188

Dinosaur An **archosaurian** reptile having an upright posture and an advanced mesotarsal (AM) ankle. 1

Dinosaur fauna All dinosaurs that lived during a specific interval of geologic time. 164

Dinosaur track (footprint) A fossilized dinosaur footprint. 184

Divergence The evolutionary splitting of one **clade** into two. 8

Ectotherm An animal that receives most, or all, of its body heat from external sources, usually from the sun. The popular term **cold-blooded** is a virtual synonym. 215

Endocast A natural or human-made cast (replica) of the brain cavity. Short for endocranial cast. 122

Endotherm An animal that generates most, or all, of its body heat internally; the popular terms **warm-blooded** and **hot-blooded** are virtual synonyms. 215

Eolian Having to do with wind. 25

Epicontinental sea Marine waters on top of continental crust. 156

Equable Marked by a lack of variation or change (roughly uniform). 149

Evolution The origin and change of organisms over time. 7

Evolutionary novelty A feature unique to a group of animals that may indicate they share a close common ancestry. 10

Extinction The disappearance of a **species** or of a larger clade of animals or plants. 8

Facultative biped An animal that is normally a **quadruped** but that occasionally walks bipedally. 33

Facultative quadruped An animal that is normally a **biped** but that occasionally walks quadrupedally. 33

Family The category in the **Linnaean hierarchy** above the **genus**; a group of genera with a shared evolutionary ancestry. 13

Feeding range The vertical height above the ground at which a plant eater forages. 205

Fluvial Having to do with rivers. 23

Foraminifera Microscopic single-celled animals that have a hard shell and live in the sea. 247

Fossil Any evidence of past life. Dinosaur fossils are bones and teeth, footprints, **coprolites, gastroliths,** eggs, and skin impressions. 17

Four-chambered heart A vertebrate heart that separates blood containing oxygen from blood lacking it; is characteristic of **endotherms.** 224

Frill A posterior-projecting shelf of bone at the back of the skull usually composed of the **parietals** and **squamosals**. 133

Function The specific contribution of a body part to the biology and behavior of an organism. 38

Furcula The wishbone of birds; the fused clavicles (collarbones). 237

Gastrolith A "fossilized" gizzard or stomach stone. 17

"Gastromyth" supposed **gastrolith** that is actually just a polished stone. 194

Genus The category in the **Linnaean hierarchy** above species. A group of species with a shared evolutionary ancestry. Plural: genera. 13

Gigantotherm A large animal with a nearly constant body temperature due to its large size; synonym: **inertial homeotherm.** 230

Gondwana The southern supercontinent of the Paleozoic-Mesozoic composed of Africa, Australia, Antarctica, South America, India, and Madagascar. 149

Grade A set of **clades** that do not share a close common ancestor. 8

Graviportal A **quadrupedal** animal with pillar-like legs and massive shoulder and hip girdles designed to bear great weight during slow and powerful locomotion. 94

Greenhouse A warm, equable, and humid climate. 161

Gymnosperm A vascular plant with a "naked" seed not enclosed in an ovary. 150

Herd A group of wild animals usually led by a dominant individual. 210

Heterotherm An animal whose body temperature varies considerably daily, seasonally, or throughout its life. 215

Homeotherm An animal that maintains a nearly constant body temperature. 215

Hot-blooded A somewhat sensational synonym of **warm-blooded**; *see also* **endotherm.** 215

Ichthyosaur Any of a group of Mesozoic reptiles that converged remarkably on a fish-like appearance and lived in the sea. 150

Igneous rock A rock that cooled from a molten state. 22

Indeterminate growth The pattern of growth of most **ectothermic** animals in which growth continues, although at a decreasing pace, throughout life. 202

Inertial homeotherm A synonym of **gigantotherm.** 93

Inoceramid A type of thin-shelled, plate-like clam of the Cretaceous Period. 247

Iridium A platinum-group metal rare on earth but more abundant in meteorites and asteroids. 253

Jurassic Period The middle interval of the **Mesozoic Era,** about 208 to 145 million years ago. 28

Labyrinthodont A type of extinct amphibian of the **Paleozoic** and **Mesozoic** with complexly folded (labyrinthine) enamel in its teeth. 151

Lacustrine Having to do with lakes. 23

Laurasia The northern supercontinent of the **Paleozoic-Mesozoic** composed of North America and most of Eurasia. 149

Lepidosaur Any of a group of **diapsid** reptiles that includes lizards, snakes, and their close relatives. 46

Linnaean hierarchy The categorical system used by biologists and **paleontologists** to classify organisms. Named after Carolus Linnaeus. 13

Locomotion The movement of an animal. 206

Maastrichtian The last time interval of the **Cretaceous Period,** about 71 to 66 million years ago. 251

Macroevolution Evolution above the species level. The origination and evolution of taxa larger than species. 15

Marine Having to do with the seas or oceans. 25

Marsupial A mammal in which the young typically are born very immature and initially live in a pouch (marsupium) on the mother's abdomen. 247

Mass-death assemblage A large accumulation of **fossils** of a single **species** of organism, often thought to be the result of a single catastrophe. 210

Mesozoic Era The middle era of the Phanerozoic eon, 250 to 66 million years ago. 28

Metabolism The chemical processes that provide energy to and repair the cells of an organism. 215

Metamorphic rock A rock that has been altered by great heat and/or pressure. 22

Microevolution Evolution at the **species** level. The evolution of populations of organisms that results in the origination of new species. 15

Mineralization The replacement of organic or inorganic matter by minerals such as silica, calcite, or iron during the process of fossilization. 18

Missing link A fossil that fills a significant gap in our knowledge of the evolution of a group of organisms. Typically, missing links bridge the evolutionary gap between two major groups of organisms. 235

Monophyletic group A taxon that includes all taxa derived from a single ancestor; synonym: **clade.** 10

Monsoon A period of high winds and rainfall. 150

Mosasaur Any of a group of extinct, giant marine lizards of the **Cretaceous Period.** 247

Natural selection The process by which an organism that is better adapted to an environment more successfully reproduces than less-adapted organisms. 7

Nest A bed or receptacle prepared by an animal for its eggs and young. 207

Numerical time scale A classification of geologic time based on numbers (usually millions) of years. 26

Opisthocoelous The condition of a vertebra with a socket (cavity) in the centrum facing posteriorly. 85

Origination The appearance of a new type of organism. 8

Ornithosuchids 1- to 3-meter-long, facultatively **bipedal,** predatory **thecodonts** of the **Late Triassic.** The likely ancestors of **dinosaurs.** 49

Pace The distance between the posterior margins of two successive footprints of the hind limbs on opposite sides of the body measured parallel to the direction of travel. 184

Pace angle The angle between a line drawn from the posterior margin of one hind footprint to an equivalent point on the next hind footprint on the opposite side, and a second line drawn to the equivalent point on the next hind footprint of the same side as the first. 184

Paleontologist A scientist who studies fossils and the history of life. 7

Paleontology The scientific study of fossils and the history of life. 7

Pangaea The supercontinent of the Paleozoic-Mesozoic comprising all of the present continents before breakup. 149

Panthalassa The single, gigantic ocean that existed when **Pangaea** was assembled. 149

Phylogenetic relationships The relationships of taxa to each other. 8

Phylogenetic tree A diagram that depicts the **phylogenetic relationships** of a group of taxa and has geologic time as its vertical axis. 11

Phylogeny The history of how a group of organisms evolved. 8

Phytosaurs A **Late Triassic** group of **quadrupedal,** meat-eating, crocodilian-like **thecodonts** having **crocodile-normal (CN)** ankles. 48

Placental A type of mammal in which the young develop in a placenta and are born relatively mature compared to newborn **marsupials.** 160

Plesiosaur Any of a group of extinct, long-necked marine reptiles of the **Jurassic** and **Cretaceous.** 150

Pneumatic Having to do with air. A pneumatic bone is hollow and perforated so air can pass into it. 234

Pneumatic ducts Openings (perforations) in the long bones of birds for the passage of air. 234

Polyphyletic group A group of organisms from which their common ancestor is excluded. 10

Postcrania The bones of the skeleton other than those of the skull and lower jaw. 35

Predator-prey ratio The biomass of predators divided by the biomass of prey. 226

Principle of biostratigraphic correlation The observation that rocks containing the same kinds of fossils are of the same age. 27

Principle of superposition The observation that in layered rocks (strata) the oldest rocks are at the bottom and the younger rocks are on top. 27

Procoelous Describes a vertebra with a socket (cavity) in the centrum facing anteriorly. 85

Pterosaur A flying archosaur of the **Late Triassic** through **Late Cretaceous.** Not a dinosaur. 46

Quadruped An animal that walks on four limbs. 33

Radioactive clock A means of measuring geologic time by the radioactive decay of unstable atoms. 29

Ratites Some of the flightless birds, including living ostriches and emus. 243

Rauisuchians A group of **Triassic,** meat-eating **thecodonts** having **crocodile-normal (CN)** ankles. 151

Relative time scale A way to measure geologic time by determining if one event is older than or younger than another by assigning each event to a named interval of geologic time. 26

Reptile A tetrapod that lays an amniotic egg and has scaly skin. 43

Resonating chamber An air space that intensifies sound waves that enter it. 110

Rudist Extinct, reef-building clams of the **Cretaceous Period.** 247

Sedimentary (depositional) environment The place and particular conditions under which a **sedimentary rock** was formed. 22

Sedimentary rock A rock formed by the accumulation and cementation of mineral grains, or by chemical precipitation. 22

Selenium A non-metallic, often poisonous, element. 248

Sexual dimorphism Anatomical differences between the male and female of a single species. 63

"Shocked quartz" A type of quartz grain with a laminar deformation known to be generated only by high speed shock in laboratories, at nuclear test sites, and near impact craters. 256

Soft-tissue anatomy That part of a vertebrate that is not skeleton, such as muscles, nerves, circulatory system, and internal organs. 38

Species The lowest grouping in the **Linnaean hierarchy.** A group of populations with a shared evolutionary ancestry. Plural: **species.** 13

Sprawling posture The posture in which the limbs are held out to the side of the body so the upper segments are horizontal to, or nearly horizontal to, the **substratum.** 1

Stratigraphy The scientific study of layered rocks **(strata).** 27

Stratophenetic phylogeny A phylogeny that relies on the relative geologic age and overall similarity of taxa to identify ancestors and descendants. 8

Stratum (plural: **strata**) A single bed or layer of **sedimentary rock.** 28

Stride The distance between the posterior margins of two successive hind footprints on the same side of the body in the direction of travel. 188

Substratum The ground surface. 185

Supernova The complete obliteration of a star in an explosion. 248

Surface area-to-volume relationship The observation that volume increases as the cube of a linear dimension, whereas surface area only increases as the square of a linear dimension. Animals of large volumes have relatively less surface area than small-volume animals. 229

Tachymetabolic The relatively fast **metabolism** characteristic of most **endotherms.** 215

Taphonomy The scientific study of the processes by which a fossil assemblage is formed and the losses of information these processes produce. 20

Temporal fenestra An opening for the passage and attachment of muscles in the skull of a reptile behind its eyes. 45

Tethys Sea The seaway between **Laurasia** and **Gondwana** during the Mesozoic. 149

Thecodont A **grade,** not a clade, of **archosaurs** that gave rise to crocodiles, dinosaurs, and **pterosaurs.** 46

Trace fossil Fossils that are not part of the actual body of an animal. Dinosaur trace fossils are **footprints, eggs, gastroliths,** and **coprolites.** 17

Trackway A series of footprints made by a single animal. 184

Triassic Period The oldest period of the **Mesozoic Era,** 250 to 208 million years ago. 28

Upright posture The posture in which the limbs are held vertically underneath the body so that they are vertical to, or nearly vertical to, the **substratum.** 1

Warm-blooded A popular term virtually synonymous with **endothermic;** *see also* **hot-blooded.** 215

INDEX